Capital, the State, and War

The history of the modern social sciences can be understood as a series of
recurring attempts to confront the challenges of social disorder and revolution wrought by the international expansion of capitalist social relations. In
this book, Alexander Anievas focuses on one particularly significant aspect
of this story: the intersocietal or geosocial origins of the two world wars
fought between 1914 and 1945—specifically, the historically unique social,
economic, and political causes of the Thirty Years' Crisis.

Standard accounts principally conceptualize the geopolitics of the era in
socially thin terms, reducing it to military-strategic factors alone and viewing the world wars as the latest chapter in a perennial interstate contest over
a Eurocentric balance of power. In contrast, Anievas examines the Thirty
Years' Crisis as a result of the internationally structured development of
global capitalism, with all its destabilizing social and geopolitical consequences. In this way, he foregrounds the intertwined and co-constitutive
nature of imperial rivalries, social revolutions, and anticolonial struggles.
Building on the theory of uneven and combined development, he unites
geopolitical and sociological explanations into a single framework, thereby
circumventing the analytical stalemate between primacy of domestic politics and primacy of foreign policy approaches.

Anievas opens new avenues for thinking about the relations between
security-military interests, the making of foreign policy, political economy,
and more generally the origins of war and nature of modern international
order.

Alexander Anievas is a Leverhulme Early Career Research Fellow at the Department of Politics and International Studies, University of Cambridge.

CONFIGURATIONS: CRITICAL STUDIES OF WORLD POLITICS

Patrick Thaddeus Jackson, series editor

Capital, the State, and War

CLASS CONFLICT AND GEOPOLITICS IN
THE THIRTY YEARS' CRISIS, 1914–1945

Alexander Anievas

The University of Michigan Press
Ann Arbor

Copyright © by the University of Michigan 2014

Published in the United States of America by
The University of Michigan Press
Manufactured in the United States of America
⊗ Printed on acid-free paper

2017   2016   2015   2014   4   3   2   1

A CIP catalog record for this book is available from the British Library.

ISBN 978-0-472-07211-8 (cloth: alk. paper)
ISBN 978-0-472-05211-0 (paper: alk. paper)
ISBN 978-0-472-12022-2 (e-book)

This book is dedicated to Arturo Anievas.
Thanks, Dad.

Contents

Foreword

IN THIS BOOK, Alexander Anievas has produced a compelling illustration of the ways that an account focusing on the shape of relations in the global political economy can explain features of the Thirty Years' Crisis period covering both world wars that remain opaque in existing statecentric geopolitical accounts of the period. He generates a compelling narrative of the origins of the First World War and of subsequent state actions centered in the United States, Germany, and Britain using the relatively spare theoretical formulation of uneven and combined development and its component international-social mechanisms of the "external whip" (the pressures generated by interstate competition) and the "privilege of historical backwardness" (the opportunities presented for less-developed states to adopt cutting-edge strategies from the leading powers in the international system rather than painstakingly developing those strategies as the leading powers did).

Standing at the intersection of these two mechanisms and locating specific events as composed of detailed, sequenced configurations of these mechanisms, Anievas's account brings to light important alliances among politicians, financiers, and industrialists that sought to mediate these pressures into concrete strategies designed to preserve these stakeholders' domestic social standing and to respond to the broader global context within which they were located. What emerges from Anievas's account is neither an overdetermined tale of power-hungry states and greedy capitalists hell-bent on war nor a tragic story of a series of wars that no one wanted but into which everyone unintentionally fell; rather, it is a more complex story in which state-led efforts to manage the tensions of a global system of production and finance made the risk of war seem less important than the risk of worldwide anticapitalist revolution.

To choose just one example, in chapter 6, Anievas argues that the British

appeasement of Nazi Germany was neither a rational calculation of state
military capacities (IR realist theory would predict that Britain would ally
with the Soviet Union to balance against Germany based purely on a calculation of military might) nor an accidental misperception of (or an idealist failure to grasp) the "real" demands of an anarchic international environment.
Instead, Anievas traces the links between the policy of appeasement and the
"City-Treasury-Bank nexus" that had come to dominate British politics because of the country's position in the global political economy—specifically,
because of the system of imperial preferences and relations of trade and production. Britain's supposed failure to balance Nazi Germany is thus not a
"failure" at all but a more-or-less rational response by British elites to international developments that threatened the entire socioeconomic structure
within which they were embedded. Once we stop looking at Britain as an
isolated state and reembed Britain within the broader political economy, it is
not at all puzzling that Britain would attempt to appease Germany and re-
fuse to ally with the Soviets against the Nazis.

In this way—and I have selected only one of the numerous points in the
book where this happens—Anievas demonstrates that his framework solves
problems and explains outcomes with which existing IR accounts have trouble. By abandoning the statecentric geopolitical-competition framework in
favor of a broader analysis of the global political economy, Anievas suggests
that the price of explaining critical events in world politics may be the abandonment of cherished scholarly illusions. In the end, that is what critical
social science is all about.

Patrick Thaddeus Jackson
Series Editor, Configurations
Professor of International Relations and
Associate Dean for Undergraduate Education in
the School of International Service at the
American University, Washington, DC

Acknowledgments

THIS MANUSCRIPT developed out of my doctoral dissertation, "Capitals, States, and Conflict: International Political Economy and Crisis, 1914–1945," prepared under the supervision of Tarak Barkawi. Without Tarak's searching and stimulating comments and unstinting support throughout my PhD, I'm not sure this work would have ever seen the light of day. Tarak was a model PhD supervisor and a good friend, and to him I owe a great intellectual debt.

When writing a manuscript such as this, one quickly realizes what a collective endeavor scholarship really is. For comments and discussion on earlier drafts of specific chapters, I am grateful to Jacques Bariéty, Colin Barker, Alex Callinicos, Michael Carley, Neil Davidson, Lloyd Gardner, Charles Jones, Rob Knox, Tor Krevor, Annie Lacroix-Riz, Mark Laffey, Richard Ned Lebow, Nivi Manchanda, Kamran Matin, Adam Morton, William Mulligan, Kerem Nisancioglu, Brian Richardson, Dylan Riley, Randall Schweller, Lisa Smirl, Jack Snyder, Adam Tooze, and Srdjan Vucetic. Particular thanks go to Duncan Bell, John Hobson, George Lawson, Mark Rupert, and Robert Vitalis, all of whom read the manuscript in its entirety at one point or another in its development. I also thank the editors at University of Michigan Press, Melody Herr and Patrick Jackson, for their very generous and professional support. I owe a special intellectual debt to Justin Rosenberg, who not only gave me detailed feedback at various points in this work's evolution but also provided me with guidance and help throughout the PhD. I am also grateful to St. Anne's College for providing me with the time and resources to finish this work.

Special gratitude is further owed to Jamie Allinson, Josef Ansorge, Adam Fabry, Gonzalo Pozo-Martin, and Luke Williams, who provided me with detailed comments on multiple drafts and chapters. They have been the best of comrades and formidable intellectual sparring partners. I also thank my dearest friends, Johnny Costello, Dominic DiFalco, Christy Kingsley, Mike

Powlesland, Vin Randazzo, Craig Schlanger, and Andy Weck as well as the late Matt Gibney, one of the most talented and beautiful people I've ever had the great fortune of knowing. Further gratitude goes to Josef Ansorge for assistance with German translations. I owe a special intellectual debt to my two wonderful teachers, Bill Cooper and Ralph Anievas, who instilled in me the desire to learn and teach. Most important, I thank my parents; my brother, Erik Anievas; and my sister, Cathy Anievas, as well as my dear Linda Szilas. Their love, support and enduring encouragement are indispensable and forever appreciated.

Some parts of this book were previously published, and I am grateful for the original publishers' permission to use them here. Sections of chapter 2 are based on Jamie C. Allinson and Alexander Anievas, "The Uses and Misuses of Uneven and Combined Development: An Anatomy of a Concept," *Cambridge Review of International Affairs* 22 (1) (2009): 47–67. Chapter 3 is a much-revised and extended version of Alexander Anievas, "1914 in World Historical Perspective: The 'Uneven' and 'Combined' Origins of the First World War," *European Journal of International Relations.* Chapter 6 is based on "The International Political Economy of Appeasement: The Social Sources of British Foreign Policy during the 1930s," *Review of International Studies* 37 (2) (2011): 601–29.

Introduction

THE CONTINUING POVERTY OF INTERNATIONAL THEORY

THE ERA OF the two World Wars persists in informing the contemporary policymaking imagination, providing powerful tropes and guideposts for thought. In Europe and North America, the Second World War (WWII) is portrayed as the "good" war, fought to defend civilization from barbarism and catastrophe. Its events, symbols, and personalities are invoked repeatedly in public and governmental discourses. If the Thirty Years' Crisis of the two world wars is a defining experience in the evolution of 20th-century world politics, its influence in the social sciences is nowhere greater than on the field of international relations (IR). The study of IR *originates within* and was a *response to* an epoch of generalized crisis and global conflagration, representing the *paradigmatic moment* in the discipline's formation and subsequent trajectory (Halliday 1989; Long 1995; Brian C. Schmidt 1998).

The tumultuous interwar years lifted "political realism" to dominance within the Anglo-Saxon academy at a time characterized by IR's intimate connections with the foreign policymaking establishment. In the United States, so the conventional narrative goes, policymakers were particularly receptive to the "intellectual compass" realism offered as they aimed to "exorcise isolationism, justify a permanent and global involvement in world affairs," and "rationalize the accumulation of power" (Hoffmann 1977, 47–48; see also Keohane 1986, 9). Though realism's triumph over liberalism in the culmination of the "First Great Debate" is a myth,[1] what *was* "exorcised" from postwar hegemonic disciplinary discourses was the question of the relationships among capitalism, interstate competition, and war.

Before they became abstract theories of IR, realism and liberalism were *political* reactions to the intersecting socioeconomic, ideological, and war-

time catastrophes engulfing "Western civilization." For politicians and policymakers of the time along with the discipline they helped shape, the problems of war and interstate conflict were perceived as inherently connected to
questions of social disorder, revolution, and ruinous economic competition.
Yet the postwar discipline that crystallized around these political responses
to the crisis chose to emphasize the problem of *war in the abstract,* as a question about why wars occur throughout history. This move abstracted from a
set of historically specific conditions facing contemporary policymakers, expunging from analyses the fundamental antagonisms between capital and
labor and their political representatives as well as those between the general
staffs and their largely working-class armies. Despite being forged in an epoch of world revolution and fierce capitalist rivalries, mainstream IR accounts of the two world wars erased the social upheavals sweeping across
and interlinking the polities of the Global North and South. Absent inquiry
into these transnational and intersocietal determinants of the geopolitics of
the era, IR explanations of the two world wars have been misconceived. As a
consequence, so too is IR theory, as it has been continually unable to adequately answer the questions it set for itself: What are the causes of war and
conditions for peace? What determines the "national interest"? How does
anarchy affect state behavior?

THE LOST HISTORY AND THEORY OF IR

This book excavates this "lost" history and theory of international relations
at a defining moment of its formation. Foregrounding the ineluctably intertwined and co-constitutive nature of imperial rivalries, social revolutions,
and anticolonial struggles evident to policymakers during the decades of crisis but subsequently lost in academic analyses, the study demonstrates how
standard interpretations and assumptions about the period have been incomplete and often mistaken. To this end, the book seeks to build on analytical tools derived from the Marxist tradition, demonstrating how they assist
in generating more adequate explanations to a number of core research questions confronting both extant IR and social theory approaches to the period.

Drawing on an expansive array of different historiographical literatures
(social, business, economic, postcolonial, and so forth) more or less invisible
to IR, *Capital, the State, and War* examines the sources of military competition
and war as formed *within, through,* and *beyond* the territorial nation-state to-
talities of conventional IR thinking. This situates the origins of great-power

wars within their multiple and interconnecting domestic, international, and transnational contexts. In doing so, the book highlights the manifold ways that the modern geopolitical system developed through the causal interface of these distinct but intersecting social-spatial fields. This shows how the deep generative grammar of modern international relations was rooted in a world-historical process of uneven and combined development—itself radically transformed over the course of the Long 19th Century by the universalizing imperatives of competitive capital accumulation unique to the spreading capitalist anarchy of an ever-invasive world market.

From this perspective, *Capital, the State, and War* examines empirically how international relations and social structures mutually entail one another. State action and interstate relations are always already socially embedded while continuously shaping and reacting back on mutating social orders. The character and outcomes of this interactive process form the basis of the analytic and explanatory account developed in the following chapters.

In these ways, the manuscript makes a major contribution to understanding the connections among development, conflict, and war in the contemporary age. At stake here are questions not only about the causes of war and great power competition but also about the fundamental nature of—and relations between—the modern international system and social order more generally. This work enriches, both empirically and theoretically, a growing corpus of literature overturning the many foundational disciplinary myths undergirding mainstream IR. For despite the productive and stimulating body of recent revisionist historiographies of the *discourse* of IR, there remains no corresponding literature reevaluating the social-historical causes and nature of the geopolitics of the period. Though the experiences and "lessons" of the two world wars suffuse the study of IR—universally referenced throughout the subject and its many subfields (foreign policy analysis, security studies, international political economy [IPE], and so on)—one searches in vain for substantive, comprehensive studies of the actual interstate conflicts of the period. *Capital, the State, and War* offers precisely this: a positive and radically alternative theorization of the origins, course, and nature of the two world wars in their historically unique global-social contexts.

THE SIGNIFICANCE OF SOCIAL STRUCTURES FOR IR

The expunging of social structure from the study of international relations has incapacitated theoretical understandings and explanations of the causes

of war and interstate conflict. Without appreciation of the deep embeddedness of geopolitics within historically dynamic configurations of social relations, the content of international politics is continually dissolved back into
generic categories ("anarchy," "balance of power," "security dilemma," and
so on) incapable of illumination. Hence, the subject of IR remains stuck
within a cyclical, premodern conception of history: the homogenous and
ultimately timeless time of perennial interstate competition and war. Mistaking causal specificity for absolute autonomy, much conventional IR visu-
alizes the international-political system in theoretical isolation.[2] The potential variances geopolitics can take from one epoch to the next are, by
theoretical fiat, denied. The result is a kind of "tempocentric ahistoricism"
(Hobson 2002) whereby a reified nation-statist ontology of contemporary
world politics is projected back in time as the suprahistorical essence of intersocietal relations in general. The underlying causes of the Thirty Years'
Crisis of 1914–45 thereby become analogous to the great-power struggles for
world hegemony throughout the millennium. The Peloponnesian War,
Thirty Years' War of 1619–48, and the Napoleonic Wars are all reduced to the
same anarchic logic of balance-of-power politics (Waltz 1979; Gilpin 1981;
Copeland 2000; Mearsheimer 2001).

Though mainstream IR increasingly recognizes that the exclusion of inquiries into the relationship between capitalism and modern international
relations has had theoretically debilitating consequences (Buzan and Little
1999, 89), conceptions of capitalism as a *historical* social structure remain remarkably thin. The fundamental role of labor-capital conflicts, social revolution, and intercapitalist competition feeding into the geopolitics of the age
simply fall out of traditional realist and liberal frameworks. This study therefore rethinks the artificial dissociation between political economy and
military-security interests so prevalent in IR. This is not simply resolved by
bringing political economy back into the study of international politics. A
number of political economy approaches lie at the heart of traditional IR
theory. Yet these approaches are overwhelmingly shaped by realist conceptions of "political economy" using *quantifiable* measures of a country's natural resources, industrial capacity, population size, number of battle tanks,
and the like (see, for example, Krasner 1978; Gilpin 1987; Paul M. Kennedy
1988; Schweller 1998; Copeland 2000; Brawley 2009).

Alternatively, more sophisticated understandings of political economy—as exemplified in some liberal, constructivist, and Weberian-inspired
studies—remain wedded to an *economistic* interpretation of capitalism as re-

ducible to "the market." Consequently, these approaches fall into a somewhat different though no less problematic tempocentric ahistoricism—a world in which the market "economy" of the Sung era (11th and 12th centuries) becomes indistinguishable from modern industrial capitalism (see McNeill 1982; Hobson 2004). From many liberal perspectives, the spread of free trade and markets is equated with the promotion of a more cooperative and peaceful international order. Economic "globalization" is viewed as transforming world politics into a series of positive-sum games whereby states can realize absolute gains. The development of market relations is in turn identified as advancing more liberal-democratic civic cultures, identities, and norms. Hence, political relations functionally follow economic integration (see, for example, Keohane and Nye 1977; Keohane 1984; Doyle 1986; Tony Smith 1994; Moravcsik 1997; Ruggie 1998a; Buzan and Little 1999; Deudney and Ikenberry 1999; Oneal and Russett 1999; Ikenberry 2004; Narizny 2007).

These pristinely liberal narratives are accepted not only by traditional IR theories but also by many self-identified "critical" and constructivist IR approaches. Alexander Wendt's (1999) account of the emergence of a Western-based "Kantian" culture of anarchy essentially repackages, in constructivist form, long-familiar liberal themes of the putatively pacifying effects of liberal-democratic identity relations (see also Booth 1991; Risse-Kappen 1995; Linklater 1998). Capitalism is conceived by Wendt (1999, 361–62) as a solely domestic attribute of states, fostering trust and peaceful relations between them. Dropping out of this picture is any *holistic* notion of capitalism as an antagonistic and hierarchical international social formation—a contradictory unity of universalizing and differentiating imperatives driven by the exigencies of competitive accumulation. Mainstream IR thus perpetuates an obfuscated conception of the effects of capitalism on processes of interstate conflict and war.

Such theoretical assumptions are misleading in examining the geopolitics of the Thirty Years' Crisis (as they are for any era of modern history), which was characterized by the complex causal interactions of social conflict, economic competition, war, and revolution. A more appropriate way to think about political economy is in terms of social structure: a specific configuration of relations constituted by a historically bound social system. Here lay the real significance of the concept of capitalism as understood from the perspective of historical materialism. As Robert W. Cox and Schechter (2002, 79) remarked, the "real achievement of IPE was not to bring in economics, but to open up a critical investigation into change in historical structures."

From this view, capitalism is not to be conceived as a solely economic phenomenon. Instead, it refers to a historically determinant form of societal organization at the heart of which is not simply "the economy" but the *social* process of production constituted by both the "vertical" relations between capital and labor and the "horizontal" relations among many capitals (Brenner 2006a, 7–8; see also Justin Rosenberg 1994; Rupert 1995; Lacher 2006). As Eric Wolf notes (1982, 97), Marx's category of production sought to simultaneously capture "the changing relations of humankind to nature, the social relations into which humans enter in the course of transforming nature, and the consequent transformations of human symbolic capability." Capitalism thus denotes much more than an economic system: it is a "definite mode of life" (Marx and Engels 1970, 42; see also Sayer 1991, 56–66).

Nonetheless, infusing the study of international relations with a stronger conception of historical social structures is still by itself not enough for a satisfactory theorization of the geopolitical. It might instead lead to the same well-worn problems of "inside-out" logics of explanation reducing the geopolitical to a preformed theory of domestic society. For an additional source of disciplinary IR's troubled relationship with sociological modes of inquiry are the peculiarities of the subject matter at hand: the decentralized and anarchic features of the international realm seem to elude theorization based on the precepts of classical social theory. This issue leads one to a direct engagement with the question of what is "the international" rendered in historical and sociological terms (Justin Rosenberg 2006). The point, then, is to demonstrate how social structures and class configurations were *generated by* and *constitutive of* the international system in ways traceable to actual foreign policymaking processes, thereby producing more complete and powerful explanatory hypotheses.

Echoing Kenneth Waltz's seminal work, *Man, the State, and War,* this volume traces a way out of the deeper methodological predicaments shared by traditional IR theory and the social sciences. This concerns the "levels of analysis" problem identified by Waltz and others common to theories of war and peace. This claimed that all theories of international politics conceptualized the causal foundations of war and peace on one of three "levels": the individual-psychological ("first image"), the domestic-political ("second image"), and the international-systemic ("third image").

While identifying the conceptual quandaries and parameters of debate, Waltz never offered a satisfactory solution to them, instead eventually proposing to disconnect unit-level ("sociological") and systemic-level ("geopolitical") theories of IR altogether (Waltz 1979). This has been the road subsequently followed by most mainstream IR students. Yet a lasting consequence of this maneuver has been a persistent oscillation and dichotomy between conceptions of the international system as an absolutely autonomous "suprasocial" sphere or a reduction of its unique qualities to a theory of domestic society (Hedley Bull's "domestic analogy" trap). Exploring the ways of overcoming this obstinate division is a major aim of *Capital, the State, and War*. The effort begins by recognizing the internationally constituted nature of capitalist modernity.

THE GEOPOLITICS OF CAPITALIST MODERNITY

The development of capitalism as a global system over the Long 19th Century (1780–1914) took place in and through an already existing plurality of states. The history of the modern social sciences can be thus understood as a series of recurring attempts to confront the challenges of social disorder and revolution wrought by this *international* expansion of capitalist relations. This book focuses on one particularly significant aspect of this story: the intersocietal or "geosocial" origins of the two world wars of 1914–45. In doing so, it tackles a number of core problematics at the center of disciplinary IR, offering new tools to explain these world-historical events of the first half of the 20th century.

Standard accounts of the period principally conceptualize the geopolitics of the era in socially "thin" terms, reducible to military-strategic factors alone. The two world wars are thus conceived as the latest saga in a timeless interstate contest over a European-centered balance of power. This has contributed to profoundly suprahistorical and asocial conceptions of the modern international system. Fundamentally overlooked, then, are the historically unique social structures and configurations of international relations as well as the sociological effects of "the international" itself.

Despite the importance of the Thirty Years' Crisis in the modern social sciences—and particularly in disciplinary IR—strikingly few studies examine the historically distinct socioeconomic causes in their interlocking domestic and international dimensions. While figuring prominently within (neo-)Marxist and world system accounts, such perspectives nonetheless exclude the specifically international determinants of these processes. Here, Marxism shares with conventional IR approaches an underestimation of the sociological effects of "the international" and war on development more generally. Moreover, political-military and security relations receive little theoretical treatment in their accounts (but see Mandel 1986; Halperin 2004). Consequently, the reciprocal interaction of domestic ("internal") and international ("external") factors in the determination of states, societies, and foreign policymaking are left largely untheorized.

By contrast, *Capital, the State, and War* examines the crisis emerging as a result of the internationally structured development of capitalism and its destabilizing social and geopolitical consequences. The tumult of 1914–45 is reconceptualized from the perspective of the "uneven" and "combined" development of capitalism as an international social formation. This renders intelligible the very different but historically connected social and political outcomes of a single world-historical process of developmental transformation.

Drawing on the theory of uneven and combined development, this text challenges standard theoretical interpretations of the crisis by distinctively uniting geopolitical and sociological modes of explanations into a single framework. In doing so, it engages with a long-standing theoretical dilemma common to classical sociology and IR theories: their shared inability to incorporate the necessarily *differentiated, multilinear* character of sociohistorical development as a *strategically interdependent* and *co-constitutive* whole. These issues go to the heart of IR and sociology debates, which have largely operated within "externalist" versus "internalist" frameworks. Here, international and social theories intersect with—and are in fact informed by—the vast historiographical debates on the origins and nature of the two world wars.

Whether a *Primat der Aussenpolitik* (primacy of foreign policy) or *Primat der Innenpolitik* (primacy of domestic politics) approach provides the best account of the interstate conflicts of the crisis era continue to dominate the historiographical debates. This is arguably the most prolific historiographical body of literature for any period of war within the modern epoch. It would then seem to illustrate a much larger problem within the social sciences: how to coherently integrate external and internal relations into a synthesized theory of interstate conflict and war.

Building from the theory of uneven and combined development, this book identifies three component sociointernational mechanisms: the "whip of external necessity" (the pressures generated by interstate competition), the "privilege of historic backwardness" (the opportunities opened up to late-developing states to adopt the most advanced cutting-edge technologies from the leading states in the international system), and the "contradictions of sociological amalgamation" (the time-compressed character of this development, taking inorganic, spasmodic, and destabilizing forms and unhinging traditional social structures). Standing at the intersection of these mechanisms, the book unravels the relations and alliances among state managers, politicians, and specific segments of the capitalist class as they sought to mediate these pressures into concrete strategies designed to preserve their domestic social standing and to respond to the broader international and global context within which they were embedded.

This book therefore opens up new sets of questions regarding how international and social theory think about the relations among security-military interests, foreign policymaking, political economy, and more generally the origins of war and nature of modern international order. For if security studies has remained fundamentally incomplete by being detached from the kind of historicized conceptions of social structures offered by critical IPE, the latter requires a rethinking of political economy through the "military-strategic" dimensions of the social. In these ways, the work will be of interest not only to IR theory but also to a much broader range of both general and specialized knowledge.

Thus far, the debates surrounding calls for an international historical sociology have been pitched at an unsustainably high level of abstraction. This is particularly the case with recent interest in the idea of uneven and combined development as a theory of "the international." As a developing research program, this literature has yet to produce any major substantive historical or empirical studies (but see Matin 2007; Green 2012). This work redresses this lacuna. It does so not simply by "applying" the idea to the crisis period but also by developing the theory itself in new directions.

Focusing on a number of key moments of the 1914–45 epoch, *Capital, the State, and War* provides new explanatory frameworks challenging many (if not most) conventional understandings of these momentous events. General theoretical arguments contributing to both IR and sociological debates are made *in* and *through* a richly developed empirical terrain of the crisis years. The endeavor seeks not to present new historical evidence or offer a "total history" of the international relations of the period but rather to deepen and broaden understandings and explanations of the causes and nature of the geopolitical conflicts and war in the modern epoch while contributing to a number of classic debates at the core of the social sciences.

STRUCTURE OF ARGUMENT

The book is divided into six chapters. Chapter 1 critically engages debates on the causes of the First World War, examining in particular the strengths and weaknesses of the four dominant schools of thought: the *Sonderweg* (special path) approach; Arno Mayer's Ancien Régime thesis; realist perspectives; and the classical Marxist theories of imperialism. The "long debate" over the war's origins offers a striking illustration of the analytically debilitating problems derivative of the persistent dissociation of "sociological" and "geopolitical" explanations common to these dominant frameworks. These dilemmas point to the need for an alternative theorization of the conflict interlinking the domestic and international as constituting a single, causally integrated, ontological whole.

Drawing on recent debates within IR and historical sociology, chapter 2 critically develops the theory of uneven and combined development, demonstrating the specificities of uneven and combined development as a genuinely holistic theory of interstate competition and war. Building from this theoretical perspective, chapter 3 then offers a historically driven analysis of the general and proximate origins of the First World War. Theorizing the international context from which the July 1914 crisis unfolded, it discusses how sociopolitical differences and intersocietal interaction were key factors in both the structural and conjunctural causes of the war. In doing so, the chapter offers a multileveled and empirically engaged analysis tracing the intersecting tendencies, trends, and events leading to the war's outbreak. This begins from the *longue durée* of development over the course of the Long 19th Century, steadily zooming into an explanation of the specificities of the immediate prewar conjuncture of 1912–14.

Chapter 4 then looks at the rise of U.S. power and "Wilsonian" diplomacy during and after the First World War. Situating these developments within the context of the international political economy and historical sociology of the U.S. modern state-formation process, it offers an anatomization of "Wilsonianism" as a distinct foreign policy ideology[3] and imperial praxis. More specifically, the chapter conceptualizes Wilsonian diplomacy as the effect and pragmatic response to the social-strategic dilemmas arising from the uneven and combined character of U.S. development and world capitalism as a whole. From this perspective, the chapter then examines in close historical detail the causes and consequences of Wilsonian statecraft during the 1919 Paris Peace Conference. Specifically, it elucidates the critical role of the Bolshevik Revolution in the making of the Versailles Treaty, which in turn reacted back on the trajectory of interstate conflicts during the interwar years.

Chapter 5 goes on to investigate the particular sociohistorical milieu giving rise to the Nazi phenomenon in interwar Germany and leading to the Second World War in Europe. This examines how the intertwining of domestic and international crises resulted in the collapse of Weimar democracy and the Nazi *Machtergreifung* (seizure of power) in 1933. Building on the structural framework of Germany's uneven and combined development offered in chapter 3, chapter 5 then turns to a close analysis of the relations among state, capital, and military in the foreign policy continuities and changes from the Weimar to Nazi regimes, focusing in particular through the prism of rearmament. This approach lends it itself to an inspection of the specific connections between Nazi ideology and the sociomaterial conditions determining the eventual *timing* and *form* that war took in 1939.

Chapter 6 analyzes the social sources of British foreign policymaking during the interwar years, specifically focusing on Chamberlain's "appeasement" policy. This investigates the evolution of British state-society relations and foreign policymaking structures concentrating on the ascendancy of a "City-Treasury-Bank nexus" within the post-1918 British state. It examines how the emergence of a hegemonic City-Treasury-Bank perspective favoring liberal economic orthodoxy and the pursuit of "Gladstonian finance" continually subordinated British military-security requirements to financial concerns and the maintenance of internal social stability. It further shows how the specific position of Britain within the world economy and international system produced a structural bias toward a dual strategy of limited rearmament and appeasement—a strategy reinforced by widespread anticommunist ideology among British elites and their persistent refusals to form an alliance with the Soviet Union. Threats to social order and the political status quo thereby overrode British policymakers' concerns regarding Nazi Germany's territorial ambitions. In short, then, appeasement policy did not proceed from strategic balance-of-power calculations, as argued by realists, but from the pressures and constraints emerging from the political economy of Britain's particular social structure and its attempts to guarantee the international conditions for its survival.

The conclusion draws out the historical and theoretical implications of the work's alternative account of the Thirty Years' Crisis for rethinking conventional periodizations of the Cold War. For contrary to conventional wisdom, it seems that the Cold War emerged not after the Second World War but rather almost immediately after the Bolshevik Revolution of 1917. Throughout the interwar years, state managers remained preoccupied with the threats of socialism at home and Bolshevism abroad in ways directly feeding into the domestic and international conditions leading down the road to 1939. Hence, the Second World War was not the cause of the Cold War but precisely the reverse: an early Cold War constituted the antecedent material and ideological conditions for the emergence of the Second World War.

CHAPTER 1

Rethinking Theories of the Two World Wars: Social Development, Geopolitics, and War

CAN THE TWO WORLD WARS be seen as forming part of a single, protracted crisis? If so, what were the origin(s) and nature of the crisis? And how have scholars conceived them? Nearly a century after the "lights went out" in Europe, such issues persist in riveting the imagination. And, for good reason: even if Hitler and the Nazis can be seen as inextricably driving Europe to war in 1939, thereby offering a seemingly straightforward explanation of the Second World War (WWII) in Europe, the circumstances leading to their arrival on the historical scene still require explanation. So too does the genuinely *global* character of the conflagration, which spread across four continents, interconnecting a multiplicity of different struggles and conflicts with their own distinct if overlapping sociohistorical temporalities (for example, the Sino-Japanese War of 1937–45). This then raises the question of whether the causes and outcomes of the First World War were inseparable from those of the Second. In other words, was the global war of 1939 a direct continuation (in one form or another) of the unresolved conflicts leading to July 1914?[1] If the question is answered in the affirmative, then an understanding of the deeper roots of the First World War is imperative to explaining the Thirty Years' Crisis as a whole.[2]

Delving into the origins of the First World War is, to say least, no easy feat. Existing literature on the subject is "probably the largest for any war in human history," representing "the most analyzed and contested case" within IR (Copeland 2000, 56; Hamilton and Herwig 2004, 1). The possibility of a "novel" theoretical contribution might seem nearly impossible. What could possibly be left to say? Notwithstanding the rich and prolific range of theoretical and historical investigations into the causes of the war, it does appear the "Long Debate" has stumbled into something of an analytical stalemate.

Whether a *Primat der Aussenpolitik* (primacy of foreign policy) or *Primat der Innenpolitik* (primary of domestic politics) best explains the war's causes remains at the heart of historiographical debates.[3] This literature intersects with and informs IR and social theories working within similar binary frameworks. Hence, within these works one continually finds a "basic methodological disjuncture between geopolitical and sociological forms of explanation" (Justin Rosenberg 2006, 312). For while geopolitical theories such as realism *externalize the social* from their general abstractions, the classical sociological tradition subsumes the ontological specificities of the international system under ideal-type notions of domestic society.[4]

Traditional diplomatic historians and realist studies generally explain the war from the perspective of a European-centered changing distribution of power. They focus attention to the anarchic nature of the international system and its effects on foreign policymaking. The disintegration of European order in the run-up to 1914 is thereby conceived as a structural crisis of the balance of power. For all their differences, classical Marxist theories of imperialism also view the war's origins as a structural crisis, one nonetheless rooted in a very different system: world capitalism. Yet a problem common to both these *systemic* approaches is their tendency to elide the question of *agent differentiation* in accounting for variations in state action. Consequently, many realists (particularly defensive realists) and Marxists have conceived the 1914–18 conflict as an example of an "inadvertent war" or explain agential differences through the addition of ad hoc factors external to their theories.[5]

Though a focus on the universal, systemic sources of the 1914 crisis is necessary, the notion of an unintended slide into war has been challenged by a wealth of evidence produced by Fritz Fischer and his students. Most historians now agree that during the immediate prewar juncture (1912–14), Austrian and German state managers engaged in a series of provocative diplomatic moves, risking if not seeking a European-wide war. This was a conflict that, as German policymakers realized (though not always consistently), would likely involve all the European great powers, including Great Britain (see Mombauer 2002; Hamilton and Herwig 2004; Joll and Martel 2007).

By contrast to these system-level approaches, a wide range of scholars (notably the Fischer School) have sought the origins of the war within the *Sonderweg* (special path) of Prussian-German internal development. This places responsibility for war squarely with the old ruling elites, locating the mainsprings of Germany's "grab for world power" in the crisis-ridden character of the country's incomplete modernization. Dominated by tenacious anachronisms, German imperialism is conceived as atavistic, rooted in the premodern illiberalism of an authoritarian state. Such explanations reveal the exact opposite problem from those of Marxist and realist studies: the tendency to fall prey to an essentializing analysis of a single state's so-called pathological development. As Fischer's critics tirelessly note, the role and effects of other states' actions leading to the start of conflict (before and during July–August 1914) still need to be taken into account in offering a satisfactory explanation. For German policymakers were not the only ones prepared to risk war in the midst of domestic crises and external pressures (see Gustav Schmidt 1990).

The changing nature of the historiographical debates has largely moved between these two poles of "internalist" and "externalist" explanations. Over their course, many scholars have recognized the need to integrate "system-level" and "unit-level" factors into a comprehensive explanatory framework (Blackbourn 2003, 335). Attempts to do so have thus far proven largely unsatisfactory, as the character of theoretical "integration" has overwhelmingly taken the form of a "mix and match" of domestic and international determinations. In the lexicon of mainstream IR, internal and external factors are conceived as relating to one another as "independent variables" incorporated at different levels of analysis. The relationship between the international and domestic is thereby shorn of any theoretical basis in the same sociohistorical process from which they emerged. They remain *analytically* and *ontologically distinct,* the objects of *separate theories* retaining only an external association to one another. Hence, a fundamental dissociation persists between "geopolitical" and "sociological" modes of explanation.

The problems with these kinds of explanations become clear enough when looking over the main issues generally cited within the historiography as decisive to the conflict: the decline of British hegemony in the face of newly industrializing powers; the time-compressed quality of Russian and German state-led industrializations, destabilizing their respective domestic polities; the steady subversion of the Ottoman Empire and its consequences in reshaping the trajectory of European geopolitics; the rising "nationalities" problem in the Balkans and its threat to the Austro-Hungarian Monarchy; and so on. All of these causal processes were inextricably interwoven in the making of war. The emergence and exacerbation of the "Eastern Question" is as much unintelligible without looking at the chain of capitalist industrializations in Europe as is the nature and path of these core states' clashing expansionist drives without examining developments within the Ottoman Empire. What is missing, then, is the formulation of an alternative logic of explanation that uncovers the historical and sociological origins of the war, one that genuinely unifies geopolitical and sociological dynamics as interlocking dimensions of a wider ontology of social development and reproduction.

In substantiating these claims, this chapter critically examines the four dominant interpretations of the origins and nature of the interstate conflicts of the Thirty Years' Crisis, with particular emphasis on their explanations of WWI. Section 1, "Feudal Ghost in the Machine," investigates the two main "unit-level" explanations provided by the *Sonderweg* and Ancien Régime theses. The next section ("Wars Will Happen") turns to "systemic-level" explanations presented by structural realists and the classical Marxist theories of imperialism. The purpose of this analysis is *not* to present a total critique of these theories or to claim that they have nothing to offer in examining the two world wars. Each of the four perspectives assists in isolating and highlighting distinctive threads of a larger explanatory narrative of the crisis period. The approaches nonetheless suffer from certain methodological and empirical weaknesses that demand a fundamental reorientation to bring these different threads together in offering a more satisfactory theoretical account—a challenge taken up in chapter 3.

FEUDAL GHOST IN THE MACHINE: WAR AS EXTERNALIZING DOMESTIC CONFLICT

German Imperialism as Pathological Anachronism

Prominent among liberal and neo-Marxist scholars, the *Sonderweg* thesis seeks to locate the origins of WWI (and the crisis in general) in the peculiarities of Prussian-German sociopolitical development, emphasizing the failure or incompleteness of an indigenous bourgeois revolution during the 19th century.[6] By the turn of the century, German society had experienced the economic transformations of an advanced capitalist society. Bismarck's state-led "revolution from above" achieved an intensive process of industrialization and urbanization, embedding capitalist property relations throughout the Reich. However, the Prussian-German state failed to undergo the normally associated political process of modernization. The state remained strong, civil society "underdeveloped," and democratization fundamentally incomplete. The Kaiserreich was thus distinguished from other developed European countries by the "powerful persistence of pre-industrial, pre-capitalist traditions,"[7] explaining the antidemocratic, illiberal, and authoritarian features of its peculiarly "premodern" state. Characteristic here was the "political abdication" (Wehler 1972, 77) of a nascent German bourgeoisie and their consequent subordination to the preindustrial Junker class in the "marriage of iron and rye" forged under Bismarck's rule. This traditional ruling elite continued to dominate German political life until the Nazi defeat in 1945 (see Moore 1966; Dahrendorf 1967; Winkler 1976).

German development thus diverged from established Western patterns displaying a number of deep historical-societal pathologies (illiberal authoritarianism, militarism, "organic" nationalism) distinguishing its foreign policy behavior. Germany's drive toward imperialist expansionism and colonialism is viewed as a particularly virulent form of "social imperialism." In Wehler's conception (1970, 153), this served to defend the traditional structures of the Prussian-German state, shielding the sociopolitical status quo from the consequences of rapid industrialization and urbanization while diverting movements for parliamentarization and democratization. Social imperialism was actively promoted by the traditional ruling class with the help of a "feudalized" bourgeoisie that was assimilated "by the agrarian-feudal forces" in staving off social reform and other threats to the status quo (Wehler 1985, 173–74; Fischer 1986, 40). If one can trace a line of continuity running throughout German history from 1871 to 1945, it is this "primacy of social imperialism from Bismarck to Hitler" (Wehler 1972, 88).

The sources of German imperialism were thus atavistic in nature. They were rooted in the fundamentally *premodern* qualities of a state characterized by the persistence of anachronistic precapitalist mentalities "steeped in a feudal value system" (Gessner 1977; Berghahn 1993, 54). The origins of the two world wars are, then, conceived as the consequence of Germany's imperfect modernization and failure to transform itself into a liberal-democratic polity—a *specific crisis* of Germany's fractured transition to capitalist modernity. If not entirely external to capitalism, the Thirty Years' Crisis is conceived as an *aberration* from it.

While the *Sonderweg* thesis continues to be advanced by historians and political scientists,[8] it is replete with various conceptual and theoretical problems. These have been meticulously dissected in the works of David Black-bourn and Geoff Eley (1984) and Richard J. Evans (1983a, b), among others.[9] The following discusses a few of the most pertinent of these criticisms.

A fundamental problem with the *Sonderweg* thesis is its *static* comparative approach to German development. Simply put, to have an "aberration" in historical development, one must first have a norm to which to compare it. The norm usually referred to in this instance is the British and French paths to modernity. The former provides the model of "normal" economic development, the latter, "normal" political development. These two normative models are based on these countries' successful "bourgeois revolutions," which Germany did not ostensibly undergo.[10]

Obscured from this static picture is a perspective that interconnects the time-space relations of capitalist development into a wider interactive totality of world development. That German development differed from those of previous states such as Britain and France is precisely explained by those earlier transitions. For "once breakthroughs to on-going capitalist economic development took place in various regions," Robert Brenner writes (1985, 322), "these irrevocably transformed the conditions and character of analogous processes which were to occur subsequently elsewhere." The sequencing of bourgeois revolutions thus "entered into the definition of their differences. *Their order was constitutive of their structure*" (Perry Anderson 1992, 116).

The comparative model assumed by the *Sonderweg* obfuscates these constitutive interrelations between spatiotemporal variations of capitalist development. In doing so, they subsume Germany's developmental trajectory under a liberal-inspired unilinear model of development. This necessarily views the German experience as an aberration. In maintaining the Enlightenment-inspired unilinear narrative of modernity, the origins of the Thirty Years' Crisis must be somehow located outside capitalism. A German *Sonderweg*, determined by premodern remnants, is the Othering mechanism through which capitalism is absolved of any responsibility.

These points directly tie to a second problem with the *Sonderweg* thesis: the unhelpful normative presupposition linking the succession of democracy, modernization, and a progressive foreign policy on the one hand with capitalism and the political ascendancy of the bourgeoisie on the other. To understand the complex relationship between the German bourgeoisie and liberalism, their interests and actions must be situated within the context of the internal conflicts and external exigencies facing the German social formation as a whole. From this perspective, the German state's authoritarian and expansionist tendencies should not be conceived as serving the *specific* interests of the Junker class and traditional political elites but should instead be seen as symptomatic of ruling classes within late-industrializing states more generally. The key difference lay in the *form* these policies took, not the interests and agents they represented (see chap. 3).

Under the compulsions of geopolitical competition, the German state was forced to industrialize as quickly as possible. Consequent to this accelerated industrialization, both the traditional ruling elites and the emerging bourgeoisie confronted the growing threat of a radicalized working-class movement. The majority of nonsocialist *bürgerliche Parteien* were thus willing to accept—and in most cases welcomed—the state-assisted industrialization drive and "revolution from above" inaugurated by Bismarck. To fend off and harness the popular discontent inevitably arising from this revolution, however, the bourgeoisie were forced to co-opt popular peasant and petit bourgeois forces, supporting if not actively promoting the antiparliamentarian elements and expansionist foreign policies of the German state. Indeed, the chief instrument of German authoritarianism and a symbol of its ostensibly premodern character—the infamous Prussian three-class franchise—was introduced and partly drafted by a commission that counted prominent liberals among its members (Blackbourn and Eley 1984, 19–20; see also Heckart 1974).

The identification of "social imperialism" and German expansionism with the specific interests of the traditional conservative elites is therefore fundamentally misleading. Contrary to Wehler's influential account (1985) of social imperialism and reform as conflicting strategies, the two were more often viewed as complementary. Social imperialism thus held a much wider resonance across the political spectrum. There were both conservative and reformist conceptions of social imperialism, and the latter can be found in Friedrich Naumann's "policy of power abroad and reform at home" (Eley 1986, 161). Naumann's program explicitly linked social imperialism with social reform as exemplified in other capitalist societies (see Semmel 1960; Scally 1975; Lebovics 1988; Fry 1996). This reformist conception of social imperialism found advocates in various sections of the German business community.

In narrowing the applicability of social imperialism to the particular interests of a Prussian-German conservative elite, the *Sonderweg* thesis ignores this much wider spectrum of debate, with its differing conceptions of social imperialism. It thereby overlooks the crucial role of the German bourgeois in promoting imperial expansion.[11] More problematically still, it fails to recognize the more general, *structural* nature of the crisis facing the German state. If feudal hangovers were the fundamental problem, then a more thorough-going modernization process to root out these pathologies from the social-political body would suffice. If, instead, the sources of the erratic (if not unusual) expansionist foreign policies of the Kaiserreich were symptoms of a deeper and wider *systemic* crisis, then such "pathologies" would be more difficult to remove.

A conception of social imperialism makes more sense when reoriented to the fact that the *general tendency* among capitalists, along with the conservative elite, was to view the extension of German power abroad as a decisive means to extinguish social conflicts at home and deter the subordinate classes from socialist radicalism. It is *only* in this sense that one can speak of social imperialism as being roughly "conservative" since "all anti-socialist strategies . . . aimed to maintain the integrity of the existing property relations" (Eley 1986, 162). What is recovered in this broader conception is the determinant sociohistorical context in which *all* politicians and business interests, liberal and conservative, had to operate.

The "flight into war" taken by the German ruling classes was the result not of Germany's lack of modernity but rather of its *overstimulation* from both below and without. This was a consequence of the particularly sudden, intensive character of Germany's industrialization and national-state formation processes, pressurized in time and space by the strategic interaction of unevenly developing societies. German development must be situated within the broader dynamics of this *international* conjuncture. Once this is recognized, the "peculiarities" of German development can be conceived as one developmental trajectory among the many variegated patterns of uneven and combined development characteristic of the conjuncture as a whole.

The recognition of this wider international terrain of German development in relation to the causes of WWI points to one final difficulty of the *Sonderweg* approach. Despite the virtues of emphasizing the substantive sociopolitical differences between Germany and the other great powers (thereby dispensing with any state qua state assumption embedded within much of the mainstream IR literature), the *Sonderweg* nonetheless too narrowly associates the cause of war with an essentializing narrative of German "misdevelopment." As Fritz Fischer puts it (1984, 183), "I look upon the July crisis from the angle that it developed specifically from the entire intellectual, political and economic position of the [German] Empire in Europe." While German policymakers' provocation to war in July 1914 seems clear, one must still focus on the more *general* and *systemic* origins of the crisis. Put simply, the German ruling classes were not the only ones prepared to risk war in a juncture of domestic crises and external pressures, as 1914 all too clearly demonstrated.

European Unexceptionalism

A second approach to conceptualizing the crisis is provided by Arno Mayer's (1971, 1981, 1990) "persistence of the Old Regime" thesis.[12] This uncovers the origins of the two world wars in the mobilization of a preindustrial, aristocratic landowning elite *throughout* Europe. Though sharing affinities with the *Sonderweg* thesis, Mayer's approach views the incomplete modernization of German society as a more general phenomenon of European (mis)development.

In emphasizing the nonexceptionalism of German development, the Ancien Régime thesis constitutes its own distinct theoretical contribution. The Thirty Years' Crisis is conceived as a general or *organic crisis* resulting from Europe's unfinished transition to modernity (Mayer 1977). Like the *Sonderweg* thesis, this was characterized by the persistence of an antiquated, semifeudalistic sociopolitical order dominated by landowning aristocratic elites, often in coalition with heavy industrial conservatives. Threatened by domestic conflicts and the imminent demise of their regimes, these elites resorted to internal repression and external expansion to maintain the status quo. In the midst of crisis, war became an "instrument of domestic policy"—a means to secure and stabilize political order through diversionary tactics (Mayer 1981, 305). The Old Regime thesis thus represents an extreme version of the *Primat der Innenpolitik,* focusing almost exclusively on the destabilizing socioeconomic and political pressures within European nation-states.

The key difference between the *Sonderweg* and Old Regime explanations is the latter's strong state qua state assumption. It was not only the German state which was ruled by prebourgeois and preindustrial elites, but *all* European states. The internal crisis of Europe's civil and political societies is seen as resulting in similar responses from different nation-states' ruling classes and policymakers: all sought to preserve the political status quo through repression at home and expansion abroad (see Halperin 2004). From this theoretical perspective, international or geopolitical factors are almost entirely absent.

While avoiding a central problem encountered by the *Sonderweg* approach—which, in focusing exclusively on the putative peculiarities of German development, lacks analysis of the broader sources of geopolitical conflict—the Old Regime thesis nonetheless offers the weakest account of the proximate causes of war in 1914. As an explanation of the origins of WWI, the approach confronts the empirical evidence and comes off the worse. Applied to the British or French cases, if not Germany itself,[13] the theory simply fails to convince. While Britain and France were experiencing domestic crises at the time of the war's outbreak, the evidence that policymakers consciously sought to escape their domestic troubles through the diversionary tactics of war is scarce if not nonexistent.[14]

Mayer's central claim concerning the similarity of responses among political actors to their domestic crises during the prewar conjuncture is very difficult, if not impossible, to maintain empirically. As Pogge von Strandmann (1988, 97) notes, "The evidence that Germany and Austria started the war . . . is even stronger than in the 1960s when Fritz Fischer published his analysis."[15] The Ancien Régime thesis's inability to register these wide discrepancies between European states' foreign policies immediately before WWI is, however, more than a mere empirical blemish in an otherwise sound theoretical framework. Rather, it reflects a deeper fault in the theoretical structure itself.

WARS WILL HAPPEN: SYSTEMIC THEORIES OF GREAT POWER CONFLICT

World Wars as Balance-of-Power Crises

While the immediate origins and dynamics of the two world wars differed, many realist scholars examine the great-power conflicts as part of a single, protracted crisis. From this perspective, the Second World War is seen "as the culmination of a disintegration of the European order, begun in the First World War and continued by the abortive peace, which left the Continent in a state of chronic instability" (P. M. H. Bell 1986, 14). But what was the nature and cause of this "disintegration of the European order"?

The following considers this question through a critical analysis of the two most prominent schools of structural realist thinking: "defensive" and "offensive" realism. Both schools theorize the origins of major wars in the structure of the international system: that is, in terms of the distribution of power (polarity). In general, these approaches conceive bipolar structures as more stable than multipolar ones.[16] For structural realism, then, "the world wars amply illustrate the risks that arise in a multipolar world" (Mearsheimer 1990, 24).[17]

For defensive realism (or neorealism), both world wars are seen as the consequence of the *alliance pathologies* symptomatic of multipolar structures. For WWI, multipolar conditions fostered a "chain-ganging" alliance dynamic in which the great powers (particularly Great Britain and Germany) were drawn into the war through conflicts among their smaller alliance partners. By contrast, the multipolar system of the 1930s resulted in states "buck-passing" the threat of German expansionism to other allies, as was the case with British and French appeasement policies (cf. Waltz 1979, 165–69; Posen 1984; Christensen and Snyder 1990; Walt 1992; Christensen 1997; Van Evera 1998; Mearsheimer 2001, 308–22).

Two questions immediately arise when considering these structural realist explanations for the two world wars. First, what explains the emergence of a great power challenging the status quo of the international system in the first place? And, second, how can structural realism explain the starkly contrasting alliance dynamics (chain-ganging and buck-passing) in the two prewar periods? Regarding the latter question, there is nothing in the *systemic* logic of international politics posited by either defensive or offensive realism that can explain these divergent alliance dynamics.

While structural realism may endogenously explain why multipolar structures produce a suboptimal operation of alliance systems, it cannot explain what *form* this might take.[18] The leading proponent of offensive realism, John Mearsheimer, remarks in a footnote that "domestic political considerations can also sometimes impede balancing behavior. For example, Britain and France were reluctant to ally with the Soviet Union in the 1930s because of their deep-seated antipathy to communism" (Mearsheimer 1990, 16n). This is quite a concession given that the failure for Britain and France to ally with the Soviet Union against Nazi Germany was more than a tertiary factor in the causes of WWII (see chap. 6). While the problem of unit-level causes of foreign policy is shared by all structural realisms, it is a particular dilemma for offensive realism, which claims to be a systemic theory of both international outcomes *and* foreign policy. By contrast, defensive realism aims (though inconsistently) to be only a systemic theory of the former.

Returning to the first question, the emergence of states attempting to dominate the international system is anomalous to defensive realism.[19] According to neorealism, systemic anarchy should result in security-maximizing states as opposed to power-maximizing behavior, as predicted by offensive realism. Hence, while structural conditions may in certain instances lead states to aim to accumulate more power, this is conceived primarily as means to another end: state survival. Defensive realism thus lacks any systemic or structural mechanism to explain why particular states would aim to dominate a given international system, particularly when faced with the risks of an overwhelmingly balancing response. If the international system impels states to act as security maximizers rather than power maximizers, as defensive realism claims, why would imperial or Nazi Germany pursue an aggressive policy of expansionism?

Considering these two issues alone would seem to pose major problems for the explanatory power of defensive realism in illuminating the causes of the Thirty Years' Crisis. Waltz and his students think not. For them, defensive realism is a structural theory of international politics intended only to explain *systemic outcomes, not* state behavior.[20] To explain the latter, one needs to supplement neorealism's systemic theory of the international with a domestic theory of the state and foreign policy. In other words, explaining any specific war or geopolitical conflict in history will require the addition of "unit-level" factors outside Waltz's sparsely conceptualized international system.

There are two relevant and related criticisms of Waltz's argument here. First, if it is impossible for a theory to *endogenously* explain the origins of the two world wars—arguably the most important period in the history of the modern international system—the more general explanatory utility of such a theory is called into question. If the "explanatory power of a theory, not its parsimony, is the criterion of a theory's success," as Waltz himself claims (1996, 57), then neorealism must be judged a great disappointment. Explaining the "dismal recurrence" of war throughout the centuries, the only deductive generalization defensive realism can claim is the refutation of Kant's "perpetual peace" thesis (Waltz 1959, 44; see also Waltz 1979, 69; 1986, 329; Justin Rosenberg 1994).

Second, there is the trouble of defensive realists' attempts to transform

Waltz's theory of international politics into a theory of foreign policy. As Waltz (1986, 1996) has repeatedly emphasized, structural realism is *not* a theory of foreign policy. For this, one needs a separate theory.[21] When states fail to act in instrumentally rational ways corresponding to the systemic logic postulated by defensive realism, neorealists must then explain this "irrational" behavior from an incorporation of unit-level factors exogenous to their theories.[22] Waltz has claimed (1986, 339) that while he did not try to formulate a theory of the state, "surely some neorealist is capable of producing" such a theory. However, following Waltz's theoretical premises, there is, according to Alexander Wendt (1987), a logical inconsistency in this proposition.

Neorealism defines the structure of the international system by the attributes of its constitutive units (the "distribution of capabilities" among states). Theorizing the content, form, and behavior of these units by recourse to system structure is thus inherently problematic. "The neorealist's individualist conceptualization of system structure is," as Wendt claims (1987, 343, emphasis added), "too weak to support a social theory of the state: system structures cannot *generate agents* if they are defined exclusively in terms of those agents in the first place." In other words, neorealism's ontological reductionism of structure to units—derivative of the methodological individualism appropriated from microeconomics—makes it impossible for them to theorize such units. Hence, the explanatory frameworks provided by neorealists attempting to offer a theory of the state and foreign policy cease to be derived from structural realist assumptions (cf. Zakaria 1992; Elman 1996; Legro and Moravcsik 1999).[23]

Wendt's critique of neorealism as being inadequate in formulating a theory of the state is, however, only partially correct.[24] One can derive a *minimal* theory of the state based on Waltz's conception of the international system. This would, above all, posit a functional convergence of state forms through the selection mechanisms of international socialization and competition. The logic of self-help systems produces a tendency toward "unit sameness" over time (Waltz 1979, 63, 66, 128). Waltz's theory of the state is then an undifferentiated one: states are conceived as functionally homogenous. The assumption is incorporated by both offensive and defensive schools of structural realism.[25] This poses a major difficulty for any structural realist explanation of the two world wars, which witnessed a variety of internally differentiated states pursuing very different foreign policies. Consequently, when neorealists aim to explain the causes of the wars, their arguments ultimately rest on nontheorized or exogenously conceived unit-level factors (for example, militarism, domestic regimes, offensive/defensive tactics, organizational dynamics, and so on). In other words, they smuggle in separately formed add-on theories that end up doing all the explanatory work. To this extent, Wendt is correct to claim that neorealists have systematically failed to produce a genuinely *social* theory of the state and foreign policy—that is, one that interweaves the international and domestic into a consistently holistic explanation of state action.

Defensive realism necessarily supplements its minimalist systemic theory with auxiliary domestic theories to explain the myriad anomalies faced when attempting to apply its theory to history.[26] To attempt to claim, as neorealists do, that this poses little problem for their theories, since what contradicts their theoretical premises is automatically discredited as a matter for another theory, is hardly a defense. As Eric Wolf put it (1982, 10) in another context, "If the models leak like sieves, it is then argued that this is either because they are merely abstract constructs and not expected to hold empirical water, or because troublemakers have poked holes in them." This is not simply a case of a "highly parsimonious" theory but one which is essentially unfalsifiable (Vasquez 1997).

The predicament of "unit sameness" is illustrative of a broader problem common to *all* structural realist explanations of WWI. This concerns their commonly shared "inadvertent war" interpretation of the conflict. Since states are conceived as functionally undifferentiated, structural realism predicts that they will, given similar structural conditions, pursue comparable foreign policies. Among those realists faithfully remaining at the systemic level of explanation, there is thus a tendency to interpret the causes of the war as the unintended consequence of the increasing difficulties of policy-making crisis management resulting from the inherent instabilities of the pre-1914 international system.[27] The idea that the great powers "slithered over the brink into the boiling cauldron of war," as Lloyd George famously pronounced (see, e.g., as quoted in Hamilton and Herwig 2004, 19), has been profoundly challenged by Fischer's "historiographical revolution." Drawing on a wealth of documentary evidence, Fischer and his students have moved historiographical debates "irretrievably away from any thesis of coequal responsibility or international anarchy" (Hamilton and Herwig 2003, 39).

Structural realism's persistent blindness to these differences in foreign policies reflects a deeper theoretical dilemma: their inability to theorize sociopolitical variations among states (see Justin Rosenberg 2008). The question is not merely one of a general structural cause having different effects as a consequence of their mediation and refraction through differentiated units. Rather, the issue is an ontologically deeper one: how a singular structural "logic" is constituted and reconstituted by the interaction of its units through which the differences among them are produced. In other words, systems are *generatively differentiating* through the interconnective plurality of their units.

These matters relate to one final problem confronting structural realist explanations of WWI. Downplaying the Balkan spark for the war, realist interpretations see very little distinct in the immediate prewar conjuncture outside of the increasing frequency of crisis events taken to be proof of the underlying structural instabilities of the European geopolitical system. As Kenneth Waltz puts it,

> In one sense the unstable politics of the Balkans carried the world into war. But that statement misses the point. Internationally, destabilizing events and conditions abound. The important questions to ask are whether they are likely to be managed better, and whether their effects are absorbed more readily, in one system than in another. (1979, 167)[28]

To some extent, such a position is indisputable: by 1912, the international system was clearly in crisis mode. The probability of a great-power war was dramatically increased. Nonetheless, the *time-space specificity* of the Balkan spark was absolutely crucial in producing a genuinely *world* war.

As historians convincingly demonstrate, there was a relatively short window of opportunity, as perceived by German state managers (approximately 1912–17), for launching a preemptive strike against Russia before it completed its strategic railway lines, making German tactical war plans obsolete (see chap. 3). The timing of the crisis was crucial to the outbreak of the war and thus needs to somehow enter into the theoretical equation. The same goes for the *geographical* location of the crisis.

Only a crisis in the Balkans directly involving both Austro-Hungarian and Russian interests could lead to a generalized war as the Habsburg monarchy's abdication of its alliance role in the Second Moroccan Crisis of 1911 clearly indicated. While it may be argued that the long-standing "Eastern Question" was destined to lead to a European-wide war at *some point,* the causal forces leading to the destabilization of Ottoman power still need to be theoretically explained. Doing so, however, means dispensing with any Eurocentric perspective on the origins of the war. This is an inherent problem for structural realists. For if the structure of the international system (polarity) is conceptualized in quantitative terms (that is, the number of great powers), then this essentially excludes the effects of "peripheral" states and societies on the nature and course of international politics (Barkawi and Laffey 2006). Hence, though the *fact* of Ottoman decline and its effects on the European geopolitical system appear throughout the realist literature, they are usually tangential to its theoretical explanations. The *theorization* of the process only goes as far as the "selection mechanisms" inherent in an anarchic international system. The Eastern Question is thus relegated to the realm of empirical contingencies. Yet there were clearly much deeper ontological linkages between the differentiated character and trajectory of European and Ottoman development. Visualizing these connections in their necessarily entwining social and geopolitical dimensions means moving beyond the realist horizon.

World Wars as Crises of Monopoly Capitalism

Despite the recent revival of historical materialist thinking within IR, classical Marxist theories of imperialism remain something of a theoretical anachronism.[29] The classical theories are seen as inapplicable not only to contemporary world politics[30] but also to the epoch in which they were originally formulated (see Gindin and Panitch 2004; Halperin 2004; Teschke and Lacher 2007). In the historiographical debates on the two world wars, it is tempting to say that the closest thing to a strong "consensus" historians have reached is that the classical Marxist theories have little if anything to offer (cf. Gordon 1974, 206; McDonough 1997, 36–37; Strachan 2001, 100; Hamilton and Herwig 2003; but see Joll and Martel 2007). Yet there is an important sense in which the classical Marxist theories have been fundamentally misinterpreted, at least within mainstream IR. Specifically, there are at least two common criticisms of the classical theories that must be overcome to seriously engage their work.

First, there is the question of classical Marxism's inherent economism or "economic reductionism." Morgenthau's (1948, 29) criticism that Marxism conceives "all political phenomena as the reflection of economic conditions" is largely accepted within "textbook" IR interpretations (see Waltz 1979, chap. 2; Kubálková and Cruickshank 1989; Tony Smith 1994, appendix). Even critical scholars such as John M. Hobson claim (1998b, 356) that "a non-reductionist Marxism is a *non-sequitur*." The second related question rests on the argument that the theories represent "unit-level" explanations of geopolitical rivalry and war. The theory most widely and comprehensively examined is Lenin's pamphlet, *Imperialism: The Latest Stage of Monopoly Capitalism* (see Morgenthau 1948; Waltz 1979, chap. 2; Kubálková and Cruickshank 1989).[31]

Briefly stated, Lenin's theory explained "interimperialist" rivalry and war as organic consequences of the development of capitalism as a world system, specifically in its transition from the "competitive" to "monopoly phase" occurring sometime around the turn of the 20th century. This marked the beginning of a distinctly capitalist form of imperialism. A basic way of distinguishing the *differentia specifica* of capitalist imperialism, as conceptualized by Lenin and further developed by Bukharin, is to say that it denoted the historical point when processes of territorial-military rivalry between states were subsumed under the competition among "many capitals" (Callinicos 2007). Geopolitical conflict was thereby transformed into a distinct species of intercapitalist competition: war as a continuation of economic competition by other means.

The monopoly stage of capitalism was conceptualized as resulting from two key tendencies of capitalism identified by Marx: the increasing concentration and centralization of capital. This led to the fusion of banking and industrial capitals into a single fraction of "finance capital." Lenin's argument here draws heavily on the works of radical liberal economist John A. Hobson, specifically in partially adopting Hobson's concept of "finance capital" as the rule of a "financial oligarchy" dominating each national economy. Hobson's extensive influence on Lenin's pamphlet has led many scholars to mistakenly identify a single "Hobson-Lenin" thesis of imperialism. This is, to a large extent, the source of their broad-brushed critiques of the classical Marxist theories as reducing international politics to "unit-level" domestic economic relations. The classic and still highly influential example of this misguided interpretation is Waltz's (1979) critique.

Lenin clearly drew on Hobson, but Lenin's conception of "finance capital" was taken more from Austro-Marxist economist Rudolf Hilferding and his overall theory similar to that of his fellow Bolshevik, Nikolai Bukharin (see Howard and King 1989; Brewer 1990; Callinicos 2009a). Whichever influence was greatest, Lenin's conceptions of capitalism and imperialism clearly differed from Hobson's. As Alker and Biersteker remark (1984, 133–34), "Waltz's concatenation of Hobson and Lenin confuses fundamental differences in approaches as well as differences of philosophies of social science."

These differences remain essentially unacknowledged in "mainstream" IR (see Barkawi 2010). For Lenin, imperialism was a *world system irreducible to its national parts* (1960, 22:272; see also Bukharin 1973, 17–18). Lenin's theory is a systemic rather than unit-level theory.

The charge of economic reductionism similarly does not hold. Lenin adopted Marx's view of capitalism as a *social structure* defined by the production process rather than liberal notions of capitalism as reducible to market transactions. In Lenin's polemics against the Marxisms of the Second International, he derided them into falling into the trap of "economism"— reducing the politics of the class struggle to the economic plane alone. Further, as Vijay Prashad notes (1995, 6), "Lenin deployed the term 'economism' to critique the economic reductionism of the bourgeoisie" in subsuming all phenomena to the techno-economic bases of society.

A fine but significant distinction, therefore, must be made between economically *reductionist* and materialistically *determinist* theories of interstate rivalry. The Second and Stalinized Third Internationals fell into the former category; Lenin's Marxism (like that of Trotsky), the latter. Lenin's perspective is consistent with a Marxist approach that conceives the "material basis"[32] as paramount in the hierarchy of mediated determinations within a holistically conceived social world and that views other moments of the "totality" as dialectically interrelated. This is not the same as reducing all phenomena to their technoeconomic foundations and conceiving them as mere epiphenomena.[33] Finally, the preponderant focus on the economic in *Imperialism* was not a result of Lenin's reductionist method but his explicit bracketing of "non-economic aspects of the question."

The causal connections between world systemic determinations and state action in Lenin's argument are, however, left murky at best. In *Imperialism,* Lenin's theory of the state is instrumentalist.[34] The crucial linkages and mediations between state and capital are never adequately worked out. The question of agents (oligopolistic businesses and states) and their interconnections are left underdetermined. However, Lenin's pamphlet was intended as a "popular outline" of already existing theories and ideas; it was not a developed piece of theoretical work. For this, one need turn to Bukharin's more theoretically rigorous *Imperialism and World Economy,* where the relations between state and capital are conceived as fused into a single unit through the transformation of national economies into "state-capitalist trusts" (Bukharin 1973, chap. 11).

Yet it is precisely Lenin and Bukharin's *upward conflation* of the international to the world systemic that renders their work so problematic. Three difficulties arise from this move. First, the theory *assumes* but does not explain the existence of plural states. The question of *why* intercapitalist conflicts take a *territorial-military* form is left theoretically unaddressed. As David Harvey remarks (2001, 326),

> To convert the Marxian insights into a geopolitical framework, Lenin introduced the concept of the state which . . . remains the fundamental concept whereby territoriality is expressed. But in so doing, Lenin largely begged the question as to how or why the circulation of capital and the deployment of labor power should be national rather than global in their orientation and why the interests of either capitalists or laborers should or even could be expressed as national interests.

Contrary to comparable criticisms made by Benno Teschke and Hannes Lacher (2007), who also quote Harvey, this problem is not solely resolvable through a historically limited account of the rise of nation-state sovereign territoriality during the feudal-absolutist epochs. Rather, it extends more broadly to a question of how a Marxist theory of international relations can capture the distinct causal determinations emerging from the coexistence and interaction of societies in general.[35]

The second problem springs from the same source as the first. By subsuming the intersocietal dimension of social development and reproduction to a world systemic level, Lenin and particularly Bukharin fall into the same realist trap of unit homogenization. The Lenin-Bukharin theory of imperialism mostly applied to the later-developing capitalist states, particularly Germany, on which much of their evidence was based. These economies were generally characterized, as Lenin and Bukharin noted, by high levels of vertical-horizontal business integration (economies of scale), oligopolistic markets (cartels and trusts), large-scale banking-industrial combinations ("finance capital"), protectionist trade policies, export combinations, and statist forms of industrialization (see Selwyn 2011). By contrast, the increasing tendency to capital export (over trade) postulated by Lenin-Bukharin was a main feature of earlier developers (specifically Britain and France). Hence, the causal connections hypothesized by Lenin and Bukharin between finance capital and territorial expansionism simply do not hold (Barratt Brown 1970, 97–107; Brewer 1990, 114–16). To take a specific example, the paradigm of "monopoly capitalism," Germany, suffered from a *shortage* rather than surplus of money capital, which weakened the economic means at the Wilhelmstraße's disposal to entice Russia into a political alliance against France (see discussion in chapter 3).

Here, the significance of Lenin's thesis of "uneven development" in the theory of imperialism needs to be addressed, as it is often conflated with Trotsky's more specific interpretation of unevenness. Although "uneven development" between nation-states played a key explanatory role in Lenin's framework,[36] it did so primarily as a cause for the persistence of interimperialist rivalries over any potential harmonization of international capitalist interests (Kautsky's "ultraimperialist" thesis"). The possibility of unevenness and intersocietal interaction *generating* sociologically amalgamated and differentiated states and in turn conditioning and feeding back into the causes of interimperialist rivalries never entered into Lenin's framework.

The problem of unit homogenization common to classical Marxists relates to a third dilemma in explaining the First World War. Simply put, while the classical Marxist theories have much to say about the "structural" and "epochal" causes of wars, they provide little help in explaining concrete conjunctures of wars.[37] As James Joll and Gordon Martel note, if the Marxist theory of imperialism is accurate "it would provide the most comprehensive explanation of the outbreak of the First World War, though *it would still leave open the question why this particular war started at that particular time in the mounting crisis of capitalism*." It would still require an explanation of the 1914 juncture "in terms of specific decisions by particular individuals" (Joll and Martel 2007, 146, 238, emphasis mine). In other words, what the classical Marxists lack is the ability to offer a theoretical analysis of the *specificities* of the immediate prewar period differentiating it as a distinct, but not autonomous, temporality. This is at least in part a consequence of the problem of "unit sameness" which identifies a single "model of expansionism" (Arrighi 1978) and foreign policy behavior common to all imperialist states.

The explanatory difficulties encountered by the homogenization of political agents are demonstrated in Eric Hobsbawm's (1987) examination of the origins of WWI.[38] This account is arguably the best English-language application of the "Leninist" theory of imperialism explaining the 1914 conjuncture. Hobsbawm's account interweaves sociological and historical factors into a rich and penetrating narrative, tracing the long-term causal forces leading the capitalist states to world conflagration. The destabilizing role of the uneven and interactive character of capitalist industrialization and its relation to economic crisis, revolutionary nationalism, and domestic class conflict is not at all lost in his analysis (see esp. Hobsbawm 1987, chaps. 2, 3, 6, 12). Yet when narrowing in to explain the causes of the July 1914 crisis, Hobsbawm's account runs into trouble.

Stopping to consider the WWI historiographical debates, Hobsbawm rightly dismisses the "war guilt" thesis identifying the Kaiserreich as the sole "aggressor." He throws doubt on the validity of the Fischerite "social imperialism" thesis and chastises proponents of that view for placing "responsibility" for war on the shoulders of German policymakers (1987, 309–10, 323–25). "The problem of discovering the origins of the First World War," Hobsbawm comments (1987, 312), is "not one of discovering 'the aggressor.'" Hobsbawm is no doubt correct in questioning the analytical validity of the "war guilt" issue. Yet this unnecessarily translates into an *ontological flattening* of the differences between sociopolitical agents and the variations in state behavior during the war juncture leading him to a restatement of the "slither into war" thesis. Claiming that no great power "before 1914 wanted either a general European war or even . . . a limited military conflict with another European power," Hobsbawm contends that WWI's origins must be sought in "a progressively deteriorating international situation which increasingly escaped the control of governments" (1987, 310–11, 312).[39] Dissolving any specificity of the war juncture, he writes: "By 1914 *any* confrontation between the [alliance] blocs . . . brought them to the verge of war . . . *any* incident, however random . . . could lead to such a confrontation" (1987, 323–24).[40]

This sets the stage for Hobsbawm's alternative theorization, which locates the causal sources of the war in the inherently expansive, infinite aims of capital accumulation. The "development of capitalism inevitably pushed the world in the direction of state rivalry, imperialist expansion, conflict and war," because the "characteristic feature of capitalist accumulation was precisely that it had no limit" (1987, 316, 318). Though recognizing that domestic troubles pushed at least one country (Austria-Hungary) to solve its internal crisis through war (1987, 323), the role of interactively generated sociopolitical differences are essentially erased in Hobsbawm's explanation of the war, which rests on this "unlimited dynamism" of the capital accumulation process. While this is surely an indispensable ingredient of any theorization of the conflicts leading to war, sociopolitical unevenness still needs to be theoretically interpolated somewhere within the analysis. Further, much more explanatory weight must be given to the particularities of the

1914 spark: it was not just "any incident" that fulfilled the time-space conditions that would lead to war, nor was it likely that any of the powers would instigate the conflict (see chap. 3).

CONCLUSION

Shedding light on different aspects of the causes of war in 1914, both "internalist" and "externalist" theories confront a number of dilemmas seemingly irresolvable within the confines of their own frameworks. Rather than continuing down the path of "unit-level" versus "system-level" polarizations, the "proper strategy is to work towards the development of . . . synthetic or integrative models of change" (Smelser 1992, 388–89) that are capable of grasping the organic linkages between the domestic and international in a wider ontology of social development and reproduction. As noted, however, the form of theoretical synthesis taken should not be the kind of mixed bag of "independent variables" incorporated at different, discretely conceived "levels of analysis" so common to the conventional IR and sociology literatures. The effect is to conceive the international and domestic as putatively separate, self-contained social spheres that only *subsequently* interact. By contrast, a genuine theoretical synthesis should capture the distinctive but in no way autonomous dimensions of social development in terms of their *mutual entailment*. As examined in the next chapter, the theory of uneven and combined development offers one route to achieve this.

CHAPTER 2

The Theory of Uneven and Combined Development: Origins and Reconfigurations

BUILDING ON Leon Trotsky's idea of uneven and combined development, this chapter demonstrates the concept's potential as an integrated theory of interstate rivalry and war. This move requires some contextualization and engagement with a number of disparate—and, until very recently, often disconnected—debates within IR, historical sociology, and Marxism generally addressing what has been termed the "problematic of the international" (Justin Rosenberg 2000, 65). Given the mutual miscomprehensions often encountered between these literatures (particularly IR and Marxism), this necessitates some clarification of the core categories of the intellectual heritage from which the proposed solution—uneven and combined development—is drawn: that is, historical materialism. For a principal claim is that while uneven and combined development provides a necessary "methodological fix" to certain anomalies faced by historical materialism, without this broader theoretical foundation, the idea remains a lifeless abstraction of the variety of such ahistorical categories as "anarchy" and the "balance of power."

So why uneven and combined development? What does it mean? And what relevance might it hold for the study of interstate conflict and war in modern world politics? Finally, what is the significance of "the international" for our theorizations of the state-capital relation and their connections to foreign policymaking ideologies and agencies? Before addressing these questions, the following section briefly lays out the "problematic of the international" as specifically manifested in Marxism before moving on to consider its broader implications for IR theory.

THE SIGNIFICANCE OF "THE INTERNATIONAL"

The Absence of International Theory

Continually frustrated with the ahistorical and suprasociological premises of mainstream IR theories, scholars in the field have recently turned to more substantive methods of historical and sociological inquiry. Marxist social theory has consequently held a renewed appeal for the discipline. Yet the revival of interest in historical materialism has revealed the persistence of a series of dilemmas present in Marxist thought on "the international." For while (neo)realist IR scholars have been charged with projecting back in time the specific characteristics of the modern international system, theorized in abstraction from their sociohistorical foundations, Marxists have confronted something of the opposite criticism. This holds that Marxist perspectives have suffered from a systematic inability to theorize what is considered the unique domain of IR: the coexistence and interaction of a multiplicity of societies (conceived in IR as sovereign states) and the distinctive causal dynamics and behavioral patterns emerging therefrom.

Irrespective of whether the particular Marxist approach in question conceptualizes social systems as operating primarily at the domestic or world level—as exemplified by political Marxism and world systems analysis, respectively—the dilemma remains the same. By working outward from a conception of a specific social structure (be it slavery, feudalism, capitalism, or whatever), the theorization of the geopolitical takes the form of a reimagining of domestic society writ large: an extrapolation from analytical categories derived from a society conceived in the ontologically *singular* form.[1] This then vanishes what is arguably unique to any multistate system: a superordinating "anarchical" structure irreducible to the historically variable types of societies constituting them. Thus, if realists have mistakenly transformed anarchy into the sine qua non of international relations, extending it back in time and projecting its effects undifferentiated across space, Marxists have traditionally subsumed anarchy under transnational capitalist hierarchies or intercapitalist competition (mediated or otherwise) or analytically separated its logic from capitalism altogether (see, for example, Chase-Dunn 1981; Arrighi 1994; Hardt and Negri 2000; David Harvey 2003; Callinicos 2007; Davidson 2010).

If Marxism's claim to a holistic philosophy of internal relations—whereby social totality is conceived as being composed of interactive and co-

constitutive parts—is to be taken seriously, then the theoretical standing of "the international" for a historical materialist approach requires further attention. For the centerpiece of historical materialist analysis rests on its unique ability to conceptually interiorize the interdependency of each element within it "so that the *conditions of its existence* are taken to be part of what it is" (Ollman 1979, 105). Hence, Marxists must be able to explain the conditions of existence for any given international system. In terms of Marx's basis/superstructure (*Basis/Überbau*) metaphor[2]—properly understood as a basic statement of philosophical materialism rather than a mechanistic cause/effect model—"the international" must be *derived* from wider sociohistorical processes.

While Marx and Engels wrote extensively on matters of world politics broadly defined,[3] nowhere did they systematically reflect on this distinctly *intersocietal* component of sociohistorical causality entering into their theorizations of development itself. Notwithstanding Marx's frequent remarks concerning the variegated forms and trajectories of socioeconomic development on Europe's "periphery" and beyond—not to mention his explicit rejection of a Western-centric linear developmentalist interpretations of *Capital*[4]—the starting point for most Marxist *theory* was the anticipated universalization of the European experience (see Löwy 1981; Shanin 1983; Kevin Anderson 2010). The problem that societal multiplicity and its multilinear effects poses to Marxism as both an explanatory theory of social change and emancipatory politics has thus emerged as a standard critique from within and without (see Waltz 1959; Nisbet 1969; Berki 1971; Skocpol 1973; Barker 1978a; Giddens 1981; Halliday 1987; Mann 1988; Martin Shaw 1988; Tenbruck 1994; Hobson 1998a; Lacher 2002; Teschke 2003; Callinicos 2004; Justin Rosenberg 2006; Davenport 2013). Writing from a historical materialist perspective, for example, Kees van der Pijl argues (2007, viii) that "the Marxist legacy as it exists has largely failed to develop its own method in the area of foreign relations."

Far from being a matter of purely scholastic concern, this missing "international theory" in the Marxist tradition has a number of directly political implications. For what modern political tradition is more unashamedly internationalist and universalist than Marxism? If the "forgotten" history of disciplinary IR is one crucially implicated in confronting the dilemmas of social disorder and revolution wrought by the international spread of capitalist social relations and empire, the subaltern history of 20th-century Marxist politics is imbricated with the manifold constraints imposed by the "interstateness" of capitalism on the potentials of emancipatory projects. For "at every point" in a revolution's development, Arno Mayer writes (2000, 534), "international politics impinges on the course of a revolution."

That capitalism emerged within—and in fact perpetuates—a world divided into a multiplicity of interactive, heterogeneous states has thus held enormous significance for revolutionary Marxist politics. For in the process of attempting to build socialism by taking state power and harnessing it to this end, Marxist-inspired revolutions have all too often transformed themselves into their very negation. Rather than constructing the emancipated society of the future, wherein the political state would dissolve into a free association of self-governing producers, the trajectories of self-proclaimed "socialist" societies witnessed the intensive perfection of the oppressive state apparatus it had originally sought to destroy. Hence the creation and consolidation of revolutionary states "perhaps best dramatizes the centrality of interstate relations and war" to modern social development (Mayer 2000, 533; see also Halliday 1999). Lenin certainly recognized such dilemmas arising from the "interstateness" of capitalism confronting any revolutionary state. As he commented to fellow Bolsheviks in March 1919: "We are living not merely in a state, but *in a system of states,* and it is inconceivable for the Soviet Republic to exist alongside the imperialist states for any length of time. One or the other must triumph in the end" (Lenin 1960, 29:153).

In the field of IR, the apparent fact that revolutionary states quickly adopted the methods of traditional diplomacy and great-power politics has been viewed as a striking vindication of the "timeless" wisdom of political realism.[5] While it would be hopelessly naive if not intellectually disingenuous to subsume an explanation of the multitude of causal forces behind any socialist "degeneration," Marxists travel at their peril without recognition of the socially transformational power of power politics. So how has this problematic of "the international" been formulated in IR?

The "Problematic of the International"

The problematic of the international has often been posed in misleading terms as a chronological question in both IR and historical sociology. From this perspective, the question is, If the existence of the state system predates the emergence of capitalism, how can this plurality of states and geopolitical rivalry be fully explained by the dynamics of capitalism? (see Skocpol 1979, 3–43; Mann 1988, 120; Teschke 2003, 264–65; Lacher 2005). Reasoning from these premises, many scholars have concluded that the transhistorical existence of geopolitical competition and war necessarily escape attempts to contextualize their causal efficacy within a historically specific logic of capital. In Theda Skocpol's words (1979, 22), "The international states system as a transnational structure of military competition was not originally created by capitalism. Throughout modern world history, it represents an analytically autonomous level of transnational reality—*interdependent* in its structure and dynamics with world capitalism, but not reducible to it."

Yet to recognize that sociopolitical multiplicity and interstate competition historically predates the emergence of capitalism does not logically necessitate imputing any transhistorical logic to geopolitics, as proponents of this form of critique often have. One could, for example, reasonably infer that relations among kin are a truly universal historical phenomenon without deducing any transhistorical logic to these relations: the social category of the "family" holds radically different meanings in different times and places. Nevertheless, the question of whether a mode of production-centered analysis of the international leaves behind an unexplained surplus of determinations arising from the fact that all societies coexist with and interact with others—thereby adding "a lateral field of causality over and above the 'domestic' determinations arising from each and every one of the participant societies"—is a legitimate one in need of further exploration (Callinicos and Rosenberg 2008, 88). To put the issue in broader terms, how can *any* social theory endogenously incorporate the specificity and efficacy of the intersocietal in the constitution, reproduction, and transformation of social structures? How might "internal" (sociological) and "external" (geopolitical) moments of social development be united into a single, coherent explanatory apparatus? What form should this theoretical integration take? And what then is the precise standing of the international in our social theories?

Formulated in these more general terms, the implications of the "problematic of the international" extend far beyond the ranks of Marxist approaches to IR. While Marx (1976, 727 n. 2) consciously abstracted the intersocietal from his conception of social development,[6] so too, at least implicitly, did all other major classical social theorists. Hence, a common problem of all social theory is a tendency to fail to theoretically account for sociopolitical multiplicity and its effects. This constitutive absence in part explains the persistence of social theories to subsume the multiplicity of variegated developmental paths under a single narrative of unilinear stages (see Nisbet 1969). This dilemma is reproduced in various forms within IR theories: the domain where the problem of difference and alterity reach their highest expression.

Within IR, engagements with these issues have taken a variety of forms, from deductive statements on the character of the international to a theory of the evolution of different intersubjectively held cultures of international relations. However, these specifically international theories have problematically excluded any historically grounded conception of society either by explicitly abstracting the international from domestic social processes (Waltz 1979) or by conceiving the former in terms of a suprahistorical, abstract sociality (Alexander Wendt 1999). Yet despite historical sociology's devout attention to pointing out the inadequacy of "societal-based theories" (Hobson 1998a, 288), they too have tended to introduce "the international" as an externality to their analyses in ways actually reinforcing the theoretical disconnect between the international and domestic. The problem thus cuts across theoretical and methodological divides, as attested to by Martin Hall's critical survey of the multitheoretical contributions of historical sociology to IR.[7] "There is a danger," Hall writes (1999, 108; emphasis added), that historical sociology "serves to strengthen the dichotomization of 'the international' and 'the domestic.' Although . . . international and domestic forces interact or combine to produce a certain outcome, *analytically they are still distinct*" (see also Halliday 2002a; Justin Rosenberg 2006).

These lacunae signal the need for a unified theory of how societies interact, of how they change, and of the relationship between these processes. Such a theory would have to capture how the operational reality of "the international," identified but inadequately theorized by realism, is itself part and parcel of a wider sociohistorical developmental process. This is particularly significant for reconceptualizing the provenance, trajectory, and character of the class conflicts, military competitions, and wars making up the Thirty Years' Crisis, a pivotal epoch in the *coevolution* and *transformation* of the modern state system and global capitalism whereby socioeconomic, ideological, and military conflicts mutually conditioned one another.

The theory of uneven and combined development offers a potential resource in overcoming the obstinate dichotomy of "geopolitical" versus "sociological" modes of explanations. It does so by uniquely interpolating an international dimension of causality as *intrinsic* to the historical process of social development itself. This renders "the international" historically and sociologically intelligible, overcoming both realist reifications of the international system as an absolutely autonomous ("suprasocial") sphere and the classical sociological tradition's tendency to falsely subsume its distinctive causal dynamics to *uni*societal abstractions. These arguments have been most rigorously advanced in the writings of Justin Rosenberg (2005, 2006, 2007, 2010) and Kamran Matin (2007, 2012, 2013). Before turning to briefly consider their spatiotemporal extension of uneven and combined development into a general theory of "the international," it is helpful to examine the concept's formation in its originating sociohistorical context, explicating its core tenets in the process.

ORIGINS: UNEVEN AND COMBINED DEVELOPMENT— THEORY OF LATE DEVELOPMENT

Despite the decisive importance of uneven and combined development in Trotsky's writings, the idea has until very recently received little attention.[8] As Neil Davidson (2006, 10) notes, while many scholars have explored the themes of "the privilege of backwardness" and "the advantages of priority," these ideas remain within the domain of uneven development. They are by no means unique to Trotsky. The principal innovation from Trotsky comes with his formulation of "combined development" and its juxtaposition with unevenness.[9]

Trotsky's Idea in Political and Historical Context

As with most advances in Marxist thinking, the genesis of Trotsky's idea of uneven and combined development was a politically strategic innovation: a means of further developing revolutionary socialist praxis within the specific context of early 20th-century tsarist Russian politics. Like other "late-developing" industrializers, the crucial question facing revolutionary socialists was whether they were "ready" for a strategy of independent proletarian revolutionary action. Had the country passed through the "necessary" stage of bourgeois-democratic revolution and capitalist development sufficient to provide the material and political bases for socialist revolution?[10]

The classical position in this debate, taken up by the Mensheviks in tsarist Russia and supported by the Second International, was that late-developing states remained unripe for socialist revolution. This was a perspective shared by virtually *all* Marxists of the period (see Walicki 1969; Knei-Paz 1978; Löwy 1981; Davidson 2006). The objective "balance of power"

within and between states militated against any successful socialist revolution outside the capitalist core. Any attempt at such a revolution was therefore deemed "utopian" (Trotsky 2007, chap. 1). The proletariat's immediate
task was then to ally themselves with progressive bourgeois forces in the
shared struggle against precapitalist forms of political rule. Such was the
"two-stage" strategy of revolution adhered to by the vast majority of Russian
Marxists, a position corresponding to Marxist orthodoxy of the time.

Significant for the discussion here is how the Menshevik strategy rested
on an *internalist* schematic of social development (the "methodological nationalism" assumption). This held that each society followed the developmental trajectory of the more "advanced" capitalist countries in the chronological succession of increasingly progressive (that is, technologically
advanced) modes of production internal to them. This took Marx's famous
"1859 Preface" to the *Contribution to the Critique of Political Economy* to its
logical reductio ad absurdum, schematically interpreting his declaration
that

> no social order is ever destroyed before all the productive forces for which it is
> sufficient have been developed, and new superior relations of production
> never replace older ones before the material conditions for their existence
> have matured within the framework of the old society. (Marx 1970, 21)

The underlying basis of these perspectives is summarized in Marx's famous
dictum directed at then "backward" Germany: "De te fabula narratur!" (This
story is told of you!). The problem was that in such states as Russia—if not
the majority of the late-developing countries—the characters of the story
were not playing their assigned roles. For it was clear by the early 20th century that the development of the more advanced societies were not destined
to show the less developed "the image of its own future" (Marx 1976, 91). In
this sense, the course of history had proven Marx mistaken. "England in her
day revealed the future of France, considerably less of Germany, but not in
the least of Russia and not of India" (Trotsky 1959, 378).

In contrast to the "methodological nationalism" adhered to by orthodox
Marxists, Trotsky's strategy of permanent revolution began from the recognition of the *international* constitution of the world capitalist system. It proposed that Russia's minority working-class movement could telescope the
supposedly indispensable stages of bourgeois democracy and proletarian
revolution into a single "uninterrupted" stage from which it would promote

socialist revolution internationally. Behind Trotsky's strategy of permanent revolution stood the theory of uneven and combined development. From this perspective, Trotsky conceived the Bolshevik Revolution as a result of the international development of capitalism, to which the trajectory of the revolution was also bound. In a sense, uneven and combined development can be viewed as a response to the emergence of particular anomalies within a Marxist research program committed to an ontologically singular conception of society. It offered a cogent *theoretical* answer to Lenin's question of why socialist revolutions arose in the "weakest links in the imperialist chain" (Burawoy 1989; Wolf 1997, 303).

Natural Beginnings: Unevenness

At its most general level, uneven and combined development can be summarized as follows. The unevenness of social development in history is perhaps its most enduring, essential feature—"the most general law of the historic process" (Trotsky 1959, 4).[11] This is represented not only by the sheer diversity of levels and tempos of development within societies but also *between* them.[12] At all points of the historical process and across its developmental spectrum, we thus find the interaction of differentially developing social temporalities. Development is, then, ineluctably multilinear, polycentric and co-constitutive by virtue of its very interconnectedness.

In the premodern period, unevenness is expressed across various dimensions and planes of internal differentiation within the ontological, though not yet causally integrated, whole of world-societal development. The natural bases of unevenness lie in the ecologically given conditions that originally confronted the human species. Ecological variations across geographical space, in turn, work to promote further processes of internal differentiation. In the case of Russia—or, more precisely, the networks of social relations constituting what is now called Russia—the "natural-historical conditions" (above all, Russia's "less than favorable geographical situation" standing between Europe and Asia) were the initial causes for the "comparative primitiveness and slowness" of its social development, stunting class formation processes and their relations with the state (Trotsky 1962, 170, 172–73; 1959, 2–3). As human societies became more complex, geographical factors become less fundamental in shaping the course of their coevolution. There are, in other words, *emergent layers* and *axes* of the unevenness of human development.

Capitalism only emerges *within* and *through* these antecedent processes of unevenness. From its origin, its expansion thereby takes a "combined" character, fusing with the plurality of existing sociopolitical forms through its internationally mediated spread.[13] Distinctly capitalist processes progressively gain mastery over this extant unevenness, reconstituting its fundamental quality as it unifies the many instances and forms of uneven development into a single, causally integrated, world totality (Trotsky 1936, 19–20). Chapter 3 examines how this progressive causal intertwining of different spatiotemporal *vectors of unevenness* accompanied the emergence of a world capitalist economy over the Long 19th Century (1789–1914). It demonstrates the causal primacy of these multiple, intersecting temporalities of capitalist industrializations and modern nation-state formation processes in explaining the crisis as a whole.

The origins of the Thirty Years' Crisis also illustrate the increasingly decisive importance of the socioeconomic sources of unevenness now fully generalized on the basis of capitalist social relations. For, unlike other social systems, only capitalism exhibits an inherent tendency toward both universalization and equalization on the one hand, and differentiation and fragmentation on the other. As Trotsky (1936, 19–20; emphasis added) put it,

> In contrast to the economic systems which preceded it, capitalism inherently and constantly aims at economic expansion, at the penetration of new territories, the surmounting of economic differences, the conversion of self-sufficient provincial and national economies into a system of financial interrelationships... By drawing the countries economically closer to one another and levelling out their stages of development, capitalism ... operates by methods of its *own*... *anarchistic methods* which constantly undermine its own work, set one country against another, and one branch of industry against another developing some parts of world economy, while hampering and throwing back the development of others. Only the correlation of these two fundamental tendencies—both of which arise from the nature of capitalism—explains to us the living texture of the historical process.

The dynamics of capitalist development thus reveals a dialectical quality expressed through the *contradictory unity* of universalizing and differentiating tendencies. Consequently, capital exerts equalizing and fragmenting pressures on social development. This is inherent to the expansionary, competitive logic of capital accumulation based on wage labor. Capitalism is therefore defined by interactive, mutually constitutive relations of homo/ heterogeneity. As Neil Smith writes (2006, 190), "Uneven economic development establishes discrete places differentiated from each other and at the same time pressures these places, across borders, into a single mode." What is more, as Trotsky's passage reveals, the "dynamics of unevenness" are now "increasingly recognized as *internal* to the dynamics of capitalism itself . . . Whatever historical remnants of pre-capitalist societies survived . . . were now enveloped, appropriated and soldered into a larger global capitalism" (Neil Smith 2006, 185–86). In other words, unevenness becomes systematized. It endows agents with specific capabilities, powers, and interests.

Encountering the International: The "Whip of
External Necessity" and "Privilege of Backwardness"

It is important to note that Trotsky's argument retains the notion of a succession of more advanced modes of production on a global scale. One might say that this presupposes stagism to scramble and subvert stagism. Here, the conceptual couplet—the "whip of external necessity" and "privilege of historic backwardness"[14] through which combined social formations are generated—are of paramount importance.

Intersocietal competition, the "whip of external necessity" (Trotsky 1957, 4), is inflicted on later-developing societies to develop in response to the military-geopolitical and economic pressures emanating from more advanced capitalist powers. Crucially, this mechanism of capitalist development *presupposes* the seemingly mundane fact of a multiplicity of interacting and differentially developing societies. The international enters into the fundamental causal conditions of each and every society's productive and reproductive logics; it thereby acts as a generative, enabling, and constraining structural feature of sociohistorical development. As Trotsky writes (1962, 170),

> It is difficult to say what shape Russian social development would have taken if it had remained isolated and under the influence of inner tendencies only. It is enough to say that this did not happen. Russian social life, built up on a certain internal economic foundation, has all the time been under the influence, even under the pressure, of its external social-historical milieu. When this social and state organization, in the process of its formation, came into collision with other, neighbouring organizations, the primitiveness of the

economic relations of the one and the comparatively high development of the others played decisive parts in the ensuing process.

Here we see how the development of Russian state and society occurred under the hostile competitive pressures of the more advanced Western European states. This indicates that Trotsky viewed the structural forces of the world economy as well as geopolitical competition as constitutive factors in Russia's internal development. Such an interpretation is further borne out when Trotsky (1962, 174) notes how "relations with other countries bore a predominantly State character" as the "influence of these countries found expression in fierce struggle for the existence of the State before expressing itself in direct economic competition." Through these directly geopolitical rivalries, the economic techniques and organizational innovations of the West influenced the Russian economy via the agency of the state. Causality here takes on a distinctly intersocietal dimension, pressurizing, molding, and transforming "internal" state-society relations.

From this first intersocietal determination (the external "whip") follows a second, compounding and rearticulating the effects of the first. This Trotsky called the "privilege of historic backwardness."[15] This represents the opportunities presented to late-developing states to adopt the cutting-edge ready-made developmental designs and technologies from the more advanced powers in the international system. Here we find the "enabling" properties of the international noted. This mechanism, too, "is a function of the overall unevenness of development, expressed as an interactive 'simultaneity of the nonsimultaneous' (Bloch) of the societies involved" (Justin Rosenberg 2007, 458). It allows for the potential "skipping" or telescoping of different "stages" of the historical process within a single social formation, producing "amalgam[s] of archaic with more contemporary forms" that "smash the limited boundaries of classification" (Trotsky 1959, 3, 1998, 77).[16] However, it does not do so in any kind of uniform manner. There is, as Trotsky termed it (1976, 582), a "hierarchy of backwardness" from which flows a multiplicity of differentiated sociological amalgamations.

Thus arrives the moment of combined development whereby the logics of different modes of production—or "phases" thereof—intermix with one another in causally consequential ways. Although Davidson (2006b, 212) argues that combination may refer to social and cultural forms, Trotsky's use of the concept derives its causal power from the foundational Marxist concept of the "mode of production." Modes of production—capitalist, feudal, slave, and so forth—form the overarching context from which people develop powers, ideologies, and interests that set them in conflict with each other. Combination involves the causal intermingling of these modes in a way that violates their hitherto assumed order of succession: societies are afforded the possibility of skipping a "whole series of intermediate stages" of development. Combined development thereby denotes a contradictory process of hothouse developmental time compression suffusing every aspect of society and usually involving "sudden, intensive industrialization and urbanization" (Davidson 2009, 15).

The possibility of skipping stages is, however, "by no means absolute." Rather, it depends on the existing levels of cultural and socioeconomic "capacities" within the borrower societies and above all on the *historical timing* and *terms* of these societies' political and economic incorporation into the world market (Trotsky 1959, 3).[17] Dependent on such capacities and timing as well as the critical factor of social agency, the "skipping" process does not automatically result in progressive effects. Instead, as often occurs, the assimilation of developmental technics by the borrower society results in their "debasement" through "the process of adapting them to" less-developed social structures. The "privilege of historic backwardness" is, then, often also accompanied by certain "penalties." For example, Trotsky (1959, 3) notes how Russia's absorption of certain Western techniques and training in the military and industrial fields under Peter the Great "led to a strengthening of serfdom as the fundamental form of labour organization." The infusion of European armament and finance was thus a contradictory process, simultaneously strengthening tsarism while undermining its socioeconomic and political foundations.

The resulting "combined" Russian social formation was characterized by the most advanced capitalist relations and productive techniques interacting with feudal relations in potentially socially and geopolitically explosive ways: mass concentrations of technologically advanced capital (particularly within the state-run military industries) imported from Western Europe and a rapidly growing proletariat existing along an unreformed absolutist monarchy and a dominant landowning aristocracy. Here, "development is no longer gradual and 'organic' but assumes the form of terrible convulsions and drastic changes" (Trotsky 1972d, 199). This accelerated industrialization, in turn, results in its own unique "class of effects," "ramifying" and unhinging social structures (Justin Rosenberg 2008, 10). These "contradictions of sociological amalgamation," as termed here, react back on the intersocietal conditions that produced them, feeding into the interior structures of other states' development while creating the conditions for revolution, interstate conflict, and war. These contradictions represent a third determination, again derivative of capitalism's differential development as a multiplicity of interactive societies.

If uneven and combined development is a universal condition of capitalism, it is then one defined by a *norm of differentiation:* there is no singular model of development. The forms of combinations are necessarily *plural* and *variegated,* with each successive modality building on the achievements and failures of its antecedents.[18] The spatiotemporal ordering of revolution and socioeconomic development are in these ways constitutive of the cumulatively graduated differences in their resulting social structures (see Gerschenkron 1962; Weaver 1974; Pollard 1981). Systemic reproduction is then necessarily interdependent and co-constitutive.

Here it is worth pausing a moment to preempt a common criticism of uneven and combined development: that it is an overly structuralist and deterministic theory with little room for political agency (see Lawson 2005; Teschke 2008, 180). Certainly, the role and direction of agency is always a partially indeterminate, *political* process. However, it is not a "structureless" one—that is, it can be explained retrodictively by invoking structural properties. One benefit of the theory of uneven and combined development is how it provides the basis for an explanation of the sociologically differentiated forms that agency takes, thereby contradicting any "predetermined" unilinear readings of sociohistorical development: an explanation of the why and how "the tasks of one class are shouldered off upon another" (Trotsky 1959, 54). Indeed, contrary to such claims of "structuralism," Michael Burawoy (1989, 784) draws attention to the intrinsically agential aspects of Trotsky's theory that capture the "accumulation of micro-processes" in explaining molecular forms of social transformation, thereby carrying "forward Marx's project of establishing the micro-foundations of a macro-sociology, of understanding how individuals make history but not necessarily in ways of their own choosing."

More generally, at the heart of such criticisms seems to be a worry that by casting uneven and combined development into a "general abstraction," as Justin Rosenberg does, it evacuates concrete human praxis, rendering it an "overly abstract and contentless register" (Teschke 2008, 180) for social theoretical explanation. As Teschke has argued elsewhere, on this conception of uneven and combined development as a transhistorical general abstraction, the theory "articulates a meta-historical law whose scientistic connotations translate into a structuralism—similar to neo-realism—which reduces agency to the faithful enactment of imperatives beyond human control or volition . . . outcomes in the social world appear as deduced from antecedent causes, leading to a conceptualization of agency as fully determined, passive-receptive and, ultimately, non-agential." Human praxis thereby becomes "objectified" (Teschke 2011, 1102).[19] And, indeed, if left at the level of a "general abstraction," this would surely be a problem: decontextualized from any conception of historically distinct social structures, the scales, mechanisms, and qualitative forms of "unevenness" and "combination"—to say nothing of the dynamics of human agency—could hardly be illuminated. Yet, as detailed below, this is certainly not the intention of the theory, which, following Marx's method, proceeds through a series of descending levels of abstraction, further approximating empirical reality in each step.

The emphasis placed in this work on the structural constraints and enabling properties of uneven and combined development, therefore, in no way seeks to erase the crucial function of agents in processes of policymaking and large-scale social change. The significance of these "first image" sources of interstate relations is further drawn out in the cases of Chancellor Otto von Bismarck and particularly President Woodrow Wilson in chapters 3 and 4, respectively. In this respect, it should be kept in mind that "to say that social structures have explanatory autonomy is to say that they cannot be eliminated from the explanations of social events. It is *not* to say that individuals and their attributes can, or should be eliminated" (Callinicos 1987b, 83). In short, agents and agency matter.

In these ways, the concept of uneven and combined development offers a cogent means of theoretically explaining the different social forms and agencies emerging from the same process of world capitalist development as well as the "geosocial" effects of their interactive differences. The following analysis further teases out these implications for IR theory. It does so in particular through a critical engagement with Justin Rosenberg's pathbreaking work.

RECONFIGURATIONS: UNEVEN AND COMBINED DEVELOPMENT—THEORY OF "THE INTERNATIONAL"?

Extensions and Reformulations

Recently, Justin Rosenberg has extended the analytical reach of uneven and combined development to propose a solution to the international problematic common to social and IR theory. Rosenberg's argument begins from the claim that the two theoretical traditions suffer from a mutual misconception. International theory, particularly in its realist guise, conceptualizes the structure of international relations (anarchy) in abstraction from its underlying constitutive social relations, thus perpetuating a reified, ahistorical conception of "the international." Classical social theory, in turn, continually suffers from a unitary conception of society, theorizing the structure and dynamics of societies *as if* they developed in isolation. Consequently, the "repressed" multilinear and interactive nature of social development returns in the form of untheorized exogenous factors (Justin Rosenberg 2006, 2007).

For Rosenberg, the answer to this dual problem facing social and IR theory is to reconceptualize social development in general as both "uneven" and "combined," thereby deriving the political multiplicity underlying the international problematic from the transhistorically variegated and interconnected nature of all development (Justin Rosenberg 2010). His formulation thus seeks to overcome the shared error of international and classical social theory by unifying their two logics in one uneven and combined social process.

Significantly, such a reconceptualization of social development as uneven and combined dispenses with any conception of "society" in the "ontological singular." Rather than viewing societies as preformed *discrete* entities that subsequently coexist and interact, Rosenberg invites us to conceive of this process of interaction as itself constitutive of these social orders. The primary unit of analysis can no longer be "society" and "societies" but social development conceptualized as a differentiated, but nonetheless, ontological whole. Thus, Rosenberg goes beyond Trotsky to account for the generic existence of the intersocietal dimension of social development.

Like Trotsky, he begins from the "universal law of unevenness." Human development—in the sense of the increase of productive capacities—is inherently differentiated and multiform. From this apparently banal premise, Rosenberg derives three substantive claims. First, "the supposedly 'irreducible' fact of political fragmentation which underlies the distinctive problematic of the international can itself be seen to be one embodiment of an analytically more general socio-historical property of human existence—its intrinsic unevenness." Second, unevenness interpolates a "more than one" ontological premise *"into the concept of development itself,"* thereby scrambling any unilinear notions of development so common to social and international theories. From these points flows another: "combination" is conceived as a universal phenomenon, consisting of the interactive and tendentially reproductive interpenetration of *all* social development. It thereby adds a distinctly intersocietal form of causality into the reproductive logics of each and every society. This both accounts for and sociologically deepens the "anarchic" dimension of causality identified but inadequately theorized by realism (Justin Rosenberg 2006, 316, 318, 320).

An important step in Rosenberg's argument is his extension of the concept of combined development. Trotsky used the notion of combination to examine the intensive hybrids of capitalist and noncapitalist modes of production within a single social formation. Rosenberg innovates by using the concept of "combined development" in three distinct but intrinsically interconnected ways. First, combined development refers to the coexistence and interactive development of all societies throughout history. Second, these processes of intersocietal development result in a tendential interdependence of "the structures of social, material and cultural life" (Justin Rosenberg 2006, 324). In other words, the "external" relations of states function as a means to transform the sociopolitical, cultural, and material institutions within society through their institutionalization beyond any given state. This combination integrates states and societies into "regional political orders, cultural systems and material divisions of labour," resulting in distinct amalgams of sociopolitical orders, cultural institutions, and economic systems that combine "preexistent "internal" structures of social life with "external" sociopolitical and cultural influences" (Justin Rosenberg 2006, 324). This is the third sense of combined development approximating Trotsky's original employment of the concept.

Rosenberg's threefold extension of combined development is both novel and useful. For it is only through the *process* of intersocietal development that combined social formations come into *effect* (Barker 2006). In particular, it dispenses with any view of societies as separate, preformed entities while also doing away with the neorealist conception of sociopolitical units as functionally homogenous. Sovereignty can instead be conceived as potentially variegated and multiform. Further, contrary to liberal arguments, it provides the basis for understanding capitalism as emerging from *within* unevenness and *reproducing* its conditions of existence: a sociopolitically differentiated and spatially fragmented system of sovereign states.

On General Abstractions: Uneven and Combined
Development as "Progressive Problem Shift"

Justin Rosenberg's approach is particularly interesting in relation to the study of the origins and trajectory of geopolitics in the era of the two world wars, as the reconceptualization of uneven and combined development provides the potential bridge linking explanations of war and interstate rivalry on the one hand and processes of sociohistorical change and revolution on the other. For Trotsky and most subsequent Marxists, these theories have remained separate despite the connections between their objects of explanation.[20] By providing a more solid foundation explaining why the same production basis could demonstrate such "endless variations and gradations in appearance" (Marx 1981, 927), the extension of uneven and combined development to a theory of "the international" offers a creative theoretical solution to the noncorrespondence of basis and superstructure explicitly linked to a theory of war and geopolitical rivalry: a framework explaining how sociological variations between agents—differences generated through their very interactivity—can itself be a source of conflict.

Nonetheless, in expanding the concept, caution is due. If uneven and combined development is a transhistorical phenomenon to be used as a "general abstraction" (Justin Rosenberg 2006), much then hangs on the precise meaning of *general abstraction,* its functions in theory, and how to conceive of the qualitative differences between capitalist and precapitalist forms of uneven and combined development and what accounts for these differences.[21] Here, a brief look at Marx's method of abstraction is useful.

It is often assumed that transhistorical categories were absent from Marx's framework. This is, however, an incorrect view of Marx's method, as numerous studies convincingly demonstrate (see esp. Sayer 1979; Fracchia 2004). Marx worked with a number of transhistorical categories: "use value," "labor," and "production in general." Nevertheless, Marx's use of transhistorical categories differs strikingly from their employment within much mainstream IR.

For realism, a theoretical abstraction such as "anarchy" or the "international system" takes the form of the primary *explanans* of the argument, from which all other relevant concepts (such as the "balance of power" and "national interest") are to be deduced. From this perspective, the *abstraction forms the theory itself.* In contrast, for Marx, the abstraction functions as an assumption that accounts for the existence of a concrete general condition whose historically specific form has to be accounted for by still further *explanans*. Marx was not seeking to build a transhistorical theory of labor or use value, for example, but rather introduced these concepts as necessary presuppositions in his construction of a historically specific social theory of value. Uneven and combined development can be utilized in a similar (though not identical) way in filling out a distinctively historical materialist theory of "the international."[22]

While uneven and combined development represents a truly *transhistorical* phenomenon, its distinct causal determinations, articulated and expressed through intersocietal competition, are in every instance historically specific to and variable across any given mode of production. Only under the specific sociohistorical conditions of generalized commodity production of the kind found in the capitalist epoch do these determinations take on their full scope and intensity. In the absence of these conditions, the instances and qualitative forms of uneven and combined development will tend to be *context-specific*. To be clear, this is not to say that "combined social formations" never existed in precapitalist times; rather, their occurrences were qualitatively different: irregular, episodic, and thus often not systematized.[23] Uneven and combined development is, then, *not a theory in itself*. It is, rather, a methodological fix in the larger research program of historical materialism.

It is, then, best to view uneven and combined development as offering a progressive problem shift *within* a historical materialist research program, introducing and then "stretching" an auxiliary theory *consistent* with the hard-core premises of that program (Lakatos 1970, 133–34). Rather than protecting these hard-core premises by limiting their explanatory scope ("monster barring") or by identifying anomalies as exceptions or pathologies—as with a degenerative research program such as structural realism (Vasquez 1997)—uneven and combined development aims to magnify the explanatory power of the original research program.[24] As Burawoy summarizes (1989, 761), "A progressive defense of the hard core takes the form of an expanding belt of theories that increases the corroborated empirical content and solves successive puzzles."

The "hard-core" premise of historical materialism is that humans are embedded within a productive metabolism with their environment. The development of this metabolism is the subject of historical materialism. It forms the basis of the "double relationship" examined by Marx and Engels in *The German Ideology* (1970). In the first instance, humans must produce and reproduce the means of their material subsistence to survive. In doing so, humans enter into an interactively transformational relationship with their natural and social surroundings, shaping and reconstituting such conditions in the process. That development is unevenly distributed; humans are consequently always dealing in some way with other "stages" or forms of such development. Unevenness—and hence the potential for "simple" forms of uneven and combined development—extends in time and space beyond modes of production. However, only the capitalist form of the metabolism contains essentially within it the impulse to transform all others. How so?

Capitalism and Uneven and Combined Development

Unlike previous modes of production, under capitalism, every productive unit is brought into a "coercive comparison" with every other unit. Indeed, the logic of capital is to bring these units into a relationship of universal equivalence (Ashman 2006, 94). This follows from the inherently expansionary nature of capitalism's "rules of reproduction," grounded in the capital relation constituted by two antagonistic relationships: the "vertical" antagonisms between capitalist and laborer and the "horizontal" relations among individual competing capitals (Brenner 2006a, 7–8). This latter dimension (intercapitalist rivalry) functions as an inbuilt mechanism in capitalism that perpetuates and intensifies the tendency toward the universalization and differentiation of social development described by Trotsky.

Each capitalist is driven to seek advantage at the expense of others. The main strategy to achieve this is by increasing the exploitation of the workers—extending the working day or introducing labor-saving technology without a commensurate reduction in working time (see Marx 1976, chap. 10). A further strategy is to expand into those areas where capitalist relations do not prevail. The competition among capitals thus leads them to search out new markets and ever-greater sources of profit across the globe, thereby unifying the world through the universalization of specific combinatory mechanisms. As Trotsky wrote, "The world is now undergoing a unified process of capitalist development which absorbs all the countries it meets on its way and creates in them a social amalgam combining the local and general conditions of capitalism" (quoted in Knei-Paz 1978, 88). In this sense, capitalism "prepares and in a certain sense realizes the universality and permanence of man's development," thereby ruling out any "repetition of the forms of development by different nations" (Trotsky 2008, 4). Indeed, as the capitalist system matures, more and more societies become locked into processes and structures of interconnection and constitution by the emergence of a genuinely global economy. In this way, capital creates "world-history for the first time" (Marx and Engels 1976, 73). As a consequence, the rules of the game, to use the rational choice jargon beloved of neorealists, are themselves changed on a global level.

After capitalism emerges somewhere, the self-expanding and totalitizing nature of capital locks all against all in the battle to cheapen commodity production through a historically unprecedented development of the productive forces. Thus, the inherently expansionary and self-valorizing imperative of capital is such that once it has come into being, the ruling classes of all other modes must submit to it or face potential peripheralization. This is only true of the logic of capitalist accumulation, rooted in the value relation. The precondition of such extensive transformations, however, is that one set of social relations is to an unprecedented degree so much more productive than another as to imperil its reproduction. Trotsky (1972b, 38) offers this logic in arguing that the Russian state was able to prevail over the nomadic Golden Horde but was then forced to adapt to Western competition. Only the emergence of capitalism opens up such an enormous *competitive gulf* between societies (Carling 2002, 110).

After the capitalist value relation has come into existence, the interactions among societies become constitutive in a way qualitatively different from the precapitalist intersocietal relations highlighted by Justin Rosenberg (2006, 321–22). The universalization of the competitive logic of capital accumulation does not, however, homogenize the units subject to its imperative. Rather, the pressurized process of "skipping" stages creates unstable amalgams of capitalist and noncapitalist relations whose instability feeds back into the geopolitical dynamics that produced them. Justin Rosenberg (1996, 12) captures the essence of these formations in describing the postdecolonization state system as "full of potential mini-Czarisms." This feedback loop is another distinguishing feature of modern forms of uneven and combined development, again hinging on the specific nature of capitalist production relations. This form exerts a set of determinations in the international sphere that are neither purely "social-internal" nor "geopolitical-external" but greater than the sum of the two.

CONCLUSION

Being committed to the *"ruthless criticism* of all that exists" (Marx 1843), historical materialists have been skeptical of claims attributing substantive transhistorical properties to structures of the social world. The slogan "Always historicize!" as Frederic Jameson (1981, 9) once put it, is "the one absolute and we can even say "transhistorical" imperative of all dialectical thought." This chapter has addressed the challenges facing not only Marxism but all social and international theories regarding the irreducibility of the constitutively intersocietal dimensions of all social development affecting explanations of interstate competition and war. In so doing, the chapter turned to an anatomization of Trotsky's notion of uneven and combined development and Justin Rosenberg's reformulation of the concept as a means to theoretically internalize "the international." While dangers of analytical overextension of uneven and combined development lurk, the chapter has demonstrated that the idea can be fruitfully employed as a general abstraction incorporated into an expanded historical materialism research program, thereby offering a *progressive problem shift* in Marxist theory. Further, the chapter claimed that although uneven and combined development represents a truly *transhistorical* phenomenon, its distinct causal determinations, articulated and expressed through intersocietal relations, are in every instance historically specific to and variable across any given mode of production. Under the generalized commodity production of the capitalist epoch, uneven and combined development tends to take on a more *intensive* and *dynamic* character. The next chapter illuminates how uneven and combined development, incorporated as a "general abstraction" into a historical materialist framework, can be *concretized* in theoretically explaining the structurally interwoven geopolitical and sociological ("geosocial") origins of the 1914–18 war.

CHAPTER 3

1914 in World Historical Perspective: The Uneven and Combined Origins of the First World War

CHAPTER 1 discussed some of the core theoretical dilemmas and cul-de-sacs confronting the dominant approaches to the causes of the Thirty Years' Crisis. The back and forth between "internalist" (unit-level) and "externalist" (system-level) theories of the First World War (WWI) within both the historiographical and IR literatures points toward the need for an alternative logic of explanation that captures the co-constitutive interaction of domestic and international relations in the developments of the period. Building on the theory of uneven and combined development outlined in chapter 2, this chapter offers such an alternative logic, illustrating how the multilinear and interactive nature of sociohistorical development fed into the causal sources of geopolitical rivalry and war. In doing so, it offers a contextualization of the opening salvo of the crisis within the broad developmental tendencies of the Long 19th Century (1789–1914) and their particular articulation during the immediate prewar juncture. The aim of this chapter is, then, to offer a "first-cut" explanation of the origins of WWI while sketching the theoretical framework *broadly* informing the analysis of the crisis period as a whole.[1]

To date, calls for an "international historical sociology"—specifically, those drawing on the concept of uneven and combined development—have inclined toward unsustainably high levels of analytical abstraction (but see Matin 2007; Green 2012). This work redresses this lacuna, developing the theory in and through the rich historical terrain of the prewar period and demonstrating uneven and combined development's utility as a theory of both international relations and foreign policymaking. It thereby provides an empirically focused contribution to recent IR debates on the relationship between history and theory (Hobson and Lawson 2008), elucidating an approach sensitive to the interaction of *structural* tendencies and *conjunctural* trends. This seeks to transcend the persistent disjuncture between the "abstract-theoretical" and "empirical-historical" while offering a means of conceptualizing "contingencies" as a theorizable object of analysis.[2]

The chapter is divided into three sections. The first section outlines the analytic framework, drawing on the theory of uneven and combined development. After discussing the distinctive character of a historical materialist methodology of conjunctural analysis, it delineates three distinct spatiotemporal vectors of unevenness that over the course of the early era of capitalist industrialization progressively interconnected, with increasingly significant effects on the nature and trajectory of international politics. From this perspective, it then identifies four *interdependent* streams of causation cumulatively leading to the July 1914 crisis.

The next section ("Advantages and Disadvantages of "Priority" and "Backwardness") examines the far-reaching "geosocial" effects of the spatiotemporally staggered process of interactive capitalist industrializations across Europe. It does so by, first, tracing the rise of the "Anglo-German antagonism" emerging from this plane of "West-East" unevenness and its intersection with the "Transatlantic" vector of development. It then elucidates how Germany's specific location in the spatiotemporal matrix of industrializations resulted in a distinct class of contradictions arising from its sociologically amalgamated development. Focusing on the nature of German class conflict and its connection to political-military relations, this section demonstrates how this particular form of capitalist "combination" directly fed into the causes of the First World War. Moving the analysis back to the wider field of great-power relations, the section concludes by looking at the more general relations among industrialization, state armaments, financing (loans), and the formation of the two military alliance blocs that eventually went to war.

The third section ("Collapsing Empires and Rising Nationalisms") considers the crucial impact of the "Eastern Question" on the changing nature and trajectory of European geopolitics. It does so by exploring the socially thick relations of interconnection and co-constitution between Europe and the Ottoman Empire over the modern epoch and their consequent destabilization of the Balkan region. It then turns to consider the rise of the nationalities question in the Habsburg monarchy, mapping out how internal-external factors combined to restructure the axes of Austro-Hungarian economic and geopolitical development eastward, thereby drawing it into direct conflict with tsarist Russia, which, over this same period, was being domestically and geopolitically pressurized into westward expansionism.

Here, the role of the collapsing Chinese Empire and its relationship to the "war-revolution" linkages in Russia's combined development are highlighted. Specifically, this section focuses on the myriad ways in which Russia's military collapse (1905–8) and rapid reemergence (1908–14) transformed the European military balance of power, pushing German policymakers to launch a "preventive war."[3] Finally, the section examines the interactive chain of diplomatic crises during the 1912–14 juncture emerging from the concatenation of developmental-geopolitical tendencies. The conclusion then considers the question of timing—the relatively short window of opportunity emerging for the successful launching of a preventive war—in relation to "radical contingency" explanations of the war.

UNEVEN AND COMBINED DEVELOPMENT OVER THE LONG 19TH CENTURY

Having detailed the most significant theoretical problems with existing explanations of the crisis period and First World War in chapter 1, there now remains the more difficult task to be accomplished: the formulation of an alternative, *positive* theorization of the war's origins. How might the theory of uneven and combined development contribute to this endeavor? To answer this, one need detail exactly what requires explanation to judge whether this alternative perspective marks an improvement on the dominant existing approaches.

Structure, Conjuncture, and Constellations of Unevenness

A satisfactory theory of the war's causes must fulfill, at a minimum, three criteria. It requires first, an analysis of the central tendencies of the epoch, setting and conditioning the international-domestic contexts leading to war; second, an account of how these structural tendencies related to and were articulated through different social formations in the immediate period leading to the war's outbreak; and, third, an elucidation of the structural specificities of the war juncture, delimiting it from the broader epochal context of which it nonetheless formed a part. What is needed, in other words, is an explanation capturing the precise articulation of a universal crisis—itself emerging from the *general* structural tendencies of the era—with the *particularities* of the prewar conjuncture differentiating it as a distinct but in no sense autonomous temporality.

This would address two questions posed by historian Gustav Schmidt in explaining why the July 1914 crisis developed into a *world* war rather than remaining a localized or even European-wide conflict. First, "What is special about the conjunction of the July crisis, apart from the simple fact that an explosion was becoming more and more likely after a series of acts of brinkmanship?" Second, "Are the general explanations of the causes of the First World War satisfactory, if the structural elements of the crisis . . . did not result in the outbreak of war during any of the other Balkan crises" of 1908–13? (Schmidt 1990, 97).

A satisfactory theorization of the war would thus need to account for why war did *not* break out under similar circumstances. The real trick, then, is formulating a methodology that avoids the dual dilemmas of a historically underspecified causality or a radically contingent historicism—that is, either subsuming the conjunctural phenomenon (in this case, war) under unmediated "abstract" sociological laws or by treating it as a hermetically sealed temporality constituted by contingently determined, self-contained causes. In other words, the account would have to weave the interaction of structural and conjunctural factors into a single explanatory whole.

Although the concept of conjuncture is in no way unique to historical materialism, the theory does offer a distinctive method for pursuing conjunctural explanations.[4] This relates to the analytical hierarchy of causality embedded within Marxism's conceptualization of social structures as historically specific "modes of production." The mode of production is the orientating theoretical abstraction for any Marxist analysis, delimiting different social systems and historical epochs from others. Of course, the concept has not been without its many theoretical confusions and controversies within the Marxist literature, particularly in regard to the category's employment in time and space.[5] For our purposes here, it is simply worth noting that the causal weight attributed to the mode of production—defined in terms of a particular configuration of relations and forces of production—in no way erases the specificities of the "changing forms and contingent interactions of the historical process." Rather, it seeks to root these forms and interactions within firm theoretic propositions about the general characteristics of modern social development as a whole, reconceived here as "uneven and combined" (Justin Rosenberg 2005, 30). These propositions relate to the organic tendencies characterizing capitalist development, including, above all, its ceaseless drive to competitive accumulation; revolutionary technological dynamism; spatial expansiveness; capital/labor antagonisms; and the recurrent nature of socioeconomic crises. The different forms these tendencies will take are, however, entirely "contingent" on the continually evolving structure of capitalism as a concrete social formation, taking a myriad of varying forms in different times and places. The sharp counterposing of the abstract-theoretical and historical-empirical is, therefore, necessarily false.[6] Theoretical categories—even the most general ones—only hold meaning in their historically determinate concrete forms.

Examining both the general and proximate causes of the 1914–18 war and taking a cue from Justin Rosenberg (2008, 25–26),[7] one can identify three distinct but overlapping spatiotemporal vectors of unevenness whose progressive entwinement had increasingly significant consequences on the nature and course of European geopolitics. The three vectors of unevenness include (1) a "West-East" plane of unevenness capturing the spatial-temporal ordering of industrializations taking place across Europe and beyond over the 1789–1914 period; (2) a "Transatlantic" vector representing the contradictory interlocking of the North American and European economies and the multiple cultural-linguistic, socioeconomic, and political links connecting the British Empire with its original white settler colonies;[8] and (3) a "North-South" constellation interlinking and differentiating the multiethnic empires from Central Eastern Europe to the Asia-Pacific (India and China) into a dynamic of asymmetrical interdependency with the capitalist-industrial powers. For each vector, a specific pattern of interdependent and co-constitutive development can be identified—respectively, the variegated patterns of interconnected industrializations; the emergence of a distinctive "Anglo-Saxon" sphere; and the deepening international impediments to modern nation-state building, resulting in partially "blocked" forms of development.[9] This gives each vector its own unique developmental inflection, permitting their demarcation as *objects of theorization* rather than simply describing a series of arbitrary instantiations of sociopolitical differences.

The accumulation of socioeconomic and (geo)political contradictions emerging from these historical processes set the conditions leading to global conflagration in July 1914. The causal interlocking of the constellations of unevenness was the effect of the dramatic expansion of the world market and spread of capitalist relations over the preceding century. "If capitalist development and imperialism must bear responsibility" for the causes of war, then it was not so much a consequence of the limitless aims of capital accumulation, as Hobsbawm suggests (1987, 315), but rather the outcome of capitalism's transformation of the preexisting conditions of unevenness, reconstituted on firmly new socioeconomic bases, into active causal determinations of "combined" geopolitical and social development. The inherited anarchic structure of the international—forming part of the interactive nature of all sociohistorical development—was in this sense both cause *and* effect of this capitalist transformation of the developmental process. This perspective provides the basis for an *international* historical and sociological analysis of the war's causes in its necessarily global dimensions.

Chains of Causation

From the intersection of these three vectors of unevenness, one can then trace four interlacing streams of causation leading to WWI. This *partly* follows Richard Ned Lebow's (2000) argument[10] that the war can be best understood as the *nonlinear convergence of multiple, interdependent chains of causation* that by the 1912–14 conjuncture affected decisive "gestalt shifts" in great-power policymaking circles.

The first causal chain centers on the decline of Britain's global primacy in the face of multiple competitors as the empire's "advantages of priority" turned into strategic disadvantages. The second stream revolves around the interrelations between the domestic sociopolitical crisis and international security dilemmas confronting German policymakers flowing from the *nature* and *timing* of Germany's industrialization process. The third centers on Russia's particular form of combined development, which, in the wake of a "confluence of external setbacks" and "internal crises," made Russian policymakers apprehensive about the foreign and domestic costs of another foreign policy defeat in 1914, thereby conditioning them to accept war (Lebow 2000, 597).[11] The fourth stream relates to the destabilization of the Balkans resulting from the weakening of Ottoman power and the connected internal/external crises facing the Dual Monarchy. The co-constitutive development of Slavic nationalist movements in the Balkans and declining Ottoman Empire enticed the Western powers to reorient expansionist strategies eastward (or westward for Russia) driving them into increasingly destabilizing interimperial conflicts within the region. The confluence of these simultaneous developments set in motion the train of events leading directly to WWI.

ADVANTAGES AND DISADVANTAGES OF "PRIORITY" AND "BACKWARDNESS": THE DEVELOPMENT-STRATEGY NEXUS IN THE MAKING OF WAR

Ascendency, Decline, Conflict: British Empire and
Alliance Formations in a World of "Many Capitalisms"

The expansion of the world market and accompanying industrialization process over the 1789–1914 period largely resulted from British development in all its *global-colonial* dimensions.[12] "Under British auspices," John Agnew and Stuart Corbridge note (1995, 27), exchange relations were "effectively globalized as production for the market replaced the mere trading of goods." That British business could develop international trade and production to such an incredible degree was overwhelmingly the result of British military power, which benefited from the almost complete monopoly on industrialization it held for almost half a century. Such were the "advantages" bestowed on the "first-comer" status of British capitalism (cf. Trotsky 1973, chap. 1).

The unparalleled position of power Britain had attained by the early 19th century was, however, relatively fleeting. For the direct corollary of Britain's worldwide expansion of market relations, commodities, and foreign investments was that it enabled other states to acquire the means to industrialize their own economies in much more intensive concentrations of time than had the original purveyor. Later-developing states no longer needed to start from scratch in their industrialization drives. Instead, they could acquire and innovate on the most advanced technologies and organizational forms pioneered by earlier developers.

Thus emerges the "West-East" axis of unevenness (Justin Rosenberg 2008, 25), representing the classical Gerschenkronite sequencing of capitalist industrializations: Britain (1780s), France (1830s), Germany (1850s), Russia (late 1880s), Japan (1890s), and Italy (late 1890s). This series of causally interwoven industrializations was characterized by an interactive "leapfrogging" process (Trotsky's "skipping of stages" accrued by the "privilege of backwardness") emanating from the "whips of external necessity." The effect was a succession of differentiated patterns of "combined" social forms. The greater spatial and temporal distance traveled from the origin of industrial capitalism's inception, the more sociopolitical differences accumulated as an "orderly system of graduated deviations" (Gerschenkron 1962, 44; see also Weaver 1974; Pollard 1981; Trebilcock 1981; Kemp 1985).

As the massive spatial expansion of an originally British-dominated world economy and European-centered state system progressed, so too did the *number* and *nature* of great powers increase within Europe and beyond. Consequently, Britain's unmatched economic supremacy soon found itself under the strains of an increasingly crowded field of economic competitors. As early as 1895, while still maintaining its dominant place in international finance, Britain was overtaken by the United States and soon thereafter by Germany in the steel and iron industries as well as in the chemical, electrical, and automobile sectors. During the decades before the war, Britain's share of world trade dropped from 20 percent in 1876–80 to 14 percent in 1911–13 as German and U.S. firms aggressively penetrated long-held British markets in Latin America, Central Europe, and the Far East (Hardach 1977, 3; Hobsbawm 1987, 46–47, 51–52; see also tables 1–4).

TABLE 1. Per Capita Levels of Industrialization, 1800–1913 (relative to UK in 1900 = 100)

Countries	1800	1830	1860	1880	1900	1913
United Kingdom	16	25	64	87	100	115
Habsburg Empire	7	8	11	15	23	32
France	9	12	20	28	39	59
German States/Germany	8	9	15	25	52	85
Italy/Italian States	6	7	8	10	15	26
Russia	6	7	8	10	15	20
United States	9	14	21	38	69	126
Japan	7	7	7	9	12	20

Source: Data from Bairoch (1982, 294).

TABLE 2. Iron/Steel Production, 1890–1913

Countries	1890	1900	1910	1913
Britain	8.0	5.0	6.5	7.7
United States	9.5	10.3	26.5	31.8
Germany	4.1	6.3	13.6	17.6
France	1.9	1.5	3.4	4.6
Austria-Hungary	0.97	1.1	2.1	2.6
Russia	0.95	2.2	3.5	4.8
Japan	0.02	—	0.16	0.25
Italy	0.01	0.11	0.73	0.93

Source: Data from Kennedy 1988, 257, table 15.
Note: Data in millions of tons; numbers for 1890 is pig-iron production, steel thereafter.

By the late 19th century, then, the international conditions for Britain's "free trade" order had largely crumbled. The Long Depression of 1873–96 inaugurated an era of neomercantilist protectionism and imperialist agitation, converting economic and geopolitical conflicts into a mutually reinforcing zero-sum game. Crucial to the depression's onset was the interconnected chain of industrializations uniting the European and North American food economies, a consequence of the contradictory interlocking of the West-East and Transatlantic constellations of unevenness heralded by the rapid, unbalanced expansion of the world market over the previous quarter century (cf. Polanyi 1957).

During the 1870s and 1880s, the development of modern transportation systems in the United States unleashed vast quantities of grain on the European market. This shock coincided with the enormous expansion of grain exports through which Russia was planning to fund its industrialization drive. Consequently, the cyclical industrial downturn that began in 1873 was transformed into a protracted crisis of downward-spiraling agricultural prices (the "Great Depression") adversely affecting British military power (Hobsbawm 1987, 36–38; Bairoch 1989, 46–51). The "advantages of priority" and "privilege of backwardness" were thus mutually conditioning and negating dimensions of the same overall geosocial unevenness of capitalist industrialization.

TABLE 3. Aggregate and Per Capita Indexes of Industrial Production and Percentage Shares of World Industrial Production, for Various Countries in 1860 and 1913 (United Kingdom in 1900 = 100)

Country	Total Industrial Output		Per Capita Industrial Output		Percentage Shares of World Industrial Production	
With 1913 Frontiers	1860 Index	1913 Index	1860 Index	1913 Index	1860 (%)	1913 (%)
United Kingdom[a]	45	127	64	115	20%	14%
Germany	11	138	15	85	5%	15%
France	18	57	20	59	8%	6%
Russia	16	77	8	20	7%	8%
All Europe	120	528	17	45	53%	57%
United States	16	298	21	126	7%	32%

Source: Bairoch (1982, table 4).

[a]The United Kingdom of Great Britain and Ireland. The values for its aggregate and per capita industrial outputs for 1900 are taken as the base 100 for all the indexes in columns 1 to 4. Note that columns 5 and 6 are percentages of total world industrial output.

The story of the origins of the 1914–18 war is often told in terms of the decline of Britain's world hegemony in the face of the manifold challenges posed by the newly emerging industrial-capitalist powers. Whether in Marxist or realist form, this largely conceives the global conflagration from the perspective of the radical changes, particularly from the late 19th century, in the conditions and distribution of power driven by the uneven development between industrializing states. Here, the emergence of the "Anglo-German antagonism," rooted in fundamentally economic causes, is generally viewed as the main axis of interstate rivalry leading to the eventual eruption of war (Paul M. Kennedy 1980).

More generally, the transition from hegemonic to polycentric international systems is often seen as a fundamental condition resulting in intensified interstate competition, increasing the overall probability for the outbreak of generalized war. This conception of the causes of war is commonly referred to as the hegemonic stability thesis (HST). According to this approach, the unequal growth of power among states results in a cyclical rise and decline of hegemonic powers dominating the international system. Out of self-interest, the hegemonic state ensures a degree of international order through the imposition of hierarchy. But as economic, technological, and other changes eventually erode this hierarchy, an international system be-

TABLE 4. Indexes of Industrial Output in the United Kingdom, France, Germany, and the United States in Quinquennial Means, 1860–64 to 1910–13

Period	United Kingdom	France	Germany	United States
1860–64	72.6			
1865–69	82.8	95.8	72.6	75.5
1870–74	100.0	100.0	100.0	100.0
1875–79	105.5	109.5	120.8	111.4
1880–84	123.4	126.6	160.6	170.4
1885–89	129.5	130.3	194.9	214.9
1890–94	144.2	151.5	240.6	266.4
1895–99	167.4	167.8	306.4	314.2
1900–1904	181.1	176.1	354.3	445.7
1905–9	201.1	206.2	437.4	570.0
1910–13	219.5	250.2	539.5	674.9

Source: Data from Lewis (1978, 248–50, 269, 271, 273).
Note: Excluding construction, but including building materials. Mean of 1870–74 = 100.

comes more fluid and unstable. Consequently, emerging great powers challenge the position of the hegemonic state. The end result is a major war for hegemony from which a new hierarchy of power will likely emerge (see, for example, Gilpin 1981; Paul M. Kennedy 1988; Arrighi 1994).

There is something to be said for these approaches, as they do capture an essential aspect of the long-term "structural" processes leading to war. They have been less successful, however, in demonstrating how the latent interstate rivalry between declining and rising hegemons (in this case, Britain and Germany) translates into the launching of war. It is quite a jump from an identification of general patterns of interstate competition to an explanation of the outbreak of a specific war. Moreover, the logic of war initiation hypothesized by adherents of the HST is often ambiguous or inapplicable in explaining the two world wars, both of which are usually cited as key exemplars of hegemonic wars of systemic transition. Robert Gilpin, a main proponent of the HST, is indeed rather vague about whether one should expect war to be initiated by the declining hegemon or the emerging power (Gilpin 1988, 163; compare Gilpin 1981, 186, 191). More problematic still is the HST's direct identification of systemic imperatives (international determinations) with state action. Here, the thesis shares with other realist approaches a pervasive analytical indeterminacy derivative of the highly parsimonious forms of theorizing common to mainstream IR. Lacking analysis of social structures and domestic politics in forming and reconstituting (rather than *translating*) systemic imperatives (whether geopolitical or economic), the link between systemic cause and agentic effect is tenuous.

The issue here revolves around the analysis of the interaction of international and social structures in their coevolution. While recognizing the myriad impacts of unevenness, neither classical Marxism nor realism theorizes its deeper *sociological* effects in determining the war's outbreak. For most Marxists, the theories of uneven and combined development and imperialism remain disassociated in their objects of explanation (national-international revolution on the one hand, geopolitical competition and war on the other) despite their clear interconnections.[13] For realists, uneven development is powerfully recognized but detached in reified form from its underlying developmental sources and social effects.[14] This severely blunts the analytical scope of its most cherished categories—that is, "anarchy," the "security dilemma," and the "balance of power."

A consequence for both theories is that the critical role of interactive multiplicity as *generative* of sociological difference and interstate conflict is obscured. Nowhere do the variegated "combinations" of development reach into an explanation of the diversity of foreign policies among the great powers leading to 1914. The following analysis seeks to rectify these issues by tracing the common foundations of these entwined geopolitical and sociological developmental processes.

By the late 19th century, the historically staggered and socially interactive character of the capitalist industrialization process had fundamentally reconstituted the conditions of state and military capability. In doing so, it also reconfigured and destabilized the European balance of power. For it was during this period that the competitive geopolitical benefits afforded to industrializing states were dramatically accelerated by the "industrialization of war" (McNeill 1982). This was in no way a one-way causal street, however. Successful industrial development did not directly and immediately translate into effective military power. Furthermore, the time-compressed character of these internationally pressurized industrializations had numerous detrimental consequences in unhinging social structures (the "contradictions of sociological amalgamation"). Particularly important for the discussion here are industrialized warfare's effects in intensifying both the geostrategic advantages *and* the disadvantages of historical "priority" and "backwardness."

With the application of industrial technologies to transportation, armaments, and communications, nation-states attained the capability to mass-produce weapons and provide more efficient means of transporting large numbers of soldiers to battle. This meant that states' military power became, more than ever before, dependent on their level of economic development. For the great quasi-absolutist empires of Central Eastern Europe, industrialized warfare thus translated into a direct interest in promoting the capitalist social relations necessary to facilitate the production of advanced military technologies and transport systems on which military success increasingly depended (McNeill 1982, chaps. 7, 8; see also Giddens 1987, chap. 9; Martin Shaw 1988, chap. 2; Murray 2005). Taking on the role of capital accumulator, state agencies sought to embed the value relation throughout their respective social structures. The state effectively came to function as "capital" (see Barker 1978b). Such was the curious historical twist by which "the tasks of one class are shouldered off upon another" (Trotsky 2008, 654).

Military and economic forms of interstate competition became not only mutually reinforcing but also socially generative (and destructive). The extraordinary changes in the production and application of the means of destruction effected by industrialized warfare set a new criterion for state power and its successful employment. These novel geopolitical and military-strategic conditions reflected the historically determinate *social logic* of the industrialization process unique to the capitalist era, a critical point often obscured by realist conceptions of technology and technological change as socially neutral phenomenon.[15]

The technological innovations of the Second Industrial Revolution transformed the organizational structures of European militaries as well as their relationship to the state and private industries. It also changed the ways state managers *strategized* and *conducted* war. The Schlieffen Plan and widespread "cult of the offensive" (Snyder 1984) in Europe on the eve of the war would have been unthinkable without these technological developments.[16] Decades of British strategic planning for an economically and politically crippling naval blockade of Germany, for example, proved a formidable weapon in the latter's eventual defeat. So too did the global reach of the British Empire and its former Anglo-Saxon colonies (forming part of the "Transatlantic" vector of unevenness), which made decisive contributions in terms of personnel, financial resources, agrarian goods, and raw materials in the Allied war effort (Hardach 1977; Offer 1989). To these factors, one need also add Britain's superior system of financing the war effort through direct taxation, which also owed much to the country's earlier nation-state formation process and development of capitalist relations (Hobson 1997, chap. 4; Daunton 2002). In these ways, both the conduct and outcome of the war were crucially determined by Britain's "advantages" of historical priority.

The timing of a state's industrialization also had a number of crucial effects on the patterns of strategic alliances in the immediate decades before the war. The growth of industrialized warfare significantly contributed to the dramatic rise in imperial defense costs, particularly affecting British military strategy. This provides a characteristic example of the "*dis*advantages of priority" of Britain's historical first-comer position in capitalist development.

The repeal of the Corn Laws in 1846 signaled London's abandonment of agricultural protectionism as part of the country's growing international strategy of capital accumulation and domestic industrialization. This made it increasingly essential for British policymakers to maintain the country's maritime supremacy as the island's growing demand for food imports and raw materials increasingly required its military control of the seas. Naval hegemony became vital not only for the country's continuing prosperity but also for its survival (Offer 1989, 218).

This was not so much a problem as long as the trade-off between cheap

imports and naval spending remained positive as during the first two decades of the Long Depression (1873–96). By the mid-1880s, however, naval
costs soared as continuing technological innovations blazed apace with the
globalization of industrialized warfare. The tide irrevocably turned as unit
costs of grain imports per year increased by 30 percent (at current prices) between 1894 and 1913 while the costs of naval defense rose by a whopping 186
percent. "Free trade no longer came free" (Offer 1989, 219–20). This marked
the point at which the "advantage" of historical priority began to turn into a
liability (see table 5).[17]

The global reach of the British Empire had been central to the formation
and consolidation of what Giovanni Arrighi (2005) calls the "UK-centred
system of accumulation," and India's role in providing England with a continual balance-of-payments surplus was particularly significant in this regard (cf. Saul 1960; Hobsbawm 1968; de Cecco 1984). The empire was essentially constituted by three strategic blocs: Anglo-Indian, the British-European,
and the Anglo-American. The fundamental aims of British strategy were necessarily twofold: the protection of overseas investments, colonial possessions, and export markets, on the one hand, and the defense against the
domination of the European continent by a single power, on the other. The
British "national interest" was thus "defined globally" (Otte 2007, 4).

This set of global relations functioned well for Great Britain as long as it
remained the preeminent world industrial power, the center of the world
market, around which other national economies orbited. However, once interstate competition for space "intensified under the impact of the transport
revolution and the industrialization of war," Arrighi notes (2005, 93), "the
protection costs of Britain's metropolitan and overseas domains began to escalate, and its imperial possessions turned from assets into liabilities." The
"vast accumulations of capital in relatively backward technologies and a fi-

TABLE 5. United Kingdom Grain Imports and Naval
Expenditure, 1871–1914

	Grains Imports to the UK		Naval Expenditure
	Weight (mil. metric tons)	Cost (£m.)	Cost (£m.)
1871	3.8	42.7	9.0
1894	7.7	48.2	15.5
1913	9.9	80.9	44.4

Source: Offer (1989, 219, table 15.1).

nancial sector geared primarily to overseas investment" was a particularly thorny dilemma for British policymakers as they faced the dual problems of reallocating this capital into newer defense technologies while simultaneously defending capital spatially embedded throughout the empire (Callinicos 1989b, 103; see also Shay 1977; Paul M. Kennedy 1981). Consequently, the admiralty sought to reduce naval expenditures by cutting the size of naval stations overseas, thereby diminishing the British presence in the Far East. Along with these developments and others, British policymakers began searching for strategic partnerships in the region. This search resulted in diplomatic agreements with the United States in 1900 and the Anglo-Japanese alliance of 1902 (Sugiyama 1988, 28–29). Britain's specific temporal location in the development of an industrial world economy thus produced a *structural incentive* for the formation of strategic agreements and military alliances in the brave new world of many capitalisms (see chap. 6).

The (Geo)Politics of Uneven and Combined Development: The "Classic" German Case

These international developmental dynamics form part of the "West-East" vector of unevenness. Here, one finds the classical Gerschenkronite sequencing of structurally interconnected and contradictory patterns of industrialization, spread out in both time and space and fundamentally transforming the texture of world politics. Crucial in this spatiotemporal sequencing was the place of the Prussian-German state. Unique among the European powers, it merged state-led, breakneck industrialization and national state formation into a single compressed "stage" of development. Squeezed between the interval of earlier industrializers such as Britain and France to the West and latecomers Russia and Japan to the east, German development was thus internationally pressurized in multiple directions at once.[18]

This middling position of German industrialization had significant geopolitical and sociological consequences for state development. To some extent, one might agree with David Calleo's (1978, 6) suggestion that "geography and history conspired to make Germany's rise late, rapid, vulnerable, and aggressive." The Kaiserreich's belated arrival on the great-power scene occurred after the world was already partitioned among the great powers into colonies and informal spheres of influence. This made German expansionism appear particularly aggressive and prone to geopolitical countermoves. A persistent disequilibrium emerged between Germany's spectacular rising economic power and its relatively limited formal empire, thereby fostering a simmering national sense of injustice and a vague search for status recognition among policymakers and their conservative social bases,[19] as demonstrated in Wilhelm's *Weltpolitik*. In these ways, the German experience represents a "classical case of an *uneven and combined development*" (Perry Anderson 1974, 234).[20]

From the early 19th century, a precapitalist Prussian state faced severe international pressure (economic, ideological, and military) emanating from industrial Britain and revolutionary France. This was particularly exemplified by the 1848–49 revolution and near annihilation of Prussia at the Battle of Jena. Consequently, the monarchy embarked on a series of agrarian reforms.[21] The "era of reform" institutionalized capitalist social relations in the countryside while strengthening the political hold of the aristocratic Junker class. It thereby left intact the essentially feudal-absolutist character of the Prussian state but endowed it with a dynamically expansive economic structure. Having defeated Napoleonic France, Prussia was awarded at the Vienna Congress the most economically developed and mineral-rich regions of western Germany, the Rhine-Westphalia. With this, policymakers "shifted the whole historical axis of the Prussian state," which "came to incorporate the natural heartland of German capitalism" (Perry Anderson 1974, 272–73). Thereafter, the Junker class harnessed itself to the burgeoning industrial-capitalist forces of western Germany. Imitating and borrowing technologies from abroad,[22] the country witnessed a dramatic acceleration of industrialization granted by the "privilege" of late development, itself *buttressed by* and *further strengthening* antiliberal, authoritarian forms of political rule (see Gerschenkron 1966; Gordon 1974; Wehler 1985; Berghahn 1993).

This socioeconomic "dualism" of the Prussian-German state played itself out politically between the liberal bourgeoisie and conservative Junkers in the constitutional conflict of the 1860s. Contemporary tendencies were, however, already laying the economic bases for the two classes' eventual political rapprochement, of which three tendencies in particular are worth noting: first, the reconstitution of agrarian *Junkerdom* on an increasingly *capitalist* basis; second, the rising economic power of heavy industry within Prussia; and third, the growing importance of heavy industry for military purposes, thereby creating a policymaking interest in their integration into the state. This eventuated in the *contradictory amalgam* of heavy industrial and Junker interests into a single hegemonic project[23] (the famous "marriage of iron and rye"), providing the decisive sociopolitical foundation for Bismarck's "revolution from above," which sought to preserve the conservative-absolutist Prussian order while unifying the German nation under its hegemony. As Seligmann and McLean note (2000, 15), "The fundamental purpose of Bismarck's constitution was to ensure the dominance of the Prussian government over its own subjects and the other German states." This *political blueprint* for Germany's combined development came to dominate German politics and society, albeit in increasingly crisis-ridden ways, right down to the war years (see Heckart 1974; Fischer 1975; Geiss 1976; Eley 1980; Wehler 1985; Berghahn 1993).

Bismarck's Constitution of 1871 encapsulated these conservative-authoritarian designs, maintaining the monarchy while concentrating political power in an Imperial Chancellery that fused the offices of the Prussian prime minister and minister of foreign affairs. As chair of the Federal Council, the chancellor further assumed ultimate responsibility for countersigning all legislation. Yet at the time of the North German Confederation, Bismarck also introduced universal male suffrage, institutionalized in the Constitution of 1871 through the formation of the Reichstag on the basis of the Prussian three-class franchise system (*Dreiklassenwahlrecht*). Counting on the overwhelmingly conservative support in the agrarian countryside to counter any creeping liberal reformism, Bismarck's strategy sought "to overthrow parliamentarism . . . by parliamentary means" (quoted in Wehler 1985, 53, 52–55). In creating an autocratic monarchy founded on a modicum of consent, Bismarck sought to preserve as much of the old order through the legitimation tactics of the new. "Although tactically brilliant," Justin Rosenberg comments (2012, 31), "Bismarck's political formula of combined development became increasingly dysfunctional over time, leading eventually to a crisis of domestic governability and foreign relations alike."

Indeed, the constitutional hybrid of the most contemporary and archaic made the Second Reich something of a political peculiarity in Europe. Though outwardly a trailblazing model of progressive parliamentary democracy to be emulated throughout Europe, the federated governmental structure essentially devolved many of the old absolutist functions to the state level, where reigning princely sovereignties were reconstituted on new foundations. At the same time, the kaiser maintained exclusive prerogatives of war-making and the right to declare martial law in times of civil disorder. Reviewing this "dual constitutional structure" of the new empire, Seligmann and McLean (2000, 16) note,

The Reich was declared to be a union of 25 separate states, with sovereignty residing collectively in the states themselves. As 22 of the states were monarchies, this entrenched the idea of princely sovereignty into the very heart of the new nation by avoiding a unitary structure and maintaining intact Germany's existing internal divisions, the constitution ensured that in practice a substantial proportion of government was conducted at the level of the sovereign federal states, whose existing constitutions were completely unaffected by the creation of the new Reich.

German state sovereignty was internally differentiated, truncated, and partially fragmented, belaying any neorealist state qua state assumption. The Kaiserreich was defined by a *semiparcelized* form of sovereignty that fused liberal-democratic and autocratic features in new and contradictory ways that "with [their] various disparate elements and conflicting authorities" made "the political system of the Second Reich difficult to control" (Seligmann and McLean 2000, 20). Indeed the contradiction-ridden nature of German political order was clear from the start.

Bismarck's state-sponsored program of rapid industrialization aimed at building a militarily powerful German state quickly undermined the socioeconomic conditions on which the Kaiserreich was founded. The conservative countryside, in which Bismarck laid his counterparliamentary hopes, was drastically depleted during the 1890–1914 period. Massive urbanization accompanied the explosive transformation of German society from a number of small, moderately "backward" principalities into the most technologically advanced European capitalist state. A numerically diminished but increasingly radicalized conservative agrarian class thereby emerged in tandem with the precipitate rise of the largest, most well organized, and most politically important working-class movement in the world.

The sudden advent of the Social Democratic Party (SPD) and working-class radicalism developed into a significant challenge to the domestic status quo, igniting near hysterical reactions within the ruling class—an ideologically inflected "siege mentality." In the December 1912 elections, the SPD gained more than a third of the vote and 110 Reichstag seats. German Conservatives were mortified. As conservative Chancellor Prince von Bülow (1900–1909) later reported, "Socialism, checked for six years in every part of the Empire . . . was alive again" and "constitut[ed] a serious menace to the future of the German nation" (1932, 85). This "menace" would require extinguishing, as the kaiser never tired of mentioning.[24] Consequently, imperialist agitation was increasingly used to ensure that bourgeois and conservative parties remained united against the "socialist threat." Yet the reconstruction of the traditional *Sammlung* was moribund. Instead, between 1912 and 1914, the Reich had reached such a political deadlock "that many Germans began to see war as a possible catalyst for stabilization at home as well as abroad before time ran out" (Beckett 2007, 26; see also Gordon 1974, 198–99; Fischer 1975, esp. 230–36; Wehler 1985, 192–233; Berghahn 1993, 156–74).

The "Geosocial" Consequences of the Great Depression

Critical to explaining this cumulative process of sociopolitical destabilization and corresponding *Weltpolitik* orientation of German foreign policy was the severe economic dislocation resulting from the Long Depression. This was itself the consequence of the interconnected chain of industrializations uniting the European and North American food economies while the continental European states were abolishing protective tariffs between 1860 and 1877. Indeed, the depression marked a major turning point in the restructuring of the rules of state reproduction within the world economy and state system, a key event undermining the fragile "free trade" period of capitalist development. As Paul Bairoch has shown, the differential effects of the depression on specific regions can be explained "essentially in terms of the *different stages of economic development*" achieved by states at the time of their economic liberalization. Since Germany was the "most liberal [commercially speaking] of the major European continental countries" at the onset of the depression, it was also the hardest hit (Bairoch 1989, 48, 41).

The long downturn of 1873–96 ushered in a chain reaction of protectionist policies, colonial expansionism, and reactionary entrenchment among the continental European powers, accompanied by an increased rationalization and cartelization of business organizations and economic concentration.[25] The idea that countries could export their way out of the crisis became widespread among policymakers, businessmen, and agrarians, as the depression was commonly viewed as a result of chronic "overproduction." Consequently, colonial expansionism and the carving out of informal economic empires were generally motivated by the widely perceived need for new markets and raw materials to escape the conditions of "excessive competition" (see Hobsbawm 1987, 34–83; Landes 2003, 232–41; Arrighi 2007, 99–101, 116–20).

In this era of renewed neomercantilism, market dominance became

widely associated with territorial control or political monopolization of target countries. In 1913, Gustav Stresemann, for example, called for the acquisition of "colonies . . . to supply the raw materials on which to base our export policy": the "struggle for Morocco was in the end a struggle for its ore
deposits" (quoted in Fischer 1975, 236). Similar views were echoed repeatedly
within important segments of the business community, policymaking circles, and influential media outlets throughout the advanced capitalist countries.[26] That most acquired colonies ended up having little immediate economic importance is irrelevant: just because the effect turned out to diverge
from the intention in no way invalidates the originating motivations or its
predominant causal forces (Hobsbawm 1987, 45).

Over the long term, the depression marked not only a decisive shift in
the character of domestic and international economic relations but also a
transmogrification of the collective self-understandings (or *Weltanschauung*)
of large sections of the bourgeois classes. Nowhere were these effects more
dramatically illustrated than in Germany, where they demonstrated an extreme of the contemporary norm. The depression shook the socioeconomic
and political foundations of Bismarck's domestic and "satiated" foreign policy, where free trade had formed the bedrock of the domestic coalition with
the Liberals. The free trade system originally provided outlets for the country's rapidly growing industries and commerce that Bismarck's laissez-faire
policies had fostered at home. As long as free trade prevailed, Germany could
remain, in Bismarck's words, a "satiated power." Under these conditions, territorial aggrandizements in Europe and colonial acquisitions overseas appeared secondary for German political and economic development (Calleo
1978, 13).

With the onset of the depression, however, German heavy industry, having been overextended during the railway boom of the late 1860s and early
1870s, now clamored for state support in the form of new markets and higher
tariffs. At the same time, Russian and U.S. grain exports threatened German
grain farming, the long-held mainstay of the Junkers. The traditionally "free
trade" Prussian agrarians quickly shifted to the protectionist camp (Calleo
1978, 14–15).[27] Consequently, throughout the Wilhelmine period, German
policymakers and capitalists continually wavered between the pursuits of
large colonial possessions overseas (*Mittelafrika*) and the creation of an informal economic empire on the Continent (*Mitteleuropa*). These two alternative
spatial strategies of capital accumulation, though not necessarily contrasting, entailed very different military strategies, the former necessitating the

construction of a world-class navy (*Flottenpolitik*), the latter focusing more on building up the army (Berghahn 1996).

Even after the economy improved in the early 1890s, capitalists continued to be haunted by fears of economic relapse as witnessed during the ephemeral recovery of 1879–82. For German businessmen, the expansion of exports coupled with state-guaranteed contracts and protected markets held out a renewed promise of sustained relief (Berghahn 1993, 39–40; see also Böhme 1967). However, the fielding of new export markets, as German policymakers never tired of pointing out, required the creation of a large-scale, modern navy. The expansion of the navy would, in turn, secure the much-needed contracts for heavy industry. Thus emerged a variety of industry-backed, jingoistic lobby groups pushing for massive increases in state outlays for enlarging the fleet (see Berghahn 1993; Eley 1980). Particularly important here was a Krupp-founded propaganda organization, the Navy League. Though not always in lockstep harmony, the Navy League did generally act in tandem with Admiral Tirpitz, who, along with other policymakers, recognized the decisive role of a strong navy as an instrument of Germany's *Weltpolitik* (Stevenson 1996).

A particularly important element of Tirpitz's strategic thinking was the obstructionist nature of British sea power to German commercial expansionism. The building of a strong navy, according to Tirpitz, could be employed as a "political lever" against England in ransoming colonial acquisitions and prying open new markets. Making the threat real meant the creation of a Reich navy that could actually rival if not defeat the British. The inauguration of *Weltpolitik* aimed at constructing a world-class navy representing the interests of the rising bourgeois classes could not but challenge British policymakers' geopolitical and economic interests, since the German navy represented direct threats both to Britain and to the empire's global position (Paul M. Kennedy 1980; Berghahn 1993).

A potentially obstructive domestic opponent to Tirpitz's proposed naval bills of 1898 and 1900 were the Junkers. As a class, the Junkers were generally suspicious, if not outright hostile, to the *Weltpolitik* orientation of German diplomacy. It not only potentially threatened their privileged position at home by giving renewed impetus to industry but also threatened a major agricultural export market (Britain) by creating renewed political frictions between the two countries (see Dietrich Geyer 1987, 152–85). The Junkers thus threatened to veto the expansion of the navy bills unless the bourgeois parties (particularly the National Liberals) and government repealed the reduced Caprivi tariffs of 1892. There was, then, a *direct link* between the naval bills of 1898 and 1900 and the increases in agricultural tariffs that the Reichstag finally passed against the opposition of the liberal-left in 1902 (Berghahn 1993, 39–40, 53–54; see also Kehr 1977). This was key in giving a new lease on life to the heavy-industrial–Junker hegemonic bloc. But, it was also a central factor in the eventual destabilization of the National Liberal Party on the eve of WWI: the party increasingly divided between liberal internationalist-oriented light industries and their conservative/protectionist heavy-industrial brethren (Eley 1980, 293–348; see also Heckart 1974), thereby setting German expansionism on a "collision course" (Gordon 1974, 207) with Russia while increasingly antagonizing British policymakers.

While the Junkers were committed to keeping out cheap Russian grain, industrialists sought to capture the Russian market. Yet as Gordon notes (1974, 206), these "two goals were irreconcilable, and the only way for the German government to try squaring them was by applying ever greater dosages of political pressure on Saint Petersburg." This was exemplified by the 1904 Russo-German commercial treaty, which imposed severely disadvantageous terms on a temporarily weakened tsarist regime and contributed to Russia's expansionist reorientation into the Balkans, where it came into direct conflict with Austro-Hungarian and German interests.

The exacerbation of international tensions resulting from the *Weltpolitik* of the Wilhelmine period, particularly in regard to the construction of Tirpitz's world-class naval fleet, grew directly out of domestic conflicts and tensions. "Despite many differences of emphasis and opinion," David Kaiser writes (1983, 443), "it is fair to say that a far-reaching consensus of German, British, and American historians now agrees that German foreign policy after 1897 must be understood as a response to the internal threat of socialism and democracy."[28] Such threats were, however, common to nearly all European states in the prewar era. Why they proved so destabilizing for Germany, contributing to the ruling classes' *Flucht nach vorn* (flight forward), must be explained by specific *political* features of its "combined" social development.

Toward "Preventive War"

One of the major effects of the 1871 Constitution was the creation of a weakly centralized federal state unable to raise the adequate tax revenues from a Junker-dominated Bundesstaat. Since imperial budgets required parliamentary consent, Junker hegemony and the emerging power of the SPD in the

Reichstag meant that increased armament expenditures came up against opposition from both ends of the political spectrum. Only by working with the SPD in 1913 was the liberal bourgeois faction able to pass joint legislation on tax reforms and increased military expenditure. This drove a wedge between the Bethmann-Hollweg government and Conservatives, thereby further destabilizing the already fragile political coalition but scarcely solving the structural dilemmas facing German public finances (Heckart 1974, 231–41; Ferguson 1994, 158, 162–64).

While the Army Bill of 1913 constituted the largest increase in military personnel and expenditure in the history of the Reich, it fell far short of the 33 percent troop increase called for by the General Staff. Given that the 1913 bill prompted similar spending measures by other European countries (most worryingly, Russia's "Great Program"), it only intensified military leaders' anxieties regarding their ability to raise funds for further military increases, thus contributing to General Moltke's and others' calls for a "preventive war" (Mombauer 2001, 151–53).[29] By the summer of 1914, German policymakers' continuing inability to provide dramatically rising tax revenues to finance the Reich's growing armaments was a major factor contributing to their decision to risk war sooner rather than later. State and military managers believed that by waiting a few years longer to launch a preventive war against Russia, Germany would lose its competitive edge as the political deadlock over tax increases continued. According to Ferguson (1999, 140), "The domestically determined financial constraint on Germany's military capability was a—perhaps *the*—crucial factor in the calculations of the German General Staff in 1914."

Further contributing to the decision for "preventive war" was the unique sociopolitical physiognomy of the imperial army. As the mainstay of aristocratic power, the Prussian army served as the "last bastion of the status quo," fulfilling the "dual function" of defending the monarchy against enemies from within and without (Berghahn 1993, 26–28). Given the geographical position of Germany as a major land power at the heart of continental Europe, it would be expected, according to "realist" logic, that military strategy would be tailored toward buttressing land armaments and manpower. However, until the army spending bills of 1912–13, the strategy pursued was exactly the opposite. As a percentage of gross national product, the 1890–1912 period saw naval armaments grow by leaps and bounds as army expenditures remained relatively stagnant.

In fact, in terms of total defense expenditures as a percentage of net national product, German spending up until 1914 (that is, even after the army bills) consistently lagged behind France and Russia (figures and tables in Ferguson 1994, 148–55; see tables 6 and 7). This was *despite* the identification of the growth of Russian power after 1908 as a clear and present danger to the European military balance of power as perceived by German military and civilian leaders. For example, Wilhelm shared his chancellor's concerns regarding the extraordinary rise of Russian power, wondering to his banker friend Max Warburg in June 1914 "whether it would not be better to strike now [against Russia] than to wait." More explicitly, on 30 July 1914, German diplomat Count Kanitz told the U.S. ambassador to Turkey that "Germany should go to war when they are prepared and not wait until Russia has completed her plan to have a peace footing of 2,400,000 men" (quoted in Seligmann and McLean 2000, 144).[30]

To explain the German armaments anomaly faced by realist balance-of-

TABLE 6. Comparison of Defense Spending of the Great Powers, 1894 and 1913 (£ million)

	1894	1913	£ increase	% increase
Britain	33.4	72.5	39.1	117.1
France	37.6	72.0	34.4	91.5
Russia	85.8	101.7	15.9	18.5
France + Russia	123.4	173.7	50.3	40.8
Triple Entente	156.8	246.2	89.4	57.0
Germany	36.2	93.4	57.2	158.0
Austria	9.6	25.0	15.4	160.4
Italy	14.0	39.6	25.6	182.9
Germany + Austria	45.8	118.4	72.6	158.5
Triple Alliance	59.8	158.0	98.2	164.2

Source: Data from Ferguson 1999, 106, table 12.

TABLE 7. Defense Spending as a Percentage of Net National Production, 1873–1913

	Britain	France	Russia	Germany	Austria	Italy
1873	2.0	3.1	—	2.4	4.8	1.9
1883	2.6	4.0	—	2.7	3.6	3.6
1893	2.5	4.2	4.4	3.4	3.1	3.6
1903	5.9	4.0	4.1	3.2	2.8	2.9
1913	3.2	4.8	5.1	3.9	3.2	5.1
1870–1913	3.1	4.0	—	3.2	3.1	3.3

Source: Data from Ferguson 1999, 110, table 13.

power theory, two interconnected factors need be taken into account. The first, already discussed in this chapter, concerns the international economic interests of German capitalists, who favored a larger navy for commercial purposes and who generally supported the *Weltpolitik* orientation of Admiral Tirpitz. The Naval Office worked closely with influential segments of the business community toward these interrelated geopolitical and economic objectives (see Berghahn 1993). At the same time, however, as a result of this rising power of the bourgeoisie within the German formation as a whole, army leaders sought to maintain the aristocratic constitution of the Prussian army (Craig 1955; Kitchen 1968, 68–69; Bucholz 1985, 132–33; Förster 1999). There was then a second *class*-based factor arising from the specificities of Germany's combined development determining military strategy and contributing to German ruling classes' putative "escape into war."

Fearing further contamination from the working and middle classes, the War Ministry repeatedly forewent any increases in manpower and expenditures as the navy was allowed to take priority from 1897 to 1912. During this period, "it was the leadership of the Army itself that had called a halt to expansion" (Berghahn 1993, 16). Despite such efforts, however, the proportion of noblemen within the Prussian officer corps fell from 65 percent to 30 percent between 1865 and 1914. While aristocrats remained overrepresented in the army's highest ranks, by 1913, 70 percent of the Great General Staff were "commoners" by birth (Stevenson 1996, 41; Craig 1955, 232–38; Ferguson 1994, 155).

Paradoxically, the *modernity* of German political and military institutions determined their outwardly "anachronistic" appearance. The "aristocratic *élan*" of the Prussian army was "a *deliberative* and *innovative* response to a new situation," Eley explains (1986, 98), "one in which great heterogeneity of recruitment, growth of technical specialization, complex divisions of administrative labor, the command of new technology, criteria of efficiency and managerial expertise . . . were all ensuring that the earlier and natural solidarities of Junker officers could no longer be automatically relied upon." The aristocratic character of the German army was thus above all a consequence of the particularly rapid nature of Germany's dual transmutation into a highly industrialized, urban nation-state. It was not a hindrance to "modernization," as traditionally assumed, but a particularly instrumental if contradictory part of the process (see Showalter 1983).

In the debate over the army bills of 1912 and 1913, the peculiarly modern yet reactionary nature of the army's aristocratic élan came to the fore as General Heeringen's position against universal conscription and other institutional changes won out. Such reforms, he reasoned, would have jettisoned the army's "permanent function as guarantor of domestic stability." As General Wandel succinctly put it, "If you continue with these armament demands, then you will drive the people to revolution" (quoted in Herwig 1994, 263–64). Revolution at that time was perhaps an overstatement. In 1914, most German civilian policymakers did not go to war to directly avert revolution. The German ruling classes were, however, far from unified in regard to the nature of the "socialist menace."

Those on the German right, including many military officials, tended to exaggerate the revolutionary threat of the SPD, viewing the party's victory in parliament as a warning sign and looking toward war as a possible means of reconstructing the domestic order in a conservative direction (see Seligmann and McLean 2000, 106–7). In response to their demands, Bethmann-Hollweg actually thought a European conflict would instead promote the cause of social democracy, noting: "There are circles in the Reich who expect of a war an improvement in the domestic situation—in a Conservative direction." In contrast, he thought that "a World War with its incalculable consequences would strengthen tremendously the power of Social Democracy . . . and would topple many a throne" (quoted in Geiss 1967, 47). Bethmann-Hollweg's prescient remarks went unheeded.

The "socialist menace" nonetheless played a significant role in German foreign policymaking calculations. At the height of the July 1914 Crisis, for example, Albert Ballin witnessed a very agitated Bethmann-Hollweg pacing around the chancellor's garden and worrying out loud about whether Germany had already declared war on Russia: "'Is the declaration of war on Russia ready yet? I must have a declaration at once! . . .' When Ballin finally asked him 'Why such haste to declare war on Russia, your Excellency?' Bethmann answered: 'If I don't I shan't get the Socialists to fight!'" (quoted in Bülow 1932, 162–63). However, the conflicts and threats to domestic stability *within the ruling classes* were the more prominent underlying motive forces behind foreign policy decisions. In particular, three axes of instability can be noted. First, as Seligmann and McLean comment (2000, 105–6), "the immediate threat to domestic stability before 1914 came from the right not the left. It originated among pressure groups such as the Pan-German League, who the Chancellor and government were insufficiently strong in standing up to German interests" (see discussion later in this chapter, under "From Agadir to Sarajevo"). A second source of instability came from the Conservative Party itself, which adamantly opposed all domestic reforms and particularly the proposed tax reforms. Third, a major threat to domestic stability came from the growing influence and power of the military elite, which increasingly came to function as a relatively autonomous social force (Seligmann and McLean 2000, 106–7).

All three axes converged around the armaments issue. Indeed, the direction of armaments provided a key *mediating link* between domestic and foreign policies (Stevenson 1996). The balance of class forces, institutionalized within the political structures of the Reich, thus proved critical in determining the character and trajectory of military strategy.

In the years immediately preceding the war, the armaments imbroglio contributed to emerging attitudes within Germany's ruling classes that a war was not only inevitable but perhaps even something to be embraced as a means to "revitalize" the currently "satiated bourgeois culture" of the Second Reich before it collapsed under the weight of unbearable fiscal burdens. As the worsening international environment after 1912 necessitated a substantial expansion of the army, "bourgeoisifying" the officer corps would, conservatives feared, inevitably sever the special political bond between the army and the monarchy. "All this raised doubts" within ruling circles "as to their ability to overcome the growing military and strategic problems without resorting very soon to the extreme solution of a major war" (Mommsen 1981, 29–30).

After the 1912 elections and subsequent fiscal crisis, German society turned into a pressure-cooker. The political consequences of these "contradictions of sociological amalgamation" were taking their toll. As Berghahn (1993, 9) puts it,

> By 1913/14 the German political system, under the impact of social, economic and cultural change, had reached an impasse. The modernity and richness of the country's organizational and cultural life notwithstanding and, indeed, perhaps because of it, in the end Wilhelmine politics was marked by bloc-formation and paralysis at home and abroad and finally by a *Flucht nach voch* (flight forward) on the part of the political leadership that was fast losing control, but still had enough constitutional powers to take the step into major war.

Even if the immediate decision for war in July 1914 was not *directly* taken to avert the multiple domestic crises facing the German government, as some historians still hold (see Hildebrand 1989; Stürmer 1990), it was a decisive factor setting the conditions under which German policymakers made the decision for war.

In sum, the German state emerging from Bismarck's 1871 Imperial Constitution formed a contradictory amalgam of autocratic and representative institutions and principles—a "combination of modern capitalism and medieval barbarism," as Trotsky characteristically called it (1945, 79). These sociopolitical relations expressed the internationally pressurized and temporally condensed nature of the empire's simultaneous traversal into an industrial-capitalist and modern nation-state formation. German development thus drastically "diverged" from those earlier roads to capitalist modernity traveled by Britain and France.

Yet the alleged *Sonderweg* of German development may only be considered "deviant" from a static comparative perspective that obfuscates the spatiotemporally variegated but interactive history of capitalist development and thereby subsumes Germany's trajectory under an implicit unilinear stagism (see Blackbourn and Eley 1984). Accordingly, the German experience (authoritarian, illiberal, and militaristic) is conceived as a *pathological anachronism* within the history of capitalism. Such an approach lacks appreciation of the ways in which the sequencing of capitalist transitions was central to the form subsequent "bourgeois" revolutions took. That German development differed from those of previous states such as Britain and France is precisely explained by these earlier developments (see chap. 1).

The putative "peculiarities" of German development must be therefore conceived as one among many different forms of uneven and combined development characteristic of the *international conjuncture as a whole*. The destabilizing effects of Germany's "modernization" were less a result of its incomplete or arrested character than a consequence of its *overstimulation* from both within and without. This was an intensified "combination of the basic features of the world process," "a social amalgam combining the local and general conditions of capitalism" (Trotsky 1962, 23, 1969, 56). Furthermore, it was a consequence of the particular spatiotemporal site of Germany's development within the interactive matrix of capitalist industrializations— that is, the *"most general product of the unevenness of historical development, its summary result, so to say"* (Trotsky 1962, 24).

Industrialization, Armaments, and Military Alliances

The rise of a dynamically industrializing and expansionist German empire was bound to provoke concern among the continental European powers. Whether the trajectory of German development was itself enough to provoke a major European war is doubtful. The alliance lineups that eventually went to war in 1914 (France, Britain, and Russia on the one side and Germany and Austria-Hungary on the other) were in no sense predetermined by the Kaiser-reich's emergence as a great power. In the colonial scrambles of the 1880s and 1890s, interstate rivalries primarily cut across subsequently formed alliance lines. Colonial conflicts in Africa and the Far East largely pitted France and Russia against Great Britain. They even promoted the possibility of an Anglo-German alliance, as demonstrated in the two countries' intermittent diplomatic talks between 1898 and 1901 (Paul M. Kennedy 1980, 223–50; Otte 2007, 133–76). Nor was it natural to assume that the traditional antagonisms between republican France and autocratic Russia could be resolved. That these long-held rivalries (Anglo-French, Anglo-Russian, and Franco-Russian) would be settled in the form of a Triple Alliance against Germany within a few decades was all but unthinkable to many contemporaries.[31]

The emergence of the Franco-German antagonism as a central axis of intra-European rivalry was much easier to predict. Bismarck's appropriation of the mineral rich Alsace-Lorraine provinces from France in the aftermath of the 1870–71 Franco-Prussian War poisoned relations between the two countries; hence, *if* a European war broke out, France and Germany would sit on opposing sides. Yet despite the humiliating loss, the French public and most policymakers of the prewar period were unwilling to risk initiating a war with Germany to regain the region (see Néré 1975; Stevenson 1982; Keiger 1983, 1997).[32]

Similarly, relations between Russia and the newly formed German state were clearly fragile, though not always antagonistic. Only with the outbreak of the tariff war in the late 1870s resulting from the onset of the Long Depression did relations between the two states become strained to the point of potential war. Bismarck had successfully concluded the Mutual Reassurance Treaty of 1887, though his successor, Chancellor Bülow, would later let it lapse. After this point, the materialization of a Franco-Russian alliance became a real possibility. To explain these geostrategic realignments, one need turn again to the staggered and interconnected chain of industrializations and its relationship to the economically unbalanced, crisis-prone nature of the world market. Here, the role of foreign finance in Russia's intensive industrialization drive presents a particularly significant example of the relationship between the sequencing of industrializations and the formation of strategic-military alliances in Europe conditioning the path to war.

State-led industrialization in Russia demanded large infusions of capital, particularly for the construction of the strategically crucial railway systems. In the wake of the empire's crushing defeat in the Crimean War, state managers viewed the building of extensive railway networks as critical to overcoming Russia's comparative economic "backwardness" and related military weaknesses. The railways would provide the vital means for transporting not only armaments and soldiers to the battlefield but also Russia's vast agrarian exports, which were crucial for the state-sponsored industrialization drive (Collins 1973; Dietrich Geyer 1987, 19–20; Trebilcock 1981, 233–36).

The railways thus played a critical part in Russia's industrialization, having an enormous impact on the form of its social development and international position. Suffice it to note here two particularly significant and interconnected points. The first relates to the intensely state-orchestrated nature of railway construction and its effects on Russian finances. According to Dietrich Geyer (1987, 37), in no other country was "railway construction so directly a creature of state initiative as in imperial Russia and nowhere did it have such a heavy impact on state fiscal policy." Despite the persistence of long-standing financial crises, the government remained committed to the railways, exacerbating the already fragile domestic position of the tsarist regime. As Finance Minister Witte put it in 1866, "Not just our currency and its rate of exchange, but also Russia's entire economy, financial system and even political importance" were tied to the railways. "Our whole future depends on the railways" (quoted in Dietrich Geyer 1987, 40).

Since Russia's railway program was so heavily influenced by military-strategic concerns, unprofitable lines were often constructed, further aggravating the tsarist regime's financial and socioeconomic problems (Collins 1973). In pursuit of the overriding aim of accelerated industrialization without paying heed to its social consequences, Witte's policy laid much of the resulting financial burden on the peasantry, sparking widespread rural discontent. At the same time, the intensity of industrialization also depended on the exploitation of a fast-emerging and geographically concentrated urban proletariat, radicalizing them in the process (Gerschenkron 1962).

A second related point concerns the intimate connection between the building of the railways and the rise of foreign financed joint-stock companies in Russia. While this was in no way distinct to Russia, what was unique—at least for a "great power"—was the exorbitant role that foreign capital played in these companies. The important part played by foreign capital in the prewar Russian economy resulted from the particularly capital-intensive character of its late industrialization. Like other late developers,

Russia was starved of the massive amounts of money required for the regime's rapid state-sponsored industrialization centered on the strategically crucial railway systems. Initially, German foreign loans satisfied Russia's money demands (Trebilcock 1981, 224–27; Dietrich Geyer 1987, 150–51). However, as Germany's rapid industrialization got under way, resources were quickly drained.

No matter how much the Wilhelmstraße would have liked to have buttressed its diplomacy by financial means, the country's permanent shortage of capital thwarted such endeavours.[33] Thus, Russia looked elsewhere. Fortunately for French policymakers—who were by this point anxiously searching for a reliable ally to balance an increasingly expansionist Germany—Paris money markets had the capital "surpluses" to spare. For a significant consequence of France's earlier, more gradual industrialization process was the country's relatively high rates of domestic savings (McGraw 1983, 243–45; see Trebilcock 1981). "By 1914 the interdependence of French investment and the Russian economy provided an essential underpinning of the Franco-Russian diplomatic and military alliance" (Joll and Martel 2007, 57).[34] Whatever other factors might have contributed to the formation of the Franco-Russian alliance, the staggered and interconnected sequencing of their respective industrializations proved crucial (Justin Rosenberg 2008, 25).

The larger volume of capital, coupled with the lower rates of interest charged by the Paris money market, also provided French state managers with a crucial competitive advantage in exporting arms to the Balkans, where the Krupp-Schneider rivalry was at its most intense. The French government cooperated with exporters in tying military contracts to loan approvals, thus assisting French businesses in capturing the much-coveted Balkans arms markets. Employing the country's strong "financial arm," Paris sought to thereby influence the political orientation of the Balkan states (Plessis and Feiertag 1999; Stevenson 1996). This served French military-strategic interests, which sought to bring the Balkan states onto the side of the Triple Alliance. As Poincaré, then finance minister, wrote to the Quai d'Orsay, "The nation that wins the loan and war material order will consolidate its influence on the Serb government" (quoted in Stevenson 1996, 39). This strategy worked in Romania, where Schneider interests took the lion's share of the country's artillery market in 1912, foreshadowing Romania's move away from the Central Powers and its eventual realignment with the Allies in 1915 (Stevenson 1996, 39).

COLLAPSING EMPIRES AND RISING NATIONALISMS: THE "PERIPHERAL" SOURCES OF GEOPOLITICAL CONFLICT AND WAR

Imperial Rivalry and Revolutionary Nationalism: The "Eastern Question" in the History of Uneven and Combined Development[35]

The twin forces of modernity—nationalism and imperialism—form two sides of the same uneven and combined process of capitalist development. By the early 20th century, the structured inequality of the world economy emerging from the uneven development between states proved a major source of friction among the great powers, a generative condition and rallying point of the nationalist bourgeois forces budding within societies, and a means through which the developed capitalist powers enforced—individually or in competitive collaboration—their domination over the "periphery." The grafting of capitalist relations onto the social structures of the comparatively "backward" countries and rapidly industrializing aspirant great powers resulted in the melding together of different social systems within a single formation. These processes simultaneously unleashed centrifugal and centripetal tendencies, uncoupling collective identities from their local and regional contexts and reconstituting them on national foundations (see Nairn 1977; Hobsbawm 1992). The interlacing dynamics of imperialism and revolutionary nationalism thus formed the basis of empire building and reconstruction, while setting the conditions for their ultimate destruction. Two cases of the latter process of empire disintegration—Austro-Hungary and the Ottoman Empire—are particularly relevant to the discussion here, as their steady decline created the overall conditions that led to the outbreak of war in 1914.

The "North-South" vector of unevenness, as Justin Rosenberg (2008, 27) terms it, interconnected and distinguished the two multinational empires whose relative power was being progressively undermined by this overall process of capitalist industrialization and nationalist effervescence. The region was characterized by an *exacerbation* of the various levels of socioeconomic and (geo)political unevenness between (and within) these states and the industrializing capitalist core. While the multinational formations of the dual monarchy and the Ottoman Empire were far from stagnant in the decades before the war, the *relative* disparities between these states and the Western European powers were nonetheless drastically increasing by the turn of the century.[36]

The effects of this intersection of the West-East and North-South vectors of unevenness were largely manifested through the series of wars, treaties, revolutions, and diplomatic crises during the period following the start of the German wars of national unification and ending before the First Balkan War. This chain of causally interconnected events configured and reconfigured the pattern of military-strategic alliances that eventually went to war in 1914. It also fixed the geographical zone where the war was ignited.

The emergence of the "Eastern Question" from the late 18th century onward constituted a particularly explosive element within European international politics as the great powers struggled to come to grips with the myriad consequences of Ottoman decline first made plain by the Russo-Turkish War of 1768-74. The clichéd "sick man" of Europe, like the later dual monarchy, was propped up by the great powers throughout the 19th century with the aim of maintaining the European military balance of power. If either empire fell, many European state managers' believed, a massive geopolitical vacuum would ensue, thus generating imperialist land grabs at the heart of the European landmass and the strategically vital commercial sea lanes in the eastern Mediterranean. The result would be a massive rearrangement of the distribution of power, leaving Germany without its only reliable ally (the Austro-Hungarians). This would then open the way for the swift application of Russian power in the Balkans and Bosporus, two prized areas long sought after by tsarist policymakers. European policymakers (particularly in Britain and Germany) long sought to avoid precisely this situation (M. S. Anderson 1966; Macfie 1996).

The artificially prolonged decline of Ottoman power, interspersed with periods of internal renewal, was intrinsically connected to the phenomenal expansion of the world market and corresponding growth of European military power during the period. Throughout the 19th century, the Sublime Porte desperately sought to reform its internal structures to meet the threats posed by the European states, which tried to open Ottoman markets to expanding trade and commerce. The British and French empires' ability eventually to impose a series of highly disadvantageous "free trade" treaties on the Ottomans in the mid-19th century was the result of the military superiority of those empires, which by that time benefited from the immense productive advantages emerging from their capitalist bases (Kasaba 1988, 55–56; see also Owen 1981, 88–99). By contrast, Ottoman attempts to regularize administration and revenue clashed with the tax-farming and tribute-taking social structures on which the empire had hitherto relied (Bromley 1994, 50–51).

The Ottoman case offers a striking example of the ways in which the self-valorizing imperative of capital pressurized ruling classes of other social formations to emulate its productive structures or face the threat of extinction. This was not only affected at the level of the societies' differential economic development, but also, crucially, in their state structures. This can be related to Michael Mann's (1993) distinction between "infrastructural" and "despotic" powers characterizing capitalist and tributary state forms, respectively.

The infrastructural power typical of the modern bureaucratic state, developed in Western Europe over the 18th and 19th centuries, permitted a more intensive state capacity to appropriate via taxation a growing fraction of the surplus produced within society; taxation, in turn, became increasingly essential in maintaining a country's military power. The tributary relations of the Ottoman state, by contrast, remained wedded to the liminal nature of its despotic power, with relatively less efficient extractive capacities. As Eugene Rogan (1999, 3) notes, "While those changes [associated with the rise of the modern state] were more characteristic of the nation-states of Western Europe, even multi-national Empires such as Russia and Austria had developed the infrastructural power to finance the modern armies which menaced Ottoman domains."

The strategic benefits afforded to the European capitalist states thus acted as the "external whip" forcing the Porte—along with other neighboring tributary states (for example, Morocco)—into a condition of prolonged fiscal crisis. This accelerated the already disintegrative tendencies in the empire's outer provinces, where the despotic power of the tributary state was ever more incapable of asserting its sovereignty in the face of increasingly bold national independence movements. The regions thus become the target of direct European colonial penetration and geostrategic manipulation in the game of great-power politics. For the Ottomans, the Long 19th Century saw continual retreat under the interconnected impacts of external interventions and internal nationalist revolts (see Bromley 1994, chap. 2).

Unable to catch up and overtake the industrializing West, the Ottoman formation suffered a form of "blocked development." While escaping formal colonization, a slowly crumbling empire eventually fractured into a multiplicity of foreign-ruled and semiautonomous areas. The centrifugal pressures and resulting crises within the Porte not only provided the opportunity for Western powers to siphon off parts of the empire but also created the conditions in which the "Young Turks" of the Committee for Unity and Progress came to power in 1908. The Young Turks' aspiration to "turn the foe into tutor," in turn, fed back into the international political crises leading to the First World War as the "new regime in Istanbul, espousing a more assertive Turkish nationalism, became embroiled in the Balkan wars, the direct prelude to August 1914" (Halliday 1999, 197). Trapped within the wider maelstrom of Eastern Mediterranean unevenness, the Ottoman formation, transformed through the geosocial ripple of capitalist industrialization, thereby came to react back on the international system in causally significant ways.

The entire "Eastern Question" was conditioned by this interwoven process of Ottoman decline and the expansion of European capitalism. The contrasting regional developments between an economically dynamic industrial-capitalism emerging in northwestern Europe (the "West-East" vector) and the relatively stagnant tributary structures of the Porte ("North-South") was not simply socioeconomically uneven but also geopolitically "combined." As Bromley (1994, 61) notes,

> The dynamic of colonial expansion and aggrandizement was itself critically determined by the "general crisis" of these land empires, and the expansion complemented the hold capitalism had already established on the Atlantic seaboard. Equally, the reformist impulses and recuperative powers of the periphery played an active role in its own incorporation into the world economy and state system. Through this process of combined and uneven development, then, a systemic antagonism between capitalist nation-states and a tributary empire was worked out in which the former achieved a decisive victory by virtue of their economic vitality and military power.

There is, however, a second sense in which Ottoman development can be conceptualized as "combined": the sociological amalgamation of different "stages" of the developmental process within the anterior structures of the Porte itself. The interventions and pressures of the capitalist powers in the Middle East resulted in the uneven grafting of capitalist social relations onto the tributary structures of the empire. This was exemplified by the last-ditch efforts of the Young Turks at state rejuvenation through a "revolution from above" modeled after the earlier German and Japanese models. Yet by this time in the development of the world economy and state system, the Young Turks were at a significant disadvantage, having already suffered successive waves of imperialist interventions from the mid-19th century onward. They were thus unable to achieve the kind of "catch-up" industrialization and state modernization projects necessary for their continued geopolitical survival. As a consequence of these changed international circumstances, the Young Turks' revolt only hastened the collapse of Ottoman power in Europe, thereby ushering in the series of events leading to 1914. Further, the empire's collapse was itself tied to changes in the international system, particularly the rise of German power and Britain's strategic readjustment away from the Ottoman Empire and toward Russia as a potential ally (Nisancioglu 2011, 29–30). Fully understanding these dynamics that turned the Balkans into the "powder keg" of Europe also requires looking at the two other great multinational empires active in the region, Austria-Hungary and Russia.

The Ausgleich, *Austro-Hungarian Development,* and the Formation of the Dual Alliance

A major outcome of the Austro-Prussian War was the *Ausgleich* (Compromise) of 1867 establishing the dual monarchy of Austria-Hungary. The *Ausgleich* was of decisive significance to the future trajectory of European geopolitics in Central and Southeastern Europe, particularly by institutionalizing Prussian and Magyar hegemony within the Austrian and Hungarian halves of the empire, respectively. This not only buttressed stronger economic-political relations with Germany, helping nurture the Dual Alliance of 1879, but also redirected the monarchy's foreign policy toward the Balkans.

Expelled from Germany and Italy, the new dual monarchy turned eastward. This was possible given the Ottoman Empire's steady withdrawal from Europe over the 18th and 19th centuries, which had gradually enhanced the confidence and aggressiveness of the Magyar landowning nobility as they extended their territorial possessions to the east and the class's overall economic importance grew in Central Eastern Europe. At the same time, the Habsburg monarchy stumbled from one foreign disaster to another, and its internal relations became ever more strained. Consequently, the dynasty was "driven, logically and irresistibly, towards its hereditary foe" (the Hungarian aristocracy), which now became the only class capable of propping up the empire's state power. The *Ausgleich* of 1867 formalized this tendency toward Magyar hegemony, thereby shifting the "geopolitical and economic axis of the Monarchy irrevocably . . . eastward" (Perry Anderson 1974, 325). Through these antecedent processes of interaction, the newly reconstituted Habsburg Empire became subject to a novel set of pressures and influences emerging from its deepening interaction into the uneven development of the Balkan region.

The crucial diplomatic event here was the Congress of Berlin in 1878. The Congress signaled the decisive retreat of Ottoman domination in the Balkans with the occupation of Bosnia and Herzegovina. Though officially remaining an Ottoman possession, the provinces inhabited by Croatian, Serbian, and Muslim populations were now administrated by the dual monarchy. With one fell swoop, the Habsburgs had *internalized the powder magazines of the Balkans into the foundations of its own "heteroclite" sociopolitical edifices* (Perry Anderson 1974, 299). Austria-Hungary's incorporation of Bosnia and Herzegovina, its annexation thirty years later, and the assassination of the archduke at Sarajevo, "though separated by decades," were thus "inextricably linked" (Williamson 1991, 59). A further consequence of the Habsburgs' eastward drive was the conclusion of the Dual Alliance of 1879, which contributed to closer Franco-Russian relations. Though originally conceived as a defensive strategy by Bismarck, the alliance over time turned into yet another factor undermining international order (Joll and Martel 2007, 54–55; Mulligan 2010, 27–29).

The exacerbation of tensions in Central Eastern Europe can be viewed as a consequence of the dual monarchy's particular combined development. Unlike Germany, the Habsburgs never achieved the twofold transformation into a fully capitalist and nationally unified modern state. The political dualism of the new monarchy was accompanied by a glaring economic asymmetry between the Austrian and Hungarian halves. Indeed, by the early 20th century, internal regional economic disparities had actually increased. The sprawling empire boasted the most modern industrial cities of the era, such as Vienna, Prague, and Budapest, and contained highly industrialized regions in the Alpine and Bohemian lands. This starkly contrasted with the immense tracts of economically primitive, semifeudal agrarian relations in the eastern and southeastern lands (see Good 1984; Berend and Ránki 1979).

The differential trajectories of regional development within the dual monarchy aggravated already strained state-society relations, further inflaming nationalist sentiments through the steady destabilizing institutionalization of the "coercive comparison" (Barker 2006) of market relations. The spread of a popular consciousness of "comparative backwardness" engendered by the uneven development of capitalist industrialization acted as a centrifugal pull within all the multinational empire-states, not least of all Austria-Hungary. As David Good notes (1986, 139), this "problem of uneven development" has been "central to interpretations of the Empire's political demise."

Formed at the interstices of the West-East and North-South vectors of unevenness, Austro-Hungarian development thereby took on a uniquely unstable hybridity of different "Western" and "Eastern" forms. The empire's "heteroclite structures" expressed "the composite nature of the territories over which it presided, and which it was never able in any lasting fashion to compress into a single political framework." As the Magyar aristocracy was the chief obstacle to either a federal or unified royal state solution, the *Ausgleich* failed to resolve the nationalities problem. Instead, the increasing power of the most "combative and feudal nobility left in Central Europe" (Perry Anderson 1974, 299, 325) within the Austro-Hungarian formation actually aggravated relations with the southern Slavs and Romanians. In this sense, Magyar hegemony was the "grave-digger of the Monarchy," as Oszkár Jászi noted (1929, 297). For example, the Magyar nobility pursued an aggressive policy of Magyarization, further poisoning Austria-Hungary's relations with its southern neighbors. Just such a policy, according to R. W. Seton-Watson (1914, 109), "led directly" to the First World War.

Perhaps more than any other country of the prewar era, the dual monarchy's foreign policy was a function of the intractability of these internal problems. Since Magyar aristocratic power blocked all reforms aimed at partially quelling nationalist discontent, Vienna became convinced that controlling the Serbian "Piedmont" was fundamental to state survival. The monarchy thus became the "one power which could not but stake its existence on the military gamble [of July 1914] because it seemed doomed without it" (Hobsbawm 1987, 323). After the Annexation Crisis of 1908–9, cracks also began to emerge in the international consensus propping up the monarchy, as subject nationalists began to look for foreign support (particularly Russia) for their claims to national autonomy. By that time, the constitutional dualism established by the *Ausgleich* was wearing down the monarchy's ability to maintain itself as a formative *military power.*

Since the constitution of the dual monarchy mandated that the parliament sanction most legislation, the only way the government could bypass parliament was to pass legislation by decree. This made the empire's common army a key institutional arena of factional disputes through which the Magyar minority could assert its independence from Vienna. Under these conditions, "the army functioned as a barometer of separatist pressures in general" (Herrmann 1997, 33). Since Franz Josef was unwilling to risk making any move that could be interpreted as a coup d'état by Vienna, domestic conflicts "practically paralyzed" the monarchy's military development until the

Second Moroccan Crisis of 1911 finally galvanized the government into rapid rearmament. Yet by that time, it was too late, as the military balance had already titled heavily against the Dual Alliance in favor of the Franco-Russian alliance (Herrmann 1997, 33–34, 173–74; Joll and Martel 2007, 152–53).

Russian Development in the Crucible of War, Imperialism, and Revolution

The 19th century witnessed the opening of a massive competitive gulf between the ancient Chinese and Indian Empires and a handful of western capitalist states. Though more geographically peripheral to European geopolitics, the slowly collapsing power of the Qing Dynasty in China, as well as the already colonized Indian landmass, were no less important in restructuring the direction and dynamics of interimperial rivalries. The Chinese Empire in particular formed the geostrategic heartland of the Asian-Pacific region, drawing the imperialist powers into a maelstrom of social upheaval with promises of its immense export market potentials and investment opportunities. The orderly, managed decline of imperial China was profoundly important to the capitalist metropoles (Mulligan 2010, 43).

The effects of the power vacuum created by the destabilization of Qing rule were perhaps most consequential for the changing direction and nature of Russian imperialism. As long as the crumbling Chinese Empire deflected Russian economic expansionism into Manchuria—Witte's policy of *pénétration pacifique*—it acted to at least partially alleviate European rivalries in the Balkans and the Ottoman Empire. This relieved tensions between Austria-Hungary and Russia, as demonstrated in their 1897 entente that pledged to secure the Balkan status quo. More generally, the "Chinese Question" offered a momentary means of great-power cooperation, as exemplified by the "ultraimperialist" experiments of the "Open Door" and the *international* policing action against the Boxer Rebellion (Otte 2007; Mulligan 2010, 43–45; see also McCormick 1967; Gardner 1984).

At the same time, by drawing Russia into conflict with Japan over Manchuria, eventually resulting in the tsarist regime's humiliating defeat by the "Asiatic inferior" and revolution of 1905–7, the disintegrating Qing Dynasty effected a dramatic reconfiguration of the European strategic balance. As David Herrmann notes (1997, 7), the "history of the balance of military power in Europe in the decade between 1904 and the outbreak of WWI was in large measure the story of Russia's prostration, its subsequent recovery, and the effects of this development upon the strategic situation." The "geosocial"

conflicts formed at the triangular intersection of the differentiated development of the Chinese, Russian, and Japanese empires fundamentally aug-
mented the geopolitical axis of European order. This Asia-Pacific "periphery" of the North-South vector constitutes an important if overlooked factor
unsettling the international system in the immediate prewar years.

Here again we witness "internal" factors (the 1905-7 revolutionary upheaval) having "external" (geopolitical) consequences. Reframed from the
perspective of Russia's uneven and combined development, the interrelations between the two spheres—the sociological (domestic) and geopolitical
(international)—takes on new light. Rather than two discretely conceived
"levels of analysis" subsequently interacting with each other, one can begin
to visualize their interconnectedness as a single theorizable whole. Here we
may retrace just one thread of this multifaceted tapestry.[37]

Under the "external whip" of Russia's near-constant contact with the
more economically advanced Western powers, the tsarist state was compelled to internalize the ready-made technologies, weapons, and ideologies
from the West in the process of adapting them to its own less-developed social structure. Reaping the "privilege of backwardness," Russia thereby came
to make tiger leaps in its own development, "skipping a whole series of intermediate stages" leading to a "peculiar combination" in the historic process.
As with the stream of French money into Russia's railways and armaments
industries, the result was "an amalgam of archaic with more contemporary
forms": "The most colossal state apparatus in the world making use of every
achievement of modern technological progress in order to retard the historical progress of its own country" (Trotsky 1969, 53). Indeed, the infusion of
European armaments and finance was a severely contradictory process, simultaneously strengthening tsarism while undermining its socioeconomic
and political foundations.

The "combined" Russian social formation was characterized by islands of
the most advanced capitalist relations and productive techniques enmeshed
within a sea of feudal relations, creating potentially socially and geopolitically explosive interactions: mass concentrations of cutting-edge technologies (particularly within the state-run military industries) imported from
Western Europe and a rapidly growing and ideologically radicalized prole-
tarianized peasantry ("snatched from the plough and hurled into the factory
furnace") existing alongside an unreformed absolutist monarchy and a
dominant landowning aristocracy. Externally pressurized, time-compressed,
and stage-skipping, Russia's development was "no longer gradual and 'or-

ganic' but assume[d] the form of terrible convulsions and drastic changes" (Trotsky 1972d, 199). The result: the rapid rise of a highly class-conscious proletariat, joining together with a majority peasant class, capable of temporarily destabilizing and nearly overthrowing tsarist power in the midst of a war-invoked domestic crisis. Such were the geopolitically "overdetermined" sociological conditions leading to the war-revolution crisis of 1904–5.

This war-revolution crisis of 1904–5 was an important factor in the evolution of the emerging rivalry between Russia and Germany. On the Russian side, the military defeat of 1905 marked a decisive *westward reorientation* in foreign policy. Policymakers now sought to avoid further antagonizing Japan over Manchuria and traditional British colonial interests in Persia, Afghanistan, and India (Dietrich Geyer 1987; McDonald 1992). The new liberal-leaning foreign minister, Aleksandr Izvol'skii, was determined to resolve a number of outstanding quarrels with Britain in the Far East and Inner Asia. This led to the conclusion of the 1907 Anglo-Russian agreement recognizing their respective spheres of influence in Persia and similar agreements with Japan in July 1907 and 1910 that did much the same in the Pacific.

Foreign policy now turned westward to the more "traditional" focal points of Russian imperialism: gaining control over the economically vital Bosporus and securing influence in the Balkans (Dietrich Geyer 1987). By the early 20th century, 37 percent of all Russian exports and more than 90 percent of the country's critical grain exports traveled through the Straits at Constantinople. With Ottoman collapse looming, Russian policymakers became intensely worried that a rival power might come to dominate the Bosporus, thereby controlling the "windpipe of the Russian economy" (Stone 2007, 13).

On the German side, state managers sought to exploit the opportunity of a momentarily prostrate Russian power bogged down in war and revolution by pushing through the Commercial Treaty of July 1904 and then by pressing economic claims in Central Africa. The latter sparked the First Morocco Crisis of 1905. While designed by German policymakers to break up the Entente Cordiale, it ended up only strengthening the Franco-Russian alliance while laying the first "bridge between the Anglo-French Entente and Russia" (Fischer 1975, 57; see also Lieven 1983, 29–31).

Moreover, the nexus of relations between these three events—the Russo-Japanese War, Russian Revolution of 1905, and First Moroccan Crisis of 1905—had a number of crucial long-term effects on German military strategy. First, it resulted in the General Staffs drawing up the Schlieffen Plan for a two-front war against France and Russia.[38] This proposed the concentration of superior German forces in the west in a knockout campaign against the French before turning their forces east to confront Russia. Originally formulated in 1905, the Schlieffen Plan was based on calculations of Russia's *current* military and industrial power—then in a condition of weakness as a consequence of war and revolution. However, the rapid recovery of Russian military power and completion of the country's western railway lines rendered the Plan obsolete (Stevenson 1996; Herrmann 1997). Indeed, with the announcement of the "Great Program" in 1913, the plan's days were numbered.

From here on, German strategists calculated that the window of opportunity to launch a successful two-front war would close *no later* than 1916-17. These developments incited growing demands within German military circles for the launching of a "preventive war" before Germany's strategic advantage was overtaken. Such arguments were part of a broader consensus forming within Berlin and Vienna policymaking circles since 1912 that the military balance had swung against them and that it was time to increase armaments with the eventual aim of striking first (Stevenson 1996; Herrmann 1997; Copeland 2000).[39] In March 1914, the younger Moltke explained to Foreign Secretary Jagow that a war *had* to come soon or everything would be lost. As Jagow reported the conversation,

> Russia will have completed her armaments in 2 to 3 years. The military superiority of our enemies would be so great then that he did not know how he might cope with them. Now we would still be more or less a match for them. In his view there was no alternative to waging a preventive war in order to defeat the enemy as long as we could still more or less pass the test. The chief of the General Staff left it at my discretion to gear our policy to an early unleashing of a war. (quoted in Berghahn 1993, 181–82)

The tightly knit Schlieffen-Moltke Plan thus enticed the General Staff to demand war before the circle of largely self-made enemies could arm in time to render the plan unviable. Despite the General Staff's continuing hopes, the plan was in fact already inoperable (Förster 1999, 361).

Since the First Moroccan Crisis, a *three-front* war had become increasingly likely since the debacle drove Britain further into the Franco-Russian camp, as revealed by the signing of the Anglo-Russian agreement of 1907. Before the German provocations at Tangiers, conditions had already emerged for an eventual Anglo-Russian détente. Specifically, the Russian defeat of 1905 diminished St. Petersburg's ambitions in Central Asia, lessening the threat posed to British colonial interests in the region. The 1904–5 war-revolution imbroglios also reduced London's fears of Russian power. For these reasons, the events provided "the essential backdrop" to the Anglo-Russian agreement of 1907 (Lieven 1983, 31). Though the issue of British participation in a future war on the side of France subsequently became a dominant question in German policymaking circles, the Schlieffen Plan, as later altered by the younger Moltke, circumvented any chance of assuring British neutrality as it called for a first-strike offensive against France through Belgium (Steiner and Neilson 2003).

The British decision for war in August 1914 nonetheless clearly reflected broader geostrategic issues, specifically those regarding the continuing menace of German power in threatening both the British Isles *and* the global interests of the empire. The latter concerns were particularly displayed by British state managers' persistent worries about Germany's expanding economic and political influence in the Middle East, which directly affected the strategic interests of the empire. Some historians have pointed to the apparent resolution of the two countries' divergent interests in the region in the immediate years before the war—for example, the agreement reached over the Berlin-Baghdad railway in June 1914, hitherto a key nodal point of Anglo-German interimperial rivalry (Strachan 2001, 33; Mulligan 2010, 202–3). Whether the Berlin-Baghdad railway agreement would have had the desired pacifying diplomatic effects had it not been for the outbreak of the Balkan Crisis less than a month later is, however, far from clear. For it seems that the most significant problem concerning the Anglo-German antagonism was much less about *specific* issues and conflicts, important as these might have been at particular junctures. Instead, it was much more about the broader challenge posed to the British Empire by the rise of an expansively dynamic German capitalism and the synchronic *interaction* of this challenge with other international-global developments (Joll and Martel 2007, 229; see also Paul M. Kennedy 1980).

Likewise, the 1905–7 Russian Revolution had crucial international sociopolitical effects. Reverberating serially across the "West-East" and "North-South" planes, it causally interconnected with and hastened structurally analogous developmental dynamics within the different polities thrown up by the same international pressures of capitalist development. Of "all the eruptions in the vast social earthquake zone of the globe," Hobsbawm writes (1987, 300), the 1905–7 revolution had "the greatest international repercussions." It "almost certainly precipitated the Persian and Turkish revolutions, it probably accelerated the Chinese, and, by stimulating the Austrian emperor to introduce universal suffrage, it transformed, and made even more unstable, the troubled politics of the Habsburg Empire." In addition, knock-on effects of the revolution fed into the series of Balkan crises immediately preceding the July–August 1914 diplomatic crisis.

From Agadir to Sarajevo: Into the Conjunctural Abyss

At this point in the investigation, we reach the moment where deep structures and world-historical phenomena appear to recede into the background noise of the frenzied chaos of the diplomatic juncture. This is the realm of "radical contingencies," where even the greatest of historically minded theorists proclaim "cock-up, foul up" as a main cause of WWI (Mann 1993, 740–802, esp. 764–66, 798). Yet in the rush to eschew all modes of monocausal explanation—if not "grand theory" altogether—scholars simply relinquish the task of theorizing the sociohistorical process as a single whole in all its richness and complexity. This section sketches how the framework developed earlier in the chapter can be used to examine the chain of events leading to the July 1914 crisis. In doing so, it analyzes the form of geopolitics as it appeared "on the surface of society" in "the ordinary consciousness" of the decision-making agents themselves (Marx 1981, 117).

In any investigation of the prewar juncture, the Second Moroccan Crisis (June–November 1911) plays a critical role. The crisis signifies the decisive caesura in the international relations of the prewar period. What were its proximate causes? Why did it *not* result in world war in 1911? And how did it nonetheless set off the chain of events leading to world war in August 1914?

The immediate background to the crisis was French colonialists' use of an indigenous revolt as the pretext for military intervention aimed at further expanding French economic interests in North Africa. The German foreign ministry in turn sought to score a diplomatic success against France to weaken Germany's external enemies while strengthening the tottering ruling political bloc against the Social Democratic challenge in the 1912 elections. Indeed, German heavy industrial interests had for some time been pushing for a more robust foreign policy (Fischer 1975).

In the short term, Germany's diplomatic move had its intended domestic effect. The "Panther's Leap" in Agadir inspired a groundswell of popular domestic support, particularly among the conservative establishment. But its eventual diplomatic failure was met by an outburst of nationalist fury, further destabilizing the heavy-industrial–Junker bloc. Among the radical-nationalist Right, the episode strengthened calls for launching a preventive war as a means to domestic unity—"War as the only cure for our people" (quoted in Eley 1980, 323; see also Mommsen 1981; Berghahn 1993). Economic interests clamored ever more loudly for decisive action, since significant segments of German business saw the raw materials of the African colonies and their potential as future markets as vital to the economy's health (see Fischer 1975, 75–81).[40] German policymakers such as Foreign Secretary Kiderlen and Gustav Stresemann shared this identification of the "national interest" with the perceived exigencies of the Kaiserreich's expanding industrial economy. Yet with the exception of Kiderlen, German policymakers were *not* yet ready to risk this "ultimate step" (as he called it) of possible war with Britain over Morocco (quoted in Fischer 1975, 76). Why?

Much of their reluctance had to do with their fears that Germany still lacked the necessary naval armaments to adequately meet the British challenge and further that the "masses" would not *yet* back a war. Further, Tirpitz had repeatedly expressed reservations, advising the chancellor and emperor "to postpone this war which was probably unavoidable in the long run until after the completion of the [Kiel] canal" (quoted in Fischer 1975, 85). Ex-chancellor Bülow's retrospective analysis was perhaps even more revealing:

> In 1911 the situation was much worse. Complications would have begun with Britain; France would have stayed passive, would have forced us to attack and then there would have been no *casus foederis* for Austria—as Aehrenthal said to the delegations—against that Russia was under an obligation to co-operate.[41]

The threat of British intervention and Austria-Hungary's abdication of its alliance role were principal issues. For most German statesmen, securing British neutrality in the case of a continental war was of the utmost importance.

During the July 1914 crisis, Chancellor Bethmann repeatedly sought to lock down such a pledge. Though remaining *hopeful* that Britain might remain neutral, in the end Bethmann risked provoking a European war, cognizant that British neutrality was unlikely (see Mommsen 1973, 33, 37–39; Trachtenberg 1991, 85–86; Copeland 2000, 64–66, 111–16). The chancellor's so-called calculated risk was largely the result of his belief that a European war was inevitable and that Germany's chance of a decisive military success was steadily declining with every passing year, given the incredible resurgence of Russian power since 1911 and specifically after the shock of the "Great Program" of 1913 (Jarausch 1969; Fischer 1975, chap. 9; Trachtenberg 1990; Berghahn 1993). As Bethmann warned on 8 July 1914, "The future belongs to Russia which grows and grows and becomes an even greater nightmare to us" (quoted in Fischer 1975, 224).

The necessity of the spark for war affecting the vital interests of the dual monarchy was made apparent by Prime Minister Aehrenthal's refusal to go to war on behalf of German colonial claims. As Chancellor Bethmann was already aware, if and when war came, it was hoped that it would be *against* the Austro-Hungarians so that they did not have to decide whether to fulfill their alliance obligations (see Fischer 1975, 86–87). This is particularly significant because it reveals the specificity of the 1914 spark involving Austro-Hungarian interests in the Balkans.[42] It was not just *any* incident that could provoke a generalized world war but only one *directly connected* with Austro-Hungarian interests—meaning some issue relating to the "Eastern Question" and thereby also involving Russia.

The Second Moroccan Crisis was also important for its effects on the industrial-arms spiral. The crisis offered the ideal opportunity for Tirpitz to introduce another naval bill as well as new demands for increases in the size and spending on the army. As a result of the already severe strains the military budget was placing on the Reich's finances, the result was a rather modest, though still fiscally damaging, rise in German army spending and plans to build only three new battleships. But most important from Tirpitz's perspective, the Reichstag moved forward the date of the fleet's battle readiness (Herrmann 1997, 167–71; see also Berghahn 1993, 115–35). This was enough to provoke a French response in 1912, when France increased its own military expenditures, coincident with the economic upswing of 1912, which motivated further German and Austro-Hungarian arms increases.

Then in 1913 came the crucial revelation of Russia's Great Program, which aimed to transform the country into a military "superpower" greater than Germany in less than four years. Already at the so-called War Council of 8 December 1912, following Britain's pledge to support France and Russia in a possible Balkan war, "Moltke wanted to launch an immediate attack," since he now "considered war unavoidable" and "the sooner the better."[43] The kaiser and General Müller backed this injunction for immediate war. "The army's position was quite clear: Germany could only lose her slight advantage over her enemies as time went on, because German army increases had led in turn to army increases in France and Russia" (Mombauer 2001, 140). Tirpitz, conversely, claimed that the navy was not ready, and the reconstruction of the Kiel Canal was not yet complete. Thus he argued that war should be postponed for another eighteen months.

Though calls for preparing the public for eventual war through a propaganda campaign were made, few concrete measures were taken. The principal significance of the December 1912 meeting lay instead with its convincing "proof that at least by this date Germany's leaders were anticipating war in the near future and were quite ready to risk it when the moment seemed propitious, even if they were not planning for a particular war at a particular moment" (Joll and Martel 2007, 130).[44] Moltke's "sooner the better" position was appreciably strengthened by the Great Program. The completion of Russia's strategic railways, allowing for the tsarist army's rapid mobilization on Germany's eastern frontier, now seemed assured and thereby undermined the foundations of the Moltke-Schlieffen Plan.

Finally, the Second Moroccan Crisis was critical in providing the chance for Italian policymakers to launch an invasion of Libya and attack a weakened Ottoman Empire. Italy's eastward aggressions were no secondary matter in the outbreak of world war less than three years later. Italian victories on the battlefield raised the clearest prospect of Ottoman collapse for some time, galvanizing the various Balkan states to assert their national interests.

Allying together in October 1912, the Balkan League won a shockingly swift victory against the Ottoman Empire, driving the army out of the region. However, the alliance soon crumbled as intra-Balkan conflicts led to a second war in 1913. This resulted in limited Turkish gains. However, the real victors were the Serbians, who cooperated closely with Russia, Greece, and the United Kingdom (Stone 2007, 12–13).

To better appreciate the causal significance of Italy's place in the matrix of events leading to WWI, the deeper sources of Italy's "drive to the East" must be considered. According to Richard Webster (1975), these can be traced back to the 1907 depression, which witnessed the intensification of Italy's industrial rivalries with the central empires in the Balkans and Turkey. Maritime competition with the dual monarchy in the eastern Mediterranean thereby became directly connected with the question of Italian naval hegemony in the Adriatic and its endangered populations in Austro-Hungary's Adriatic ports. The irredentist movements of the Adriatic thus came to mirror the growing conflict between Austro-Hungarian and

Italian interests, reflecting the two countries differential but interconnected "combined" developments.

Italy's policy reorientation was further strengthened by the mass exodus of German capital from Italy's industrial and banking sectors during this same period as French money markets took a growing share. This was a consequence of Germany's chronic shortage of banking capital and France's high rate of savings, both of which derived from the nature and timing of both states' industrialization. The result was a weakening of the already fragile strategic ties between Germany and Italy, with the latter titling toward the entente camp. Italy's new "industrial imperialism," as Webster writes (1975, 125), "meant colonial expansion to the East, alliance with the Entente, divorce from the Central Powers, and eventual war against them." This was particularly the case as Italian heavy industry and its financial backers increasingly came to rely on state military contracts and subsidies, in turn contributing to the industry's chronic overproduction during the immediate prewar years. The lines connecting Agadir and Sarajevo thus ran through Tripoli. In this sense, Italy's eastward drive was a key mediating link between the West-East and North-South configurations of unevenness.

CONCLUSION: TIMING IS EVERYTHING

In a fascinating piece, Richard Ned Lebow (2000, 600) emphasizes the coincidental character of the various causes coming together in 1914 to make a world war possible. According to Lebow, Russian security threats facing both Germany and Austria-Hungary were largely "independent" in their causal sources. There was, moreover, "no particular reason why they should have become acute at the same time." He thus concludes that "timing was everything in 1914, and time was fortuitous . . . For this reason alone, the First World War was highly contingent."

Accordingly, Lebow charges structural theories of IR as being both underwhelming and overdetermining in their inability adequately to account for contingent, system-altering catalysts in the causes of war. Yet despite his insistence on the "multiple streams of independent causes" (2000, 597) that came to produce the war, there is a very different reading that can be gleaned from his analysis, and it was least partially and ambiguously formulated by Lebow himself. For if the *general* argument regarding the various relations between the different configurations of developmental dynamics is correct, then the supposedly "contingent" sources of the conflict's origins become rather suspect.

To retrace just one thread of this interconnected picture, as detailed earlier, Western European and Russian expansionism drove the disintegration of Ottoman rule in the Balkans. The Young Turks' revolt in turn fed into the causal conditions resulting in the Bosnian Annexation Crisis of 1908–9 and the Second Moroccan Crisis of 1911. The former irrevocably damaged Austro-Serbian relations, while Russian policymakers became determined to avoid the domestic and international costs of yet *another* humiliation (a major legacy of the Russo-Japanese War, which had reoriented Russian strategy westward in the first place). The Second Moroccan Crisis, largely the product of Germany's worsening domestic and international position, which pushed the country toward diplomatic brinkmanship, then resulted in the Italian occupation of Tripoli, aggravating the Ottomans' precipitous decline and thereby also worsening Austria-Hungary's external/internal "security dilemma" by setting off the two Balkan Wars. Further, Italy's eastward expansion was (at least) in part an effect of its place in the historically staggered and interactive chain of European industrializations, as the plentiful French money market came to make up for the departure of German investments from the Italian economy (itself a consequence of Germany's late, hothouse industrialization eating up its domestic disposable finances). A further effect of the Moroccan Crisis was the dramatic acceleration of the continental arms race into a classic action-reaction spiral, as German rearmament set off Russia's Great Program, leading to the widespread perception among German policymakers that a preventive war against the "Slavic enemy" must be risked sooner rather later.

The concatenation of events producing the strategic window of opportunity to be exploited by German and Austro-Hungarian policymakers was the result of the interconnected character of these sociohistorical processes. The conception of causality here is thus necessarily "multiperspectival" (Justin Rosenberg 2006, 322)—a parallax view of the "synergistic interaction" of different causal chains arising from "geosocial" development and change over time. In this sense, Lebow is generally correct in claiming that a world war would *not* have resulted from any one single stream of causation but would only have resulted from the interaction of multiple streams. But how this translates into an interpretation of the intersection of discretely constituted independent causes is much less clear. This is not to make the banal point that everything in the world is related, and thus nothing can be considered an independent cause: the precise *links* connecting each stream have been pinpointed, as has their shared basis in a theorizable developmental process.

What is to be made of Lebow's argument that "timing was everything"? The temporal specificity of the conjuncture was no doubt important. Earlier crises did not result in world war, and had a Sarajevo-like crisis erupted some years later, it might not have resulted in WWI, since the military window of opportunity was quickly closing. Yet given the fragility of the geopolitical and domestic environments of Central and Southeastern Europe after the Balkan Wars of 1912–13, it seems difficult to imagine that some crisis *in the region* would not have developed before the window closed. Once the "gestalt shifts" in European policymaking circles occurred, a world war became the likely (though not inevitable) outcome.

This is not to repeat the "slide into war" thesis, since this crisis needed to fulfill both the particular time (1912–17) and space (Balkans) conditions necessary to draw the two alliance blocs into war. Existing structural explanations of the crisis, as chapter 1 argues, fail to meet these criteria. The chapter has constructed an alternative framework combining international and domestic-based processes to more adequately fulfill these conditions.

CHAPTER 4

Between War and Revolution: Wilsonian Diplomacy and the Making of the Versailles System

THE PEACE TREATIES of 1919[1] retain a prominent place within the study of IR, provoking more debate and controversy over the origins, nature, and limits of "international order" than any other major postwar settlement in modern history. The theoretical significance of Versailles for IR can hardly be overstated. For much rests on the question of whether the postwar settlement was problematic because or in spite of its liberal nature. Historians and IR scholars have long emphasized the fundamental flaws and illegitimacy of the Versailles settlement as a central factor in the geopolitical instabilities of the interwar years. Yet explanations about why Versailles diplomacy was so problematic vary significantly. What were the central factors affecting policymaking at Versailles? And what does Paris peace diplomacy tell IR theory about modern foreign policymaking processes? Given the many similarities between the two postwar eras, it is productive to inquire into the conditions and factors that resulted in such different conclusions: the problematic "Versailles system" as compared to the more durable and relatively peaceful (at least within the capitalist heartlands) international order after WWII.[2]

Despite the differing explanations of the "Lost Peace" at Versailles, most interpretations stress the problems caused by the unprecedented divergence of policymakers' conceptions of postwar international order. Unlike previous peace settlements among the great powers, such as the Treaty of Westphalia (1648), the Peace of Utrecht (1713–15), and the Congress of Vienna (1815), the Versailles peacemakers held "fundamentally different perspectives about the nature of international politics, significantly diverging diagnoses of the causes of the Great War, and largely incompatible recipes for constructing the peace" (Holsti 1991, 178; see also Ikenberry 2001, 117). In standard IR interpretations, these conflicting perspectives are associated with specific statesmen—Clemenceau, Lloyd George, and Wilson—conceived as ideal-type representations of the two dominant IR paradigms, realism and liberalism. IR debates over the nature and problems of the peace settlement are thus largely formulated from this perspective of a "realist/idealist" (or "power/utopianism") dichotomy. Nation-states are conceived as characters in a Greek tragedy: characters identified by the ideological attributes of their most prominent policymakers whose ideas and actions reflect IR theories themselves.

In IR interpretations, it is not surprising that the role of Woodrow Wilson in the making of the peace figures prominently as what became commonly referred to as "Wilsonianism" is synonymous with idealism/utopianism. The outcome of Wilson's diplomacy at Versailles is well known: his proposal for U.S. entry into the League of Nations was defeated in the Senate. Thereafter, successive Republican administrations rejected all security alliances in Europe as U.S. policymakers retreated into so-called hemispheric isolationism. In explaining these events, standard IR and historical narratives stress their contingent if not idiosyncratic and "irrational" causes: Wilson's political intransigence during the League of Nations debate, resulting in part from debilitating illness; the mood of disenchantment prevailing in the country by the fall of 1919; and the inflexibility of a parochial, shortsighted Congress (Dueck 2006, 44). While such contingent factors are important, they remain inadequate for explaining the construction of the Versailles system and its consequences. This requires a systematic examination of the structural and social forces in the making and unmaking of the postwar international order, particularly focusing on the contradictions of intercapitalist rivalry and labor-capital conflicts in the context of the uneven and combined development of capitalism on a world scale.

This chapter is divided into three sections. The first section provides a critique of standard IR interpretations of Wilsonian diplomacy at Versailles, illustrating how realists' and liberals' uncritical acceptance of Wilson as the quintessential "idealist-liberal" statesman obfuscates a core contradiction at the heart of Wilsonian diplomacy: the wielding of power politics to transcend power politics. The next section offers an alternative "anatomization" of Wilsonianism, examining the historical and sociological conditions from which a distinctive Wilsonian foreign policy ideology and imperial praxis emerged. In doing so, it conceptualizes Wilsonian diplomacy as the *effect* and *pragmatic response* to the social-strategic dilemmas arising from the uneven and combined nature of U.S. development and world capitalism as a whole. The final section ("The Making of a Social Peace?") examines the effects of the Bolshevik revolution as a paradigm-rupturing event transforming the nature and dynamics of WWI. This traces the unique sociological patterns of uneven and combined development thrown up by the war and the geopolitical problems this created for Wilson and the Allies in forging a new international order.

WILSONIANISM AND VERSAILLES IN IR THEORY

An essential continuity in U.S. strategic thinking since WWII has been the imperative to remake the world in the American image. Central to this has been the distinct belief that the flourishing of U.S. democracy, prosperity, and security are necessarily connected with the maintenance of a liberal-capitalist international order. The origins of this thinking can be traced directly back to Woodrow Wilson and his injunction to "make the world safe for democracy." If only in this sense, "Wilsonianism" can be credited as *the* fundamental component of post-WWII American foreign policy ideology (see Holsti 1991; Moravcsik 1991; Kissinger 1994; Tony Smith 1994; Ruggie 1998a; Ninkovich 1999; Bucklin 2001; Ikenberry 2001; Ambrosius 2002).

It is, then, hardly surprising that Wilson(ianism) holds such a prominent place in the "American discipline" of IR (Hoffmann 1977). Perhaps no other modern policymaker is as often evoked as a canonical liberal statesman than President Wilson (Waltz 1959; Russett 1993; Tony Smith 1994; Ruggie 1998a; Ikenberry et al. 2009). His role in the creation of the postwar international order at the Paris Peace Conference remains a central issue in both historiographical and IR debates on the Versailles settlement. Yet the nature of Wilson's vision for the postwar international order as well as the means through which he pursued this vision have been issues of great dispute among historians (see Coogan 1994; Steigerwald 1999).[3] This is anything but apparent when approaching these issues through the lens of IR studies. As Michael Cox notes (2000, 235), "While realists and liberals might disagree about nearly everything else, both seem to accept at face value the claim that Wilson was a true enlightenment figure whose ultimate goal was to make the world a more democratic place." How so?

The Unbearable Lightness of Realist Critique

For the new deans of postwar U.S. realism, Walter Lippmann, George F. Kennan, and Hans J. Morgenthau, Wilsonianism was synonymous with the interwar "utopianism" E. H. Carr so bitterly attacked.[4] Wilson was viewed as the paradigmatic "idealist" thinker in U.S. foreign policymaking history, an unworldly man both ignorant and disdainful of the realities of power politics. Wilsonianism was thus perceived as a doctrine inherently antithetical to "America's national interest," a pathological *deviation* from traditional U.S. foreign policy thinking (see Lippmann 1944; Morgenthau 1950, 1977; Kennan 1951).

From the realist perspective, the "traditional guarantee" of European geopolitical order was the balance of power. Eschewing this, Wilson's "legal-moralistic" approach to international relations was doomed to failure *irrespective* of domestic conditions. After having entered the war to counter immediate threats to U.S. security, Morgenthau claimed, the logic of Wilson's "moral position" drove him to substitute the national interest in the pursuit of constructing a "community of interests comprising mankind." Yet in the end, Wilson "consent[ed] to a series of uneasy compromises," thereby betraying "his moral principles" and resulting in an inherently unviable European balance of power. "Thus Wilson returned from Versailles a compromised idealist, and empty-handed statesman, a discredited ally. In that triple failure lies the tragedy not only of Wilson . . . but of Wilsonianism as a political doctrine" (Morgenthau 1950, 849). For these realists, Wilsonian diplomacy was thus a central factor in the making of the flawed peace and its destabilizing consequences during the interwar years (Kennan 1951, 68–69).

There are three principal problems with this "classical" realist critique of Wilsonianism. First, there is a key inconsistency in Kennan and Morgenthau's formulation. On the one hand, the Kennan-Morgenthau thesis argues that the peace was flawed *because* of its Wilsonian nature. On the other hand, they claim that Wilson failed to implement his peace plan at Versailles. There is, then, an underlying ambiguity regarding whether the peace was problematic because or in spite of its "Wilsonianism" (see Bucklin 2001). Second is realism's view of Wilsonian diplomacy in terms of the "idealism/utopianism" couplet. This conception of Wilson as the characteristically naive idealist statesmen, shunning power politics in the name of abstract moral principles, is itself hopelessly naive. The importance of "Wilsonian slogans" for Wilson's actual diplomacy, as Michael Walzer notes (2006, 111), "has been much overestimated in the realist literature."[5] In mistaking Wilson's rhetoric for the core substance of his policies, realist critics inadequately consider the sociohistorical determinations accounting for the emergence of Wilsonianism as a foreign policy ideology. From the latter perspective, Wilsonian diplomacy can be conceptualized as an organic response to U.S. development in the context of the significantly altered international and socioeconomic conditions of early 20th-century world capitalism.

In true "realist" fashion, the critiques of Wilson(ianism) offered by Carr, Lippmann, Kennan, and Morgenthau were explicitly *political-strategic* interventions into debates concerning the conduct of U.K. and U.S. foreign policymaking, respectively.[6] As such, one would expect the construction of a "straw man" Wilsonian idealism with which to contrast their "realist" alternatives. Yet even granting this strategic rhetoric, the substance of their criticisms reveals realism's own shallow theoretical foundations. This ties to a third difficulty concerning the discontinuity in U.S. foreign policy proponents of this view attribute to Wilson(ianism).

According to Kennan and Morgenthau, the rise of a moralistic-expansionist foreign policy at the turn of the century and its continuation under President Wilson constituted a fundamental *aberration* from U.S. foreign policy tradition. This view has been discredited by more recent historical literature, which overwhelmingly views Wilsonianism as representing an essential continuity in U.S. foreign policy (see, among others, Williams 1972; Leffler 1979; Emily S. Rosenberg 1982; Gardner 1984; Offner 1986 [1975]; McDougall 1997; Steigerwald 1999; Ryan 2000; Ambrosius 2002; Hannigan 2002; Cohrs 2006). Kennan and Morgenthau's inability to see this continuity is symptomatic of a more elementary theoretical problem with realism in general.

Whether in its "classical" or "structural" forms, realism works from the strong assumption that all things being equal, states are instrumentally rational actors. The logic of such rationality is deduced from the changing international distribution of power, which, in turn, informs policymakers' pursuit of the "national interest." State interests are thus conceived as the maximization of a particular variable—security for defensive realists, relative power for offensive realists (see, respectively, Waltz 1979; Mearsheimer 2001). From this perspective, foreign policy outputs that do not conform to these interests are explained by exogenous (largely domestic-level) factors. To the extent that ideology plays any explanatory role in (neo)realist accounts of state behavior, it does so as a subsidiary variable "layered in" to explicate deviations from expected state actions derivative of international systemic determinations (see, for example, Snyder 1991; Schweller 1998; Zakaria 1998; Dueck 2006; Layne 2006). In other words, when states fail to act in accordance with their rational interests determined by the distribution of power within a given international system, (neo)realism attributes this to "irrational" factors such as ideology. In the case of Wilson's diplomacy at Versailles, realist approaches thus point to the corrupting influence of Wilson's idealist-legalistic ideology—viewed in discontinuous terms from the more prudent foreign policies of previous U.S. administrations.[7]

These realist approaches to ideology have a number of problems. Primary is the lack of any adequate understanding of historically determinant forces, irreducible to the international system alone, explaining the emergence of Wilsonian ideology and the precise relation of this ideology in determining state interests and action. As historian Lloyd Gardner (1967, 205–6), writes, while radicals "may criticize [Wilson's] naïve moralism and idealism along with the realists . . . a full account of the development of that outlook is a much more difficult problem." This "outlook" had "developed from a much keener insight into the nature of his society (and its needs) than would appear from the realist critique." There is, then, a *social-historical embeddedness* of Wilsonianism escaping realism's rather oblique conception of ideology and its function in foreign policymaking. Put simply, state interests cannot be read off "brute material" forces such as the distribution of material capabilities among states. The great contribution of constructivist IR has been to highlight the necessarily *interpretative* dimension in understanding the formation of state interests. Specific foreign policy ideologies are developed through collective identity formation processes among state managers, which are, in turn, constitutive of state interests (see especially Weldes 1996; Vucetic 2011). Ideologies work as a kind of filter through which state managers select from a menu of potential interests themselves embedded in specific sociohistorical conditions, such as the changing balance of class forces. This interpretative dimension of state interests is entirely consistent with a Marxist approach, which works with a much more sophisticated materialist ontology than realist IR does (cf. Rupert 1995; Callinicos 2009a).

Liberal-Realist Convergence

In contrast to realist approaches to Wilsonianism, liberal IR stresses the visionary nature of Wilson's diplomacy. Proponents of democratic peace theory (DPT), conceive of Wilson as a kind of modern-day prophet expounding Kant's vision of "perpetual peace." The "normative basis of Wilson's vision of world order," Bruce Russet writes, "grew naturally from his progressive inclinations in domestic politics . . . his Fourteen Points sound almost as though Kant were guiding Wilson's writing hand" (Russett 1993, 4; see also Doyle 1997). Across a wide spectrum of liberal IR approaches, Wilson's fight to extend the institutions of national sovereignty and international law is viewed as a decisive step in the progressive realization of a normatively regulated global civil society (see, for example, Bull 1977; Mayall 1990; Tony Smith 1994; Kratochwil 1998; Reus-Smit 1999; Robert H. Jackson 2000; Clark 2007). His legacy in U.S. foreign policy is thus widely praised—a model for how America should conduct itself in world politics (Kegley 1993; Ruggie 1993; Tony Smith 1994; Ikenberry 2001; Mandelbaum 2002; Ikenberry et al. 2009).

More broadly, Wilsonianism is conceived as a paradigm shift: from the "old diplomacy" of European secret treaties, imperialism, and balance-of-power alliances to the "new diplomacy" of collective security, open covenants, self-determination, and the creation of a law-based international order predicated on a community of liberal democratic states. On this account, the fundamental problems of Versailles were not a result of its Wilsonianism but rather were a consequence of Wilson's inability to fully implement his liberal internationalist peace program. Further compounding these problems was Congress's subsequent rejection of the Versailles Treaty and thus U.S. membership in the League of Nations. Consequently, the United States failed to play a leading and stabilizing role in the international relations of the interwar years, retreating into geopolitical isolationism (Kindleberger 1981). Wilson's failure is then overwhelmingly seen as a *failure in political leadership:* a function of the inability of self-organizing political elites to implement a liberal internationalist agenda on an overwhelmingly conservative Republican Congress (Ikenberry and Kupchan 1990; Holsti 1991; Ruggie 1993; Ikenberry 2001; Art 2003; Legro 2005; Kupchan and Trubowitz 2007).

A fundamental problem with these liberal analyses of Wilsonian diplomacy, one shared by realist approaches, is their apparent willingness to uncritically accept the idea that Wilson was indeed a truly "progressive" liberal thinker whose primary goal was to "make the world safe for democracy." The key difference between realist and liberal assessments of Wilson(ianism) is that whereas realists critique Wilson for having pursued a progressive vision of international order, liberals applaud him. Yet the obvious question is "to what extent is this portrait an accurate one?" (Michael Cox 2000, 235). Or, more precisely, what *kind* of liberal was Wilson? While liberal interpretations are correct in linking Wilson's conception of domestic politics with international order, there is a persistent misunderstanding (or one-dimensional understanding) of this conception. Did Wilson's foreign policy thought *and* action conform to the canonical status of liberalism associated with him? If Wilson is indeed the quintessential liberal statesman IR conceives him as, what then is the significance of his diplomacy for liberal IR theory?

Once such questions are penetrated, the idealism/realism-power/utopianism edifice on which "textbook" IR narratives of Versailles diplomacy are built quickly crumbles. The reason for this is clear: working within these dichotomous understandings of Wilsonianism, its relation to Versailles, and the interwar years more generally, conventional IR studies exclude what is key to any inquiry into the determining role of foreign policy ideologies: their constitutive social relations. For precisely what is "Wilsonianism" and liberal internationalism *for* and *about*? What forms of social relations do they seek to extend, defend, and legitimatize? There is, in other words, a need to systematically rethink Wilsonianism through the social category of capitalism. As a comprehensive corpus of thought, liberalism only arises with and indeed presupposes capitalist social relations. This crucial context is either uncritically assumed or altogether excluded from these IR frameworks (Holsti 1991; Ruggie 1998a; Kegley and Raymond 1999; Tony Smith 1999; Ikenberry 2001). Yet only by linking the emergence of Wilsonianism as a foreign policy ideology with the development of capitalism as a tendentially global but internationally fragmented social system can one begin to explain its *social conditions of possibility* as well as decipher its social content. From this perspective, Wilsonianism can be interpreted as the flip side of realism, not its inherent negation.[8]

The liberal confrontation with "the international" as a dimension of human existence where the problem of difference reaches its apogee necessitates "realist" policies, exemplified by the historically pervasive use of force and power politics to extend and maintain capitalist social relations in competition with other capitalist states. From the "so-called primitive accumulation of capital" Marx traced in the emergence of capitalist property relations in late seventeenth century England to President Wilson's many interventions in the Global South to the contemporary U.S.-led wars in Afghanistan and Iraq, the use of state power and "brute force" remain "economic powers" integral to the world-historical development of capitalism (see Marx 1976, chap. 26).[9] The reproduction of the liberal state's sovereign assumptions—the differentiation of economic and political and the "internal" and "external"—depends on the systematic use or threat of *Gewalt* (force/violence) in both its domestic and international spheres. Similarly, liberal states employ *Gewalt* in the international sphere, maintaining international law and open trading regimes, as President Wilson's many military interventions to uphold the rule of law or sanctity of private property in the Global South demonstrate.

Obscuring the role of *Gewalt* in the extension and reproduction of capitalist relations, standard IR approaches inadequately grasp the social origins and purpose of Wilsonian diplomacy and the means through which it was pursued. If realism is deficient in appreciating the sociohistorical embeddedness of Wilsonian diplomacy within the U.S. foreign policy tradition, liberal interpretations unreflexively reproduce its presuppositions, thereby failing to explore the inherent limits and contradictions of its policies. Assuming the combination of American "exceptionalism" with unilinear and stagist conceptions of social development, liberal IR approaches—like Wilson—conceive the U.S. system as a universal phase of development through which all countries must pass. Liberal IR thereby replicates many of the contradictions of Wilsonian diplomacy, illustrating, in Andrew Hurrell's words (2007, 264), the "easy slippage between liberal internationalism and liberal empire." Is this "slippage" inherent in liberalism internationalism? While no definitive answer can be provided here, analysis into the social sources and character of Wilsonian ideology should shed some light on these definitive issues facing contemporary world politics.

AN ANATOMY OF WILSONIANISM: THE ORIGINS AND NATURE OF WILSONIAN DIPLOMACY

Given the centrality of these notions of "liberty," "democracy" and "self-determination" to IR conceptions of Wilson(ianism), the absence of any systematic analysis of Wilson's understanding and use of these concepts is surprising.[10] How, then, did Wilson understand these concepts, and for what purposes did he seek to employ them? More broadly, what were the core tenets of Wilsonianism? To answer these questions, it is essential to examine more seriously than IR has hitherto the historically determinant socioeconomic and political origins of Wilsonian diplomacy. Often overlooked in IR is the fact that the formation of Wilsonian diplomacy was a reaction to the revolutionary conditions produced by the uneven and combined character of U.S. and global capitalism. In this sociohistorical milieu, Wilsonianism was a strategy of "progressive" counterrevolution both at home and abroad. "If you want to oust Socialism you have got to propose something better," as Wilson put it in 1912.[11] This perspective would guide Wilson's later designs in creating a "liberal-capitalist internationalist" order (Levin 1968). In these ways, Wilson was perhaps the first U.S. statesman to offer a *holistic* conception of foreign policy, thoroughly integrating domestic and international dimensions. This foreign policy—what became known as "Wilsonianism"—had four key components or pillars: (1) American exceptionalism; (2) corporate liberalism; (3) Open Door "frontierism"; and (4) racial hierarchy.

American Exceptionalism

So what was the sociohistorical content of Wilsonianism? At its most fundamental level, Wilsonianism represents both the result and intended solution to the geosocial consequences of the uneven and combined development of U.S. and world capitalism. Contrary to his realist critics and (some) liberal proponents, the central guiding principle behind Wilson's thought and action was *not,* however, an attempt to transcend the anarchic effects of capitalism's uneven and combined development as much as to ameliorate its more explosive elements. For Wilson, this was to be achieved through the construction of a rule-governed liberal capitalist international order modeled on an idealized notion of the U.S. system itself. Such thinking was based on a unilinear, stagist model of social development rooted in 19th-century Enlightenment thinking fused with the unique historical experience of U.S. development—which, in Hegelian prose, was viewed as the end goal of history.[12] This ideology of American "liberal-developmentalism," as Emily S. Rosenberg (1982) terms it, was characterized by a firm conviction in the superiority of the U.S. social system and a faith in the ability of other nations to repeat the American developmental experience.

Lacking the feudal-aristocratic baggage of its European ancestry, such thinking assumed U.S. development as "exceptional" in its purely liberal-democratic constitution. The United States thereby escaped the exclusively European phenomenon of imperialism and militarism. This idea of an "American exceptionalism," coined by Louis Hartz, represented a kind of "inverted Trotskyite law of combined development" whereby America skipped "the feudal stage of history as Russia presumably skipped the liberal stage" (Hartz 1955, 3, 236–37). The notion of a pristine culture of liberal capitalism shorn of any feudal elements is fundamental to "myths of American identity," forming the basis of a "culturally constructed consensus" enabling militarist imperial policies, and reinforcing domestic hierarchies (Hixson 2008, 8; see also Rupert 2010). This interpretation of U.S. development is historically suspect (see Byres 1996). Yet despite—or perhaps because of—the mythical nature of American exceptionalism, its role in the perpetuation of a certain liberal "cultural hegemony" is undeniable, in part helping to explain the general continuity of U.S. foreign policies during the 20th century. Moreover, the uniqueness of U.S. capitalism as *comparatively* ideal in its constitution was more the result of the *intersocietal context* in which it developed—specifically, through the safety valve of frontier expansionism (near and abroad) and the transformational affects it had on the U.S. body politic (see discussion later in this chapter, under "Open Door Frontierism and Racial Hierarchy").

Presupposing American exceptionalism, Wilson viewed U.S. institutions and values as politically and morally superior to all others. "America" represented a higher stage of historical development. Given the opportunity, the rest of the world would naturally adopt the U.S. developmental model. It was possible, then, for Wilson to fuse, with perfect internal consistency, U.S. "national interests" with universal ones—he saw the two as naturally identical.[13] "American principles, American policies," Wilson claimed, "are the principles and policies of forward looking men and women everywhere, of every modern nation, of every enlightened community. They are the principles of mankind and must prevail" (quoted in Hoff 2008, 13). U.S. commercial expansion was thus conceived as acting in the service of human progress. "Lift your eyes to the horizons of business," Wilson told a "Salesmanship Congress" in July 1916,

> let your thoughts and your imaginations run abroad throughout the world, and with the inspiration of the thought that you are Americans and are meant to carry liberty and justice and the principles of humanity wherever you go, go out and sell goods that will make the world more comfortable, more happy, and convert them to the principles of America. (quoted in Levin 1968, 18)[14]

As the natural vanguard of modernity marching toward progress, the uses of U.S. power were by definition virtuous if not divinely sanctioned. As a Christian nation, Wilson averred, America "exemplif[ied] that devotion to the ele-

ments of righteousness . . . derived from the revelations of the Holy Scrip-
ture" (quoted in Ambrosius 1987, 12). America's historical exceptionalism
thus combined with a moral uniqueness derivative of the nation's perceived
flawless Christian-Puritan foundation.

From this perspective, Wilson never considered U.S. interventionism
abroad as imperialist or recognized the pursuit of a liberal internationalist
capitalist order as involving U.S. domination. Both were perceived as alternatives to European-style imperialism and radicalism, which circumvented
individual self-determination (Levin 1968, 9–10, 25–26; Ambrosius 1990).
For Wilson, there was simply no conflict of interest between "the needs of a
bourgeoning American political-economy to expand commercially and
morally throughout the world" and the creation of a U.S.-dominated liberal
internationalist capitalist order. The two were complementary as "a world of
open economic access, growing American economic might, and international cooperation led by the United States would ultimately bring prosperity and development, peace and liberal democracy to most people" (Levin
1968, 5; Emily S. Rosenberg 1982, 63).

Corporate Liberalism

For Wilson, the defense of U.S. social order and stability against projects of
"radical" change at home and abroad was to be achieved through *limited* and
necessarily *gradual* social reforms designed and implemented by a white,
"enlightened" technocratic elite. Gradual reform was a means of buttressing
rather than transforming the domestic status quo and social hierarchies. According to Walter Lippmann, Wilson often used one particular metaphor to
illustrate his understanding of how progressive ideas were really conservative: "If you want to preserve a fence post, you have to keep painting it white.
You can't just paint it once and leave it forever. It will rot away" (quoted in
LaFeber 1994, 278). In other words, liberal capitalism required continual re-
making.

In view of the unprecedented years of social divisiveness within the
United States at the turn of the century,[15] a central focus of Wilson's writings
and public addresses was the necessity of re-creating social order and transcending factionalism. This was to be achieved through the revitalization of
America's political institutions and crucially economic expansionism. To
these ends, Wilson sought strengthened executive leadership capable of re-
solving antagonistic sectional interests and subsuming class conflict through

the forging of a robust common national consciousness (Sidney Bell 1972, 17–21; see also Thorsen 1988). Wilson did not so much reject the idea of a balance of power as radically expanded its framework to embrace both internal and external dimensions. From Wilson's liberal conception of states and societies as discrete but interacting entities, the aim of enlightened governments was to reconcile competing class interests in domestic and international affairs.

Wilson articulated an understanding of democracy thus explicitly formulated to address the perceived failings of the U.S. democratic order, which he viewed as a "mixed blessing and of limited validity" (Sidney Bell 1972, 14; see also Gardner 1984, 25–44; Sklar 1988). The ideal of U.S. government was conceived in terms of a technocratic vanguard guiding and shaping public opinion. The role of government, Wilson wrote, was to *"instruct the understandings* of the people" (Thorsen 1988, 61; Diamond 1943, 48–50).

Connected to this was Wilson's reconceptualization of the notion of progress vanquishing the term's historically "radical" or progressive meanings. As Niels Thorsen notes (1988, 159) "Throughout the eighteenth and nineteenth centuries, the term *progress* was the catchword for the struggle against an inherited feudal order, the hierarchies of church and monarchy, and the suppression of popular majorities. Wilson's hope was to make progress a term for the modern dependence upon leadership." Political liberty and individual freedom were associated not with democratic political institutions but with the reconciliation of the particular with the universal interest: the forging of a "common political consciousness" (nationalism) and purpose through the imperial presidency. As liberty existed "only where there is best order," the truest freedom was realizable through "obedience" to the laws of the state (Wilson 1925, 9:103; 8:335, 337–38, 340). Further, democratic orders were "not so much . . . a form of government as a set of principles" attained by communities through a necessarily *gradual, linear* organic developmental process. Specifically, U.S. democracy was "not a body of doctrine: but a *stage of development*" based on the nation's superior Anglo-Saxon pedigree. Its "process was experience," emerging from the "long discipline which g[ave] a people self-possession, self-mastery, the habit of order and peace . . . the steadiness and self-control of political maturity" (Wilson 1966–94, 6:229; Wilson 1908, 103–4).[16] The superiority of this Anglo-Saxon model was its fundamentally elitist nature, posited on the rule of the chosen few of "character." Had the men "who colonized America" not "sprung of a race habituated to submit to law and authority," Wilson wrote (1908, 103), they could have never "taken charge of their own affairs and combined stability with liberty in the process of absolute self-government."

Wilson's understanding of national self-determination was thus always a partial if not contradictory one. Only after the less developed nations underwent a long process of Western-led instruction did Wilson conceive of self-determination as a possibility for them. This was well demonstrated in Wilson's proclamations regarding the status of the Philippines after the Spanish-American War. Although the United States had "shown the world enlightened processes of politics that were without precedent," Wilson wrote, America could not simply "give" the Filipinos self-government. For, as he went on, "Self-government is not a thing that can be 'given' to any people, it is a form of character . . . Only a long apprenticeship of obedience can secure them the precious possession" (Wilson 1966–94, 18:104). The "consent of the governed," Wilson wrote elsewhere, was not the same for the "politically undeveloped races" as for the Anglo-Saxons. The latter needed to teach the former the ways of democracy before they could govern themselves (quoted in Hannigan 2002, 11; see also Pomerance 1976; Hunt 1987).

In Wilson's thinking, one finds the incomplete adaptation of classical liberalism to the changing conditions of an emergent industrial-corporate capitalist society. As economic relations were *fundamental* to all spheres of social life, Wilson believed,[17] such transformations necessitated a reconfiguration of liberal principles. Though never entirely abandoning his attachment to laissez-faire economics, Wilson sought to amend its principles to new historical conditions, to harness the American "way of life" to the exigencies of modern industrial capitalism. He believed that community and executive leadership could set the parameters of economic competition without eliminating it altogether. Wilson's "New Freedom" called for government to function as the ultimate guarantor of "fair competition," free enterprise, and the "opportunity for self-development" in the service of national community and efficiency (Diamond 1943, 92, 87–88; Wilson 1966–94, 2:25, 29).

From this perspective, Wilson emphasized the crucial differences between a "good capitalism" and "bad capitalist" (see Sklar 1988). This differentiation between systemic soundness and individual corruption was fundamental to his views of the origins of WWI and later support for a moderately punitive settlement at Versailles. The tensions between Wilson's lifelong commitment to classical liberal doctrines and his emphasis on the impor-

tance of national community and cooperation would have severe consequences, particularly in Wilson's foreign policies. In these ways, Wilson's
thinking organically connected to a distinct if internally diverse corporate-
liberal "hegemonic project" formed primarily of businesspeople from large-
scale financial institutions and capital-intensive, internationally oriented
industrial corporations. These social forces ideologically converged with the
emergent strata of political allies among state bureaucrats, academics, and
corporate lawyers who sought to challenge the traditional dominance of
conservative laissez-faire capitalism (Noble 1985).

Open Door Frontierism and Racial Hierarchy

Wilson's conception of the role of the U.S. economy and power in the world
was intimately connected to the sociomaterial conditions facing U.S. capitalism at the time. Already by the turn of the 20th century, U.S. political and
business leaders had concluded that the marketing of America's increasing
manufacturing surpluses was necessary both to maintain economic growth
and domestic prosperity and to circumvent radical sociopolitical and economic reforms at home. In other words, to avoid any substantive redistribution of the *relative* shares of national income, there had to be an *absolute* increase in its volume. This was only possible if U.S. state managers and
capitalists developed outlets for U.S. goods and services commonly viewed as
having developed in surplus of what could be *profitably* employed domestically (see LaFeber 1993).

An early advocate of Frederick Jackson Turner's "Frontier Thesis," Wilson
viewed America's natural political-economic development as a function of
its continual westward expansion. The "meeting point between savagery
and civilization," as Turner famously called it (1966, 3), the Western frontier
had been integral to America's unique reconciliation of liberty and democracy into a project of imperialist expansion. The frontier's closing in the last
quarter of the 19th century necessitated U.S. overseas economic expansionism to provide markets for the nation's surplus goods, investment, and ener-
gies. "For nearly three hundred years," the American people's "growth had
followed a single law—the law of expansion into new territory." As Wilson
continually reiterated, "Our domestic market no longer suffices. We need
foreign markets" (Wilson 1966–94, 12:11, 25:16).

For Wilson, the Philippines and other "backward" countries provided the U.S. with a new frontier. The Spanish-American War was thus perceived as a means to forge a sense of national solidarity within the United States.[18] In "Democracy and Education" (1907), Wilson wrote,

> Since trade ignores national boundaries and the manufacturer insists on having the world as a market, the flag of his nation must follow him, and the doors of the nations which are closed against him must be battered down. Concessions obtained by financiers must be safeguarded by ministers of state, even if the sovereignty of unwilling nations be outraged in the process. Colonies must be obtained or planted, in order that no useful corner of the world may be overlooked or left unused. Peace itself becomes a matter of conference and international combinations. Cooperation is the law of all action in the modern world. (Wilson 1966-94, 17:135)

There are few more revealing passages illustrating the ambiguities and contradictions of Wilson's conception of economic expansionism and its relation to state power and international cooperation. After noting the dialectic of (transnational) capitals and (nationally embedded) states resulting in the employment of state power in the service of the former, Wilson concludes with an injunction for the necessity of international cooperation. Colonialism and interimperialist rivalry thus ultimately demanded ultraimperialist responses.

Avoiding the shame and inefficiencies of formal territorial control inconsistent with narratives of "American exceptionalism," an explicitly colonial strategy of U.S. expansionism was relatively short-lived. Instead, U.S. policymakers, supported by leading factions of capitalists, soon adopted "nonterritorial" forms of expansionism modeled after Secretary of State John Hay's famous "Open Door Notes" (1899-1900). Originally formulated for the Chinese market but subsequently globalized by Wilson, the Open Door stipulated an equality of opportunity for the commerce of all nations. For Wilson and others, the Open Door was viewed as key means of both promoting U.S. interests and creating a world "community of interests," which were viewed as mutually complementary. Given the vast economies of scale and the technological efficiency of the U.S. economy, Wilson was confident that the extension of the Open Door abroad would disproportionally benefit U.S. capital, as "the skill of American workmen would dominate the markets of all the globe" (Wilson quoted in David M. Kennedy 1980, 299).

In its *pretenses* to nonterritoriality, the Open Door concept is unique if somewhat misleading. Indeed, its distinctiveness as a spatial concept of accumulation is that it *ideally* presupposes a formally sovereign *international* system through which a *transnational* process of capital accumulation is facilitated. In this way, the Open Door reflected in ideal-utopian form the structural logic of capitalism's differentiating and equalizing tendencies. The reconstitution and transformation of state sovereignty under capitalist conditions in no way impinged on its political territoriality or de facto sovereignty in the juridical sense (see Justin Rosenberg 1994, 2005). Instead, as the Open Door strategy demonstrates, it could actually promote it. Under capitalism, anarchy and hierarchy are mutually conditioning: one need not beget the other. The international is thus constituted by a nexus of antagonistic relations of competition *and* domination.

In ideological and economic ways, the Open Door was preferable to other accumulation strategies that suffered from the material inefficiencies and ideological discomfitures of formal empire.[19] "The brilliance of liberal U.S. internationalists in this period, with Woodrow Wilson as their flagbearer," Neil Smith writes, "lay in the implicit realization that the wedding of geography and economics undergirding European capital accumulation was not inevitable . . . and that economic expansion divorced from territorial aggrandizement dovetailed superbly with U.S. national interests." In these ways, Smith goes on, "U.S. internationalism pioneered a historic unhinging of economic expansion from direct political and military control over the new markets" (Neil Smith 2003, 141–42).[20] Given the massive economies of scale, enormous domestic market, and advanced mass-production techniques characterizing the U.S. political economy by the turn of the 20th century, state managers and corporate capitalists viewed the global equalization of trade and investment conditions as necessarily favorable to U.S.-based capital.

This peculiarly *trans*spatial yet territorializing character of America's "imperialism of anti-imperialism" (Williams 1972) must be further qualified by another important fact: the Open Door strategy *presupposed* a crucial moment of *Gewalt* analogous to the origins of capitalism itself. The forcible and often violent expropriation of land from the Native Americans and Mexicans on the North American continent, the colonial wars and formal occupations in the Philippines (1898–1913) and Cuba (1898–1902, 1906–9), and annexations of Hawaii and Puerto Rico all crucially *preceded* the consolidation of a consistent Open Door strategy. As Gareth Stedman Jones remarks, "The whole *internal* history of United States imperialism was one vast process of territorial seizure and occupation. The absence of territorialism 'abroad' was founded on an unprecedented territorialism 'at home'" (1972, 216–17).

Indeed, a fundamental difference setting U.S. imperialism apart from its European counterparts was *not* primarily its lack of precapitalist origin but rather U.S. capitalism's unique ability to expand through a process of "internal colonization." The dispossession of the Native Americans and later Mexicans from the North American continent constituted a single, drawn-out process of (so-called) primitive accumulation (Byres 1996, chap. 5). The scale of unevenness between the colonial settlers and native population was thus crucial in the subsequent development of U.S. capitalism, as was their violent interaction in the cementing of a "white American" identity.

After the closing of the Western Frontier and Long Depression, the often-reinforcing dynamic of racialized imperialism[21] and class conflict became even more marked. Adapted to the changed sociohistorical conditions of industrial capitalism from the Civil War onward, the frontier "myth" justified U.S. expansionism abroad into "backward," "racially inferior" regions, while rationalizing class and racial hierarchies and oppression at home against threats from below, whether from the "white savages" of urban (often immigrant) laborers and farmers, half-freed "African savages," or the Amerindians themselves (Slotkin 1998, 16–21; see also Hunt 1987; Hannigan 2002; Hixson 2008). As Wilson put it in 1900 during the Spanish-American War,

> The East is to be opened and transformed . . . standards of the West are to be imposed upon it; nations and peoples which have stood still the centuries through are to be quickened, and made part of the universal world of commerce and of ideas . . . It is our peculiar duty, as it is also England's, to moderate the process in the interests of liberty: to . . . teach them order and self-control in the midst of change . . . the drill and habit of law and obedience which we long ago got out of the strenuous processes of English history. (Wilson 1966–94, 12:18)

Teleological conceptions of history, American exceptionalism, commercial expansionism, and Anglo-Saxon chauvinism all neatly intertwined here in Wilson's rendition of the "white man's burden" at the heart of his liberal internationalism.

Indeed, as president, Wilson reconstructed racial hierarchy within "America's global mission" on firmly liberal-internationalist foundations. It is no secret that Wilson and many within his administration were ardent Anglophiles and outright racists. "Racial hierarchy" and "paternalism" were among the most important features of the administration and Wilson's ideology, with Wilson himself a "genteel white supremacist" (Coogan 1994, 74–75; Steigerwald 1999, 91; Ambrosius 2007, 698; Offner 1986 [1975], 5). The Anglo-Saxon powers were conceived as the top of a pyramid-like global racial hierarchy naturally bestowed with the task of managing the turbulent waters of international politics. Such thinking would guide Wilson in his League of Nations plans and in particular in the colonial mandate system.

The initial moment of *Gewalt* entailed in America's frontier expansionism also prefigured subsequent trajectories of U.S. foreign policymaking. The disintegration of social structures in the Global South, corollary to American attempts to impose market forces and capitalist relations, came to "require" later waves of U.S. interventionism against the "nationalist revolutionary" social forces it engendered, thus perpetuating a vicious cycle of revolution and counterrevolution. In these many ways, U.S. Open Door expansionism formed peculiar combinations of nonterritorial and territorial means of control serviced through an uneasy but potent mix of unilateral and multilateral tactics geared toward the construction of a "liberal-capitalist international order." Thus, far from moderating the uneven and combined character of social developments in the Global South, an unintended consequence of the Open Door was to exacerbate these very tendencies: implanting market forces and capitalist relations onto such societies in inorganic ways, their development took convulsive and destabilizing forms unhinging traditional social structures. In these ways, U.S. foreign policymakers were often the unknowing "agents" of combined development.

Assuming the Open Door concept, Wilson viewed U.S. economic security as fundamentally tied to the reorganization of the international political economy along more cooperative and formally democratic lines. While the Open Door formed an essential continuity in U.S. strategic thinking beginning with Secretary Hay's notes, Wilson's innovation was to globalize the concept and integrate it into a holistic liberal internationalist strategy. Wilsonianism was, then, much less a radical departure from established U.S. strategic thinking than the hyperbolic concatenation of tendencies within that tradition. Wilson transformed the "American way of life" into a universal public good to be brought to all peoples of the world, and he harnessed considerable U.S. economic and military might to that end, as is illustrated by the administration's record in enforcing the Monroe Doctrine in Central and South America, where Wilson would set out, as he put it, "to teach the South American Republics to elect good men" (quoted in Knock 1992, 27).[22]

The promotion of the globalized Open Door was seen as a means to depoliticize international economic conflicts and secure the adequate socio-economic and political institutions to contain social pressures accompanying less-developed industrializing countries. "Wilsonianism" was, then, the direct predecessor to U.S. foreign policy thinking of the Cold War era. This was a unique synthesis of Realpolitik and modernization theory that sought to employ U.S. power to create a system of "coordinated economic interdependence, based in part on the replication of aspects of the American model of capitalism in the rest of the capitalist world, from which many states could derive positive benefit" (Bromley 2008, 9).[23]

Wilsonian diplomacy followed an "expansionist-interventionist security logic" posited on the imperative to intervene in transforming the internal conditions of societies abroad for both socioeconomic and "security" reasons.[24] This focused on the necessity to facilitate the ceaseless accumulation of capital perceived as integral to U.S. social order and democracy. The *security motive*, in turn, sought to manage the anarchic consequences of international development as expressed in the "revolutionary" nationalist movements in the developing world. The "tragedy of American diplomacy," as Williams (1972) called it, lay in how these two aims of U.S. policymaking continually contradicted each other. America's expansionist-interventionist security logic resulted in the destabilization of international order, registered in the waves of revolutionary nationalist movements following U.S. interventions. These resulted in further U.S. interventionist measures to maintain social order and the rule of law necessary for the continuing existence of capitalist social relations. Cumulatively, these policies continually exacerbated international disorder and the centrifugal tendencies of political and economic power within U.S. society, which, in their limited ways, the policies had been designed to ameliorate (see LaFeber 1993).

THE MAKING OF A SOCIAL PEACE? WILSONIAN
AND INTER-ALLIED DIPLOMACY AT VERSAILLES

Peace Diplomacy as Prelude to Crisis in IR Theory

Most standard IR analyses of the Thirty Years' Crisis emphasize the fundamental flaws and illegitimacy of the Versailles settlement as a central conjunctural factor contributing to the geopolitical instabilities of the interwar years (Carr 1939; Kennan 1951; Morgenthau 1951; Hinsley 1963; Gilpin 1988;

Schweller 1993; Clark 1997). While accounts vary as to why such an unfavorable outcome resulted from the postwar settlement, the few IR studies[25] examining the Paris Peace negotiations largely attribute its flaws to the sharp divergence of interests among the Big Three (United States, United Kingdom, and France) and the failure in elite political leadership, particularly on the part of President Wilson. In the textbook rendition, French and British positions largely prevailed through a series of uneasy compromises whereby a diplomatically outmaneuvered and domestically embattled President Wilson acquiesced on a number of his core principles. The result was a Carthaginian peace dressed in Wilsonian garment, scarcely veiling the European victors' imperial gains. This dictated peace sustained the illegitimate status quo international order, nurturing an intense dissatisfaction among three of the four strongest Continental states (Germany, Russia, and Italy) and thus sowing the seeds for the next major war.

In the conventional IR literature, the politics of the peace settlement are overwhelmingly conceived in socially "thin" terms, reducible to military-strategic calculations and/or abstract-ideological presuppositions. This is most dramatically exemplified in IR treatments (or nontreatments) of the Bolshevik Revolution's impact on the course and outcome of the Paris Peace Conference. The very real threat of communist revolutions "spreading" westward from Russia to the vanquished nations during the peace negotiations scarcely figure into dominant IR narratives.[26] Missing, too, are the severity of labor conflicts and social struggles within the victor countries themselves, as evidenced by the mass of strikes and violent demonstrations in Britain, France, and the United States immediately after the war. In the absence of any examination of these social processes, IR accounts of Versailles tend to conceptualize state agency as if it were entirely autonomous from social forces. Foreign policymaking is viewed as determined by discretely conceived geopolitical determinations (the "balance of power") and/or domestic regime types. When social forces are given explanatory weight, they are filtered through the narrow prism of partisan politics: unreflexively reproducing Wilson's own truncated conception of politics (see, for example, Holsti 1991; Ikenberry 2001). Yet the class-based dynamics of revolution and counterrevolution cut across party politics and transcended national borders.[27]

Narrowly focusing on the strategic-military interactions *among* sovereign nation-states, both conventional historical narratives and IR theoretical perspectives largely exclude these dimensions of modern international

order formation arising from the historically pervasive crucible of war, imperialism, and revolution. By contrast, this section demonstrates how revolutions and *social* conflicts have been not only central factors in the creation of
the postwar international order but also defining features of its social content and purpose. As Wilson's press secretary at Versailles and official biographer, Ray Stannard Baker, put it (1922, 2:64),

> The effect of the Russian problem on the Paris Conference . . . was profound:
> Paris cannot be understood without Moscow. Without ever being represented
> at Paris at all, the Bolsheviki and Bolshevism were powerful elements at every
> turn. Russia played a more vital part at Paris than Prussia.

At Versailles, the Allied-associated powers spent more time on the Russian
question than any other issue. Of all the dilemmas facing Versailles policymakers, the *social* problems of revolution and disorder at home and abroad
were most decisive in the making of the peace. Policymakers were continually unable to "reach an understanding with the Bolshevik revolution or to
crush it." This largely explains why Versailles produced such a particularly
fragile and unstable postwar international order, particularly in its creation
of such an "uneasy stalemate of power in Eastern Europe" (Stevenson 1988,
237; John M. Thompson 1966, 8). The dual threat of Bolshevism abroad and
socialist revolution at home crucially intersected with the other chief dilemma facing the peacemakers: how to treat the defeated Central Powers
(above all, Germany) and reintegrate them into a stable and prosperous international capitalist system. But, why did the Bolshevik Revolution have such
consequential international effects? And where were these effects most felt?

Versailles Diplomacy: A Case Study in the Sociology of International Capitalism

While the Russian Revolutions of February and November 1917 were domestic affairs, their causes were decidedly international in scope. In studying
these causes of the Bolshevik Revolution, Trotsky coined the phrase "uneven
and combined development" to explain the origins and socialist nature of
revolution as fundamentally determined by the *international* constitution of
the capitalist system. For Trotsky, the sociological effects of the internationally mediated nature of capitalist expansionism held the key to why semipe-
ripheral revolutions would precede metropolitan ones, and, moreover, why
their fates were inextricably interconnected. *"Without a more or less rapid vic-*

tory of the proletariat in the advanced countries," he proclaimed, "the workers government in Russia will not survive" (quoted in Löwy 1981, 72).[28] The Bolshevik Revolution was thus international(ized) from its inception.

It might have taken much less than the mass destruction of WWI for the tottering Russian tsarist regime to collapse. Yet this is how it turned out. As military conflict dragged on to seemingly inexhaustible lengths, it "transform[ed] the whole of Europe into a powder magazine of social revolution" (Trotsky quoted in Mayer 1959, 32). Mass mobilization during the war strengthened organized labor and the radical Left within all belligerent countries, temporarily shifting the balance of social forces in their favor (Hardach 1977; Halperin 2004). These effects of war were, however, not uniform.

The earlier-developed capitalist states, such as England and France, endured the trial of war relatively well in comparison to their Russian ally. The tsarist regime collapsed in the March Revolution of 1917, which was soon followed by the Bolshevik Revolution. Stimulating further sociopolitical upheavals and counterreactions, both Russian Revolutions transformed the dynamics of the war effort while simultaneously changing the sociopolitical conditions within the advanced capitalist states themselves. The international reverberations of the November Revolution were particularly acute, as the ideological force of Bolshevism rallied radical leftist and socialist revolutionaries throughout Europe and the United States. The revolution's impact was most decisive in the vanquished states of Central Eastern Europe where military defeats were swiftly accompanied by liberal-democratic and in some cases subsequent Bolshevik-style revolutions.[29]

What explains these differential effects of Bolshevism across Europe? Some scholars have sought to explain the impact of Bolshevism in spreading these revolutions as a mere epiphenomenon of the Central Powers' military defeat. Yet such military reductionist explanations immediately run up against the simple but fundamental fact that states' military capabilities depend on their sociopolitical and economic development. Hence, a state's military capacities and performance—and thus their likely success in war—cannot be detached from their underlying social structures. One must look to these social structures for an explanation as to why the Central Powers were more susceptible to distinctly telescoped bourgeois cum socialist revolutions. The decisive impact of the November Revolution on the vanquished Central Eastern Europe states was a consequence not only of these countries' *geographical* proximity to revolutionary Russia but, more important, of their *structural* similarities resulting from the societies' analogous forms of "combined development" (Justin Rosenberg 1996, 11). This was indeed Trotsky's explanation of the time-space relations of socialist revolutions. The spatial and temporal patterning of revolutions was the result of the dynamic, interactive nature of social development, for which it was "possible to interpret dialectically the course of a country's development, including its revolutionary development, only by proceeding from the action, reaction and interaction of all the material and superstructural factors, national and world-wide alike" (1972a, 51–52). Beginning from these "reciprocal relations" of determinations, Trotsky thus viewed "the proletarian revolution[,] after starting in the most backward country of Europe," as "mounting upwards, rung by rung, toward countries more highly developed economically" (51–52).

The chief sites of revolutionary upheaval between 1917 and 1920 indeed ran in approximately *reverse geographical and temporal order* from the origins of industrial capitalist development. This corresponded to the configurations of unevenness constituted by the spatiotemporal sequencing of capitalist transformations and industrialization processes taking place in Europe over the Long 19th Century—through the intersection of the West-East and North-South vectors. The growing significance of "ethnic nationalism" within Europe in the four decades preceding 1914 proved crucial in the steady destabilization of the old multinational empires of Austro-Hungary, tsarist Russia, and the Ottomans. For the expansion of capitalist social relations throughout Europe entailed not only the *quantitative multiplication* of differentially developing capitalist states but also the *qualitative reconstitution* of their antecedent social conditions of unevenness. These became part of the "causal mechanism" of their "'combined development,' both within the non-capitalist societies affected, and as a feature of the expanding international system as a whole" (Justin Rosenberg 2005, n. 28). This combined development conditioned and fed back into the existing texture of unevenness (the international), reconfiguring it in the process, as witnessed by the effects of Bolshevik Revolutions in the making of the postwar international order.

Strategies of Counterrevolution: "The Geopolitical Management of Combined Development"

After the war, Allied policymakers faced a number of seemingly intractable dilemmas. Despite the outcome on the battlefield, fears of German imperial ambitions and the renewal of fierce economic competition in Europe remained. The territorial and economic threat of German power loomed particularly large for the French, who had arguably suffered the most in terms of the material, financial, and human devastation wrought by the war. At the same time, Allied policymakers were concerned about America's newfound industrial and financial supremacy, which had dramatically reversed the traditional debtor-creditor relationship. Yet of all the dilemmas facing the Paris peacemakers, the rise of an increasingly radicalized and organized left-wing movement was the most immediately pressing and decisive factor in the forging of the postwar international order. If WWI had "transformed the whole of Europe into a powder magazine of social revolution," then the primary challenge facing the peacemakers was how to extinguish it. Bolshevism represented what Lord Milner described as "the greatest danger of the civilized world" (quoted in Mayer 1967, 310), an opinion shared by the vast majority of high-ranking Allied statesmen. According to Herbert Hoover, Bolshevism "was a spectre which wandered into the Peace Conference almost daily" (1958, 115–16), threatening "to overwhelm and swallow up the world of revolutionary chaos" (R. S. Baker quoted in Mayer 1967, 10).

During the peace proceedings, policymakers were plagued by a barrage of labor strikes, protests, soldier mutinies, and localized uprisings as well as by communist revolutions in Germany and Hungary (Mayer 1967, 326–28, 609–11; Middlemas 1979, 118–20). The threats of international Bolshevism and domestic socialism thus resolutely impacted the peace negotiations at Versailles and after, as demonstrated by decisions made regarding the German and Austro-Hungarian territorial settlements, Polish border disputes, reparations, territorial arrangements in the Baltic, the formation of the International Labor Organization and League of Nations, and the handling of the Eastern Question, among other matters.

From the outset, debate among the Big Three over intervention in Russia was thus shaped by extramilitary questions. Despite their anti-Bolshevik consensus, the Allies nevertheless disagreed regarding the precise means of containing the revolution and the form and scope their interventions would take. Generally speaking, traditional conservatives preferred direct military intervention, while the liberal Wilsonians favored more limited, indirect efforts employing combinations of financial-economic aid and covert action (see Mayer 1967; Gardner 1984).[30] With some exceptions, their positions remained relatively fluid, adjusting to the changing configuration of domestic and international forces.

The interlocking of the domestic and international dimensions of the "Bolshevik problem" was extremely contradictory. The threat of international communism challenged Wilsonian liberals and reformist socialists in both the United States and Europe, effectively radicalizing their political rhetoric for a moderate peace settlement. At the same time, policymakers sought to ameliorate threats to the existing domestic order emanating from leftist labor and socialist movements—themselves radicalized and encouraged by the Bolshevik Revolution—by initiating piecemeal social reforms financed through reparations and indemnities from Germany. The result was a consistent back-and-forth from a relatively moderate to harshly punitive peace with Germany, most dramatically exemplified in the persistently wavering "pragmatism" of Premier Lloyd George (see esp. Bunselmeyer 1975; Kent 1991; Douglas J. Newton 1997). The fused linkages of these domestic and international dynamics in their interconnected temporal and spatial dynamics, filtering through the arena of each Allied-associated power's domestic politics, proved crucial for Versailles decision making.

For the Wilsonians, the best strategy of countering social revolution was to contain and channel it into Burkean modes of gradualist change buttressed by an open and expanding international commercial society. Indeed, in Wilson's view, the primary challenge of U.S. foreign policy since the turn of century had been expanding U.S. capitalism and market relations globally while managing their most geopolitically and socially explosive effects. During and after the war, Wilson's foreign policy thus sought to hold together the world economy under the dual strains of imperial rivalries among the advanced industrial states and the attendant uneven but hastened capitalist transformations thrusting House's "waste places of the earth"[31] in the direction of (often socialist) revolutionary nationalism. The chief social substance of Wilsonian policy was, then, not *only* the reordering of geopolitical anarchy under the auspices of rule-based international institutions or the promotion of de facto constitutional democracies—Wilson's "consent of the governed" (quoted in Manela 2007, 35). It was, rather, the attempted "geopolitical management of combined development" (Justin Rosenberg 1996, 12),[32] necessitating the reform of traditional atavistic forms of imperialism into a Kautskian ultraimperialist order of international capitalist cooperation among the great powers.

With these aims in mind, Wilson's primary objective at the peace conference was to ensure the establishment of the League of Nations as well as the inclusion of his cherished covenant into the treaty's structure. All other U.S. peace aims were subordinate to these overriding objectives, as Wilson viewed U.S. long-term economic and strategic interests as ultimately facilitated by the League framework. Wilson conceived of the League as a way of institutionalizing peaceful and orderly social and territorial change: an "American-inspired international social contract, guaranteeing a world liberal order made safe from traditional imperialism and revolutionary-socialism" (Levin 1968, 9–10).

In particular, Wilson envisaged the colonial mandate system established by the League as a means of ameliorating interimperial rivalries over investment outlets and raw materials in the Global South. Under the mandate system, colonies were divided into different classes (A, B, and C) based on their level of development. As understood by Wilson, the Allies would be obligated to administer their areas immediately within the framework of the Open Door (as for Class B mandates) or soon restructure them along these lines. Either way, the eventual result would be to open floodgates of investment and trade from the United States and other advanced capitalist states to the formerly closed colonial regions (Parrini 1976; Safford 1978, 201–2).

From Wilson's perspective, the mandate system would thus function to harmonize frictions over sovereignty and equalize development between advanced and developing societies. Providing for the "indigenous political self-development under the disinterested tutelage of the advanced countries," the mandate system, in paternalistic Wilsonian fashion, sought to channel revolutionary aspirations into gradualist processes of American-inspired orderly change (Levin 1968, 245–46; Parrini 1976, 431). As Article 22 of the covenant read, the "tutelage" of those peoples "not yet able to stand by themselves under the strenuous conditions of the modern world . . . should be entrusted to advanced nations who by reason of their resources, experience or their geographical position can best undertake their responsibility."[33]

Self-Determination, Order, and Intervention

The eventual reintegration of a reformed German republic into the community of liberal capitalist states created by the League was essential for the Wilsonians. Pacifying and rebuilding a strong German economy was integral not only to the revitalization of the world economy but also to prevent the further spread of Bolshevism (Leffler 1979, 4; Costigliola 1984, 26). At the same time, Wilson believed that the militaristic imperialism of Germany ("bad capitalist") required punishment, a conviction paradoxically reinforced by the Bolshevik rise to power. Challenging the totality of the capitalist imperialist system, the Bolsheviks made it all the more imperative for Wilson to condemn Germany action's alone as pathological rather than symptomatic of capitalism writ large. In this regard, Wilson favored a punitive (or therapeutic) peace requiring some "probationary period" before Germany could enter the League of Nations. The perceived necessity of punishing German militarism was reinforced by the harsh settlement imposed on the Bolsheviks at Brest-Litovsk. Wilson's "just peace" is thus not to be confused with a "soft peace" (Levin 1968, 123–25; Gardner 1984, 161; Offner 1986 [1975], 23–24; Steiner 2005, 19).

The steady consolidation of Bolshevism as an ideological threat to Wilsonianism also simultaneously challenged U.S. policymakers to evoke calls for a more moderate and progressive peace settlement than they ever actually considered implementing. Here, the question of Wilson's use of the "self-determination" slogan becomes paramount, as the employed forms of the concept increasingly contradicted its intended content. On 9 April 1917, under pressure from the Bolshevik-dominated Petrograd Soviet, the Russian provisional government became the "first among the belligerent governments to call officially for a peace settlement 'on the basis of self-determination of peoples.'" In contrast to "textbook" IR accounts, it was, then, the Bolsheviks, not Wilson, who introduced the concept into the international discourse of the period (Manela 2006, 1331; see also Mayer 1959, 71–75).

After assuming power, the Bolsheviks continued these demands for the right to *national* self-determination and the breaking-up of colonial empires as the cornerstones for any peace settlement (see Lenin 1969). Their message found strong support among Europe's anti-imperialist Left, provoking widespread fears within the Allied camp that popular support for the war would be comprised. In averting such an outcome, official Allied pronouncements of war aims took a decisive leftward turn (see Mayer 1959). Here lay the origins of Wilson's 8 January 1918 Fourteen Points speech, which was "primarily designed to counter the Soviet ideological assault on the bastions of civilization" while also seeking to divert the Bolsheviks from making a separate peace with the Germans (Gardner 1984, 163; Schwabe 1985, 12).

Wilson never used the term "self-determination" in the address. At this point, he opposed doing so because he still sought to maintain the territorial integrity of the Austro-Hungarian Empire (Ádám 2004, 12–13). A month later, the president shifted his position further to the left, explicitly employing the principle in his call for a "just peace." A central rationale for Wilson's change of heart were reports from advisers suggesting the Fourteen Points speech's profound impact on the leftist parties of the Central Powers. If the president adopted the political slogan they favored, his advisers suggested, then the drift to the left could be accelerated, paving the way for the overthrow of the monarchy and thus peace negotiations. Despite Wilson's reservations about the socialist parties of Europe, the President nonetheless saw the *tactical* value of his advisers' suggestions (Schwabe 1985, 18).

When Bolshevism threatened to overwhelm Europe in late October 1918, however, Wilson favored maintaining the kaiser in power to "keep [the Bolsheviks] down—to keep some order," as Wilson told his interior secretary. This position was echoed by the fiercely anti-Bolshevik secretary of state, Lansing, who continually asserted that of the "two great evils at work in the world today" (German absolutism and Bolshevism), the latter was to be more feared because it was destructive of law, order, and private property. Bolshevism was, as Wilson put it, "the negation of everything that is American," a decisive threat to the essence of "modern civilization," which he defined in terms of "democracy, capitalism, and Christianity" (quotes in Levin 1968, 133–34; Ambrosius 1990, 343; Foglesong 1995, 44–45; see also Gardner 1984, 197–202; Schwabe 1985, 67–71; Donald E. Davis and Trani 2002, 151–54).

After December 1917, Lansing's rampant anti-Bolshevism formed the basis of the U.S. administration's policy. For all its ambiguities, the administration's handling of the Russian question set the precedent for future U.S. Cold War policies. While Wilson originally sought to recover the "true" Russia of the liberal internationalist sorts of the short-lived March Revolution, Lansing and the State Department began their search for a "strong man" to reassert domestic order by military dictatorship if necessary. In contrast to the genuine "democratic" aspirations of the Russian people, the Bolsheviks were perceived as the willing or unconscious agents of German imperialism. Such conceptions of a foreign-influenced radicalism found clear resonance with contemporary U.S. domestic discourses that almost universally viewed foreign-born radicalism and recent immigrants as conspirators in their own labor unrest (Levin 1968, 197; Gardner 1984, 144–45, 156, 260; Foglesong 1995, 85–88; Donald E. Davis and Trani 2002, 100, 202). Despite the seeming fluidity of Wilson's positions during the war and Versailles, a striking continuity can be discerned: whenever the forces of radicalism and revolution threatened stability, Wilson chose to maintain social order over change.

The self-determination concept initially formulated in socialist discourses as a means of challenging the capitalist-imperialist system was thus appropriated and transformed by Wilson and other Allied policymakers as a means to preserve this system. By adopting self-determination as the basis of his own peace program, however, Wilson ran the risk of promoting social changes he in no way sought and in fact hoped to prevent. "If Lenin saw self-determination as a revolutionary principle and sought to use it as a wrecking ball against the reactionary multi-ethnic empires of Europe," Erez Manela notes (2006, 1333), "Wilson hoped that self-determination would serve precisely in the opposite role: as a bulwark against radical, revolutionary challenges to existing orders."

Secretary Lansing was keenly aware of the potential perils of Wilson's tactical utilization of a political slogan intended for opposite ends. In a confidential memorandum written on 30 December 1918, Lansing expressed his increasing convictions regarding the "dangers of putting such ideas into the minds of certain races. It is bound to be the basis of impossible demands on the Peace Congress, and create trouble in many lands . . . The phrase is simply loaded with dynamite" (Lansing 1971, 80).

As with Wilson's earlier interventionist crusades for "democracy" in Mexico, Nicaragua, Santo Domingo, and elsewhere, considerable dissonance between the rhetoric and the reality soon emerged. Although most national liberation movements in the Global South interpreted Wilson's evocation of "self-determination" as support for their causes, these hopes were quickly dashed.[34] At Versailles, Wilson did little if anything to champion the cause of national sovereignty. While he eventually supported the nationalist aspirations of the Central Eastern Europe states, he did so only after they declared sovereignty and broke away from the Habsburg Monarchy (see Ádám 2004). There was a distinctly Wilsonian "balance of power" dimension to national self-determination, one aimed to "balance" forces internally and externally. Shifts in U.S. policy toward national independence movements thus followed, not led, the emerging consensus among Allied policymakers to establish a cordon sanitaire against the Bolsheviks.

During the war period of "Red Hysteria," Wilson would, despite his repeated statements against intervention in Russia, continually aid anti-Bolshevik forces with financial and material resources. Finally succumbing to Allied pressure for full military intervention, Wilson ordered four thousand U.S. troops to Siberia under the humanitarian pretext of rescuing a stranded Czech legion—whose members were, incidentally, fighting the Bolsheviks.[35] The U.S. military intervention illustrates the interlinking of the military-strategic, economic, and ideological aspects of Wilson's diplomacy. It was simultaneously aimed against German and Japanese expansionism, at enhancing U.S. access to Russian markets through the maintenance of the Open Door, and at the establishment of a non-Bolshevik regime (see

Levin 1968; Gardner 1984; Foglesong 1995; Bacino 1999; Donald E. Davis and Trani 2002).

Wilson's foreign and domestic policies toward the Bolshevik/socialist threat helped tip the balance of social forces at home in a more conservative direction, contributing to the failure of Wilson's more "progressive" peace plans.[36] During the Paris negotiations, when Wilson most needed support from the liberal left in moderating some of the Allies' harsher policies, many of his most likely supporters were jailed, weakened through government harassment, or alienated from the administration by its own policies. This same dilemma also scuttled Wilson's subsequent fight for Senate ratification of the treaty (Knock 1992). Hence, it was more than just a "failure" of elite leadership that undermined Wilson's proposals for a liberal internationalist postwar order, as mainstream IR narratives suggest. Rather, the administration's antiliberal policies worked against such efforts.

The effects of the Bolshevik Revolution on the direction and conduct of Wilson's diplomacy were ultimately contradictory. On the one hand, the revolution radicalized the Wilsonian peace discourse beyond anything Wilson and other higher-ranking U.S. officials wished to implement in policy. On the other hand, it simultaneously cemented opposing tendencies within the administration for a more punitive peace settlement against Germany. Moreover, at the Paris conference, the "Bolshevik question" imposed a time imperative to negotiate the peace as quickly as possible to stem the revolutionary tide, thereby further pushing the U.S. delegation to more readily compromise on the more progressive aspects of its peace conception, as numerous Versailles delegates and commentators recognized at the time. "As a recurrent undertone throughout would run the rumble of Time's winged chariot," Harold Nicholson wrote, "incessantly reiterant would come the motif this time-pressure . . . the flames of communism flaring, now from Munich, and now from Buda-Pesth" (quoted in John M. Thompson 1966, 20).

The "time-pressure" factor emanating from the necessity to reestablish social order before socialism spread further was key to the final compromised form that Versailles took. In response to criticism from within the U.S. administration that Wilson was compromising too much during the negotiations, Colonel House claimed, in terms "undoubtedly reflecting Wilson's views," that "if the President had pulled out of the conference, it would have meant revolution in every country in Europe and that the President was not ready to take this responsibility" (quoted in John M. Thompson 1966, 390). After news of Belá Kun's coming to power in Hungary, Wilson stated that he was faced with a "race between peace and anarchy" (quoted in Schwabe 1985, 256).

The president's signing of a compromised peace settlement some three months later was the result of widespread fears within the U.S. administration that further delays in concluding the peace would destabilize the German government, opening the door to Bolshevik rule or possibly a military dictatorship. Wilson felt that if an uncompromising line was taken at the conference, "he might precipitate domestic political developments for his allies and his opponents which could undo everything had been gained in Paris so far" (Schwabe 1985, 295). In other words, Wilson needed a "quick peace" to stabilize Europe and "stop the epidemic of revolution that threatened to spread from Russia to the Atlantic" (Costigliola 1984, 26–27). The "series of uneasy compromises," as Morgenthau called them (1950, 849), that Wilson was forced to make at Versailles was, then, the direct result of *social* rather than narrowly defined military-strategic factors. In these ways, the intersocietal dimensions of development resulting in the war-revolution linkages conditioned and reacted back on the making of the peace and the next war.

CONCLUSION

The tragedy of Wilsonian diplomacy in the making of Versailles was not so much the betrayal of a liberal statesman's moral or idealistic principles but the squandering of a historical moment in which radical emancipatory change was a genuine possibility. Having ended one war, the European powers and United States began another. The military conflict between nation-states was now overlaid by a class civil war operating both within and through the sovereign national-states system. As the "secret war against Bolshevism" (Foglesong 1995) began almost immediately after the October Revolution turned into a direct military intervention by the Allied-associated powers, the prospects for a more peaceful European (if not international) order receded. The intervention signified the beginning of the first Cold War, which in less than twenty years would lead to the next global military conflagration. In their attempts to make the world safe from Bolshevism, European and U.S. policymakers instead contributed (in both direct and indirect ways) to the conditions conducive to the rise of fascism[37] and another world war. In all this lies the great tragedy.

CHAPTER 5

Nazism and the Coming of World War II in Europe: Change and Continuity in German Foreign Policymaking during the Interwar Years

WITHIN MUCH OF the historiographical and IR literature the descent into war in Europe 1939 and later "Final Solution" seems to defy rational explanation. Only a "madman" such as Hitler could have started another great-power conflict in the midst of a war-weary Europe.[1] Misperception or miscalculation by individual Western policymakers *must* have played a crucial role (Mueller 1988, 75; see also Brown 2001, 30). Even among structural realists, the causal role of individual pathologies looms large. "A small-number system can always be disrupted by the actions of a Hitler and the reactions of a Chamberlain," as Waltz put it (1979, 175).

The causal emphasis on the individual runs throughout the conventional historiography of the origins of the war, as exemplified by the aptly labeled "intentionalist" school of interpretation. These approaches accord a stark "primacy of politics" in explaining Nazi foreign policy. Hitler is seen as firmly in the driver's seat, steering Germany toward total war, "bending foreign policy to his determined will to accomplish long-term but clear-cut ideological goals" (Kershaw 1993, 62). Whether concentrating on the psychological or ideological dimensions of the Führer's role as "Master of the Reich" or the more general desire for power rooted in an invariant human nature, such perspectives share a Hitler-centric explanation of the origins of World War II (WWII) (Waltz's "first image").[2]

In disciplinary IR, offensive realists have instead focused on changes in the international distribution of power as the primary determinant in Germany's decision to go to war. These accounts have largely downplayed the individual capacity of Hitler as well the more general question of the relationship between Nazism and the causes of WWII. This reflects structuralist predispositions to conceive a strong line of continuity in German foreign policymaking.[3] Granting the peculiarly racist nature of the Nazi regime, such realist approaches parallel A. J. P. Taylor's (1983) argument that Hitler's foreign policy objectives differed little from past Prussian-German policy-makers. Since "Powers will be Powers," Taylor wrote, it was "perfectly obvious that Germany would seek to become a Great Power again" (1983, xiii). It was only a matter of time until a militarily weakened but still unified German state would attempt to overthrow the "harsh" strictures of the Versailles settlement and again challenge the European status quo.

The fascist physiognomy of the German state is thus seen as inconsequential to the outbreak of WWII. Nazism was *not*, in other words, a necessary condition for war. It was "irrelevant or epiphenomenal to the outcome" (Schweller 1998, 5, 6). "German geopolitical vulnerability and the desire to eliminate the Russian threat," Dale Copeland writes (2000, 120), "would have existed with or without Nazi ideology." Whether focusing attention on the division of great powers into "status quo" and "revisionist" states resulting from the Versailles settlement, the pathologies of military alliance dynamics, or the inherent instabilities arising from the interregnum period of hegemonic power transition, structural realist explanations converge in their emphasis on the particular configuration of the interwar international system as making war "inherently more likely" (Mearsheimer 1990, 22; see also Waltz 1979; Posen 1984; Gilpin 1988; Christensen and Snyder 1990; Schweller 1998, 2001b; Copeland 2000).[4]

Nearly every historian agrees that Hitler sought war in Europe. This factual observation, however, provides very little in the way of a satisfactory explanation of the 1939 war. As E. H. Carr put it (1961, 81), "To say that the Second World War occurred because Hitler wanted war . . . is true enough but explains nothing." To this extent, realists are correct in downplaying the "Hitler factor" in the origins of WWII. Explanations evoking Hitler's personal idiosyncrasies or the "irrational volunteerism" of Nazi ideology are insufficient. Yet the specific social-historical milieu that brought Hitler and the Nazis to power still needs to be explained.

Despite the foreign policy similarities between the Weimar and Nazi periods, one point seems indisputable: while Weimar policymakers sought to revise Versailles peacefully, the Nazis sought to do so through military force. Realist accounts emphasizing the identity of military and Nazi interests fail to convince as proof of an exclusively *systemic*-level explanation (see Copeland 2000, chap. 5). For the activation of such "systemic-level" determinations still required the *overthrow* of Weimar's political framework. Only this could allow German military managers to pursue a full-scale rearmament program aimed at overturning the Versailles settlement by force. Thus, "domestic-level" factors were decisive in preparing the way for war.

Political elites' capacity to overthrow the Weimar order depended on the changing *balance of social forces,* which were, in turn, bound to developments in the capitalist international economy. The fragmentation of the Left; the sustained attacks on organized labor and parliamentary democracy by the ruling classes; the world economic crisis and radicalization of conservative agrarians; and the increasing disaffection of the "dying middle" were all *necessary* causal conditions in the downfall of Weimar, opening the door to the Nazi war drive. How if not by some recourse to this changing balance of social forces can one explain Germany's massive rearmament in the 1930s, which transformed the international distribution of power? Uncovering the causes of the Second World War in Europe thus requires an explanation of how Nazism could arise in the first place. This demands a theoretical perspective going beyond structural realist approaches incapable of providing a social theory of the state that could account for how Nazi ideology developed with such widespread resonance. Such an interpretation also necessitates a theoretical framework capable of locating the National Socialist phenomenon within the more *general tendencies* of world development, given the emergence of similar regimes in Italy, Japan, and elsewhere.

This chapter probes these critical issues in explaining the Nazi *Machtergreifung* (seizure of power) and its geopolitical consequences. Rather than downplaying the role of National Socialist ideology, it seeks to explicate how Nazism's vehemently racist ideas could stick in interwar German society. In other words, what were the social-historical conditions from which National Socialism could emerge as a mass movement and sustain itself in power? This entails, as Patrick Finney notes (1997, 2), "locating the Third Reich within the broad context of modern German history and analysing the nature and dynamics of Nazi expansionism." It also involves an elucidation of the precise relationship between National Socialist ideology and the sociomaterial conditions determining the eventual *timing* and *form* that Hitler's war took in 1939.

Answering these questions, this chapter examines German state and society relations during the interwar years, building on the structural framework of Germany's uneven and combined development offered in chapter 3.

This focuses close attention to the nexus of state-capital-military relations in the foreign policy continuities and changes from the Weimar to Nazi regimes. The first section investigates the historically particular geosocial conditions leading up to the collapse of functioning parliamentary democracy in 1930, investigating the intersection of social forces and foreign policy-making in the shifting international constellations of the 1920s.

The second section focuses the analysis on the decisive events and issues of the interregnum conjuncture of 1930–33, which led to the rise and consolidation of Nazi state power. Crucially, it shows how the fusion of specific domestic and foreign policy objectives of different factions of industrial capital, the military, and landowning Junkers led them to make common cause in removing the political impediments (democracy, organized labor, reparations) to reconstituting their social dominance. In the third section, the questions of politics/economics primacy and "intentionalist/structuralist" divides central to the historiography are reconsidered in interrogating the "immediate" origins of WWII. This examines Nazi foreign policy objectives, the rearmament drive of the 1930s, and their relation to the specific timing of Hitler's decision for war in 1939. The conclusion further draws out the implications of the analysis vis-à-vis IR theories.

WEIMAR DEMOCRACY BETWEEN EAST AND WEST: SOCIAL FORCES AND FOREIGN POLICY IN THE MAKING AND UNMAKING OF THE REPUBLIC

The emergence and eventual destruction of the Weimar Republic forms an integral part of historical inquiries into the causes of WWII. The short-lived democracy played a formative role in both Hitler and the NSDAP's ideological and political development while laying the social foundations for Nazism's emergence as a mass movement. The fallen republican "experiment" colored the contemporary international political landscape. For traditional conservatives and the radical Right, it was taken as proof of the inherent excesses of social democracy. For the far Left, it was seen as a sign of the intrinsic weaknesses and limitations of the reformist path to socialism. The collapse of Weimar thus reflected and further exacerbated the ideological civil war raging across Europe. As the fabric of European interstate relations progressively deteriorated over the 1930s, Weimar's fate also came to be seen as symptom and critical turning point within the international system. With the Nazi ascent to power, the postwar "Versailles system" was doomed as a new era of geopolitical rivalry and war appeared on the horizon.

Weimar Democracy in the Balance: Baptism by Fire

The Bolshevik Revolution of November 1917 transformed the interimperial rivalries of the war into a broader *"intersystemic* conflict" (Halliday 1999) articulated within, through, and across national boundaries. The battle between antagonistic social systems was crucial in the making of the peace settlement and the Weimar state, as German policymakers confronted the immediate task of establishing democracy in the midst of a Europe-wide struggle between revolution and counterrevolution. Consequently, the Allied-led fight against Bolshevism in Germany led to "the survival of the leading Wilhelmine elites and their influence on the infant German republic" (Lee and Michalka 1987, 49; see also Carsten 1973). Germany's social conflicts thus held a distinctly geopolitical component bound to the international dynamics of revolution and counterrevolution.

The republic was, in the first instance, the result of a *failed socialist* revolution—that is, a political compromise between the Social Democratic Party (SPD) and the traditional ruling elites to maintain social order. Faced with the possibility of revolution from below, German policymakers sought to preempt any fundamental transformation to the existing order by a revolution from above. This entailed ending monarchical rule, eliminating the Prussian three-class franchise, granting the eight-hour workday, and institutionalizing parliamentary democracy while leaving intact capitalist property relations and essentially preserving political power in the hands of the Reich's ruling classes (see Harman 1982; Broué 2005).

The establishment of parliamentary democracy thus failed to end the struggle between the forces of the revolution and those of the status quo (reformed or otherwise). From 1918 to 1923, the republic experienced a series of attempted—and sometimes temporarily successful—communist and left-wing uprisings, along with the counterrevolutionary Kapp (1920) and Beer Hall (1923) putsches. During these years, the specific circumstances of high profit rates in industry spawned by inflation, the devaluation of the mark, and widespread fears of mass unrest provided the *temporary* foundations for a collaboration between moderates within the labor movement (particularly the SPD and its associated free trade unions) and corporate industrial circles.[5] This was exemplified by the November 1918 Stinnes-Legien Agreement and the subsequent cooperative project known as the Zentralarbeitsgemeinschaft (Central Working Association), which, as Hugo Stinnes put it, provided industry with a much-needed "breathing space" (quoted in Geary 1983, 90; see also Feldman 1970; Maier 1975; Geary 1990).

The "class truce" worked *out from above* in the face of popular *challenges from below* was short-lived. The domestic and international foundations on which it was built were inherently unsustainable. When the exceptionally favorable production conditions of the inflationary boom period and immediate threat of communist revolution subsided and export opportunities diminished, powerful segments of the business community began orienting themselves toward dismantling labor's gains. This was already evinced in the 1922 Reichsverband der Deutschen Industrie (RDI) program, which looked forward to reductions in taxation, social security provision, and wages as well as the eradication of the statutory eight-hour working day (Geary 1990, 99).

Only after the German mark's stabilization in 1924–25 did heavy industry's long-term structural problems, significantly exacerbated by the Versailles settlement, become apparent as the sector fell into a protracted crisis of overcapacity and low profits. The Ruhr industrialists blamed overly generous wages and welfare benefits for their troubles, which they saw as a direct consequence of the Weimar "trade-union state" (Peukert 1992). By this time, heavy industry's political power was, however, at least partially counterbalanced by the ascendancy of the more dynamic export-oriented, capital-intensive sectors of industry (chemicals, machine building, engineering, and textiles), which allied themselves with the Stresemann-led cabinets between 1923 and 1929 (Geary 1983; Abraham 1986).[6] This "liberal internationalist" hegemonic project sought expanding export markets in the West and could afford more conciliatory relations with the unions given the relatively low labor costs.[7] Even if the conservative nationalist heavy industrial faction retained a kind of veto power over industrial policy, as Bernd Weisbrod claims (1979), a number of domestic and international factors merged to create conditions favorable for Stresemann to pursue the liberal internationalist foreign policy preferred by the dynamic, export-oriented faction.

Stresemann's Atlanticist Strategy of "Fulfillment": The Dawes-Locarno Nexus

Moving on from the protectionist and Eastern-oriented policies of the early Weimar years,[8] German policymakers between 1923 and 1929 pursued a more internationalist strategy aimed at cementing a transatlantic partner ship by which Germany could achieve a "peaceful" revisionism. This Western reorientation of German policymaking is associated with Gustav Stresemann, who served as chancellor in 1923 and subsequently as foreign minister until his death on 3 October 1929. While focused on forging closer ties between the two Anglo-Saxon powers and Germany, Stresemann's "Atlanticist strategy" nonetheless sought to achieve territorially revisionist goals along Weimar's western and eastern borders.

Stresemann's strategic thinking was shaped by an attentive focus on the changing dynamics of international capitalism. "Politics," as Stresemann noted, is "today first of all the politics of the world economy" (quoted in Tooze 2007, 3). His foreign policy was based on a keen appreciation of the strategic dilemmas arising from the structural interdependency binding nation-states together through the "combinatory" mechanisms of the world economy.

During WWI, Stresemann was one of the foremost advocates of German territorial annexations in the East. Like many contemporary businessmen and policymakers, he called for the creation of an extensive German-dominated *Mitteleuropa* capable of politically safeguarding the import and export opportunities "essential" to German survival. He also supported colonial expansionism and its corresponding *Weltpolitik*-orientation, which could complement a land-based German *Mitteleuropa* economic empire. Yet after Germany's defeat in 1918, Stresemann turned into a leading spokesman for the more "progressive," liberal-imperialist sections of the business community, which sought to overturn Versailles by cooperative relations with Britain and, above all, the United States (Lee and Michalka 1987, 74–75; see also Wright 2002). From his most annexationist moments to later "peaceful revisionism," a key line of continuity in Stresemann's strategic thinking was a focus on harnessing German economic forces in the service of power politics. To this end, Stresemann was primarily motivated by an "economic logic centred on the United States" (Tooze 2007, 4). As chancellor and then foreign minister, Stresemann recognized that it was to "Germany's economic and political advantage to develop the closest possible ties with the United States, while simultaneously working to undermine French economic and military power" (Lee and Michalka 1987, 77).

Hjalmar Schacht, the Reichsbank president appointed in 1923 who would later serve under the Nazi regime, shared this strategic vision. Together, Stresemann and Schacht sought to use U.S. capital to redress Germany's strategic weaknesses while meeting reparations obligations. Binding

U.S. financial interests to German prosperity, they hoped to employ U.S. power to the ultimate end of overturning the entirety of the Versailles settlement (Tooze 2007, 3–8, 13–15, 657; see also Schuker 1976, 265; Cohrs 2006, 121–28). However, the impetus for this reorientation of German foreign policy originated not in Berlin but instead in London and Washington, as international political and economic conditions facilitated concurrent shifts in British and U.S. policymaking circles.

In the context of the continually depressed economic conditions of the early 1920s, Anglo-American policymakers began reconsidering their relations with Germany. London officials came to believe that German economic recovery was a necessary precondition for sustained European growth and British prosperity as well as a necessary counterweight to France's renewed drive to Continental hegemony after the Ruhr invasion. This signaled a turning away from the Anglo-French alliance and a more collaborative approach with U.S. political and financial interests (Cohrs 2006, 71–74). To this *limited* end, London forged a common front with Washington and Wall Street against French aims on the Continent (see Schuker 1976; McDougall 1978; Costigliola 1984).[9]

U.S. policymakers and business leaders had long made the connection between U.S. economic recovery and a stable European settlement. "The prosperity of the United States" depends on the economic settlements which may be made in Europe," Charles Hughes proclaimed in 1921, "and the key to the future is with those who make those settlements" (quoted in LaFeber 1994, 121; see also Van Meter 1971, 28–34, 57–58). This meant restimulating the German economy, the engine of any general European recovery, through reparations relief and large infusions of foreign capital. The short-lived Harding administration had already made moves in this direction, as exemplified in the Washington Treaty of 1922 (see Van Meter 1977). Yet French and British demands for full cancellation of their war debts remained a tenacious obstacle in American-Allied negotiations. Repeatedly rejecting any official link between repayment of inter-Allied war debts and German reparations, successive Republican administrations continued Wilson's policy set at Paris. This aimed at "moderate change and stability" to "rekindle prosperity" in Europe and the United States, thereby reducing political tensions and the prospects of renewed war and revolution (Costigliola 1984, 96).[10]

In 1923–24, international conditions ripened for U.S. policymakers to finally intervene decisively in European affairs to resolve the reparations issue. As Germany's economic troubles grew under the strains of the French-

Belgian occupation, U.S. exports fell disastrously, tipping the U.S. economy back into recession between May 1923 and June 1924 (Costigliola 1976, 482–84). France's mounting internal economic problems—also exacerbated by the occupation—resulted in the collapse of the franc in the autumn of 1923. Thereafter, French policymaking was held hostage to Anglo-American finance (McDougall 1979, 21; see also Schuker 1976, esp. 173–81; Costigliola 1984, 114–24).

French policymakers desperately sought continued access to U.S. capital markets. The Poincaré government was thereby compelled to accede to the Republican administrations' demands for a new reparations settlement, ultimately resulting in the Dawes Plan. The French government accepted scaled-down reparations payments and committed to liquidating the Ruhr occupation (at a later date) on relatively unfavorable terms. France's military hegemony on the Continent was essentially terminated and the course set for eventual German revisionism (Schuker 1976, 178–80; see also Marks 1976; McDougall 1978; Artaud 1998). The Locarno Treaties of 1925, the geopolitical corollary of the Dawes Plan, soon demonstrated this.[11] By the mid-1920s, German revisionist strategies thus came to neatly intertwine with U.S. interests in their shared attempts to create a liberal "Open Door" capable of heading off the connected dangers of interimperial war and revolution (see Buckingham 1983; Costigliola 1984; Werner Link 1986, chap. 1).

Triumphing toward Disaster: The U.S.-led Reconstruction of
German Capitalism and Its Geosocial Consequences

From 1925 to 1928, the Dawes Plan had its intended effect. Unprecedented flows of U.S. capital poured into Germany, stimulating its economy and spurring a massive upturn in international trade. The result was a generalized if uneven recovery of the world economy. Along with Locarno, the plan stabilized European interstate relations, inaugurating a renewed "age of normalcy"—the "golden years" of the Weimar Republic. Some scholars have argued that the international architecture developed at and after Locarno provided the potential basis for a *sustained* period of peace had it not been for the onset of the Global Slump in 1929 and the rise of Nazism (see Cohrs 2006). Yet how stable was the international order established by Dawes and Locarno? Was the Great Depression an *exogenous* shock or a consequence of this order?

Between the May 1921 London Schedule of Payments and the 1924 Dawes

Plan, German policymakers faced a series of obstacles in fulfilling their reparations obligations. Central to this was the question of how German businesses could export enough to meet reparations payments given the relative
inelasticity of world market demand for German goods. Without a massive
expansion of world trade or an increase in domestic productivity, German
policymakers would have to regulate and restrict capital expenditures and
domestic consumption. In the 1920s, such goals were unachievable, as German politicians were hard-pressed to accommodate the competing demands
of labor and capital (Kent 1991, 1–18; see also Maier 1975; McNeil 1986).

Moreover, the Allied-associated powers remained generally reluctant to
alleviate the transfer problem by creating the necessary demand conditions
outside of Germany. In the immediate postwar years, France and Britain
aimed to eliminate Germany as a potential rival in international trade. In
Britain, significant fears emerged in business and policymaking circles that
after the war Germany would retain its foreign markets and possibly even
strengthen its international trading position. The theme that Britain might
"win the military but lose the trade war" resonated throughout the conflict's
duration (Daunton 1996, 897). A "community of interests" thereby emerged
between policymakers in the Foreign Office, in the economic ministries, and
in certain banking and industrial circles concerning the necessity to pene-
trate former German markets and "thus prevent a renewal of Germany's prewar economic, financial and diplomatic position" (Teichova 1979, 368; see
also Scott Newton 1996).

Further, during the war, the Allied-associated powers had adopted protectionist policies to defend their markets against the Central Powers and
each other. After Versailles, they appropriated German assets in Central Eastern Europe and expanded into once German-held markets (see Teichova
1979; Kaiser 1980; Ránki 1983; Segal 1987; Hehn 2002). Though conceived as
temporary measures, the turn to protectionism never quite died and was actually strengthened by the recurrence of recessions and generally depressed
economic conditions continuing over the next two decades. In Britain and
France, reparation claims became a means by which the economic "war after
the war" was continued as conservative politicians, joined by powerful business interests, sought to defer the domestic costs of war. Since these costs had
been overwhelmingly financed by U.S.-backed loans, rather than direct taxation or capital levies, Allied reparations policies were in part determined by
U.S. war debt policies (Kent 1991, 2–4).

For their part, U.S. policymakers were also keenly aware of the political domestic problems of displacing the costs of war onto a reluctant American "taxpayer"—that is, the business community. While officially rejecting any official war debt–reparations link, consecutive Republican administrations wielded the war debts issue (and access to U.S. capital markets) as a means to reduce Allied reparations claims, as exemplified by the Dawes-Locarno nexus (Leffler 1972; Hogan 1991). Yet U.S. officials continually insisted on the repayment of European war loans while pursing tariff policies that *in effect* if not intention denied its debtors sufficient access to the U.S. domestic market, the *largest* consumer market in the world. U.S. trade policies thereby contributed at least indirectly to the European victors' unwillingness to abandon their financial claims on each other and Germany (Kent 1991, 265; see also McNeil 1986; Artaud 1998).

The U.S.-backed proposal for the Dawes Plan was designed to ameliorate these problems by providing a more robust and flexible political-economic framework. Though the transfer mechanism detailed in the plan was *not* intended to rely on a continual stream of U.S. loans, this is how it ended up functioning. For what the plan's architects failed to realize was how America's "limited, initial loan to inaugurate the reparations plan would quickly and uncontrollably mushroom into a massive and on-going obligation to keep the system going" (Costigliola 1984, 118), thereby generating a speculative frenzy on Wall Street. The net effect of the Dawes Plan was to temporarily conceal the intractability of the transfer problem through an "artificially induced and short-lived flow of foreign funds to Germany" (Kent 1991, 261). If anything, Dawes exacerbated the underlying weaknesses of the German economy, as the indirect recycling of international liquidity enabled German policymakers to make their reparations payments without forcing the country to produce the necessary export surpluses. As the speculative fury of U.S. finance capital into Germany began to slow down in late 1928, eventually halting with the October 1929 Wall Street crash, the German economy was left in tatters. The Dawes Plan thus held an intrinsic relation to the Great Depression.

The persistent structural disequilibria were also aggravated by policies pursued by the great powers in the 1920s. The global trajectory, scope, and duration of the depression *cannot* be understood without attention to these conjunctural developments.[12] The idea that the depression emerged as some sort of "exogenous" shock undermining an otherwise stable (or "stabilizing") postwar international system is therefore misleading. As Gilbert Ziebura notes (1990, 6), the "structural flaws inherent in the world economy and political system in consequence of the Great War were in fact growing more serious beneath the surface of seeming reassurance throughout the era of 'relative stability.'"[13]

The collapse of Weimar retains a *fundamental* relation to the Dawes-Locarno framework. Indeed, a central factor in the recrudescence of antirepublican forces after 1928 was the swelling disillusionment with the U.S.-sponsored "stabilization" programs represented by the Dawes and later Young Plans. The continuing credibility of Stresemann and Schacht's Atlanticist strategy depended, above all, on the expectation that America's political influence in Europe would continue to grow and eventually lead the way to a comprehensive reparations settlement (Tooze 2007, 13). These anticipations failed to materialize.

Announced in early 1929 and adopted in 1930, the U.S.-backed Young Plan reduced reparation annuities only *marginally* below the original level fixed by Dawes. Further, the plan abolished the transfer protection clause stipulated by Dawes. The risk of future default or rescheduling now squarely rested with Germany's commercial creditors. Moreover, the negotiations of 1928 prompted widespread rumors about the future reparations scheme, sparking a rise in U.S. interest rates. Thus, even *before* the Young Plan's implementation, much of the damage to the German economy and politics had already taken place, as long-term capital lending began to dry up (Ritschl 1996, 3–4; Tooze 2007, 14–15). During this time, heavy industry launched a frontal assault on the Weimar "compromise." This aimed at nothing less than the systematic dismantling of Weimar's "corporatist" system of industrial relations and welfare benefits, together with the eventual destruction of parliamentary democracy.[14]

Conservative business circles had been horrified by the stunning success of the SPD in the 1928 parliamentary elections, which put the Socialists back into government for the first time in eight years. The "grand coalition" formed thereafter represented the last political gasp of the compromise order between the SPD and "liberal internationalist" faction of capital. Holding it together was the common goal of a substantially reduced reparations settlement. Once these negotiations drew to their bitter conclusion, the coalition's "grace period" came to an end (Mommsen 1996, 266–67; Richard J. Evans 2004, 247).

During its time in power, the coalition presided over a series of arbitration settlements perceived by heavy industrialists as favoring labor, as exemplified by the Ruhr lockout of 1928. For many corporate capitalists, this confirmed that Weimar was the instrument of "trade-union interests." Alongside the reparations burden, representatives of the heavy industrial sectors ramped up their crusade against "artificially" high wages and "overly" generous social welfare programs associated with the republic (Weisbrod 1979; Geary 1990, 103; Richard J. Evans 2004, 115–17). In a 1929 RDI memorandum, "Decline or Ascent?" Ruhr industrial magnate Paul Reusch summarized industry's demands for relief from these economic burdens and implored industrialists to unite in a common front "promoted against Marxism . . . by all means" (quoted in Stegmann 1976, 31). And so they did. Between 1929 and 1930, the heavy industry faction worked through its political dominance of the Deutsche Volkspartei (German People's Party) to undermine the Müller coalition government on the issue of unemployment benefits, thereby paving the way for the Brüning dictatorship (see Weisbrod 1981; Geary 1983, 94–95; Mommsen 1996, 263–68, 276–77; Kershaw 1999–2000, 2:323–24; Baranowski 2011, 156).[15] In the final instance, opposition from heavy industry was crucial in breaking Weimar's parliamentary democracy.

Consequently, even before Stresemann's death in October 1929, German policymaking began shifting away from its Atlantic orientation. The former champion of the Atlanticist strategy, the Reichsbank's President Schacht, became a ferocious critic of the Young Plan. Resigning in protest in the spring of 1930, Schacht joined a growing chorus of the radical Right to demand unilateral treaty revision. His shift to the hard right was soon on display in his "surprise" participation in the self-styled "nationalist opposition" meeting at Bad Harzburg on 11 October 1931. There, Schacht spoke alongside Hugenberg and Hitler, denouncing the Young Plan and the economic policies of the Brüning administration (Henry Ashby Turner 1985, 167–68).

Though he never officially joined the NSDAP, Schacht began openly promoting Nazi ideas by 1932. Together with the Keppler circle, the internationally renowned economist worked to transform the NSDAP into a party amenable to the interests of German big business (Henry Ashby Turner 1985, 144–45, 239–46; see Stegmann 1976). Reappointed Reichsbank president under the Nazi regime, Schacht thus forms the "'missing link' between Stresemann's strategy of economic revisionism and the unilateralist military aggression that replaced it after 1933" (Tooze 2007, 15).

FROM BRÜNING TO HITLER: ENTERING THE NAZI CONJUNCTURE

The international order forged under the "spirit of Locarno" had already dissipated before the October 1929 Wall Street crash. Yet the onset of world de-

pression was fundamental in catapulting the Nazis into the political lime-
light. Without the collapse of the "capitalist world economy," Eric Hobsbawm
writes (1994, 86), "there would certainly have been no Hitler."[16] Nor, for that
matter, would there likely have been another world war breaking out a decade later. In this sense, the Global Slump of 1929–33 was indeed the water-
shed event in the history of interstate relations between the wars. It marked
the point where the "postwar era" ended and "another prewar era" began as
"long term strategic interests gave way to ostensibly short run economic necessity" (Boyce 1989, 88–89; see also James 2001; Boyce 2009).

Viewed from this international perspective, the pervasive "primacy of
politics" explanations of Nazism and the origins of WWII seem rather problematic (see discussion later in chap. 5, under "The 'Internalist' Trap"). This
section examines these international economic conditions accounting for
the emergence of Nazism as a mass political movement *from below,* leading,
then, to a consideration of the narrowing of political options available to the
besieged industrial and Junker capitalists in their attempts to maintain their
hegemony *from above.*[17] In doing so, the analysis elucidates how structural
forces operated *through* the terrain of the conjuncture, itself articulated and
overdetermined by the international (uneven and combined) character of
capitalist development.

World Economic Crisis and the Social Bases of Nazism

Until 1914, most European powers were able to pay off current-account deficits through the invisible surpluses generated by foreign investments
throughout the Global South.[18] After the war, the European economies became heavily indebted to the United States, while much of their foreign
trade and investments had been entirely lost (e.g., Russia) or substantially
reduced in value (as in Central and Eastern Europe and Central Asia). This
dislocation of world investment and trade patterns, coupled with the unprecedented growth of countries' productive capacities during WWI, resulted in conditions of *global overproduction* that persisted throughout the
interwar years (see Kaiser 1990, 354–62; Hobsbawm 1994, chap. 3).

Specifically, as a consequence of this global surplus of key primary commodities, the export earnings of the primary producing economies—such as
those in Central and Southeastern Europe—were substantially reduced.
Hence, as the primary producing nations went into a slump in the late 1920s,
the industrialized countries lost a major market for their export surpluses.

The collapse of worldwide agrarian prices at the end of 1920s—*interconnecting* with the Soviet Union's intensified steps toward state-forced industrialization—was then in part a consequence of the "uneven development" between the agricultural and industrial nations, "shifting the terms of trade between primary products and manufactured goods" (Bernstein 1987, 10; see also Lewis 1949, 55–56; Aldcroft 1977, 268–84; Kindleberger 1986, 273, 292–93; Hobsbawm 1994, 89–91).[19]

A credit crisis in world markets originating in American financial markets—itself reflecting the persistence of structural deficiencies within the U.S. industrial economy—resulted in the Global Slump of 1929–33. The vast contraction of credit for the developing nations combined with the general tendency toward trade protectionism among the industrial states (most dramatically exemplified in America's Hawley-Smoot Tariff of 1930) further exacerbated the problem of insufficient export markets. Over the 1930s, the global economy fractured into a number of fiercely competing protectionist trade blocs configured along regional lines (James 2001).

The severity of the agricultural crisis within the new states of Central Eastern Europe was further worsened by government "modernizing" strategies of land redistribution, which rapidly broke up large-scale landed estates and redistributed them among peasants engaged in small-scale subsistence farming and animal husbandry. By the 1920s, the economic effects of these policies were plain: sharply reduced crop yields, declining wheat quality, and a general diminution of export earnings. "The southeastern states' problems," David Kaiser writes, "reflected the difficulty of *telescoping countries' political and economic development into a few short years*" (1980, 18–19; emphasis added). In short, the problems resulted from these countries' variegated and peculiar forms of "combined development."

The structural conditions leading to the Global Slump can be conceptualized as emerging through the accumulated contradictions arising from the causal interaction of the *partially reconstructed* West-East, North-South, and transatlantic vectors of unevenness. The different "combined" forms of social development in the Central Eastern European region (including Russia) in turn facilitated an eastward reorientation of German foreign policy toward the creation of the kind of *Grossraumwirtschaft* along the lines envisaged by the Brest-Litovsk Treaty.

Together with Brüning's brutal deflationary measures, a number of long-term sociological factors[20] combined with the world depression of 1929–33 to effect an irreversible fragmentation of the bourgeois and agrarian parties, opening the way for a series of major Nazi electoral successes from 1930 on-ward. The impact of rapid industrialization and its attendant "rationaliza-tion" on the different aspects of German society "was extremely uneven," as Larry Eugene Jones writes (1972, 24), "and in the long run it generated an ele-ment of structural instability which played a crucial role in the rise of Na-tional Socialism in the period before 1933." The course of German develop-ment was, however, in no way "deviational" from capitalist modernity but rather was *internal* and *constitutive* of it: the "national peculiarities" crystal-lizing through the overall unevenness of the developmental process (Trotsky 1962, 23–24).[21]

This unevenness of German development was significantly intensified during the Weimar period as the severity of socioeconomic dislocations of war and then inflation rendered the old middle class of artisans, small-scale manufacturers, shopkeepers, and peasants in a state of competitive disad-vantage and overall decline. The rationalization of heavy industry climaxing in the mid-1920s aggravated its inherited structural weakness that, existing alongside and interacting with the perpetuation of a technologically and or-ganizationally "backward" agricultural sector, resulted in the "scissors price crisis" of 1926–32. This "extreme rationalization of German industry after the war," as Trotsky noted (1971, 272), "resulted from the necessity of over-coming the unfavourable conditions of historical delay"—that is, German capitalism's belated development—"the geographical situation, and mili-tary defeat."

As a consequence of more than four decades of protectionism, German agriculture developed a structural bias toward the continued production of 19th-century food staples. An upshot of this was that the agrarian econo-my's development of the dairy economy significantly lagged and the tradi-tional technological structures of the agrarian economy underwent little change up to WWI (Gessner 1981; see also Tooze 2007, 166–99). With the emergence of a global food economy, this translated into a serious strategic disadvantage for the country. As the Allied blockade in WWI demonstrated, the German agrarian economy was dangerously dependent on the world market (Hardach 1977; Offer 1989).

Despite interspersed periods of attempted rationalization, protectionist tariffs and state subsidies remained throughout the Weimar years, thus per-petuating German agricultural "backwardness" in a condition of overall stagnation. Consequently, Germany remained a highly "industrialized state whose social formation only partly met the needs of a modern industrialized economy" (Gessner 1977, 760; see also Gessner 1981; Abraham 1986, 42–106). Interwar German society was thus characterized more by the kind of "dual economy" typical of late industrializers than by the most "advanced" capitalist economy in the world.[22] As Adam Tooze (2007, 167) notes, "A substantial minority of the German population continued to eke out a living from the soil, under conditions, in many cases, of extraordinary backwardness."[23] The radical agrarianism of Nazi ideology and Hitler's *Lebensraum* expansionism thus addressed (in fantastical-racist form) *real* material grievances. "Even under the most favourable assumptions," Tooze writes (2007, 167), "the territory of Germany was not sufficient to support an agricultural population substantially larger than that to which German had been reduced by 1933, at standards of living that were acceptable in relation to those prevailing in the cities." In other words, without dramatic domestic structural reforms, German prosperity necessitated expanded *Lebensraum* (Tooze 2007, 179). Yet Nazism as both an ideology and political movement was *not* so much the "product of a society still in transition," as Tooze concludes (2007, 168) but more the consequence of a particular trajectory of capitalist development overpressurized in both time and space.

Interwar German development can be thus conceptualized as a kind of sui generis form of *capitalist* combination. The sociologically *amalgamated* character of German capitalist development and its socially and geopolitically explosive effects were "artificially" perpetuated during the interwar years through the interrupting influences of recurrent war, crisis, and (failed) socialist revolution. The accumulated contradictions of antecedent developmental tendencies in Germany were thereby extended in time by the specificities of the conjuncture marked by the "organic crisis" of capitalism in its intersecting domestic and international dimensions. Mastering the techniques of the modern mass election, the Nazi leadership transformed themselves into the "catchall" party of the pool of dissatisfied suffering from the burdens of this conjuncture.[24] The NSDAP thereby raised itself to power "on the backs of the petty bourgeoisie," the "most *backward* part of the nation, the heavy ballast of history" (Trotsky 1971, 405, 402). In power, Trotsky (1971, 405) writes,

> Fascism opened up the depths of society for politics. Today, not only in peasant homes but also in city skyscrapers, there lives alongside the twentieth century the tenth or the thirteenth . . . Everything that should have been eliminated from the national organism in the form of cultural excrement in

the course of the normal development of society has now come gushing out from the throat; capitalism is puking up the undigested barbarism. Such is the physiology of National Socialism.

Rather than counterposing the "material" and "ideational" sources explaining the German population's susceptibility to Nazi ideas, one needs to take into account the *specificity* of Germany's crisis of hegemony developing within the broader context of world economic depression. The reemergence of the perceived threats of revolution and counterrevolution between 1930 and 1933 again posed the issue of how the ruling capitalist classes could protect their *social* dominance.

Brüning the "Bonapartist": A Balancing Act[25]

Between 1930 and 1933, Nazism emerged as a mass political movement, challenging the dominance of the traditional bourgeois parties. It became apparent to leading echelons of the business community that the coalescence of an antisocialist *Sammlung* of mainstream bourgeois parties *excluding* the Nazis was no longer a politically viable option. Only a government with Nazi participation could offer the modicum of political legitimacy required in a period of widespread social upheaval. This meant a Hitler chancellorship, which the Führer stipulated as an absolute condition of Nazi participation in any government.

Moreover, the Nazis offered a feasible means of achieving a number of crucial aims promoted by different strata within the ruling classes. However, throughout the 1920s, NSDAP economic policies were met by widespread skepticism in German big-business circles. Corporate capitalists were on the whole deeply suspicious of the party's proclaimed socialization programs, ultraprotectionism, and fiery anticapitalist rhetoric. Only with the beginning of the Global Slump did business attitudes toward the Nazis slowly begin to change. Explaining these shifts entails examining the progressive narrowing of political options facing capitalists following the fall of the "grand coalition" in March 1930.

With the depression, a number of decisive and interconnected shifts in the institutional and ideological configurations of German corporate capital led to the reemergence of nationalist-conservative forces coalescing around the *tenuous* dominance of the heavy industrial faction (see Weisbrod 1979; Neebe 1981, 200–201). This retrenchment of heavy industrial power was made clear by 1930 as the RDI was internally reorganized, giving heavy industry a significantly increased share of representation. A year later, the RDI leadership passed from the "progressive" Carl Duisberg (head of IG Farben) to the conservative Krupp (Abraham 1986, 146).

By this time, leading figures associated with the dynamic export-oriented industries were already changing gears in both their domestic and foreign policy orientations. As Duisberg declared in January 1930, "Capital is being destroyed through the unproductive use of public funds . . . Only a radical reversal in state policies can help" (quoted in Geary 1990, 103). The demolition of parliamentary democracy and organized labor at home and imperialist expansionism abroad thereby came to be seen as a way of restoring business profitability while providing the potential basis for the eventual "social reconsolidation of German capitalism."

Formed in March 1930, the Brüning cabinet seemed set to pursue these goals. Lurching towards a "monarchist restoration," Brüning evoked Article 48 of the Weimar Constitution, allowing him to govern by emergency presidential decree. The chancellor employed these powers to pursue an uncompromising deflationary policy, a dismantling of the welfare state, and revival of the traditional *Mitteleuropa-Politik* through an attempted resuscitation of a Austro-German customs union (*Anschluss*) potentially incorporating the entire Danubian-Balkan region.[26] Many contemporaries and later historians saw Brüning's deflationary policy as the only way for the government to meet reparation obligations without immediate foreign assistance.[27] In the long term, the policy would demonstrate the infeasibility of continued reparations. Yet whatever the extent of the structural economic constraints weighing on the government, it seems clear that Brüning's policy also held an explicitly *political* goal. Rapid deflation made it possible to undermine the power of organized labor through strict wage and price reductions, alongside a piecemeal dismantling of welfare legislation (Lee and Michalka 1987, 112–23; Weisbrod 1990, 47–48).

The social consequences of the deflationary strategy were devastating. It aggravated the already severe process of socioeconomic stratification within the *Mittelstand* and peasant classes, thus ripening the conditions for a Nazi electoral breakthrough onto the national scene. In the September 1930 elections, the NSDAP garnered 18.3 percent of the vote (up from 2.5 percent), making it the second-largest party in Parliament, behind the Socialists who placed first with 24.6 percent of the popular vote.[28] After two years of severe austerity measures, the NSDAP took 37.4 percent of the vote in the July 1932 elections, making it far and away the largest party in the Reichstag, with 230 seats.[29] Most shocking for the ruling classes, however, was the steady rise of the Communist vote from 13.1 percent (77 seats) to 14.6 percent (89 seats) to 16.9 percent (100 seats) over the last three elections. Hence, by mid-1932, it appeared to many within the ruling classes that the ultimate choice was between Bolshevism or Nazism, as the two largest parties of the far Left (SPD and Communists) made the SPD-Communist combination the largest force in Parliament with 221 seats (37.3 percent of the vote) behind the NSDAP (Volkmann 1990, 188–89; see also Geary 1983).[30]

During the Brüning chancellorship, a number of leading sections of capital began to grow impatient with the pace of institutional "reforms." The cabinet was seen as too slow in undoing welfare taxation, and the proposed labor legislation of 1932 was regarded as unnecessarily timid. Though challenges from the nationalist-conservative heavy industrial faction ended up contributing to the Brüning government's collapse, his final removal was largely driven by Junker-led forces that had already identified themselves with the extreme Right (see Neebe 1981; Henry Ashby Turner 1985; Geary 1990; Mommsen 1996).[31]

Eastern Promises: From Grossraumwirtschaft to Lebensraum in Central Eastern Europe

For the most part, between 1930 and 1933, corporate industrial and agrarian interests diverged. However, one significant area saw the emergence of a broadly shared realignment toward the economic penetration and further development of Central Eastern European markets. A consequence of the severity of the agricultural crisis in the Danubian and Baltic regions, these countries sought economic relief through German "assistance," which, with Brüning's ascent to power, the Germans were only happy to exploit (Kaiser 1980, 17–56; Volkmann 1990, 173–94).

For many German capitalists, export possibilities to the West momentarily appeared exhausted, while conditions in the East seemed much better. Both heavy *and* light industries, along with large-scale agrarian interests, turned their attention to cultivating the export opportunities offered by Central and Southeastern Europe, where politically safeguarded markets could be more easily achieved (Frommelt 1977, 87–103; Stegmann 1978, 213; Berghahn 1996, 16–17). Capital accumulation and geopolitical strategies thus again began to converge around the *Mitteleuropa* concept. Emblematic of this reorientation in leading industrial circles was a speech given in March 1931 by IG Farben chair Carl Duisberg. "In Europe, the goal of a regional economic space seems to take gradually firmer forms," declared the onetime proponent of liberal internationalism. "Not until there is a united economic bloc from Bordeaux to Sofia will Europe receive the backbone from which it can retain its importance in the world" (quoted in Schumann and Nestler 1975, doc. 81, 219–20).

The eastward imperialism in the late Weimar period was a critical precursor to the militarily expansionist course subsequently taken by the Nazis. Here, a key link between the foreign policies from the Brüning to Hitler periods can be found in the activities of the Mitteleuropäischer Wirtschaftstag (Central European Economic Congress, MWT). Already in 1929, the German section of the MWT was advocating the creation of a "central economic union," noting that "Germany's interests primarily lie in attainting in *Mitteleuropa* an equivalent to the lost markets in the East, to its lost colonies, and, also, as compensation for the increasing tariff barriers of the large economic empires, England, the United States, and other relevant states." In a confidential memorandum written the same year, the MWT claimed "that the complete economic *Anschluss* of Austria would create the necessary economic '*Lebensgrossraum*,' as a first step in establishing the future '*Grossreich*'" (quoted in Brechtefeld 1996, 51–52).

Members of the business community representing almost all sectors of big industry, agriculture, and finance headed the MWT. Through its internal reorganization in 1931, it became dominated by heavy industrial interests (Frommelt 1977, 91). According to Alfred Sohn-Rethel's (1978) controversial account, under heavy industry's leadership, the MWT acted as a "unique vehicle" for the *partial* reunification of the hitherto divergent interests of the various factions of German capital on the basis of a renewed eastward imperialist policy (see Stegmann 1978; Abraham 1986, 215–19).[32]

The MWT also acted as a point of Nazi contacts with big business, specifically through the personal connection between Schacht and Paul Silverberg.[33] Together, they edited the association's private newsletter, the *Deutschen Führerbriefe*, a biweekly "political-economic private correspondence" circulated to the "the ruling circles of leading financial and industrial capitals, including their political confidants: Cabinet members, upper echelons of the *Reichswehr*, leading big landowners, and the circle around Hindenburg."[34] The *Führerbriefe* steadily represented the "social and economic policies" of the Ruhr industrialists, particularly in their "anti-Marxism and anti-unionism," though it did not always articulate their political positions (Neebe 1981, 154, 155). From 1932 onward, the *Führerbriefe* advocated for a coalition government with the NSDAP that would provide for the "social re-consolidation of German capitalism," as the title of a two-part September 1932 article called it. "If [it] were possible for Nazism to assume leadership" over the unions, the article argued, and to bring them "into a compulsion-based social structure in the way that the Social Democrats were introduced into the liberal system, the Nazis would thus provide an indispensable function becoming the carrier of the future for any bourgeois rule, and would in the socio-political system of this rule necessarily find their organic place" (quoted in Neebe 1981, 160).

In the early 1930s, the NSDAP's increasing calls for a more intervention-ist economic policy favoring capital over labor and the turn to an autarkic German-dominated economic bloc in Central Eastern Europe seemed to of-fer an alternative program to German corporate interests. In a January 1932 address to the Dusseldorf Industrial Club, Hitler emphasized the business-friendly character of the Nazis' program, promising to cut labor costs, curb the descent into "Bolshevism," and improve economic conditions through territorially expansionist methods (the attainment of new "living space").[35] During this time, Schacht had also begun refining the NSDAP's economic ideas, seeking to bring them into greater accord with the business commu-nity (Volkmann 1990, 186–88).

Hegemony in the Balance: Toward the "Social Reconsolidation of Capitalism"

From mid-1932 onward, leading corporate capitalists were beginning to swing in favor of *some* form of cabinet including the Nazis, particularly after Chancellor Schleicher's flirtations with organized labor raised "the spectre of an alliance of the military and the working class against propertied ele-ments of society" (Henry Ashby Turner 1969, 67).[36] Heavy industrial leaders were "horrified" by General Schleicher's plans for a reflationary collabora-tion with the unions. In an infamous November 1932 letter to President Hin-denburg, leading business representatives and industrialists demanded that Hitler be appointed chancellor. Denouncing Schleicher's policies as social-ist, the heavy industrialists thereby played a critical role in the chancellor's eventual dismissal by President Hindenburg on 30 January 1933 (Geary 1990, 100–103; see also Weisbrod 1979, 260–61; Volkmann 1990, 189).[37]

In early January 1933, arrangements were being made between the NS-

DAP and the DNVP for the formation of a coalition government with Hitler as head without the calling of new elections. This arrangement had been preceded by negotiations between the Keppler circle and industrialists that resulted "in a broad agreement on the National Socialist economic program" (Volkmann 1990, 188). The inclusion of Hitler in a future cabinet was also discussed at a 7 January 1933 meeting between von Papen and leading representatives of Ruhr heavy industry (Krupp, Springorum, Reusch, and Vögler). Whether the industrialists were merely informed of Hitler's appointment or actively promoted it is unclear (see Stegmann 1976, 57; Neebe 1981, 144–45; Mommsen 1996, 515). What is clear, however, is though many industrialists did not *directly* support the Nazis before taking control, their "politically myopic and self-serving" actions, as Ian Kershaw writes (1999–2000, 1:435), "significantly contributed to the undermining of democracy that was the necessary prelude to Hitler's success." Furthermore, once in government, big business was a *decisive* factor in the NSDAP's consolidation of power.

At a secret meeting with leading members of the business community on 20 February 1933, the new Chancellor Hitler proclaimed the Nazis' willingness to crush the German Left by physical force if necessary (see Stackelberg and Winkle 2002, 130–33, doc. 3.3). The Nazis sought to solicit donations from the capitalists at a time when the party was in dire financial straits and preparing for the upcoming 5 March 1933 elections. As Göring explained at the time, these elections would "surely be the last for the next ten years [and] probably even for the next hundred" (quoted in Richard J. Evans 2004, 325). To these ends, Tooze notes (2007, 100–101), "German big business was willing to make a substantial down-payment," thereby providing a "large injection of cash" when the NSDAP needed it most.

The relationship between capitalism and the emergence of fascist regimes in the interwar period was, however, much more systemic. The disintegration of parliamentary democracy and the emergence of an authoritarian solution was a consequence of a particular crisis *within* capitalism. What was at stake in Germany's turn to authoritarianism and later fascism was nothing less than the "social reconsolidation of capitalism" in a qualitatively novel form. As a 1932 article in the *Deutschen Führerbriefe* put it,

> The problem of consolidating a bourgeois regime in post-war Germany is in general determined by the fact that the leading group—namely the bourgeoisie operating the economy—has become too narrow to account for its own rule. For this hegemony it needs . . . to bind itself to a layer that is not

part of it socially but which provides the essential service of anchoring its hegemony within the people, thereby becom[ing] the actual or final support of that hegemony. (quoted in Neebe 1981, 160)

German society was engulfed in what Gramsci termed an "organic crisis" representing a fusion of a *structural* socioeconomic crisis and a *conjunctural* crisis of political legitimacy. By the early 1930s, the principal political representatives of the bourgeoisie no longer provided an adequate solution to this crisis. The ruling classes could no longer rule for themselves, as internecine rivalries opened the door to their relinquishment of the reins of government. This "incapacity of the political representatives of the propertied classes to formulate and implement their own policies" led to their abdication in favor of National Socialism (Mason 1995, 59). The emergence of Nazi power in Germany thus shares certain characteristics with other fascist movements, which, as Geoff Eley points out (1983, 78), "prospered under conditions of general political crisis in societies that were dynamically capitalist, but where the state was incapable of organizing the maintenance of social cohesion." Such conditions paved the way for the geopolitical conflicts of the coming years. The Nazi seizure of power can thus be best conceptualized as a particular instantiation of a passive revolution whereby new forms of capitalist discipline and rule are established under conditions of generalized organic crisis at home and abroad.

THE INTERNATIONAL POLITICAL ECONOMY OF NATIONAL SOCIALISM: STATE-CAPITAL RELATIONS, REARMAMENTS, AND FOREIGN POLICY IN THE THIRD REICH

The "Internalist" Trap: Rethinking Questions of Primacy

The long-running debate among historians regarding the nature and trajectory of Nazi foreign policy largely revolves around two overlapping axes of contrasting perspectives, one between a "primacy of politics" versus "primacy of economics" approach, and the other between an "intentionalist" versus "structuralist-functionalist" interpretation. As developed within much of the historiographical literature, both sides of these two debates reveal an instrumentalism (residual or otherwise) whereby the question of primacy is ultimately resolved by an identification of the core *agents* dominating the policymaking process. In other words, the question is whether big business or the Nazis ultimately governed the Third Reich. Cast in these terms, the answer appears clear enough. At least in the foreign policymaking realm, historians now generally agree that most major foreign policy directives were made by Hitler or required his consent (Kershaw 1993, 111).

This line of inquiry has lent itself to an "intentionalist" interpretation of Nazi foreign policy as being bent to the will of Hitler's "programmatic aims." Simply put, the Führer desired war, and once in power, he relentlessly pursued this objective. This "intentionalist" perspective emphasizing the "free agency" in Nazi foreign policymaking has found much resonance in liberal-inspired IR accounts.[38] From this perspective, the nature and dynamics of Nazi foreign policy and economy are conceptualized in terms of an absolute "primacy of politics." While there is debate among these interpretations regarding the consistency of Hitler's program (whether it was set by a stage-by-stage plan or "timetable for war") and its final objectives (world domination or continental hegemony), the key question is thus narrowed to "whether it was considerations of racist ideology or pure power politics which decisively influenced Hitler" (Hildebrand 1973, 20; see also Luža, Campbell, and Cienciala 1985; Weinberg 1985b).

By contrast, "structuralist-functionalist" interpretations emphasize the pressures emanating from different rival groups *within* the Nazi state, with domestic social conflicts and the institutional discord characterizing the Third Reich as central determinants of Nazi foreign policy. Whether Hitler held clear and persistent objectives, the dictator's foreign policy decisions were more often than not "pragmatic" responses to these structural and institutional forces. On the structuralist account, Nazi expansionism is viewed as unfolding through its own "uncountable dynamism and radicalizing momentum" (Kershaw 1993, 108).[39] Particularly interesting here is how, unlike the debate over the origins of the First World War, the two conceptual axes of interpretation dominating the WWII debate have overwhelmingly operated within an "internalist" logic of explanation. The perspectives assume a "methodological nationalism" whereby the concepts of "primacy" (whether political and economic), "intentionalism," and "structuralism" all operate solely within the *domestic* sphere.[40]

Even the most theoretically sophisticated positions fall prey to this "inside-out" explanatory framework, as exemplified in Tim Mason's more nuanced "primacy of politics" thesis. This holds that "from 1936 onwards, the NSDAP in both its foreign and domestic policies became increasingly independent of the influence of the economic ruling classes, and even in some essential aspects ran contrary to their interests" (Mason 1995, 54). While the statement is certainly accurate, the point is that Mason presupposes "primacy" in terms of its *domestic agents*. Yet surely this does not exhaust the realm of methodological framing (the nation-state) by which one may determine what is in fact causally decisive. What happens when the field of analysis is widened beyond the confines of the domestic?

Race into Space: Nazi Geopolitics through the
Looking Glass of Uneven and Combined Development

From the moment Hitler took power, the fascist regime was set to pursue a comprehensive program of rearmaments, destruction of the Left, and imperial expansionism congruent with the interests of military managers and leading factions of capital. The chancellor made these intentions clear as early as February 1933 in a secret meeting between Hitler and the top German military generals. At the meeting, Hitler reiterated a number of long-held Nazi goals, including the "root and branch" extermination of Marxism and the building up of the German armed forces. Once political power was consolidated, the regime's aim would then turn toward "perhaps fighting for new export possibilities, perhaps—and probably better—the conquest of new living space in the east and its ruthless Germanization." Either way, Hitler made it clear "that only through political power and struggle can the present economic circumstances be changed" (Noakes and Pridham 2001, doc. 472).

Unlike Stresemann, who sought to use the accumulation of economic resources to redress Germany's strategic-military deficiencies through German capitalism's reintegration into the world market, Hitler wanted to rebuild German military power to compensate for its economic weaknesses through the partial delinking (autarky) of German capitalism from the world market. Attached to a program for the political acquisition of a large-scale economic space in the East, autarky would strengthen the domestic German market and its competitiveness vis-à-vis other imperial powers—that is, the United States, Japan, and Britain, which were already carving out their own closed economic blocs (see Volkmann 1990, 188, 172–74; Baranowski 2011, 193–94). This would restore German capitalism on fundamentally reconstructed *sociospatial* foundations, a goal shared by the Nazis, the military, and corporate capital. In other words, Germany's great-power status would be founded on expanded economic power.

The recent works of Adam Tooze (2007) and Christian Leitz (2004) have emphasized these long overlooked *economic* dimensions of Hitler's geopolitical thinking. These works, among others, have underlined the importance of international economic factors in Hitler's thought and in conditioning the Nazi drive to war in the 1930s. Tooze's study in particular hones in on the understated importance of the Nazi regime's perception of the threat posed by the world economic ascendancy of the United States. These fears help explain both the motives behind Hitler's aggressions and the reasons why it was likely to fail.

According to Tooze (2007), the "originality" of National Socialism lies in the regime's rejection of the inevitability of continued Anglo-Saxon hegemony under U.S. economic supremacy. In his unpublished *Second Book,* dictated in the summer of 1928, Hitler locates the sources of the sociopolitical problems facing Germany as fundamentally rooted in the uneven and combined development of capitalism on a world scale conceived through the ideological prism of a hyperracialized social Darwinist conception of world politics. The spectacular rise of America's industrial power vis-à-vis Europe as a whole and Germany in particular was seen by Hitler (and many of his contemporaries)[41] as both a *material threat* and *model to be emulated.* Here, one finds a striking recognition of the competitive logic of capital accumulation binding every productive unit—whether an individual firm or an entire country—into a universal relationship of "coercive comparison" (Barker 2006). As Hitler writes,

> The standard of living of cultured peoples is a general standard that is *not* determined by a people's quantity of individual goods; rather, it is subject to the assessment of surrounding nations and, vice versa, [jointly determined] established by their condition. Today's European dreams of a standard of living that is derived just as much from the possibilities of Europe as from the actual circumstances in America. Through modern technology and the communication it enables, international relations between peoples have become so effortless and intimate that the European—often without realizing it—takes the circumstances of the American life as the benchmark for his own life. (Hitler 2003, 21)

He goes on to emphasize the abundant resources and mass internal market of the North American continent, which undergird America's unparalleled productivity. This favorable ratio of land to population size was viewed as indispensable to a nation's productive power. Hitler particularly focused on America's superior productivity in the automobile industries, in which he took a personal interest as a car enthusiast (see König 2004).

For Hitler, Germany was simply in no position to survive against U.S. competition on the world market. The "size of the internal American market," abundance of raw materials, and vast purchasing power "guarantee the American automobile industry internal sales figures that alone permit production methods that would simply be impossible in Europe due to the lack of internal sales opportunities" (Hitler 2003, 107). For Hitler, then, a fundamental prerequisite to the productive supremacy of American Fordism was the *spatial scale* of its internal market. He saw the productive logic and tendency of economies of scale as playing out at an *international* level. Put simply, to be a great power in economic and military terms, size mattered.

Typical of many far-right political and academic circles in interwar Germany and elsewhere, Hitler's foreign policies were guided by the belief that the world was fracturing into large-scale, self-sufficient, economic empires. The larger the internal market, the more productive and self-sufficient a country could be.[42] "Fordism, in other words, required *Lebensraum*" (Tooze 2007, 10). No amount of technological or scientific development in increasing agricultural and industrial productivity in Germany would, Hitler believed, make up for the country's "disproportionate population in relation to land" as "measured by the proportion of the population of the American union in relation to the territory of the union" (Hitler 2003, 21). This problem of "inadequate *Lebensraum*"[43] confronting the German nation was all the more insufferable given the contemporary conditions of intensified intercapitalist competition in a world of contracting markets. "Competition for the limited market is naturally beginning," Hitler wrote (2003, 25), "and it will become ever fiercer as the number of industrially active nations increases and as the market constricts."

Hitler's thinking on national autarchy, *Lebensraum,* and the challenges emanating from Anglo-Saxon hegemony were hardly novel. Nor was his conception of territorialized space as expressing the "dynamic unity of culture and race" (Murphy 1997, 59). Propounding well-worn social Darwinist conceptions of a biologically determined struggle among states for hegemony, Hitler followed a number of contemporary German geopolitical thinkers[44] who envisaged eastward expansionism as essential to the survival of the German nation and race. *Lebensraum* offered the "necessary" food sources and raw materials, along with the essential outlets for the country's "overpopulation." Building a German-controlled continental economic empire would thus provide the launching pad from which Germany, in alliance with other "revisionist" nations, could challenge Anglo-Saxon imperialism (see Stoakes 1986; Murphy 1997; Ó Tuathail 2006, 23–27; Baranowski 2011, 150–52).

The economic problems confronting Germany—of which Hitler identified insufficient domestic food supplies as the most important—were viewed as derivative of its "limited internal market." In other words, German economic security necessitated expanded *Lebensraum*. This was all the more imperative given the imminent threat posed by America's economic ascendancy. As Hitler put it, to "prevent the world hegemony of the North American continent," the "duty of the National Socialist Movement [is] to strengthen and prepare our own fatherland to the greatest degree possible" to "stand up to the American union" (Hitler 2003, 114, 116).[45] Expanded *Lebensraum* in the East would not only offer Germany the food supplies, raw materials, markets, and economies of scale necessary to effectively compete with the U.S. and other industrializing powers in the "struggle for the world market" (Hitler 2003, 26) but would also eliminate the other primary force menacing Germany, communist Russia.[46]

Hitler had long regarded Bolshevik Russia as the key military and existential enemy of the German people. The importance of anticommunism in the Nazi Weltanschauung and its relation to Hitler's overall grand strategy cannot be overstated.[47] Hitler's "obsession with Russia," as Dale Copeland notes (2001, 124), was in one sense a "straight-forward extension of traditional German geopolitical thinking." The caveat, however, was that this geopolitical "tradition" had been significantly transformed with regard to its strategic aims in Russia since the Brest-Litovsk Treaty—that is, *after* the emergence of Bolshevik Russia.[48] The interwar socioexternal milieu fundamentally informing German geopolitical thought on the conservative and radical Right was, then, from the outset, inculcated with implicit (and often explicit) anticommunist assumptions.

Like all other aspects of Hitler's thinking, the fear and hatred of the communist threat was infused and combined with that of the Jew. From the early 1920s onward, the identification of Bolshevism with the "international Jewish conspiracy" against Germany was a constant theme of Hitler's thought.[49] These ideological constructions entwined with Hitler's economic thinking on the need for expanded *Lebensraum* in the East to enable the Reich to compete with other capitalist powers in the struggle over the world market.

"What India was for England, the territories of Russia will be for us. If only I could make the German people understand what this space means for our future!" Hitler exclaimed (9–11 August 1941, in Hitler 1973, 24).[50]

For these reasons, the Nazis would attempt to telescope over the course of a few decades the territorial imperialisms other European countries had pursued over the previous three centuries. Through this one "last great land grab in the East," Tooze writes, the Nazis could "create the self-sufficient basis both for domestic affluence and the platform necessary to prevail in the coming superpower competition with the United States." The Nazi regime's aggressive expansionism "can thus be rationalized as an intelligible response to the tensions stirred up by the *uneven development* of global capitalism" (Tooze 2007, xxiv–xxv). Indeed, as Hannah Arendt observed, this long history of European colonial plunder, conquest, and genocide was the *direct forebear* of the Holocaust (Arendt 1951; see also Traverso 2003).

The uniqueness of Nazi imperialism and its internally radicalizing dynamics that resulted in the "Final Solution" was not so much the level of violence perpetuated against its victims. Rather, it was the *time-compressed quality* by which the Nazis sought to achieve their expansionist ends and the *people* (white Europeans) against whom it pursued them. As Sven Lindqvist notes (1996, 158), "The Holocaust was unique—in Europe. But the history of Western expansion in other parts of the world shows many examples of total extermination of whole peoples."

The State-Capital-Force Connection: The Changing Nature of Nazi, Industry, and Military Relations

The first few years of Nazi dictatorship saw a number of aggressive moves in foreign policy, the most significant of which included Germany's steps toward rearmament, its withdrawal from the League of Nations (November 1933), and its reoccupation of the Rhineland (March 1936). While it is clear that capitalists played no direct role in these decisions, to narrowly focus on this point would obscure the fact that these policies nonetheless reflected common objectives *shared* by big business, the NSDAP, and the military. This point is further evidenced by the high level of cooperation between heavy industrialists, the military, the civil service, and the NSDAP in rearmament plans. Moreover, there was no effective resistance to Nazi foreign policies within industrial circles during this early period of Nazi rule, even though these groups occupied a social position that gave them the maximum scope for such action (Mason 1995, 61–62). Ignoring these crucial points makes it impossible to explain "why German private capital came to such a speedy arrangement with National Socialism as soon as the latter came to power," Volkmann writes (1990, 193), "or why during the Third Reich [an] almost *complete identity of economic objectives* was achieved."

The "identity of economic objectives" Volkmann notes did not entail an *absolute* identity of interests. Nor should one assume that the relationship between the Nazis and capitalists was static—that their relations were the same before and after the Nazis took power. It is clear that neither Hitler nor the Nazis were the simple "tools" of monopoly capitalists acting at the behest of business interests.[51] Though the Nazis were never *their* party, corporate capitalists *actively* collaborated in bringing the Nazis into power and dutifully served their aims in government.[52] "Rather than obstructing political change as it had done in Germany's first revolution in 1918–19," Adam Tooze writes (2007, 134),

> big business was an active partner in many key facets of Hitler's National Revolution . . . in virtually every context, even settings in which one might have expected some resistance, the regime's political representatives found active collaborators in German business. The autarchy programme, rearmament, even the mass of new regulatory authorities were all backed up and energized by managerial expertise supplied courtesy of German industry.

The complexity of relations between the Nazis and German big capital might be best characterized as one of "conflictual partnership," as Alex Callinicos terms it (2001). This partnership was predicated on a "limited convergence of interests" between the Nazis, the Reichswehr, and specific segments of capital (particularly those allied with the heavy industry faction), all of who shared a number of common objectives—most notably, the elimination of organized labor by force, a rapacious and comprehensive rearmament program, and the pursuit of an imperialist program of expansionism in Central and Southeastern Europe (Callinicos 2001, 395–96; see also Geary 1983, 92–98; Deist et al. 1985, 352–53; Lee and Michalka 1987, 141–48; Berghahn 1996, 17–18; Tooze 2007, 101–6; Baranowski 2011, 155–71). The key point to bear in mind here is that each set of agents (Nazis, capitalists, and military managers) pursued these shared objectives for their own *specific interests,* which corresponded to their particular positions within the German sociopolitical structure, itself part of a wider international capitalist system.

The Nazis sought above all *political* power through the destruction of all potential enemies at home and abroad. To these ends, they needed the economic, political, institutional, and later technological support and capacities of big business and the military. The impetus for members of the military elite to pursue these aims was also primarily a function of their *social* position as the "subject and object at the interface of domestic and international affairs" (Michael Geyer 1983, 108). Nazi-military cooperation developed out of the commonly perceived threat of the revolutionary Left. "Reichswehr officers and the National Socialist leadership readily took for granted the workers' ability to organize another revolution and replayed in their minds the events of 1918 and 1923 again and again" (Michael Geyer 1983, 104).

In Weimar's final years, distributional conflicts over resources and civilian recruitments pitted military leaders increasingly against the so-called agents of the welfare state, tilting them toward the Nazis, the loudest party promoting the obliteration of the organized Left and a massive rearmament campaign. Not surprisingly, a systematic rearmaments program was *the* main goal of Reichswehr policy throughout the Weimar years, as leaders sought to reestablish Germany in the position of a world power (see Deist 1981; Michael Geyer 1985). This external policy also had a distinctly social-domestic component.

A critical corollary of industrialized warfare developing over the Long 19th Century was the profound strengthening of the structural interdependency between a state's military power and industrial capabilities. Under these distinctly modern capitalist conditions, military managers' traditional prestige deriving from their direct organization of the means of violence became overwhelmingly dependent on "their ability to employ society and economy for their own purposes" (Michael Geyer 1983, 108). Moreover, after clearing out the older generation of Reichswehr officers between 1928 and 1930, the officer corps became much less a self-contained caste of Wilhelmine leftovers and more a group of "remarkably young, remarkably bourgeois, and upwardly mobile . . . men who *wanted to become* the German elite through the resurrection of the German army which, in turn, meant rearmament" (Michael Geyer 1983, 111). The institutionalized bias within the Reichswehr toward the revolutionary Left and organized labor was, however, no less extreme, as these younger officers were primarily groomed in the Weimar years under the leadership of the old guard. By 1930, the "stab in the back" myth had been entirely internalized (see Carsten 1973).

Corporate capitalists were, in turn, primarily motivated by profit motives that they believed required a reduction of the social costs of production (i.e., labor) and politically secure markets. Many businessmen within the heavy industrial and automobile sectors also sought the state-guaranteed contracts that a massive expansion of armaments would provide (see Volkmann 1990, 188–89; Michael Geyer 1983, 113). As with the pre-1914 era, rearmaments was a key mediating link between the domestic and international as well as one of the central nodal points of institutional and personal contacts between different agents. "Figures closely associated with Daimler Benz," Neil Gregor notes (1998, 57), were, for example, "among those who played a role in facilitating links between the Reichswehr and industry in the 1920s." Later, these same figures would play a pivotal role in the Nazi rearmament effort.[53] Moreover, state-capital relations crystalized around the *functional* role played by industrial technological innovations in the drive toward national autarky in preparation for war, particularly after 1936–37. The nature of state-capital-military relations was symbiotically connected to the changing technical and sociopolitical exigencies emerging from the rearmaments program.

According to Tim Mason, from the end of 1936 onward, the Nazi regime became increasingly independent of German capitalists. A turning point in this politically autonomizing process was the implementation of the Four-Year Plan in the summer of 1936. During this time, the Wehrmacht was placed under the leadership of Hermann Göring, who supplanted Schacht as the central figure in running the Nazi economy. These developments progressively brought the German economy under party control to serve entirely political-military ends. Hitler sought dramatically to accelerate the drive for autarkic self-sufficiency in preparation for a future war. With these changes, Mason argues, the Nazi state assumed a fully autonomous position, standing over and subordinating all economic interests to its own (Mason 1995; see also Overy 1995).

Mason's thesis is a powerful interpretation of the relationship between big capital and the Nazis. It serves as a useful corrective to orthodox Marxists' crude portrayal of Hitler as the mere puppet of monopoly finance capital.[54] Mason's approach has a number of shortcomings, however. First, it is problematic to reduce the complex relations between private German capital and the National Socialist regime to the more general categories of "politics" and "economics," as Mason does with his "primacy of politics" thesis. This not only constructs a misleading dichotomy between "state" and "society" (see Kershaw 1993, 48–58) but also inadequately takes into account the historical specificities of the international economic context within which the Nazi state operated. For a paramount tendency, witnessed in varying degrees and scales within all capitalist states during the interwar years, was the increasing *statization* of economic life and the simultaneous privatization of the state.[55] This tendency toward the direct *interpenetration* of state and capital was dramatically accelerated during the 1914-18 war. Despite the dismantling of the war economies in the early 1920s, increased levels of state interventionism generally remained: the era of "organized" or "state" capitalism had emerged, however *uneven* its effects and *differentiated* the forms it took.

State interventionism has been a characteristic of capitalism since its inception. The conditions from which capital first emerged were the direct result of the concentrated violence employed by the state. From this process of so-called primitive accumulation, capital, as Marx put it (1976, 926), "arrived *dripping from head to toe,* from every pore, with blood and dirt." What changed over the course of capitalist development was not the existence of state interventionism (both internal and external) but the *forms* this interventionism took. As noted in chapter 3, with the spread of the industrialization process over the 19th century and particularly with its application to military affairs, the structural symbiosis between state and capital reached a qualitatively new level (see Bukharin 1982).

With the fragmentation of the world economy during the 1930s, policymakers, economists, and business interests began to look to alternative models of organizing the economy, and the experience of wartime "collectivism" proved instructive. From these *general* tendencies operating at the world economic and international levels emerged a number of *differentiated* state forms, from the Stalinist "degeneration" of the Soviet Union to FDR's New Deal liberalism to Hitler's National Socialism. Common to all these states was the qualitatively transformed nature of state interventionism: the state now played a *direct* role in the process of production itself. Indeed, in Nazi Germany, "a key feature of the 'radicalization' of the regime in 1937-8 was the development of the state as an independent source of economic power" (Callinicos 2001, 397).[56]

Yet the structural exigencies emerging from both international capitalist competition from above and class struggle from below continued to constrain Hitler's domestic and foreign policies.[57] In other words, the competitive logic of capital accumulation persisted in imposing its own unique imperatives and limits on the Nazi regime. The interesting and rather novel feature of the Nazi regime was the means in which the dictatorship used its power over the state to *gain direct access to the capital accumulation process.* In this way, the Nazis transformed their *political power* into *economic power.* "The Hitler regime's success in setting the parameters for private capital was no mere act of ideological levitation," Callinicos notes (2001, 398), "but was rather closely associated with its success into entrenching itself in control of a large and expanding state capital."

This was most dramatically exemplified in the creation of the Reichswerke in the summer of 1937. This state-controlled, multinational corporation competed in the international economy with other private German capital in its drive to secure the productive assets made accessible by the Nazis' territorial expansion into the East and subsequently France (see Overy 1995, 93–118). Obtaining these productive assets was vital to the Nazis' rearmament drive, especially after its acceleration from 1936 onward, when raw materials and labor inputs were scarce. The drive to autarchic self-sufficiency initiated by the Second Four-Year Plan also shifted the loci of power within the Nazi-capital partnership away from the heavy-industry faction to the newer chemicals and electrical industries (above all, IG Farben and Siemens).[58]

Of all the individual enterprises, the position enjoyed by IG Farben in the Third Reich was truly unique. Despite having been one of the most significant industrial advocates of Stresemann's liberal internationalist strategy during the 1920s, the IG Farben management's acute interest in developing expensive synthetic technologies intersected with the Nazi obsession with national self-sufficiency. After three years of rapacious crude oil production, the regime was still far from achieving its ultimate goal of absolute energy independence. The Nazis thus turned their attention to the chemical industry, which was "not only to be Germany's saviour from dependency on foreign mineral oil but was further intended to meet the economy's overall requirements" (Volkmann 1990, 265). As a consequence of a series of technical decisions, IG Farben managers in turn positioned themselves in an ever-closer alliance with the Nazi regime. After the introduction of the Second Four-Year Plan, this self-serving alliance "took on a new intensity" as the leaders of IG Farben intimately collaborated with the regime's stepped-up efforts for self-sufficiency and rearmaments in preparation for eventual war (Tooze 2007, 227, 115–19; see also Hayes 2001, 163–212).

Despite all the National Socialist rhetoric about working-class gains from the *Volksgemeinschaft,* and contrary to those interpretations of the Third Reich as heralding some kind of "socialist-capitalist" hybrid, a direct predecessor to the postwar German welfare state,[59] at *no time* during the Nazi period did German society ever cease to be capitalist. In fact, the rate of return on capital in German industry dramatically increased after the Nazis took power in 1933. Indeed, profits *surged* in almost all sectors of industry. Despite increasing taxation on private enterprises, the "well-established picture" is that of a sharp "redistribution of income *away* from the working class and in favour of capital over the course of the 1930s" (Tooze 2006a, 7, emphasis added; see also Spoerer 1998, 2007, 106–9). National Socialist policies clearly disproportionately favored corporate capital over all other segments of society.

These points regarding the "pristinely" capitalist character of state-society relations under the Third Reich are particularly significant given the tendency within liberal IR studies to equate capitalism with liberal democracy. For proponents of the democratic peace thesis (DPT), this (implicitly or explicitly) identifies capitalism with cooperative international relations and peace. The example of Nazi state capitalism, however clearly contradicts this "capitalism-democracy-peace" syllogism.[60] Moreover, the DPT argument that had Germany (as well as Italy and Japan) remained a liberal-democratic polity, war would have been highly unlikely is unsatisfactory. This position simply defers the question of *why* these democracies broke down in the first place while ignoring the crucial role *capitalist social forces* played in their disintegrative course.

The Nazi Arms Economy and the Immediate Origins of the Second World War

The central dispute dividing intentionalist and structural-functionalist approaches within the historiographical literature is *not* whether Hitler sought war from the moment he took power. This is largely taken for granted. Instead, the main controversy surrounds the extent of Hitler's room for maneuvering, particularly after 1936–37, when international and domestic circumstances worsened. In other words, was the war Germany ended up fighting in 1939 the one Hitler wanted? According to Tim Mason (1995, 229), it was not that Hitler was "forced to war" but rather that the "wars that the Third Reich actually fought bore very little relation to the wars which he appears to have wanted to fight." From Mason's "structuralist" perspective, this was a consequence of "domestic pressures and constraints which were economic in origin and which also expressed themselves in acute social and political tensions" (229). The main issue of contention thus involves why Hitler decided to launch military aggressions in 1939, thereby risking war with Britain, after having so long sought an alliance with Britain and having planned for a major European war sometime between 1943 and 1945.[61] What, then, were the primary causal forces explaining the specific *timing* of this war?

When explicating these discrepancies in Hitler's ideal *plan* for war from the actual timing it took, focus must be placed on the reinforcing domestic and international dynamics emerging out of the Nazi rearmament drive. Hitler always sought to reclaim the empire's pre-1914 western borders and expand into Central Eastern Europe along the lines of the Brest-Litovsk borders. Only after having secured German continental domination would Hitler then turn the Third Reich's attention outward to challenge North America's rising world economic hegemony.

German policymakers and military managers sought a staggered two-front war against France and Russia, *hoping* for British neutrality.[62] Hitler's immediate strategic focus—one shared by the military generals—was to destroy France and then immediately turn the Wehrmacht's attention to its primary objective: "to shatter the universal danger of Russian Bolshevism at its centre of power," thereby allowing for "the conquest of new living space in the east and its ruthless Germanization" (Hitler quoted in Copeland 2000, 125). Crucially, this was to be achieved *before* Soviet leaders could complete the country's rapid industrialization and translate its vast economic potential into military power (see Copeland 2000, chap. 5). Such were the *broad* contours of Hitler's geopolitical thinking stretching from at least 1928 to WWII and dramatically radicalized thereafter. This was *not* a stage-by-stage plan for war, and even if there had been such a plan, events unfolded very differently.

On three separate occasions over the 1930s, the Nazis sought dramatically to hasten the intensity and speed of Germany's armaments-fueled economic recovery. In each instance (1934, 1936–37, and 1939), the regime confronted a potentially paralyzing balance of payment constraints, raw material and (later) labor shortages, and production bottlenecks.[63] The acceleration of the armaments program in 1936–37 is generally viewed as the critical point of no return for the Nazi regime. The Four-Year Plan (in its first and especially second incarnations) marked a qualitatively new phase in Nazi economic policies, "one that was bound to have drastic consequences because its objectives were set so high that they inevitably exceeded Germany's economic potential and could not but lead to territorial expansion" (Volkmann 1990, 279).

Hitler's decision to intensify the Nazi armaments drive in 1936 must be situated within the entwining domestic-international contexts linking the Nazis' changing socioeconomic and political circumstances to the rapidly altering international constellation of forces of which it also formed a constituent part. The key international events here included Italy's war against Ethiopia; the outbreak of the Spanish Civil War; and the steady destabilization of the Japanese government, culminating in the military coup against liberal prime minister Okada Keisuke on 6 March 1936, opening the door to the Japanese invasion of Manchuria the following summer.

The Italian-Ethiopian conflict of 1935–36 provided the necessary cover for the long-held German conservative aim of remilitarizing the Rhineland, which the Nazis successfully pursued in March 1936. The timing of Hitler's move in the Rhineland was also a result of the increasing *social unrest* in Germany, which made a potential foreign policy conquest particularly attractive to Nazi leaders at the time. As Kershaw explains (1993, 119),

> The opportunist exploitation of the diplomatic upheaval—which Hitler feared would be shortlived—arising from Mussolini's Abyssinian adventure was coupled with internal considerations: the need to lift popular morale, revitalize the sinking élan of the Party, and to reconsolidate the support for the regime which various indicators suggested had seriously waned by early 1936.[64]

Thus, already in early 1936, a number of domestic and international factors were coming together to progressively subvert an already fragile European balance of power. With the outbreak of the Spanish Civil War in July 1936, however, the balance of geosocial forces in Europe was irrevocably destabilized. Not since the Bolshevik Revolution had the *fusion* of ideological, socioeconomic, and geopolitical-military conflicts taken such an acute and unadulterated form. The Spanish Civil War represented the reignition of an open "war of maneuver" (in Gramsci's terms) between the forces of revolution and counterrevolution in Europe.

The Spanish war brought fascist Italy, Japan, and Nazi Germany into an ever-closer alliance against the Soviet Union. The November 1936 Anti-Comintern Pact between Japan and Germany, with Italy joining a year later, exemplified this unifying tendency (Overy 1999b, 99–100; Whealey 2005, 27–28). Within this nascent reconfiguration of strategic alliances, the civil war tipped the balance of power between Italy and Germany in the latter's favor. For Italy, bogged down in two simultaneous small-war fronts (Ethiopia and now Spain), the bleeding economy became dependent on the Third Reich. This brought the Nazi regime significant economic and political gains at Italy's expense, eventually rendering the Italian economy subservient to Nazi interests. "The costs of the Ethiopian War, the East African pacification campaigns, and involvement in Spain," Brian Sullivan writes (1999, 189), "combined to gravely weaken Italy's economy and military . . . The result was a rapid decline in Italian strength from a high point in 1934–35, when Mussolini could have prevented the *Anschluss* and defied Britain in the Mediterranean, to a position of near-impotence in 1938–9."

The Spanish Civil War significantly undermined Italy's position in Central and Southeastern Europe while dramatically exacerbating internal divisions within British and French society (see chap. 6). By dividing Western Europe, the Spanish war opened the way for the Nazis to pursue territorial gains in the East (Whealey 2005). Further, by bringing Germany and Italy together on the side of Franco's Falangistas, the European fascist powers became engaged in a kind of proxy war with the Soviet Union. The effect was to bolster calls within leading Nazi circles for an immediate stepping-up of Nazi rearmaments in anticipation of the coming "showdown" with Bolshevism.

The inevitability of war with a rising Bolshevik-Russian power now became an increasingly prominent theme in Hitler's meetings and personal conversations. The Four-Year Plan was based on the essential premise of the coming "historical conflict" with Bolshevism, as Hitler made clear in the secret August 1936 Four-Year Plan memorandum: *"Since Marxism, through its victory in Russia, has established one of the greatest empires in the world . . . this question has become a menacing one. . .* The means of military power available to [Soviet Russia] are in the meantime increasing rapidly from year to year" (Stackelberg and Winkle, doc. 4.3, 196).

At a December 1936 cabinet meeting, Hitler again depicted the threat of Bolshevism, arguing "Europe is already divided into two camps . . . Germany can only wish that the danger be deferred till we're ready. When it comes, seize the opportunity." As with the 5 November 1937 "Hossbach memorandum," Hitler anticipated "a great world showdown" in "five or six years," according to Goebbels's reported comments in February 1937. In late January, Hitler had said that he hoped Germany would have six years to prepare but that the country would act early if an advantageous situation arose (quoted in Kershaw 1993, 124–25). In other words, the race was on. Henceforth, Germany would rearm at breakneck speed.

Yet as the intensified pace of rearmaments proceeded, the resources

needed for its continuation far surpassed those available in the German domestic economy. Schacht's original plans, drafted in the summer of 1933, for
rearmaments within the limits set by German capitalism's productive capacities were now scrapped. Fault lines opened within the Nazi leadership, eventually leading to Schacht's dismissal as he increasingly voiced his concerns
over the "economic limits" hindering the continuation of Nazi armaments
policy (Schacht quoted in Tooze 2007, 209). At this critical juncture, the German economy was again hovering on the edge of economic crisis.

In 1936–37, the German economy was suffering from a massive shortage
in foreign currency reserves (a balance-of-payments crisis), raw materials,
and food supplies. Indeed, already in 1935, butter and meat were being rationed in major German cities. In January–February 1937, the regime imposed rationing of nonferrous metals and steel (Tooze 2007, 231–32, 659). A
dramatic increase in raw material inputs was thus required not only directly
to channel into rearmaments but also to export.[65] The shortfall in foreign
exchange became so severe that substantial quantities of weapons and machine tools for their production were exported (Mason 1995, 62–63; see also
Volkmann 1990; Leitz 2002). "In early 1937 and then again in early 1939,"
Tooze notes (2006b, 4),

> it was the armaments programme that bore the brunt of the Nazi regime's
> efforts to live within the balance of payments constraint. Armaments pro-
> duction was cut back, in the first instance to reduce the demand for imported
> materials, most notably iron and copper ore, and at the same time to release
> industrial capacity, labour and raw materials for the production of exports. At
> its most crude the trade-off involved exporting weapons intended for the
> Wehrmacht, or machine-tools with which to make them, to pay for imports
> of food and raw materials.

Nazi rearmaments, then, remained vitally dependent on fluctuations in the
international economy. Despite the regime's commitment to prioritizing rearmaments within a framework of national self-sufficiency, its ability to do
so was continually constrained by the economic limits imposed by the uneven and interactive development of capitalism on a world scale. The Nazis'
acceleration of armaments from 1936–37 onward was further propelled by
the pressures of an international arms race with the Soviet Union—and subsequently the Western powers—that the regime itself had unleashed (see
Dülffer 1976b; Michael Geyer 1985).[66]

Increasing signs of the regime's sociopolitical destabilization coupled with the structural disequilibrium within the Nazi economy in 1936–37. By the latter half of 1938, an overheated German economy, with more than one million unoccupied jobs, created a precarious socioeconomic situation for the Nazi regime. During this time, the German working class began to show signs of passive resistance via declining work discipline and productivity, while the general legitimacy of the Nazi regime seemed increasingly in question. Having internalized the "stab in the back" myth of WWI, Nazi leaders "felt it necessary to purchase at least the passive acquiescence of the much-abused German working class" (Mason 1995, 297). The ghoulish specter of November 1917 continued to haunt the Nazi leaders, as indicators pointed to a lack of any general enthusiasm for war among the public between 1936 and 1939. According to Albert Speer (2003, 300), Hitler had indicated in private conversations "that after the experience of 1918 one could not be cautious enough."

While the severity and scope of these economic and sociopolitical problems facing the Nazi regime in 1936–37 remain the subject of great debate, it seems clear that the frantic pace of armaments could not have lasted much longer or it would have resulted in a collapse of the German economy, if not the regime itself. Without territorially expanding the Nazis' productive base to incorporate new sources of raw materials and labor, the war economy would be brought to a halt. As Mason put it (1995, 51), a "war for the plunder of manpower and materials lay square in the dreadful logic of German economic development under National Socialist rule."

This was in fact made clear in a report by Major General Friedrich Fromm on the economic consequences of the proposed expansion of Nazi rearmaments outlined in the summer of 1936. According to Fromm's report, "Shortly after the rearmament phase the Wehrmacht must be employed, otherwise there must be a reduction in demands or in the level of war readiness." Thus, before committing to the hasty expansion entailed by the Second Four-Year Plan, the Nazi political leadership had to first answer the question of whether there was "a firm intention of employing the Wehrmacht at a date already fixed?" (quoted in Tooze 2007, 213).

Fromm's report is particularly significant for two reasons. First, it made clear the point of no return that Nazi policymakers were passing. This would seemingly add credence to the "intentionalist" school. Since the Four-Year Plan of 1936 called for the Wehrmacht's readiness by 1940 (thus the title), it apparently suggested a clear timetable for war. Such an interpretation would be mistaken, however, because Hitler soon modified the time scale suggested in the plan in view of the numerous economic setbacks the Nazi armaments economy faced in 1936–37.[67] This was made clear in the "Hossbach meeting" of 5 November 1937.[68] At the meeting, Hitler made plain Germany's need to resolve the *Lebensraum* problem by no later than 1943–45. By that time, Hitler anticipated that Germany's relative advantage in the international arms race would be in *decline* given the continuing economic and fiscal constraints facing the regime. "If we did not act by 1943–45, any year could, owing to a lack of reserves, produce the food crisis, to cope with which the necessary foreign exchange was not available, and this must be regarded as a 'warning point of the regime'" (quoted in Noakes and Pridham 1974, 526). Hitler also outlined the multitude of sociopolitical and economic problems facing the regime. Pointing to the decline of popular morale, expressed in Hitler's usually mystical terms, he argued that "sterility was setting in, and in its train disorders of a social character must arise in course of time, since political and ideological ideas remain effective only so long as they furnish the basis for the realization of the essential vital demands of a people." He also emphasized the "difficulties of food supply" and the need to acquire "areas producing raw materials" in close geographical proximity. If "the security of our food situation" was "the principal point at issue," then "the space needed to ensure it can be sought only in Europe" and not through the liberal-capitalist means of distant colonies (quoted in Noakes and Pridham 1974, 523–26).

The *Anschluss,* the annexation of the Sudetenland, the occupation of Prague, and finally the attack on Poland were all "risks" Hitler was willing take to solve the myriad socioeconomic problems confronting the regime in the midst of a progressively hostile and well-armed international environment. The *Anschluss* and subsequent incorporation of the Czech industrial heartlands provided the much needed replenishing of German economic resources. The precocious timing of such overt acts of Nazi expansionism was, above all, "dictated by the dynamics of rearmament and directed towards safeguarding 'major requirements in the event of war'" (Volkmann 1990, 327, in part quoting General Thomas).[69]

Despite the economic benefits accrued from these Nazi acts of expansionism, such stopgap measures were not enough in light of the increasingly strenuous demands armaments were placing on the overall German economy. The economy continued to be plagued by severe structural problems. In October 1938, the Reich Defense Committee reported that *"in consequence of Wehrmacht demands* (the occupation of the Sudetenland) and unlimited construction on the Westwall so tense a situation in the economic sector occurred (coal, supplies for industries, harvest of potatoes and turnips, food supplies) that continuation of tension past 10 October would have made an [economic] catastrophe inevitable" (quoted in Murray 1992, 90). German military generals feared that such overt Nazi foreign policy aggressions would lead to a Europe-wide war that the regime was militarily unprepared to fight given the unyielding problems in the armaments economy.

After the *Anschluss* (March 1938), a degenerating international milieu took on a new urgency as it became increasingly apparent that the United States was now aligning against Germany. President Roosevelt's 17 May 1938 decision to sign into law the Naval Expansion Bill, which spent $1.15 billion on the navy, represented the "largest peacetime military appropriation in history" (Tooze 2007, 249). France and Britain also finally began to show *some* signs of emerging from their military slumber,[70] while Stalin continued to pursue a breakneck Soviet rearmament program (see Harrison 1988). From the summer of 1938 on, the Nazis were thus facing, as Göring ominously proclaimed, the prospect of a "world war, in which" Germany's enemies would "include France and England, Russia, [and] America" (quoted in Tooze 2007, 255).

As Göring and almost everyone else in the Nazi leadership recognized, the material superiority of such a grouping was overwhelming. So, too, was the economic case against war in 1938, as Hitler's closest economic and military advisers (including Göring) made clear. The financial and economic capacities of the Reich were stretched to the breaking point, and the Wehrmacht was unprepared for war. In September 1938, Hitler reluctantly backed down from conflict and accepted the Munich Agreement. The full military-industrial implications of fighting a war first against *both* France and Britain and then the Soviet Union only became apparent *after* Munich. Hitler and Nazi policymakers not unrealistically continued to seek British neutrality but now *planned* for war against the United Kingdom. On the day of Munich, Major General Thomas received "the instructions: all preparations for war against England, target 1942!" (quoted in Tooze 2007, 288).

Like much of the military leadership, Major General Thomas was, however, extremely pessimistic about the international balance of forces in late 1938 and after. In a May 1939 report, Thomas detailed how Britain, France, and the United States would outspend a German-Italian combination by no less than two billion Reichsmarks in the following year. As Britain had at its disposal "the entire Empire and the United States as an armoury and reservoir of raw materials," Germany was clearly outmatched (quoted in Tooze 2007, 310).[71]

The devastating supremacy of power represented by this military combination of liberal-capitalist empires and the Soviet Union meant that the paramount diplomatic question facing Nazi policymakers in 1939 was how to consolidate their alliance partners while putting off a war against the Soviet Union. Faced with such an overwhelming superiority of forces, Hitler thus decided to seek a temporary alliance with Stalin. This was a *tactical* rather than *strategic* shift. Hitler and the Nazi leadership never ceased viewing the destruction of the Bolshevik-Soviet threat and the expanded *Lebensraum* it would provide as their primary objectives.[72] "Everything that I undertake is directed against Russia," Hitler notoriously told the Swiss commissioner of the League of Nations in 1939; "If those in the West are too stupid and too blind to understand this, then I shall be forced to come to an understanding with the Russians to beat the West, and then, after its defeat, turn with all my concerted force against the Soviet Union" (quoted in Kershaw 1993, 125).

As the balance-of-payments crisis in Germany worsened in 1939, leading Hitler to proclaim that the Reich must "export or die!," and steel shortages became ubiquitous, procurements for the Wehrmacht actually *decreased* over the spring and summer. Hence, from approximately 1939 on, Nazi political leaders no longer believed that time was on their side. Further postponements of war would put Germany at a disadvantage in the international arms race as the country's industrial-financial resources were near fully exhausted. Foreign exchange and the goods to pay for them would have run out within a few *months* had the Nazis not gone to war in September 1939. Ammunition stockpiles for the Wehrmacht covered a meager fourteen days of heavy fighting, and estimated labor shortages had now reached approximately one million workers (Volkmann 1990, 365–72; Tooze 2007, 293–304).

Given the persistence of clear *economic* limits hampering any further acceleration of German rearmaments and the Nazi political leadership's intent on the "inevitable showdown" with the international Jewish conspiracy now stretching from Moscow to Washington,[73] the time for war was now. This was necessary before the productive-military gap between the liberal-capitalist and fascist powers turned any more unfavorably against the latter.[74] As even Hitler recognized, no further substantial increases in economic potential were possible. Making explicit reference to *economic* pressures, Hitler told the commanders in chief on 22 August 1939, "We have nothing to lose; we have everything to gain. Because of our restrictions [*Einschrank-ungen*] our economic situation is such that we can only hold out for a few more years. Göring can confirm this. We have no other choice, we must act" (Germany. Auswärtiges Amt. 1949, doc. 201).

CONCLUSION

The political economy of Third Reich is perhaps best conceptualized as one of "permanent crisis," reflecting and reinforcing what Giorgio Agamben (2005) has referred to as the "permanent state of exception" politically insti-tutionalized by the Nazi regime.[75] The specificity of the crisis in the Nazi arms economy in the middle of 1939, however, may not have represented a generalized, "organic crisis" that threatened to bring down the entire Nazi sociopolitical system, as suggested by Kaiser (1989) and Mason (1989). It would be a mistake to conceive the war as the regime's *only* option for avoid-ing imminent sociopolitical collapse.[76] Nonetheless, the gravity and persis-tence of the structural disequilibrium within the Nazi economy was serious enough to make Hitler, as he retrospectively told Mussolini in March 1940, to "begin immediately with the counterattack [*Abwehr*] even at the risk of thereby precipitating the war" with "the Western powers two or three years earlier" than he had originally envisioned (quoted in Tooze 2007, 317).

In sum, the Nazi regime's rearmament drive to prepare itself for a Euro-pean war by 1943–45 and free itself from its dependency on the world econ-omy made it increasingly difficult for the German economy to reproduce it-self. Under these circumstances, Hitler expedited his expansionist policies and risked drawing Britain into a war earlier than he had originally planned. Hence, the historiographical and IR consensus on a total "primacy of poli-tics" emerging after 1936 must be called into question as *international eco-nomic pressures* continually constrained and in many instances determined Nazi foreign policymaking. If there was a causal primacy involved here, it was the "primacy" of the international political economy. This is in no way to *deny* the significance of ideology in Nazi foreign policymaking. Rather, ideology was always rooted and reproduced through social processes and sets of relations that determined how and to what extent its efficacy could be felt as a "material force" itself.[77]

In contrast to deterrence theorists' claims, Hitler's invasion of Poland was not a consequence of "miscalculation" or "misperception." Though Hit-

ler still wished for British neutrality, he and the Wehrmacht nonetheless prepared for war with Britain and in fact likely expected it.[78] As examined in the
next chapter, if there was any fundamental "misperception" among policymakers in the coming of war, it was the persistent inability of British and
French conservatives to recognize the Soviet Union as a necessary and willing alliance partner against the Nazi-fascist powers. In a very different way
from the Nazi case, the role of "anti-Bolshevik" ideology was thus decisive in
the outbreak of war.

CHAPTER 6

Class, Security, War: The International Political Economy of Appeasement

FOR POST-WWII realists in the United States, there was nothing more tragic than British appeasement policy. During the Cold War, the historic failure of this policy guided U.S. foreign policymakers in their resolve to counter, by force if necessary, the perceived aggressions of the Soviet Union. Even after the demise of the Soviet Union, the "Munich analogy" remains a particularly effective discursive battering ram for justifying interventionist policies and criticizing political opponents.[1]

For most classical realists, appeasement represented the "corrupted policy of compromise" that had mistaken "a policy of imperialism for a policy of the status quo" (Morgenthau 1993, 78; see also Kissinger 1957, 3). For contemporary structural realists, appeasement is conceptualized as a pathological consequence of the alliance dynamics of the 1930s multipolar system. Instead of forming a balancing coalition against Nazi Germany, between 1933 and March 1939 both Great Britain and France preferred a strategy of "buck-passing" or "distancing" that sought to place the burden of defense on the other (see Waltz 1979, 165–67; Posen 1984; Christensen and Snyder 1990; Walt 1992; Christensen 1997; Schweller 1998; Mearsheimer 2001).

In the liberal historiography, appeasement is primarily conceived as a result of the idiosyncratic shortcomings and misguided thinking of Chamberlain and his closest advisers. From both realist and liberal perspectives, appeasement is viewed as a consequence of policymakers' *misperceptions* of the Nazi threat (see Alexandroff and Rosecrance 1977; Jervis 1982; Rosecrance and Stein 1993; Powell 1996). In the post-WWII IR literature, appeasement is thus conceived in almost entirely negative terms—a misguided policy that allowed dangerous threats to fester and grow.

Although numerous IR texts uncritically repeat these liberal and realist interpretations (see Holsti 1992; Snow and Brown 1996; Kegley and Wittkopf 2004) or at best remain firmly embedded within realist-dominated state-centric theoretical assumptions (Beck 1989; Treisman 2004; Ripsman and Levy 2008), there are many problems with these accounts, particularly the lack of social and historical contextualization. In IR, the concept of appeasement has been developed without due attention to the socioeconomic, ideological, and political conditions faced by policymakers. Consequently, analyses have mistakenly identified what, given these conditions, policymakers hoped to achieve by appeasing Nazi Germany.

In this chapter, I show that threats to social order and the political status quo overrode British policymakers' concerns regarding Nazi Germany's territorial ambitions. These concerns were, in turn, rooted in the British ruling classes' desire to shore up the "UK-centred system of accumulation" (Arrighi 2005, 103), a goal that entailed the defense of the empire and reconstruction of a London-centered international financial order. Appeasement was a form of "crisis strategy," a preventative diplomacy that sought to ward off multiple socioeconomic and (geo)political crises by assuming limited foreign policy commitments (Gustav Schmidt 1983).

Conventional IR accounts exclusively focusing on the territorial threats posed by German power miss this multidimensional nature of British policy, which was both inward and outward looking. From a pure balance-of-power perspective, the label *appeasement* is itself a misnomer. At least until January 1939, the central threat that concerned key British policymakers was not German *territorial* expansion but the *social* threat of Bolshevism abroad and the emergence of a strong Left at home (Halperin 1996). For many British elites, "fascism was not an unmitigated evil" but "an effective weapon against communism and socialism and a barrier to the expansion of bolshevism beyond the borders of the Soviet Union" (Carley 1999a, 3–4). British policymakers were not appeasing German interests but actively and strategically using Nazi power, in Lloyd George's words, as a "bulwark against communism in Europe" (quoted in Schuman 1939, 340). Hence, if appeasement is defined as a "policy of making unilateral concessions in the hope of avoiding conflict" (Treisman 2004, 345), then *conflict* must be conceived in broader social terms that transcend strategic balance-of-power calculations.

In rethinking the origins and aims of British appeasement policy, this chapter problematizes a defining moment in the ideological self-representation and development of Anglo-Saxon IR theory after WWII.[2] More particularly, it demonstrates the fundamental deficiencies of mainstream IR's state-centric theoretical assumptions. From such presuppositions, IR scholars have inadequately understood the origins of appeasement policy, its purpose, and its meaning to the actors involved.

The challenge in analyzing British appeasement policy and the foreign policymaking process more generally is to provide a theoretical framework capable of conceptualizing these multifaceted determinations (socioeconomic, strategic, ideological) of state actions as constituting a single, internally related social totality. Overcoming this challenge, a distinctively historical materialist approach to appeasement offers a social theory unique in its methodological commitment to radical historicism and a holistic, social-relational ontology. Against criticisms of Marxism's alleged "class reductionism" and/or "economism" (Ruggie 1998b, 859; de Goede 2003, 40; Narizny 2003, 204; Hobson 2007; see also Bieler and Morton 2008), this chapter emphasizes the central role of ideology and ideas, particularly the anticommunist (or anti-Bolshevik) ideologies guiding and legitimating British (and French) foreign policies.

Ideology and socioeconomic structure (and class interests) are *not* "independent" or "autonomous" causal factors relating to separate, discretely constituted ideational and material spheres but are *internally related* within a single social totality. The British and French elites' anti-Bolshevism is only understandable when we ask what kind of social structure they saw themselves defending and what position they held in its hierarchy of social relations. Anti-Bolshevism was not some irrational prejudice but rather was immanent to the process through which individuals are socialized in capitalist societies. The emergence and sticking power of anti-Bolshevik ideology among British policymakers was a form of identity production structurally inscribed within capitalist state-society relations. That Bolshevism and capitalism were perceived as antithetical socioeconomic and political orders was, then, hardly a coincidence.[3] The inclusion of ideology in a historical materialist analysis, therefore, can be viewed neither as a contingent causal factor (as in much constructivist analysis) nor as trumping other "materialist" determinations—a kind of "get out of jail free" card for an otherwise materialist explanation of British policymaking. Both of these views would assume an *external* relationship between ideology and socioeconomic structure.

The analysis in this chapter proceeds in four sections and is structured along specific theoretical themes. The first section provides an international historical sociological account of the British state and foreign policymaking structures. It examines the evolution of foreign policymaking structures, particularly the ascendancy of a "City-Treasury-Bank nexus" in the post–First World War British state. It then analyzes the various mechanisms linking state and capital in a relationship of *structural interdependence,* compelling state managers to identify military-security interests with the maintenance of capitalist social relations. These points are illustrated in the second section, which offers a reconceptualization of the relations between military-security and political-economic interests in terms of capitalist social structure through an analysis of the pace and scope of the British rearmament effort. This shows how the City-Treasury-Bank perspective, favoring liberal economic orthodoxy and the pursuit of "Gladstonian finance," continually subordinated British military-security requirements to financial concerns and the maintenance of internal social stability.

The third section analyzes how the hegemony of the City-Treasury-Bank nexus engendered an institutional bias against conflict with Germany (Nazi or otherwise). It details how British elites sought to strengthen economic and financial relations with the Nazis to deter the spread of Bolshevism abroad and fight socialism at home through a revival of the domestic and world economy. The section elucidates the theoretical claims regarding the internal relations between capitalist political economy and ideology, a point further explored in the final section, which illustrates how the debates over the creation of an Anglo-Franco-Soviet alliance were deterred by the fundamental role of anti-Bolshevik ideology and the fear of war-generated revolution. The conclusion draws out some of the more general theoretical conclusions for IR emerging from a historical materialist account of appeasement.

THE BRITISH STATE IN AN INTERNATIONAL
CAPITALIST CONTEXT

In examining British policymaking during the 1930s, attention must be paid to the changing configurations of social forces and structures of policymaking power within the state. After the First World War, the British Foreign Office lost its dominant position in the foreign policymaking process, as the center of power decisively shifted to the Treasury, which worked in close collaboration with the Bank of England and City interests (Shay 1977, 25, 91, 282; Paul M. Kennedy 1981, 231, 252; Gustav Schmidt 1983, 111; Forbes 2000, 13). This shift in policymaking power was symptomatic of long-term socioeconomic and political changes connected with the rise of the world economy during the 19th century.

During this period, the interconnected processes of industrialization and the progressive development of an externally oriented British capitalist system resulted in the "workshop of the world" continually running a commodity trade deficit—a deficit offset by the invisible surpluses generated by the City and the profits it derived from its interests in banking, insurance, shipping, and overseas investments (Hobsbawm 1968, 144–45; Cain and Hopkins 1993b, 91). These economic developments were, in turn, achieved through a series of monetary and commercial reforms that transformed the central institutions in the British state and society. This resulted in the institutionalization of a set of key common economic objectives uniting the Treasury, Bank of England, and City interests to a policy of "sound money," free trade, and a strict adherence to the gold-standard regime.

The Development of the British State-Capital Nexus

By the early 20th century, a particular form of "structural interdependence" emerged between these financial institutions and those segments of capital (finance, shipping, insurance, and colonial capital) at the heart of the City. The "pursuit of fiscal and monetary orthodoxy by the Bank and Treasury sustained the gold standard and later sterling's exchange value" and underpinned the City's international financial role. These policies further served as an "independent source of power for the Bank and Treasury in their own respective domains—that is, in the banking system and the state bureaucracy" (Ingham 1984, 6–8).

The development of this special relationship between the Treasury, Bank of England, and City was further reinforced through institutional, familial, and social links.[4] With the implementation of the Northcote-Trevelyan reforms in 1870, the Treasury was converted into the "superintending" department in Whitehall. At the same time, the social composition of the entire civil service took on a more uniform color as departmental staffs were now recruited almost exclusively from a small elite class of students passing through the doors of the major public schools and Oxbridge (Gowan 1987). Consequently, the proportion of permanent secretaries from public schools climbed to two-thirds between 1900 and 1919 (Scott Newton 1996, 12–13). From the 1870s on, this same elite educational system was flooded with the sons of financiers and bankers. In addition, it began producing its own stream of new entrants to the City, resulting in a close and personal inter-mingling of present and future economic and administrative elites (see Ing-ham 1984; Lisle-Williams 1984; Perry Anderson 1987; Cain and Hopkins 1993b).

The upshot of these developments was the formation of a City-Treasury-Bank relationship constituting the "core institutional nexus" (Ingham 1984) within Britain. This came to be the chief proponent of a liberal-internationalist hegemonic project and capital accumulation strategy based on free trade and a London-centered gold standard.[5] With the institutional changes within the British state resulting from the exigencies of the WWI, the long-term trend toward City-Treasury-Bank hegemony in foreign policy-making became a reality.[6] Even after the Great Depression of 1929–33 and Britain's turn toward imperial trade preferences (institutionalized in the "Ottawa System"), the City-Treasury-Bank nexus's hegemony largely survived.[7] This resulted, in part, from the increased interpenetration of financial and industrial interests that had developed with the emergence of an oligopolis-tic economy during the interwar years (Hobsbawm 1968; Barratt Brown 1970, 97, 144; Overbeek 1980; Hannah 1983; Cain and Hopkins 1993a, 14–20). This financial-industrial bloc was further cemented by a common ideologi-cal animosity against the threat of Bolshevism abroad and socialism at home, a crucial component of a larger Weltanschauung instantiated within capitalist class relations.[8]

For these reasons, the formation of a Conservative-dominated national government in 1931 and its foreign policies found widespread support in fi-nancial and industrial circles throughout the 1930s. Evidence of pro-appeasement sentiment within the City as well as export-oriented industries is abundant (see, for example, Einzig 1941; Bernd Jürgen Wendt 1983; Gustav Schmidt 1986; Scott Newton 1996; Forbes 2000; Kirshner 2007; Ferguson 2008). While segments of the capitalist class differed over *how* to appease German interests, they were broadly united with the majority of British pol-icymakers in their efforts to secure peace at almost any price. Indeed, even the most traditionally anti-German businessmen, such as the Anglophile partners of the House of Morgan, became "ardent backers of appeasement" (Horn 2005, 536). The extensive sources of the national government's social power base, along with the hegemony of the City-Treasury-Bank establish-ment within British policymaking, helps explain why alternative strategies to appeasement were continually ignored.[9]

The "Structural Interdependence" of State and Capital

The problem of how to theorize the "state-capital" nexus and it relation to foreign policymaking, geopolitical rivalry, and war requires some attention, particularly given the long debates in state theory.[10] A clear point that emerged from these debates (and that was accepted by Marxists and non-Marxists alike) was the potential for a divergence of interests between capitalists and state managers (see Poulantzas 1973; Barker 1978a; Miliband 1983; Block 1987; Jessop 1990; David Harvey 2003; Ashman and Callinicos 2006). So-called instrumentalist theories of the state (Marxist or otherwise) have largely proven overly simplistic if nonetheless illuminating in pointing to the sociological links between state managers and capitalist classes (Miliband 1969; Domhoff 1983).

Indeed, tracing the many ways in which particular factions of capital come to encroach on specific state apparatuses is an important piece of the puzzle but leaves much unexplained. Simply put, policymakers and business interests do not always see eye to eye on many issues, and the latter's influence in actual foreign policy decision making is often far from clear. The potential transformation of capitalists' *economic* power into *political* power must be explored from a structural perspective.

A more sophisticated theory of the capitalist state is thus required. This would, among other things, necessarily allow for as well as *explain* the formation of interests *specific* to state managers and capitalists arising from their distinct location within the matrix of sociopolitical relations in their interlocking domestic and international environments. What is needed, then, is some form of *structural* theory of the state that also offers the analytical tools to identify *who* the major capitalists (or factions of capital) are and *why* they act the way they do. This would aim to uncover the often hidden social ontology of capitalist agents in their concrete relations to state action and foreign policy outputs within the "external social-historical milieu," as Trotsky (1962) called it, of a strategically interdependent plurality of differentiated societies.

From this perspective, state managers and capitalists can be viewed as constituting two distinct groups of actors who are drawn into strategic alliances with one another in pursuit of their own *distinctive interests* (Block 1987; Callinicos 2007). Broadly speaking, capitalists need state support to secure the necessary general conditions for capital accumulation and more particularly to advance their specific interests in the international economic arena. State managers, in turn, seek to maintain and increase the relative power of their state, which necessarily depends on the various resources produced by the capital accumulation process, most obviously taxes (Ashman and Callinicos 2006, 113–15). State managers and capitalists are, therefore, mutually dependent on one another. The state-capital relation can be thus best understood as one of *structural interdependency* (Harman 1991).

Following Fred Block (1987), the relation of structural interdependency can be further specified through the identification of various "subsidiary" and "structural" mechanisms engendering state managers to serve capitalist ends *irrespective* of whether capitalists directly intervene in the policymaking process.[11] Subsidiary mechanisms include, among other things, the institutional and social channels through which capitalists and state managers directly relate. This results in the ideological inculcation of state managers as "capitalists" through the encroachment of capitalist norms and social logics on state structures. These subsidiary mechanisms alone are, however, inadequate in explaining foreign policy outputs. For even when the "ruling class" does not directly rule, policymakers overwhelmingly tend to serve capitalist objectives—above all, continued capital accumulation (Davidson 2010).

Addressing this issue, Block identifies two further *structural* mechanisms. The first is captured by the idea of "business confidence." The survival of the state apparatus depends on the maintenance of a certain level of economic growth since (1) the capacity of a state to finance its own activities directly depends on the conditions of the economy (that is, the state needs taxes); (2) public support for a government will decrease if the economy declines; and (3) if a state fails to safeguard the interests of capitalists by pursuing policies resulting in economic decline, capitalists can invest elsewhere (Block 1987, 58–65).

A second structural mechanism is the level of class struggle within and beyond the state. In the British case, this mechanism dissuaded state managers from working with labor in rearmament efforts as they feared both the expansion of state functions, as experienced during WWI, and a consequent intensification of class conflict. State managers thus sought to maintain as much policymaking autonomy as possible to avoid power-sharing agreements with labor. Such policies ended up crippling Britain's military preparedness for war and hence provided additional support for policymakers' logic of appeasement. Further, Whitehall's dual strategy of limited rearmament and appeasement was structured through the *international* level of class conflict, which also tied into the *transnational* role of revolutionary ideology.

A third structural mechanism Block does not consider is that of direct geopolitical-military rivalry, the external whip that compels each state to facilitate a certain level of capitalist development or face potential peripheralization. In the face of interstate exigencies, state managers will thus *likely* pursue policies generally congruent with sustained capital accumulation.

These arguments are not, however, intended to suggest that in *every* historical case, capitalists and state managers will promote policies entirely harmonious with the successful reproduction of capitalist social relations. In the case of Nazi Germany (chap. 5), state managers and capitalists were "conflictual partners," and the policies that they pursued were not always in the best interests of capital (either in the particular or general long-term sense) (see Davidson 2014). The Holocaust in particular provides at least one example where state policies were antithetical to the long-run interests of capital in general: the extermination of the Jews was certainly not dictated by the needs of German capitalism. But even in this case, at least an indirect connection can be made between capitalism and the Holocaust. For Nazism became a mass movement during the Great Depression and was supported by significant sections of big capital that were motivated to crush organized labor. Hence, as Alex Callinicos notes (2001, 406), "German big business allied itself to a movement whose racist and pseudo-revolutionary ideology drove it towards the Holocaust, particularly because of its failure to transform German society. Thus—not directly, but in this nonetheless important way— capitalism was causally implicated in the process that led to the extermination of the Jews."

It is therefore important to note that the form structural interdependence takes varies in space and time. The "marriage of iron and rye" and its relationship to the Kaiserreich before the First World War and the City-Bank-Treasury nexus that emerged in interwar Britain represented two very different historical expressions of this relationship (see chap. 3). Their differences were as much a product of the differential timing and tempo of capitalist development characterizing the two social formations as their strategic interactions. In other words, the spatiotemporal location of different societies within the uneven and combined nature of capitalist development is absolutely crucial in explaining the different character and trajectory of their state-capital relations.[12]

Rather than viewing state managers and capitalists in an external relation to one another—as do pluralist and neo-Weberian theories—this conceptualization situates them within the international context of the dynamics of capital accumulation. Further, a key shortcoming of existing class-based or ideological analyses of appeasement is their inadequacy in specifying such structural mechanisms facilitating state policies to capitalist ends (see, for example, Narizny 2003; Schweller 2004; Haas 2005). This is a problem common to Marxian analyses of appeasement. For example, Sandra Halperin's otherwise excellent neo-Gramscian analysis of appeasement explicitly conceives the state in instrumentalist terms. This follows from her argument that European states remained dominated by preindustrialist classes. For Halperin, appeasement was a defense of the Old Regime (Halperin 2004, chap. 1). While this chapter develops particular arguments made in Halperin's study, it rejects these two assumptions.

REARMAMENTS, FINANCE, AND INDUSTRY

A problem with conventional IR approaches to appeasement is the failure to explain why, if British military power was so inadequate in confronting the territorial threats posed by the Nazis, British policymakers did not quicken the pace and scope of their own rearmament program. If states' foreign policies are ultimately determined by the changing international distribution of power, it would be logical that in the face of three simultaneous threats (Germany, Japan, and Italy), British policymakers would have undertaken a much more comprehensive and prudent rearmament program earlier than they did. Thus, appeasement represents a "leading empirical anomaly" for IR theories of "preventive war" (Ripsman and Levy 2008, 33). For between 1933 and 1939, successive British administrations pursued a limited rearmament program that continually subordinated speed and direction to financial, socioeconomic, and political concerns. These concerns had little if anything to do with geopolitical and security factors as narrowly defined by conventional IR theories. Rather, they were geared toward securing the socioeconomic status quo and the international conditions supporting it.

The City-Treasury-Bank Perspective and Rearmament

The point of convergence between the socioeconomic and financial concerns of the City-Treasury-Bank establishment and foreign policymaking is nowhere better demonstrated than in the debate over rearmament. The direction, speed, and ambit of Britain's rearmament program during the 1930s was largely dictated by the Treasury, which pursued orthodox policies based on its shared perspective with the City, Bank of England, and significant sectors of Britain's export-oriented industries. During this period, the City-Treasury-Bank nexus maintained that rearming too rapidly would weaken business confidence by dislocating production and threatening an inflationary spiral, potentially destroying the Sterling Area and undermining Britain's fragile domestic status quo. This perspective gained widespread acceptance in foreign policymaking circles (Shay 1977, 96, 125–26; Middlemas 1979, 254; Peden 1979, 85–86; Gustav Schmidt 1983, 109; Bernd Jürgen Wendt 1983, 161; Post 1993, 317–30; Ferguson 2008, 458). Policymakers were thus committed to a strategy of restrained defense spending and maintaining the principle of business as usual—that is, rearmament should interfere as little as possible with the normal export-oriented and free market British model of capitalism. Committed to this principle of business as usual, "the government was generally sympathetic to employers and their preference for limited government intervention" (Imlay 2007, 19, 31–32). Britain's rearmament program exemplifies how the capital-state encroachment process imbued state managers with a specific conception of political economy and "national interest."

Throughout the 1930s, the opinion of the City-Treasury-Bank establishment that an accelerated rearmament project would destroy business confidence by dislocating production and threatening an inflationary spiral gained widespread acceptance in foreign policymaking circles. This was exemplified in the wake of the Manchurian Crisis, when the Committee of Imperial Defence requested on 17 March 1932 that the Ten-Year Rule be suspended and that expenditures be made for "purely defensive commitments" in the Far East. The Treasury's response to the committee's request for increased funding, signed by Neville Chamberlain, then chancellor of the exchequer, was a "classic statement" of its basic rationale in denying the military's repeated requests for funds (Shay 1977, 23). It argued that under the present circumstances, the British state was no more in a position financially and economically to engage in a major war in the Far East than it was militarily. It concluded "that today financial and economic risks are by far the most serious and urgent the country has to face and that other risks must be run until the country has had time and opportunity to recuperate and our financial situation to improve" (quoted in Shay 1977, 23–24; see also Christopher Price 2001, 7–8).

In 1934, the Defence Requirements Committee identified Germany as Britain's main potential long-term enemy while recognizing Italy and Japan as potential opponents. Despite the identification of these multiple threats, the pace and direction of rearmaments as recommended by the committee's November 1935 "Ideal Scheme" was continually stalled by the Treasury (Christopher Price 2001, 71–74; see Shay 1977). The Treasury's reasoning was clear: too rapid a rate of rearmament would result in intolerable levels of in-flation, undermine the fragile sociopolitical status quo, and "wreck the Ster-ling Area by precipitating a financial crash equal to, or greater than, that of 1931" (Cain and Hopkins 1993a, 96).

Furthermore, British policymakers not only limited the speed of the rear-mament program throughout this period but also directed military spend-ing on primarily financial and economic criteria, overwhelmingly concen-trating on Royal Air Force defense of the home islands and the British Navy to secure the empire. This was "by no means an accident or an oversight." Chamberlain had forcefully argued that the air force's powerful striking ca-pabilities "offered the greatest security for the amount available to be spent" (Shay 1977, 78; Paul M. Kennedy 1981, 293). He therefore suggested that spending on the air force take priority, with the navy given second priority and the army a distant third.

This allocation of spending was based not on British security priorities conceptualized in realist balance-of-power terms; rather, it was born out of financial and economic orthodoxy and a willingness to sacrifice Europe to save the empire (Shay 1977, 91; Post 1993, 65–66; Ruggiero 1999, 99–101). As the chiefs of staff put it in 1936, "The greater our commitments to Europe, the less will be our ability to secure our Empire and its communications" (quoted in Murray 1984, 104).[13] Further, the Treasury continually denied in-creased defense expenditures on the grounds that it would be a "shock to business confidence," often citing City and business organizations' opposi-tion to Chamberlain's proposed National Defence Contribution, which would have implemented a graduated tax on business profits (quoted in Middlemas 1979, 259; see also Shay 1977, 288–89; Peden 1979, 95; Gustav Schmidt 1983; Bernd Jürgen Wendt 1983, 161; Post 1993, 317–30). Decrying such a policy as "socialist," City interests were successful in defeating the measure, which was quickly withdrawn after Chamberlain's accession to the premiership. Rationed defense spending and appeasing Britain's external enemies were two sides of the same coin (Adams 1993, 61; Peden 2000, 287). Together, they formed a two-pronged strategy "rooted in the Government's desire to maintain the economic and social status quo" (Shay 1977, 196; see also Gustav Schmidt 1983; Bernd Jürgen Wendt 1983; Imlay 2007).

These geopolitical and socioeconomic challenges facing Britain in the 1930s as well policymakers' strategies for addressing those challenges were conditioned by the uneven and combined character of capitalist development. From this perspective, Paul M. Kennedy's (1988) "over-stretch" thesis sheds new light. By the interwar period, Britain was suffering from what has been termed the "disadvantages of priority" as "the historical first-comer" of capitalist development (see chap. 3). With "vast accumulations of capital in relatively backward technologies and a financial sector geared primarily to overseas investment," British policymakers faced the dual problems of real-locating this capital into newer military and other technologies while defending capital fixed in the Empire (Perry Anderson 1987, 71–72; Callinicos 1989b, 109). "Britain's far-flung empire" had been key to the "formation and consolidation of a UK-centred system of accumulation," particularly through India's role of providing a continual balance-of-payments surplus. Yet "as soon as interstate competition for 'living space' intensified under the impact of the transport revolution and the industrialization of war, the protection costs of Britain's metropolitan and overseas domains began to escalate, and its imperial possessions turned from assets into liabilities" (Arrighi 2005, 93; see also Hobsbawm 1968, 146–49). Given the earlier timing of British imperial expansion, a key aim of British foreign policy was maintaining the territorial gains that had already been consolidated. In the words of first sea lord Admiral Chatfield, "We have got most of the world already, or the best parts of it, and we only want to keep what we have got and prevent others taking it away from us" (quoted in Reynolds 2000, 57).

With the emergence of multiple geopolitical threats, the defense and financial costs of Britain's vast and dispersed spatial fixes of capital embedded throughout the empire and elsewhere became a critical problem for policymakers. Consequently, Britain's specific position in the world economy produced a *structural incentive* toward a dual strategy of limited rearmament and appeasement—a strategy reinforced by widespread anticommunist ideology among British elites. Hence, throughout the 1930s, the Treasury's rationale remained the same: financial and socioeconomic considerations took precedence over military ones. Or, more precisely, military-security interests were inherently linked to these considerations that necessitated a moderately paced rearmament program; the economy was Britain's "fourth arm of defense."

IR scholars have noted connections between economic and geopolitical power but have failed to recognize that the specific intertwining of military-security and socioeconomic interests as a means of appeasement are *unique* to capitalism. This is not to imply that military-security and socioeconomic interests were disassociated in precapitalist epochs; rather, their dynamics held a radically different significance. In the feudal epoch, for example, lords had little systematic incentive to increase their income through the introduction of productivity-enhancing technological innovations. To increase returns, they turned to the redistribution of "wealth and income away from their peasants or from other members of the exploiting class." This meant "building up their *means of coercion*—by investment in military men and equipment" (Brenner 1986, 31). Feudal production relations therefore reveal a marked tendency toward state building and war posited on the direct fusion of political and economic power in the lord-serf relation. In contrast, while war may be used as a means to acquire colonies and open markets, the structured separation of the "political" and "economic" spheres distinctive to capitalism allows state managers to use economic and financial incentives to induce political effects in adversarial states. Consequently, *the systematic use of "economic" appeasement makes sense as a foreign policy tool only in the capitalist epoch.* Drawing broad historical analogies between Chamberlain's appeasement policy and, for example, Thucydides' account of the Peloponnesian War (Gilpin 1981, 206–7; Mearsheimer 2001, 163) fails to take account of these radically different structural contexts.

While capitalism demonstrates a definite tendency toward competition and rivalry, its patterns of cooperation and conflict are much more intricate than those of less complex social structures. The abstract logic of capital provides incentives for both war and peace. One cannot simply read off policy outputs from this logic or, for that matter, from any "static" picture of state-capital relations. These logics alter in relation to the changing constellations of social forces and their relation to foreign policymaking processes within the context of capitalism's uneven and combined development.

A Crisis of Capitalist Sovereignty

British state managers' concerns regarding the economic and financial consequences of rearmament fundamentally connected with political and social problems. Policymakers feared the loss of the state's relative autonomy vis-à-vis industry and labor resulting from the necessary government collaboration with these groups in reorganizing the economy for war. By "steering towards rearmament with the hand-brake on," the government sought to avoid becoming dependent on employers and organized labor, as had happened in WWI (Gustav Schmidt 1983, 105). Extensive government collaboration with labor, chief economic adviser Horace Wilson warned, could "carry us very far in the direction of interference and control" (quoted in Imlay 2007, 32–33). Moreover, there was widespread dread that by potentially engaging in a long, drawn-out war, the liberal capitalist system defining Britain society would be entirely transformed. As the president of the Board of Trade put it to Member of Parliament Harold Nicolson in September 1938, "Whether we win or lose [a war], it will be the end of everything we stand for." As Nicolson went on to note (1980, 132), "By 'we' he means obviously the capitalist classes." What was at stake for the British ruling class was a particular social order and conception of national identity embedded in capitalist social relations.

The concerns regarding the loss of autonomy in policymaking were particularly directed toward labor. The government had no intention of giving workers the same considerations as the business community in the rearmament drive. Rather, "organized labor" was treated as "an adversary with whom the Government had no wish to become involved" (Shay 1977, 127; Peden 1979, 82; see also Imlay 2007). Policymakers knew that they would need labor's support for their industrial war mobilization plans. This would, in turn, increase labor's bargaining position and demands from the government.

Drawing on the experiences of the First World War and the General Strike of 1926, policymakers feared that labor would exploit the war emergency as a means to enhance its social power. Despite potential shortages of skilled workers, the Ministry of Labour advised the government to avoid "direct contact with the trade unions . . . as consultation would encourage the unions to demand a high price as regards conditions and wages in return for cooperation" (Peden 2007, 142). Exacerbating these concerns was the ongoing Spanish Civil War, which further stoked the flames of class conflict within Britain and throughout Europe. Chamberlain thus proposed that "it would be necessary to wait for European events to sweep away Labour's sectional prejudices, making unnecessary such forms of appeasement [to labor] as a wealth tax or an attack on employers' profits" (quoted in Middlemas 1979, 262).

An additional anxiety among policymakers was that engaging in a close collaborative rearmament effort with industry and labor would unwillingly draw the government into industrial disputes. In explaining the problems involved in mobilizing labor for the rearmament drive, a government labor adviser claimed,

> If . . . it is decided that the maximum speed must be applied to the [rearmament] programme then a warning must be given that labour difficulties are probable . . . *The more the Government are directly involved, the more they will be put into the position of solving the employer's difficulties by buying off the Trade Unions.* (quoted in Shay 1977, 126–27; emphasis added)

The underlying problem confronting policymakers was that by directly entering the production process and thereby politicizing formally economic issues, state sovereignty would be weakened and potentially contested. This is a problem unique to the liberal capitalist state: for the very structural specificity of capitalist state sovereignty "lies in its 'abstraction' from civil society which is constitutive of the private sphere of the market, and hence inseparable from capitalist relations of production" (Justin Rosenberg 1994, 123–24). Once the state becomes directly involved with organizing production relations and surplus-value extraction, this formal separation of "economic" and "political" spheres collapses. Consequently, the transformation of industrial disputes into directly political conflicts would call into question the legitimacy of the state and thus put an end to the necessary illusion of its social neutrality.

To the detriment of British security, policymakers did everything possible to avoid collaborating with organized labor in the rearmament drive until the "government found its back to the wall in 1938." Consequently, the assistance of labor, a "major productive force," in the rearmament effort "was denied the nation for two full years" despite the fact that organized labor had been willing to collaborate with the government since 1937 (Shay 1977, 125, 128; Peden 1979, 82). These political concerns were reinforced by threats of industrial disputes, social unrest, and revolution continually brought up in government-level discussions of the rearmament issue. As Chamberlain wrote in an April 1937 personal letter, "All the elements of danger are here . . . we might easily run, in no time, into a series of crippling strikes and finally the defeat of the Government . . . Industrial unrest is only just round the corner." Similar views were expressed by key government officials such as Sir John Simon, Thomas Inskip, and others (quoted in Middlemas 1979, 256–57; Peden 1979, 89; Gustav Schmidt 1983, 103).

The potential reignition of intense labor-capital conflicts resulting from

a rapid rearmament process and its expected economic consequences fig-
ured prominently among policymakers. Oliver Harvey, Halifax's private secretary, recorded in his diary (1970, 222),

> the real opposition to re-arming comes from the rich classes in the [Conser-
> vative] Party who fear taxation and believe Nazis on the whole are more con-
> servative than Communists and Socialists: any war, whether we win or not,
> would destroy the rich idle classes and so they are for peace at any price.

The issue could not be more clearly stated: war would signal the end of the
political status quo and social structure that the British elites were desperately trying to save. Policymakers were convinced that Britain could more
easily survive foreign policy risks than a conflict with labor (Gustav Schmidt
1983, 112). The fact that Whitehall continually subordinated the speed, direction, and scope of the rearmament program to myriad financial and socioeconomic concerns is a fatal problem for IR accounts of appeasement,
which explain it primarily in balance-of-power terms. In addition, Whitehall's actions point to the need for a substantive reformulation of IR theory's
basic concepts of "security" and "security interests" as well as "political
economy" that reconceptualizes them as interdependent in specifically capitalist ways.

THE "ANGLO-GERMAN CONNECTION" AND APPEASEMENT

With the success of the Bolshevik Revolution in 1917 and intensification of
labor-capital conflicts across Europe during and after World War I, the City-
Treasury-Bank nexus became infused with an ideology of radical anticommunism. In conjunction with key industrial interests, it formed the bastion
of anti-Bolshevik and pro-German sentiment in British policymaking circles
during the interwar years. It was "committed to the defence of free enterprise and the limited state against the internal threat of socialism and the
external menace of Bolshevism" (Scott Newton 1997, 293–94).

The Creation and Aims of the "Anglo-German Connection"

For many British elites, the rise of the Nazis was perceived as less of a danger
to British interests than a necessary evil in keeping communism at bay and
maintaining social stability at home. The Soviet Union was essentially per-

ceived as Europe's Other. In contrast, many considered Nazi Germany "an integral part of the Western capitalist system, particularly when contrasted to 'half-Asiatic' Russia" (Middlemas 1972, 73–74; Bernd Jürgen Wendt 1983, 164). Bolshevism was viewed as an existential threat to Western civilization, whereas German and Italian fascism were perceived as an aberration *within* capitalist modernity. Many British business interests and state managers—including those at the highest echelons of policymaking—thus hoped that maintaining and strengthening the channels of Anglo-German economic intercourse would cement a natural congruity of interests that might act to settle political differences. As long as the Nazis continued to trade profitably, avoided socialist experiments, and guaranteed reliability in business, Britain's ruling classes were prepared to overlook the regime's criminal aspects (Bernd Jürgen Wendt 1983, 165). These views were reinforced by prevalent sentiments that Germany had been unfairly treated by the Versailles settlement, further encouraging a political atmosphere favoring appeasement.

After the First World War, the Bank of England, under the governorship of Montague Norman, actively cultivated closer economic and political relations between Britain and Germany, particularly through the key role London played in financing German trade. Norman was well known to hold deep anti-Bolshevik convictions and pro-Nazi sympathies (see Hargrave 1939, 219–20; George 1965, 174–81; Scott Newton 1996). "Hitler and Schacht are the bulwarks of civilization in Germany and the only friends we have," said Norman; "they are fighting the war of our system of society against communism. If they fail, communism will follow in Germany, and anything may follow in Europe" (quoted in Chernow 1990, 398). The rebuilding of a strong German economy through the creation of an "Anglo-German connection," as Norman called it, was viewed as a bulwark against the Bolshevik threat (quoted in Scott Newton 1997, 293). In addition, this connection formed an integral part of the City-Treasury-Bank establishment's strategy for rebuilding a London-centered international financial order that would eventually revive the free trade system on which the empire was built. This required the construction of a strategic partnership with Europe's largest economy (Germany) to face the challenges stemming from America's ascendancy as a global power (Scott Newton 1996, 58–59).[14] The facilitation of the "Anglo-German connection" was thus essential not only for British socioeconomic interests but also for Britain's ability to maintain its financial-economic autonomy and hence its security-defense sovereignty.

The 1920s witnessed a "spectacular increase" in the magnitude of business British banks did with Germany. By the early 1930s, British capital made up a significant share of Germany's external debt. Consequently, the high levels of capital withdrawals from Germany in 1931 caused grave concern in City circles. Germany's external debt problems led to an international Standstill Agreement in September 1931, whereby all existing credits to Germany (amounting to approximately three hundred million pounds, including sixty-two million of the one hundred million pounds in acceptances held by London banks) were frozen on their original terms but with interest payments guaranteed (Diaper 1986, 64). The agreement was originally intended to last for only six months, though it would be open to renewal thereafter. However, as a result of the intense lobbying efforts by particular sections of capital with direct economic interests in Germany and the British capitalist class's more general support for maintaining close economic relations with the Nazis, the agreement was annually renewed until 1939 (see Forbes 1987; Scott Newton 1996). "There was," as Niall Ferguson notes (2008, 458), "a measure of self-interest as well as macroeconomic pragmatism in the City's support for appeasement."

In 1934, these financial relations were formalized with the Anglo-German Payments Agreement. Under its terms, the Nazis were permitted to go on collecting a considerable sum of earnings from the maintenance of Germany's export surplus with Britain. This provided the Nazis with vital funds to purchase raw materials for Germany's war economy, either through English transit trade or directly on the world market (Bernd Jürgen Wendt 1983, 168).

The Payments Agreement and the Nazi "Moderates"

Among the various agreements regulating Anglo-German business relations during the 1930s, the Payments Agreement of 1934—the "first act of economic appeasement" (Einzig 1941, 94)—was the most important. While the Payments Agreement served multiple aims at once,[15] its most important function for the City-Treasury-Bank establishment was its role in maintaining a significant fraction of German trade within the international economy. The "active interest" taken by British banking interests in slackening the economic restrictions on Nazi Germany was necessitated by the fact that those credits frozen during the depression could be released only if the Germans opened up their economy and earned additional foreign exchange. The potentially devastating economic effects of canceling the agreements were recognized by many in both policymaking and business circles (see Forbes 2000, 97–132). If successful, the Payment Agreements might stimulate a revival of international trade and a recovery of the British economy, particularly by raising the "purchasing power of commodity producers in the interest of British exports" (MacDonald 1972, 114–17; Scott Newton 1997, 298).

British policymakers also sought to pull the Nazis away from their warlike behavior through the liberalizing influence of increased trade, particularly by increasing Anglo-German trade and agreements in third markets. This would act to "modify autarky and pave the way to a political settlement" (MacDonald 1972, 114). Such appeasing efforts were primarily directed toward the Nazi "moderates"—initially Hjalmar Schacht and subsequently Hermann Göring—who, it was hoped, would positively influence Hitler and steer the Nazis away from placing the entire economy on a war footing, which would result in economic catastrophe. Economic appeasement thus constituted a continuation of political appeasement by other means.

Widespread fears among British policymakers that the Nazis' rapid rearmament would end in economic collapse were concerned not solely with its effects on the international and British economy but also with its effects on Germans' general living standards. It was believed that this would "ultimately create a situation in which Hitler would be faced with the choice of "internal revolution or external adventure" (MacDonald 1972, 107; see also Gustav Schmidt 1986). The Payments Agreement was thus designed ultimately to strengthen the Nazi regime from internal socioeconomic shocks while protecting Britain's socioeconomic interests. This was explicitly recognized by Norman, who, during a meeting with British bankers in early 1934, pledged the Bank of England to the agreement, citing the "stabilization of the Nazi regime" as its key objective (Hargrave 1939, 222). London thereby sought to "fatten" Germany and strengthen the stabilizing influence of the moderates as a deterrence against the connected dangers of revolution and war—as expressed by such British officials as Sir Maurice Hankey, Sir Bolton Eyres-Monsell, Orme Sargent, Admiral Chatfield, Lord Swinton, Thomas Inskip, and others (Gustav Schmidt 1986, 85–88).

British assessments of the crises facing the Nazis,[16] pushing them toward "internal revolution or external adventure," are significant in illustrating the extent to which state managers were themselves aware of the socioeconomic causes of war and how this factored into their decision making. This is further demonstrated in the British policymaking process vis-à-vis the resolution of the Sudeten problem, which, from the summer of 1938 onward, appeared to Whitehall to offer an opportunity to create a solid foundation from which the "appeasement of Europe" could finally be achieved.

For Chamberlain, the cost of Czechoslovakian sovereignty was a small price to pay for preserving peace. For some time, British policymakers had expected the Nazis to expand eastward, a prospect that did not overly trouble many British leaders as long as it was done peacefully. The logic was that it was better for the Nazis to move east and come into conflict with the Soviets than to expand west. In 1936, Prime Minister Stanley Baldwin told his Conservative colleagues that the "German desire . . . to move east" was well known, adding that if Hitler "should move East I should not break my heart": "if there is any fighting in Europe to be done, I should like to see the Bolshies and the Nazis doing it." Shortly after Munich, Cadogan affirmed that Britain should "let Germany . . . find her 'Lebensraum' and establish herself, if she can, as a peaceful economic unit" (quoted in Wark 1985, 212; Carley 1999a, 31–32).

After Lord Halifax's November 1937 diplomatic mission, Hitler was left with the impression that an eventual Nazi expansion to the East would *not* encounter British interference. According to the German interpreter's report of the meeting, "Halifax admitted of his own accord that certain changes in the European system could probably not be avoided in the long run. The British did not believe that the status quo had to be maintained in all circumstances." In his introductory remarks to Hitler, Halifax described "Germany as the bulwark of the West against Bolshevism" (quoted in Eden 1962, 578; see also William Young 2006, 228–29).

Other policymakers viewed Germany's eastward drive as a welcome move, since it would deflect German attention from Britain. At best, it could provide new order to the chaos of Eastern Europe. Since Russian pressure westward was always a perceived danger, the construction of a strong bloc "between her and the West was to be welcomed." The British were thus "often closer adherents to German expansionist policy than the German themselves" (Gilbert and Gott 1963, 35; Middlemas 1979, 137–38; quoted in Gustav Schmidt 1986, 84–93). For British policymakers who viewed Nazi aggressions as a result of "economic bottlenecks" attributable to its "lack of *Lebensraum*," substantive appeasement effects could be derived from conceding German hegemony in Central Eastern Europe. These region's markets could provide the kind of spatial fix needed to ameliorate Germany's supposed need for expanded living space (MacDonald 1972; Gustav Schmidt 1986, 87).

The Sudeten crisis was eventually settled with the signing of the Munich Agreement in the early hours of 30 September 1938. British elites perceived

the agreement as a "first step in the creation of an international environment which would sustain continuing recovery from the Depression in a
manner compatible with the maintenance of the *status quo* in British society" (Scott Newton 1996, 86). In March 1939, the Nazis occupied Bohemia
and Moravia. Many expected the Czech crisis to signal the end of London's
appeasement efforts. However, the Nazi invasion did little to modify Norman's "Anglo-German connection." On 22 May 1939, a new agreement was
signed between British short-term creditors and the Nazis that was intended
to renew the Standstill Agreement until 31 May 1940 (Scott Newton 1996,
113). In addition, throughout 1938–39, British industrialists actively supported by the Board of Trade sought closer trade relations with the Nazis.
Increasing trade relations became not only a favored means of reviving British exports but also a stepping-stone toward the more general political settlement sought by Chamberlain (Holland 1981).

After Munich, Whitehall's dual strategy of deterrence and détente remained unaltered and overwhelmingly skewed toward the latter. While London increased spending on the Royal Air Force, it continually resisted calls
for the establishment of a Ministry of Supply and the introduction of conscription. This reflected Chamberlain's belief that the rationale behind the
Munich Agreement was *not* to postpone war but to *prevent* it (Scott Newton
1996, 86–87, 100–101; Carley 1999a, 78–79; see also Halperin 1996). IR interpretations of appeasement as a strategy of "buying time" for increased British rearmaments to better prepare for an "inevitable" war with the Nazis are
thus questionable (Mearsheimer 2001, 165; Ripsman and Levy 2008).
"Rather than doing away with 'the present rule' [business as usual], the minister for the coordination of defence maintained, 'it would be better to press
forward as rapidly as possible with the methods that had already proved not
unsuccessful'" (Imlay 2007, 31–32). If Munich had "swept away all doubts
about Hitler's aims and removed the remaining restrains on Western rearmament efforts" (Walt 1992, 453), why did policymakers continue appeasement
efforts well after the formal declaration of war? Further, what explains British policymakers' readiness for war with the Soviets after the start of the
Winter War in spite of their (continuing) reluctance for war with Germany?

THE FAILURE OF THE ANGLO-FRANCO-SOVIET ALLIANCE

For almost three centuries, British strategy had been directed toward preventing the emergence of a hegemon on the European continent. Yet despite

Britain's time-honored "special role" of holding the balance of power in Europe, policymakers in the 1930s continually shunned Soviet efforts to form a collective security alliance against Germany and consistently undermined French moves toward closer Franco-Soviet relations. Why Britain, despite all historical precedents, failed to balance against German power and uphold the international status quo of Versailles is a central anomaly to IR approaches to appeasement. This stems from their fundamental misidentification of the determining forces behind British policy, which, in turn, reflect a deeply nation-statist ontology embedded within mainstream IR theories.

IR Approaches to the Alliance Dynamics of the 1930s

These problems are well exemplified in recent neorealist interpretations of appeasement. From this perspective, appeasement was the result of British policymakers' perceived "defensive advantages" in military technology, making the country less vulnerable to attack and policymakers more willing to free ride on France's balancing efforts (Posen 1984; Christensen and Snyder 1990; Walt 1992, 458; Christensen 1997, 83–91; Van Evera 1998, 31–33). The logic behind the claim that perceived defensive advantages explain Britain's buck-passing strategy is, however, contradicted by Christensen and Snyder's own arguments (1990, 165) for Britain's partial policy reversal after Munich, as pointed out by Schweller (1993, 85). Yet Schweller's "distancing" thesis fails to provide a more convincing answer to the key question: if the combined strength of Britain and France was clearly overmatched against German power, why did they not ally with the Soviets?

After Germany's occupation of the Czechoslovakian provinces of Moravia and Bohemia, British policymakers and their French counterparts issued a "guarantee" of Polish independence, eventually signing a treaty to secure the defense of Poland's western borders against German aggression. The question of how to obtain Russian cooperation for the Polish guarantee now became the principal issue in Parliament. Yet without a Soviet alliance, Britain would be "walking into a trap" if called on to honor its commitments (quoted in Parker 1993, 219). The time had seemingly come for British and French policymakers to put aside their ideological animosities toward the USSR and form the tripartite "collective security" alliance for which Maxim Litvinov had been calling since the mid-1930s. Indeed, by the summer of 1939, British public opinion strongly supported an alliance with the Soviets, as did the chiefs of staffs and a majority in Parliament as well as officials in Paris (Neilson 1993, 212; Parker 1993, 233; Scott Newton 1996, 108).

Despite this overwhelming support, the Chamberlain administration remained skeptical of a Soviet alliance. According to Alexander Cadogan,
Whitehall sought Soviet support only "to placate our left-wing in England,
rather than to obtain any solid military advantage" (quoted in Parker 1993,
227). When faced with the choice of forming an alliance with either the Soviets or Poland but not both, Chamberlain persistently chose the latter for
fear of alienating the Germans. In negotiations, Chamberlain and Halifax
tirelessly cited Polish reservations that a Soviet alliance would be more likely
to provoke than deter German aggression.

According to Schweller (1998), Chamberlain's decision to prioritize the
Polish over the Soviet alliance was based on the latest British intelligence
that Soviet military capabilities were extremely weak (see also Ripsman and
Levy 2008). Therefore, there was no reason to risk provoking the Nazis and
losing Poland as an ally. This explanation is problematic in numerous
ways. First, despite Stalin's purges of the military, Soviet military capabilities remained overwhelmingly superior to those of Poland. In pure "balance of power" terms, the rational ally for Britain should have been the
Soviet Union (see esp. Neilson 1993, 2006; Carley 1999a).[17] Second, any
participation of Poland in a defense against Germany *depended* on Soviet
military support. As the deputy chief of staff reported in August 1939,
"Without early and effective Russian assistance, the Poles cannot hope to
stand up to a German attack . . . for more than a limited time." An alliance
with the Soviets was therefore "the best way of preventing a war" (quoted
in Carley 1999a, 199–200). Third, Schweller's interpretation of Chamberlain's decision is predicated on a one-dimensional and uncritical acceptance of Chamberlain self-justifications. Yet Chamberlain's decision was
made in spite of overwhelming evidence to the contrary and was based in
part on explicitly expressed socioeconomic reasons. "Not wanting to ally
with the Soviet Union, Chamberlain made use of any argument to justify
his position" (Carley 1999a, 117). For some time, Soviet military support
had been sought by the British chiefs of staff. As Commander Bower told
the Commons, "I know they have shot a lot of people but there are some
170,000,000 of them left . . . we cannot do without her now" (quoted in
Paul M. Kennedy 1975, 155).

In early March 1939, British ambassador Sir William Seeds wrote to Lord
Halifax that the Soviet régime was "as firmly established as any régime can
reasonably expect to be." A subsequent memorandum from the British military attaché in Moscow reported that that the Red Army was loyal to the re-

gime and that although it had "suffered severely from the 'purge,'" it would "still prove a serious obstacle to an attacker." The document claimed that the Red Army would be capable of mobilizing at least one hundred infantry and thirty cavalry for the Western Front within three months and that its "numerical superiority" would be of "great value" in the "defense of the Soviet territory." The memorandum ended by stating that the "Red army considers a war inevitable and is undoubtedly being strenuously prepared for it" (Great Britain, Foreign Office, and Woodward 1946 3rd ser., vol. 4, doc. 183, pp. 188, 194, 195). The perceived necessity of Soviet military power in a war against Germany was supported by various other British and French military reports (see Neilson 1993; Carley 1999a, chap. 4). The subsequent failure to find a suitable formula alliance was based more on ideological and socioeconomic concerns than pure "balance of power" considerations.

The Role of Anti-Bolshevik Ideology

The failure of the Anglo-Franco-Soviet alliance was a consequence of the ideological bifurcation of Europe that had arisen during the First World War with the Bolshevik Revolution and the Allied powers' subsequent invasion. This "European civil war" was simultaneously *intra*national, *inter*national, and *trans*national, as illustrated in the determining role of "anti-Bolshevism" on appeasement, a policy aimed not only at the British government's domestic opponents (socialism at home) but also at its "external" ones (Bolshevism and the Soviet Union abroad) (see Halperin 2004).

Though many historians have questioned the role of "anti-Bolshevik" ideology in deterring the formation of the alliance (see Lammers 1966; Paul M. Kennedy 1981, 299–301; Watt 1989, 120), the evidence to the contrary seems quite overwhelming. Anti-Bolshevik ideology was deeply rooted in Whitehall. As the head of the Central Department put it, "All at No. 10 are anti-Soviet" (Oliver Harvey 1970, 290). Anti-Bolshevik views were repeatedly expressed by numerous notable British policymakers and leading capitalists, including Foreign Secretary Halifax, Hoare, Hankey, Cadogan, Henderson, Phipps, Sargent, Simon, and Chamberlain himself (see Aster 1973, 184–85; Post 1993, 20; Scott Newton 1996, 110–11; Thomas 1996, 99; McDonough 1998, 47, 51; Carley 1999a, 12, 43, 163; Louise Grace Shaw 2003, 21–22, 90–91, 187–88). As Lord Philip Kerr Lothian said, "Of the two evils threatening Europe—German aggression and communism . . . communism is the worst evil." Furthermore, the British Secret Intelligence Service and French General Staff considered the Soviet Union to be the real "Enemy Number One" (quoted in Carley 1999a, 32; Halperin 2004, 203).

While Conservatives found neither the Nazi nor the communist systems particularly pleasant, they did, all things considered, prefer Nazism, since it did not represent a major threat to the existing social order. In fact, many Conservatives held significant sympathy and admiration for Mussolini's variant of fascism though less for Nazism, which they hoped would eventually reform itself along Italian lines. For Soviet Russia, however, there was "nothing but thinly disguised fear and hatred" (George 1965, 139–41, 161–63; Neville Thompson 1971, 38, 40; Robert J. Young 1978, 199; Post 1993, 203; Thomas 1996, 95–99). Fears of the "Red danger," "communist expansionism," and the general "hatred of socialist revolution" were dominant themes among French ruling elites (see George 1965, 141–45, 196, 171–72, 206–12; Kuisel 1967, 126–33; Irvine 1979, 194; Jordan 1992, 228; Alexander 1992, 294–95; Robert J. Young 1996, 60, 67; Carley 1999a, 14–15, 45–47). Indeed, many in French policymaking circles considered the defeat of fascism at the expense of increased Soviet influence in Europe entirely undesirable. As French premier Édouard Daladier put it to the German chargé d'affaires in September 1938, after the fighting ceased, "revolution, irrespective of victors or vanquished, was as certain in France as in Germany and Italy. Soviet Russia would not let the opportunity pass to bring world revolution to our lands" (quoted in Carley 1999a, 46). As Charles de Gaulle scornfully noted, "Some circles were more inclined to see Stalin as the enemy than Hitler" (quoted in Richardson 1973, 140).

British policymakers shared the idea of a "war-generated" revolution. In the wake of the remilitarization of the Rhineland in March 1936, Prime Minister Stanley Baldwin claimed that the French "might succeed in crushing Germany with the aid of Russia, but it would probably result in Germany going Bolshevik." Baldwin noted in his diary at the time, "Naturally we [Britain] shall win and enter Berlin. But what is the good of that? It would only mean communism in Germany and France" (quoted in Leibovitz and Finkel 1998, 107). Such comments were quite common among British conservative politicians (see esp. Carley 1993, 1999; Louise Grace Shaw 2003). More radically, some British and French policymakers sought to use Nazism as a bulwark against the spread of Bolshevism. Such were the sentiments (if not always consistent) of Baldwin, Chamberlain, Norman, Hankley, Henderson, Daladier, Pierre Laval, General Gamelin, and others (see George 1965, 140–41, 163, 174–76; Middlemas 1972, 73–74; Irvine 1979, 194; Alexander 1992, 294–95; Scott Newton 1997; Carley 1999a, 14–15, 45–46, 84).

The determining role of anti-Bolshevik ideology in preventing the formation of an Anglo-Franco-Soviet alliance is borne out not only by policy-makers' admissions (expressed in varying contexts to a multitude of different audiences) but also by their actions during the alliance negotiations. Throughout these, Chamberlain remained "very disturbed" by the prospect of concluding an agreement. During the critical phase of negotiations in the summer of 1939, British representatives were directed "to go very slow," as demonstrated by the British government's infamous decision to send its mission to the USSR via leisurely merchant ship (Carley 1993, 321, 325).

In sum, French and British policymakers' persistent refusals to form an Anglo-Franco-Soviet alliance were primarily the result of ideological considerations rooted in socioeconomic and political interests. The principal "misperception" of British and French policymakers was not their assessments of the Nazi threat but rather their persistent inability to perceive the Soviet Union as a necessary and willing ally instead of the enemy. Anti-Bolshevism thus took the role of a material force blinding British policymakers to such cooperative opportunities. As Carley argues (1993, 332), "Mistrust motivated Anglo-French policy, but anti-bolshevism was its most important component."

The traditional causal links between the Second World War and Cold War must be questioned. The Second World War did not cause the Cold War; instead, the "early" ideological Cold War contributed to the Second World War. This determining role of ideology must not be, however, conceptualized in any way as "autonomous" from its capitalist context.[18] The emergence and sticking power of anti-Bolshevik ideology in policymaking circles is inexplicable without recognition of its class content. Anti-Bolshevism formed a crucial ideological component of a larger Weltanschauung instantiated within capitalist social relations.

The War-Revolution Nexus: Prewar to "Phony War" to Real War

British and French elites also viewed the continuation of appeasing Germany and avoiding war as necessary since the only gains from a European war would come to the domestic Left and the Soviet Union. The logic was simple: war in Europe would spark socialist-inspired revolutions throughout Europe as Soviet prestige and influence would spread. This idea of a "war-revolution nexus" (Irvine 1979) was ubiquitous among British and French policymakers. Baldwin argued that even if France and Britain defeated Germany, the war "would probably only result in Germany going Bolshevik." Similarly, in the midst of the Czech May Crisis, Lord Halifax warned Ribbentrop, "We should not let it get out of hand, for then *the only ones to profit would be communists*" (quoted in Lammers 1966, 20; Post 1993, 204). Such opinions stemmed from the widespread view that the Soviets strategically wanted war to break out between the Western powers and the Nazis as it would provide them the opportunity to spread Bolshevism westward. According to the British deputy chief of staff, the Soviets would probably intervene in the war "to advance [the communist] ideology on the ruins of a civilization weakened by war." As his French counterpart put it, "Stalin will do anything to destroy capitalism" (quoted in Carley 1993, 83; Robert J. Young 1996, 67).

So ubiquitous and powerful were these views of war-generated revolution that even *after* the outbreak of war with the Nazis, French and British policymakers remained unsure about which posed the greater threat. This was demonstrated in both the Allies' early conduct of the war and their reactions to the outbreak of the Finnish-Soviet conflict in November 1939. Six months after the declaration of war, neither France nor Britain waged an offensive against the Germans. This "phony war" was best summarized in the words of the Italian ambassador in Paris: "I have seen several wars waged without being declared; but this is the first I have seen declared without being waged" (quoted in Colville 1985, 28).

During this period, British policymakers continued to explore the possibility of peace with Germany. On no fewer than five occasions during the fall of 1939, Whitehall officially sought peace terms with the Nazis (Halperin 2004, 214). British appeasement policy had yet to be fully exhausted. It was dictated by the same logic as its prewar predecessor: defense of the existing social order and political status quo against socialism at home and Bolshevism abroad. As Sir Arthur Rucker, chief private secretary to the prime minister, argued five weeks after the declaration of war,

> Communism is now the great danger, greater than Nazi Germany . . . It is thus vital that we should play our hand very carefully with Russia, and not destroy the possibility of uniting, if necessary, with a new German Government against the common danger. (quoted in Colville 1985, 40)

Similarly, in February 1940, Chamberlain argued that he did not want to beat the Germans too hard for fear that doing so would "create chaos which would open the door to Bolshevism" (quoted in Oliver Harvey 1970, 338). Similar sentiments were found in France.[19] British and French statesmen had yet to decide who the real Enemy No. 1 was.

The outbreak of the Finnish-Soviet "Winter War" in November 1939 further complicated matters for British and French policymakers, who remained indecisive about which power constituted the greater threat. While continuing to wage phony war against the Nazis, policymakers began planning a real war against the Soviets in Finland. On 15 February, the Anglo-French Supreme War Council decided that each country would send fifteen thousand soldiers to the Norwegian port of Narvik, whence they would advance into Finland. The official joint objective for the British mission was to complete the northern blockage of Germany and aid the Finns against the Soviets (Richardson 1973, 136; Keeble 1990, 159; Halperin 2004, 214). Policymakers also considered preemptive strikes on the Russian oil fields at Baku, and the British government contemplated subversive activities in the Caucasus in combination with Turkish efforts. In early November, the British ambassador to Finland even suggested that Japan should be encouraged to attack the Soviets (Richardson 1973, 136; Carley 1999a, 238–45).

Had the Finnish-Soviet war not ended before the Allies could complete their preparations, an Anglo-French invasion would have taken place (Richardson 1973, 137). What is most noteworthy, however, is the readiness with which British policymakers were willing to attack the Soviet Union compared to their years of appeasing the Nazi regime. Most accounts of British policymaking during the interwar years "neither recognize nor explain the fact that Britain seemingly preferred 'appeasement' to war with respect to Germany (in 1936, 1938, and 1939), but not with respect to the Soviet Union (in 1918, 1920, and 1939)" (Halperin 2004, 200). Whitehall's behavior during the interwar years is essentially anomalous to (neo)realist approaches, which view external security concerns conceived in balance-of-power terms as primary in determining state behavior. Any adequate theory of IR needs to transcend the confines of "second" and "third image" conceptions of international relations since this is exactly what the war-revolution nexus combines.

CONCLUSION

For proponents of U.S. global expansionism, evoking the "Munich analogy"[20] remains a discursive force foreclosing legitimate noninterventionist policy options. Lest policymakers forget the lessons of Munich and waver in the face of aggression, they risk sacrificing the "national interest." IR analyses implicate themselves in such ideological obfuscations by constructing theories based on false historical analogies.

Focusing on the nature and dynamics of British society and its place within the world economy, this chapter offers an alternative explanation of appeasement to those traditionally found in IR. While the gamble of appeasement failed, it was far from irrational. British fears of the socioeconomic and political consequences of war were largely borne out. The "appeasers" were correct in their assessment that war would cost them their British-centered liberal capitalist world order, dissolve the empire, and upturn the political status quo at home. In this narrow sense, the Chamberlain administration was more "realistic" than its American realist critics ever understood. Yet appeasement strategy was pursued despite the fact that throughout the 1930s and particularly after the Nazi invasion of the Rhineland in 1936, the severity of the German threat was widely acknowledged in both British and French policymaking circles.[21]

While this chapter examines the multiple *structural* factors shaping British policy,[22] the conclusion that there was simply no alternative to appeasement must be rejected. At the apex of appeasement efforts (1936–39), the creation of an alliance with the USSR against the Nazis remained a genuine possibility.[23] Appeasement neither was the result of contingent misperceptions nor was aimed at buying time adequately to rearm. The chief "misperception" of British elites was not their assessments of the Nazi threat but rather their persistent inability to view the Soviets as a necessary ally in balancing against the Nazis. The same anti-Bolshevik ideology that led to the Cold War thereby also fed into the causal conditions producing the Second World War.

British policymaking miscalculations were structurally conditioned and overdetermined by myriad socioeconomic and ideological factors, including the hegemonic position of the liberal-internationalist City-Treasury-Bank nexus; concerns regarding the maintenance of the (relative) autonomy of the state; a bias toward protecting access to commercially strategic sea-lanes and the empire rather than Continental Europe; and an assessment of Bolshevism abroad and socialism at home as greater threats than German territorial aspirations. Appeasement policy was designed to shore up both the British and world economies while maintaining the domestic status quo. It was, above all, a strategy designed to protect a capitalist social order in the midst of potentially revolutionary turmoil. From this perspective, Britain's external security was inextricably connected to its internal security and social stability.

Conclusion

THE ERASURE OF social structure from the study of IR has incapacitated theoretical understandings and explanations of the two world wars. Conceiving the geopolitics of the era as yet another interstate struggle over a perennial military balance of power obscures more than it illuminates. Typical IR rehearsals of transhistorical resemblances can no longer suffice as explanations of historically specific geopolitical conflicts and wars. The historical identity of the international relations in the era of the two world wars far outweighs any putative transhistorical comparisons evoking spurious analogies with such classic great-power conflicts as the Thirty Years' War (1619–48) or the Peloponnesian War (431–404 BC).

The two world wars were not merely the result of unstable multipolar systems, alliance pathologies, spiraling arms races, or policymaking misperceptions. Nor were they simply an effect of authoritarian regimes, illiberal ideologues, out-of-control military elites, or other aberrational symptoms of modernity's so-called incompleteness, as argued by many domestic-based IR theories. Visualized in *isolation* from the wider field of historically distinct social relations, both of these sets of external and internal factors offer necessarily partial and often misleading conceptions of the great modern upheaval of the first half of the 20th century. IR has thus continually and systematically failed in uncovering the deeper meanings of the geopolitics of these world historical events.

How then might the era of the two world wars be understood historically and sociologically? Antonio Gramsci (1971, 178) perhaps captured it best in viewing the epoch as one of "organic crisis": the hegemony of capitalism as a social system simultaneously experienced a crisis both in its material conditions and in its legitimacy and authority. More precisely, the world wars can be said to have represented an organic crisis of the totality of structures constituting capitalist modernity in its spatiotemporally uneven and combined development as a global, internally differentiated, sociohistorical whole.

The period of "classical imperialism" (1896–1945) was characterized by a fundamental contradiction between the simultaneous *internationalization* and *statization* of capitalist productive powers whereby the abstract logic of the world market came increasingly to dominate the fates of each and every state. This process was driven by intensified geopolitical competition ensuing from the synchronized collective outward thrust of rapidly industrializing and newly emergent capitalist states of the time. With the *quantitative* multiplication of "autonomous" centers of capital accumulation, politically rooted in national-state spaces, came the *qualitative* transformation of the rhythms and dictates of geopolitical rivalry. Different states pursued different foreign policy strategies to compete effectively in this changing international milieu. These variations were themselves bound to specific trajectories of capitalist development and processes of class formation related (in time and space) to the overall history of world capitalism. Local manifestations of the ensuing *universal* crisis thus sharply varied from one sociopolitical order to the next, shaping and conditioning the changing contours of the Thirty Years' Crisis itself.

This book offers a number of very different explanations of some of the most important events of 20th-century world politics. The diplomatic juncture of July 1914 was not the result of a geopolitically determined "slide" into war or the consequence of Germany's "special path" of (mis)development. Nor was it produced by the transition to the "monopoly" stage of capitalism or the continuing "feudal" legacies of the old European regimes. Rather, it should be conceived as the nonlinear convergence of *multiple, interdependent* chains of causation emerging from the socially and geopolitically destabilizing consequences of the internationally structured (uneven and combined) spread of capitalist relations.

As examined in chapter 4, the essence of U.S. "Wilsonian" diplomacy was to further expand capitalism internationally while managing these explosive effects. During and after the war, Wilson's diplomacy aimed to hold the world economy together under the dual strains of interimperial rivalries and the attendant uneven but hastened capitalist transformations thrusting the Global South in the direction of revolutionary nationalism. The chief social substance of Wilsonian policy was, then, not *only* the reordering of international anarchy under the auspices of rule-based international institutions or the promotion of de facto democracies. It was also the attempted "geopolitical management of combined development" (Justin Rosenberg 1996, 12), necessitating the reform of atavistic forms of imperialism into a cooperative international order of joint rule and exploitation of the Global South by northern power.

The inability to reconcile continuing imperial rivalries and the challenges of rapid social changes led to the diplomatic imbroglio of the Paris Peace Conference of 1919. Domestic and international order remained unhinged after the signing of the Treaty of Versailles despite the revival of the world economy during the mid-1920s. The emergence of fascism and Nazism offered alternative, reactionary means of temporarily stabilizing these social orders—means that were tolerated (if not actively cultivated) by key policymakers and business elites of the capitalist democracies.

While the uniquely racialized anti-Bolshevik ideology played a significant role in Hitler's ultimate decision for war, it was also fundamentally rooted in the sociomaterial circumstances in which the Nazi regime found itself. The timing for war organically arose out of *reinforcing* domestic and international dynamics emerging out of the Nazi rearmament drive aimed at simultaneously challenging North America's rising world economic hegemony and the rapidly industrializing Soviet menace. Despite the Nazi regime's commitment to prioritizing rearmaments within a framework of national self-sufficiency, its ability to do so was continually constrained by the "economic limits" imposed by the uneven and combined development of capitalism on a world scale. Hence, without territorially expanding the Nazis' productive base to incorporate new sources of raw materials and labor, the war economy would be brought to a halt. As this was ideologically unacceptable, some way forward had to be found. Given the persistence of clear *economic* limits to any further acceleration of German rearmaments and the Nazi regime's ideological intent on the "inevitable showdown" with the international Jewish conspiracy stretching from Moscow to Washington, the time for war was now—that is, before the productive-military gap between the liberal-capitalist and fascist powers turned any more unfavorably against the latter. Consequently, in the final instance, the combined weight of world economic and international systemic forces gave Hitler the incentive to risk war sooner rather than later.

As examined in chapter 6, the British-inspired policy of "appeasement" was not a consequence of policymaking "misperception" or an unwanted product of an unbalanced multipolar geopolitical system, as recounted in numerous liberal and realist texts. The "appeasement" label is in fact misleading, as British policymakers actively sought to use Nazi power as a bulwark against communism in Europe. At least until January 1939, the central perceived threat within Europe was not German *territorial* expansion but the geosocial menace of Bolshevism abroad and the emergence of a strong Left in domestic politics. The chief "misperception" of British and French policymakers was thus not their assessments of the dangers of Nazi power but their continual inability to see the Soviets as a necessary and willing alliance partner. This failure to form an Anglo-Franco-Soviet alliance against both fascism and Nazism was a key outcome of the "international civil war" bifurcating Europe during the interwar years.

The account provided in this volume necessitates a fundamental rethinking of conventional periodizations of the evolution of the modern international system. The origins of the Cold War, usually dated to sometime during the mid-1940s, needs to be pushed back to the immediate years following the November 1917 revolution. The Cold War was therefore not the "tragic" consequence of WWII; rather, precisely the reverse holds true: the antagonistic policies toward the Soviet Union inaugurated by the Allied intervention in Bolshevik Russia produced the geopolitical and ideological conditions leading to the Second World War. An early "first" Cold War of the interwar years was thus a major force driving the great powers into WWII, resulting, in turn, in a "second" Cold War emerging thereafter.

In uncovering the continually obscured, historically unique geosocial origins of the crisis period, this book maps a way out of the deeper theoretical and methodological problems shared by social and international theories. However, a number of crucial issues call for much further exploration. While some examination of racism and ideology has been offered in this work, the linkages among culture, agency, and identity in the nexus of North-South imperial relations feeding into the geopolitics of the era are in need of much further attention. Here, a historical materialist sociology[1] would benefit from a more extensive engagement with the constructivist IR literature, which has been notable by its absence in studying the 1914–45 period (but see Kier 1997; Legro 2005).

Widening the analysis to a thoroughly global, non-Eurocentric perspective would also problematize my own rather conventional periodization of the crisis as lasting from 1914 to 1945. For much of the Global South, the anticolonial and revolutionary struggles for self-determination emerging out of WWII lasted until well after 1945. Moreover, while this work has sought to further flesh out Trotsky's concept of uneven and combined development into a theory of interstate conflict and war, many more productive avenues for research remain. To mention just one example, research into the role of uneven and combined development in the colonial world (particularly India and China) during the interwar years would provide much-needed studies of the ways in which international systemic pressures contributed to domestic conditions generative of revolution and war, shedding further light on the "war-revolution" nexus so prevalent in modern international relations.

The collective and individual experiences of the two world wars obliterated straightforward narratives of progress. For many, it represented an irreversible caesura in history, a regression into generalized barbarism and systemic transformation. Though a different era emerged from its ashes, the intellectual, political, and moral challenges raised by the world crisis remain as salient as ever. Confronting these challenges will mean, among many other things, tackling the unexplored horizons of the intersocietal, where the problems of difference and alterity find their ultimate and most destructive expression.

Notes

Introduction

1. On these disciplinary myths and the intertwining of liberal and realist perspectives in IR studies during and after the 1914–45 period, see Ashworth 2002; Long and Schmidt 2005; Duncan Bell 2008, 2009.

2. Kenneth Waltz's vision of a scientific neorealism laid out in *Theory of International Politics* is the most influential and extreme version of this. It is far from alone, however.

3. Given the many meanings the concept of ideology holds in IR and particularly in the Marxist literature, it is helpful to clarify that ideology will be used in subsequent chapters to capture the ways in which agents "posit, explain and justify ends and means of organized action, and specifically political action" (Martin Seliger quoted in Eagleton 2007, 6–7).

Chapter 1

1. Here I leave aside the important question of whether the July 1914 crisis was itself the result of the intersection of various *contingent* factors. This issue is taken up in chap. 3.

2. The title of this chapter would suggest rather clear-cut answers to these questions. However, both the temporal and conceptual parameters of the notion of a singular Thirty Years' Crisis will be shown to be more fluid than is first assumed. The great difficulty in any periodization of the two world wars as forming part of the same era is how the Great Upheaval of 1914–18 marked both the concatenation of antecedent world-historical causal forces and the simultaneous reconfiguration of these causal coordinates. The latter is most strikingly demonstrated by the October Revolution of 1917, the hastened ascendency of U.S. hegemony, and the acceleration of national self-determination movements in the Global South, all of which came together in the making of the Cold War.

3. For overviews of these debates, see Koch 1984; Mombauer 2002; Hewitson 2004; Joll and Martel 2007.

4. Marxist theories of imperialism sit uneasily within this binary perspective.

Unlike the self-limiting parsimony of contemporary realist theory, the classical Marxist notion of "dialectical totality"—however slippery and abused at times—does aim to capture the indivisibility of the social world, including the geopolitical, while preserving an irreducibility or "relative autonomy" of different dimensions of the social (see Jay 1984). With this said, however, I find it more interesting and fruitful, both politically and intellectually, to begin from the possibility that "the international" is more of a problem for Marxist theory than has been hitherto recognized.

5. Notable exceptions include Levy 1990; Trachtenberg 1991; Copeland 2000.

6. Important works associated with the *Sonderweg* thesis include Veblen 1915; Taylor 1946; Gerschenkron 1966; Moore 1966; Dahrendorf 1967; Wehler 1972, 1985; Fischer 1974, 1975; Kehr 1977, esp. 97-108; Puhle 1986; Kocka 1999b.

7. Jürgen Kocka quoted in Childers 1990, 332.

8. See the more recent (if heavily qualified) restatements by two of its most indefatigable advocates, Kocka (1988, 1999a) and Wehler (1996). In the IR literature, see Snyder 1991.

9. See also Eley 1986, 1996 and contributions in Blackbourn and Evans 1991.

10. The argument that Germany lacked a bourgeois revolution in the 19th century has been, to my mind, definitively refuted. This position assumes an idealized representation of the earlier English and French cases, which have been shown to have "diverged" from the normative model of bourgeois revolution they supposedly set. More important, the argument for the absence of a German bourgeois revolution rests on a direct identification of revolution with its agents rather than its *structural consequences:* the idea is that "bourgeois revolutions" can only be made by the bourgeois themselves. This then excludes the most common form of capitalist transitions from the mid-19th century onward: that is, "revolution from above," or what Gramsci termed "passive revolution" (see Stedman Jones 1977; Blackbourn and Eley 1984; Richard J. Evans 1985; Callinicos 1989a; Mooers 1991; Davidson 2012, chap. 19).

11. In the revised second edition of *Germany and the Approach to War,* Volker Berghahn (1993) attributes much greater weight to industrial capitalists in driving German naval expansionism (see Berghahn 1996; Tooze 2001).

12. For similar perspectives in IR, see Halperin 2004; Lacher 2006, 138-39. The Old Regime interpretation of the two world wars is also amenable to the "democratic peace thesis."

13. In all three cases, the emphasis on the persistence of a hegemonic aristocratic landowning classes is misplaced. The problem of forces from below pressurizing the German ruling classes into imperialist expansionism and war is a separate question examined in chap. 3. The Austro-Hungarian and Russian cases better fit Mayer's model, though the tsarist regime clearly feared the revolutionary consequences of a European war resulting in the regime's collapse.

14. On French policy vis-à-vis Mayer's thesis in the origins of the war, see Keiger 1983; Hayne 1993; on Britain, see Lammers 1973; Gordon 1974; French 1982; Steiner and Neilson 2003.

15. Similarly, Herwig notes (1991, 59) that while some of Fischer's views remain controversial, "three-quarters" of his empirical arguments are now accepted by the majority of historians.

16. There are two principal reasons for this. The first is relatively straightforward: fewer conflict dyads result in fewer possibilities for war. Under conditions of bipolarity, the negative externalities of the security dilemma are diminished, since states are less likely to misperceive the relative power, actions, and intentions of others. Under multipolarity, the risks are increased. The second factor concerns the prevalent *form* of balancing under these two international structures. Deterring aggressive states is easier under bipolar conditions, since great powers need not rely on external balancing (alliance formation) and can instead focus more on internal balancing (military spending). Structural realists identify three consequent positive effects on systemic stability. First, a focus on internal balancing greatly diminishes the possibility of states chain-ganging themselves into major wars over disturbances involving relatively minor powers. Second, it decreases the chances that great powers pass the buck or hide when faced with aggressive challenges. Third, it reduces the prospect that great powers will disregard military spending and thereby allow a superior power to emerge (Copeland 2000, 12).

17. See also Waltz 1979, chap. 8, 2008, chap. 4; Posen 1984; Christensen and Snyder 1990; Van Evera 1999.

18. This much is tacitly admitted by Christensen and Snyder (1990) and Schweller (1998).

19. This is a key critique of neorealism put forth by offensive realists. See Mearsheimer 2001.

20. On the important question of Waltz's conflation of systemic and structural theory, see Buzan, Little, and Jones 1993.

21. As Waltz put it (1986, 340), "Students of international politics will do well to concentrate on separate theories of internal and external politics until someone figures out a way to unite them."

22. See, for example, Snyder's (1991) reliance on domestic regime types, Posen's (1984) incorporation of organization theory, and Van Evera's (1984) emphasis on militarism. All claim to be consistent with the assumptions of neorealism, however this seems disputable.

23. One might retort that such unit-level theories are nonetheless *consistent* with the assumptions of neorealism. But given the sparseness of these very assumptions, what add-on theories would be inconsistent? Very few I suppose.

24. Waltz's conception of the international system is unable to account for the production of units because it lacks any generative mechanisms explaining the existence of sovereign states. Waltz agrees that his account of structure is "individualist in origin" but argues that one can nonetheless distinguish between a system's origins and its structural reproduction (1979, 91). Waltz's justification of this move by recourse to Durkheim's sociology, from which Waltz explicitly builds his theory of the international-political, is unconvincing (see Ruggie 1983; Justin Rosenberg 2008).

25. "Neoclassical" realists such as Randall Schweller (1993, 1998) have sought to loosen Waltz's "state qua state" assumption by differentiating between "status quo" and "revisionist" states. I discuss the problems with this approach vis-à-vis interwar balancing dynamics in chap. 6.

26. As one structural realist put it, "We still lack a theory that can explain, without invoking ad hoc unit-level factors like 'lusting for power' and 'dissatisfaction with the status quo,' why preponderant states in multipolarity attack the system in face of staggering risks and costs" (Copeland 2000, 15).

27. Notable exceptions include Levy 1990; Copeland 2000.

28. Waltz here echoes a number of realist-inspired historians (see Paul M. Kennedy 1984; Lowe 1994; Hinsley 1995).

29. Notable exceptions include Halliday 2002b and the many works of Callinicos (1987a, 2007, 2009).

30. See, for example, Wood 2003; Panitch and Gindin 2004; Kiely 2006; Lacher 2006; Lacher and Teschke 2007. Theories of the "new imperialism" are often inspired by the classical Marxist theories, but few actually claim that lineage (but see Callinicos 2009a; Davidson 2010).

31. The subtitle referred to the "latest," not final, stage of capitalism (Hobsbawm 1987, 367).

32. Throughout this book I employ the term *basis* rather than *base,* since Marx used the former metaphor when writing in English. Pointing this out, James Furner (2008, 4) notes, "'Basis' has the advantage over 'base' in rarely being used to refer to the bottom of physical objects" but rather denoting "that by which something else is sustained or supported."

33. My conception of the basis/superstructure views them as standing in a relationship of "mutual entailment" (Barker 1987) whereby their determinations form a "hierarchy of conditions of possibility" (Sayer 1979, 110).

34. In *State and Revolution,* by contrast, Lenin (influenced by Bukharin) developed a more structuralist conception of the state (Sawer 1977).

35. Teschke and Lacher's (2007, 567) argument that Marxists need provide *"either* a theoretical derivation or a historical specification of the conditions under which capitalist class relations took shape, politically, in the form of multiple and competing sovereign states" gives the game away. This counterpositioning of the "abstract-theoretical" and "concrete-historical" runs throughout Teschke and Lacher's work, where theoretical explanation goes the way of Ancien Régime/*Sonderweg,* in which social relations take the form of undying "historical legacies." On their account, uneven development is a historical hangover from the feudalist-absolutist eras. Thus the sovereign states system is viewed as entirely *contingent* to capitalism. Yet this theoretically conflates the transhistorical fact of unevenness (in part accounting for political multiplicity) with the particulars of European feudalism-absolutism (see Allinson and Anievas 2010a).

36. This is a distinguishing feature of Lenin theory's vis-à-vis Bukharin, as "uneven development" is entirely missing from the latter's static framework (see Howard and King 1989, 249–50).

37. With the very notable exception of Hobsbawm (1987, 302–27), scholars

drawing on the classical theories have offered little in the way of thorough historical analyses of WWI. Even the more historically sensitive works do not spend much time on the war's origins (see most recently Callinicos 2009a, 156–58). On the differences between the "structural," "structural-conjunctural" (or epochal), and "conjunctural" moments of analysis in Marxist theory, see Callinicos 2005.

38. The critique here is informed by Justin Rosenberg 2008, 23–24.

39. To reiterate, Hobsbawm's historical account here is suspect: both Austria-Hungary and Germany actively sought such a war (see chap. 3).

40. Hobsbawm's analysis of WWI is anything but unique within the Marxist literature. Illustrative of the many problems noted earlier, Robert Brenner writes (2006b, 85) in regard to the causes of WWI that "the action of any state can easily set off responses by other states that detonate a chain reaction controllable by none of them. Chain reactions of this sort are the stuff of international history and, though not in contradiction with standard historical-materialist premises . . . they are not fully illuminated by those premises, but require analysis in their own terms." This account not only is historically problematic but also illustrates the untenable detachment of theory from history. The internationally constitutive character of capitalist development (producing the classic "security dilemma" Brenner highlights) is merely *assumed* but in no way explained. Are conjunctures of war merely the object of history but not Marxist theory?

Chapter 2

1. For an excellent critique of political Marxist and World Systems Theory (WST) approaches from a uneven and combined development perspective, see Nisancioglu 2011. Though an important aim of Wallerstein's world systems analysis was to overcome the "methodological nationalism" of the traditional social sciences by rescaling the "unit of analysis" from the nation-state to world system, the intersocietal nonetheless remains an untheorized residual (see Skocpol 1977; Zolberg 1981). The analysis of capitalism as a domestic social system is simply transposed to the world level as exemplified by WST's employment of such categories as the "division of labor," "core/periphery," "town/country," and "unequal exchange." Further, international exchange relations take prominence over the character of production in defining social structures. Consequently, the existence of a world capitalist system predetermines the identity of its national-state parts (Brenner 1985). This leaves no room for noncapitalist social configurations and "combined developments" of the sort that the perspective developed in this volume can elucidate.

2. An examination of Marx's basis/superstructure architecture is far beyond the scope of this discussion; but see Allinson and Anievas 2010a. Chris Harman (1986) provides a concise interpretation of how best to understand Marx's basis/superstructure metaphor when he writes:

The distinction between base and superstructure is not a distinction between one set of institutions and another, with economic institutions on one side and political, judicial, ideological, etc. institutions on the other. It is a distinction between relations that are directly connected with production and those that are not. Many particular institutions include both.

3. According to Justin Rosenberg (1994), Marx and Engels's works on war, diplomacy, and colonialism approximated eight hundred pages. For a judicious review of Marx and Engels's writings on international relations, see Kendel 1989.

4. See, for example, Marx's 1877 letter to the editor of *Otyecestvenniye Zapisky,* where he argues against an interpretation of *Capital* as a "historico-philosophic theory of the *marche generale* [general path] imposed by fate upon every people." Found at http://www.marxists.org/archive/marx/works/1877/11/russia.htm.

5. As Andrew Linklater put it (1990, 3), "The merits of political realism had been exemplified by the role that international relations had played in the transformations of Marxist politics in the twentieth century. What had been intended as an instrument of revolutionary change had become an agent of the reproduction of the international system."

6. At the beginning of *Capital,* chap. 24, Marx writes, "In order to examine the object of our investigation in its integrity, free from all disturbing subsidiary circumstances, we must treat the whole world as one nation, and assume that capitalist production is everywhere established and has possessed itself of every branch of industry" (1976, 727 n. 2). The idea that Marx based his theory of capitalism on a conception of society as a "closed national system" has been forcefully challenged by Lucia Pradella (2013). Basing her interpretation on a wide-ranging reading of Marx's notebooks kept while he was writing *Capital,* Pradella claims that the abstraction Marx employed was *not* the English nation-state (as traditionally assumed) but the British Empire. Marx thus internalized North-South imperial relations and the development of the *modern state system,* particularly in the chapter on "so-called primitive accumulation," into his theory of capital accumulation. The processes of empire-building and state-building are therefore conceptualized within a single analytical optic whereby the concentration of force monopolized by the modern state is wielded to exploit and oppress workers from both within (domestically) and without (internationally). This offers the foundations for rethinking the emergence of the sovereign international system on the basis of the drive for capitalism accumulation on a world scale. There is much to take away from Pradella's constructive interpretation, not least of which is her drawing out of Marx's conception of states and violence as socially generative and relatively autonomous forces of historical transformation. On this view, states and state interventionism (internal and external) are clearly "functionally promiscuous," as Michael Mann (1986) put it, critiquing Marx's putative economism. Nonetheless, whether Pradella's reading of Marx is more immanent than exegetical is debatable. But more important for my discussion here and irrespective of the character of Pradella's interpretation (brilliant as it is) is the extent that this directly engages the "problematic of international." In other words, why does the "political" in Marx's "critique of political economy"

take the spatial expression of a plurality of societies (in its contemporary form the states system)? And to what extent does Marx theoretically incorporate the distinctive causal pressures emerging from this form?

7. Hall's essay was a review of books by John M. Hobson, Hendryk Spruyt, and Sandra Halperin.

8. Thanks in part to the works of Neil Davidson and Justin Rosenberg, the past few years have witnessed a great revival of studies on uneven and combined development cutting across disciplinary and theoretical boundaries (see, among others, Ashman 2006; Barker 2006; Linden 2007; Matin 2007, 2013; *Cambridge Review of International Affairs* 2009; Joseph 2010; Steel 2010; Heller 2011; Hobson 2011; Makki 2011; Glenn 2012; Kiely 2012; Luke Cooper 2013). The issues raised here are, then, far from merely contributions to internecine Marxist debates.

9. I am not concerned here with the various internal debates within Marxism over the differences between the ideas of "unequal development," "combined and uneven development," and "uneven and combined development." The former two are central to many studies in the *dependencia* and world systems perspectives (see, for example, Amin 1977; Chilcote 1984; Brett 1985; Arrighi 2007). In no way do I wish to downplay the significance of these studies. My basic point here is that neither the distinct determinations of the international nor a sociological conception of combination is explicitly present in these works. On the uniqueness of the law of uneven and combined development and its often confused uses, see Davidson 2012, 284–308.

10. For an anthology of these early debates sketching the origins of the strategy of permanent revolution, see Day and Gaido 2009.

11. For the original theory on which the following exposition draws, see esp. Trotsky 1936, 1959, chap. 1, 1962, 1969, chap. 1.

12. The "*unevenness* of historical development of different countries and continents," Trotsky wrote, "*is in itself uneven*" (1936, 15). Therefore, "the force of [uneven development] operates not only in the relations of countries to each other, but also in the mutual relationships of the various processes within one and the same country" (Trotsky 1962, 131).

13. For studies highlighting the role of unevenness in the emergence of capitalism, see Heller 2011; Anievas and Nisancioglu 2013.

14. The use of the term *backwardness* is in no way intended in a moral and/or pejorative sense (see Knei-Paz 1978, 63).

15. The idea of a uniquely Russian "privilege of backwardness" was first coined by Russian populist V. P. Vorontsov in *The Fates of Capitalism in Russia* (1882) and was prefigured in the writings of Alexander Herzen four decades earlier. In Vorontsov's formulation,

> The historical peculiarity of our large-scale industry consists in the circumstance that it must grow up when other countries have already achieved a high level of development. It entails a two-fold result: firstly, our industry can utilize all the forms which have been created in the West, and, therefore, can

develop very rapidly, without passing at a snail's pace through all the successive stages; secondly, it must compete with the more experienced, highly industrialized countries, and the competition with such rivals can choke the
weak sparks of our scarcely awakening capitalism. (quoted in Walicki 1969,
115–16)

I thank Neil Davidson for alerting me to this citation.

16. The flip side of this privilege—the "advantages" and "penalties" of historical "priority"—is examined in chapter 3.

17. I have greatly benefited from my discussions with Adam Fabry on the importance of the terms of incorporation and the crucial role of political agency in
this process. For an excellent discussion of the case of contemporary Hungary, see
Fabry 2011.

18. Take the classic example of the interwar Chinese Revolution. Simultaneously pressurized through geopolitical competition and war into "catch-up" development, the Maoist revolutionaries drew inspiration and built on the achievements of the already "degenerated" Stalinist model (see Deutscher 1984, 181–212).

19. By contrast, Teschke (along with Hannes Lacher, among others) has sought
to demonstrate the utility of Robert Brenner's theory of social property relations
(also known as Political Marxism) as a theory of IR, in particular by providing a
historicized account of the rise of and interconnections between capitalism and
the modern states system. According to Teschke (2003) and Lacher (2006), the
inauguration of a genuinely modern system of sovereign states was *not* a product
of the Treaty of Westphalia (1648), as conventional IR narratives assume, but instead connected to the emergence of capitalist property relations in England after the Glorious Revolution of 1688 from which they spread out internationally
through a long-term process of "geopolitically combined and socially uneven
development." From their historical analyses of the emergence of capitalism
within the context of an antecedently formed system of plural states, Lacher and
Teschke claim that the "interstate-ness of capitalism" *cannot* be derived from the
nature of the capital relation itself. Rather, it must be "regarded as a 'historical
legacy' of precapitalist development" (Lacher 2002, 148; 2006, 60; Teschke 2003,
145–46). "Taking the international character of global capitalism to be a *contingent* aspect of capitalism," the states system is conceived as being structurally internalized within the totality of capitalist social relations through the spatiotemporally differentiated and geopolitically mediated development of capitalist
property relations (Lacher 2006, 60, emphasis added; see Teschke and Lacher
2007). For Lacher and Teschke, then, there is neither any structural connection
between capitalism and a multistate system nor anything inherent to the nature
of capitalism that would necessarily perpetuate it; rather, the relationship is conceived as an entirely contingent one. As Teschke (2003, 144–45) puts it, "there is
no constitutive or genetic link between capitalism and a geopolitical universe."

While there is much to applaud in Teschke and Lacher's works, particularly
their rigorously historicized account of the origins of the modern states system

and capitalism—which, within IR studies at least, is probably one of the best available—many of their empirical findings, along with the theoretical framework underlying them, are problematic. The first problem concerns the theoretical tools on offer from a Political Marxist perspective in *theorizing* the existence of the variegated and interactive process of sociohistorical development as a whole. There is, in other words, no *theoretical* (as opposed to historical) explanation of the existence of "the international" in the first place and, consequently, like neo-Weberians and other approaches to historical sociology, the distinct behavior patterns and causal determinations arising from the interaction of a multiplicity of political communities remain theoretically exogenous to the Political Marxist framework. Teschke's *Myth of 1648* remains trapped within an essentially "inside-out" logic of explanation by which different geopolitical systems reflect and express the internal attributes of "domestically" constituted social property regimes. As he puts it, "the nature and dynamics of international systems are governed by the character of their constitutive units, which, in turn, rests on the specific property relations prevailing within them" (Teschke 2003, 46; see also 7, 73). Indeed, Teschke and Lacher's (2007, 567) argument that Marxists need provide *"either* a theoretical derivation or a historical specification of the conditions under which capitalist class relations took shape, politically, in the form of multiple and competing sovereign states" is inherently problematic. For without the prior theoretical derivation of "the international," thereby internalizing its causal determinations within the anterior structures of theory itself, any historical account of the emergence of a multiple, competitive sovereign states system remains theoretically underdetermined. Or, to put it another way, it *assumes* rather than explains a key causal factor that needs to be theoretically incorporated into the analysis: that is, the antecedent existence of a multiplicity of interactive political communities. For the unevenness of sociohistorical development is a crucial condition in the development of both capitalism and the modern states system itself.

Second, and following from this partial disconnect between historical and theoretical analysis, Teschke and Lacher's argument that capitalism retains a wholly *contingent* relation to a multistate system is entirely unconvincing. While one might legitimately question the historical connection between capitalism and the modern states system—claiming, as Teschke and Lacher do, that the latter emerged prior to the former—this in no way invalidates the systemic connection between the two as capitalism's "laws of motion" perpetuate political multiplicity through its deepening *systemization* of developmental unevenness (see Callinicos 2007; Anievas 2008; Davidson 2010). In other words, uneven development must be viewed as a *constitutive property* of capitalism whether conceived as an abstract or historically determinate system of social relations. Thus, even *if* capitalism had emerged within a universal empire, it would have *necessarily*, by its own logic of process, created a system of multiple states, though the precise form that such states would have assumed is an open question (see Davidson 2010). In this sense, one can indeed theoretically derive political multiplicity from capitalism itself. By contrast, Teschke and Lacher base their claims on the contingency of capitalist social relations being mediated and expressed through a plurality of political states from their strict definition of capitalism as constituted by the substantive separation of the political and economic spheres. Thus, according to Teschke and Lacher (2007, 579),

> capitalism developed unevenly not because it is in its nature—conceptually, of course (that is, abstracted from history and agency), it should even itself out internationally through world-price formation and the long-term equalization of profit rates—but because its spatio-temporally differentiated historical origin and expansion was from the first suffused with non-capitalist (and often anti-capitalist) elements that produced and kept reproducing unevenness, manifested in differential strategies of late development and catching-up.

Consequently, they claim that "it is perfectly possible to imagine that had capitalism emerged within an imperial formation—let us say, the Roman Empire—it would *not* have required its political break-up into multiple territorial units" (Teschke and Lacher 2007, 574). It seems then, according to Teschke and Lacher, that both the contemporary system of sovereign states and uneven development are "historical legacies" of a distant feudal-absolutist past. In turn, they view the emergence of a fully capitalist international order after the Cold War as potentially heralding a kind of Kautskian era of ultraimperial peace as capitalism, unlike feudalism or absolutism, does not require the war-assisted process of (geo) political accumulation. Hence, Teschke writes (2003, 267), "we should expect [capitalism] to bring about the decline of external geopolitical accumulation that defined the war-driven international conduct of the feudal and absolutist ages." He goes on to describe international organizations as a providing an "arena of peaceful inter-capitalist conflict resolution," concluding that "the major lines of military conflict run between states that are locked out of the world market and those that reproduce the political conditions of the world market, backed up by the principle of collective security" (Teschke 2003, 267). This would seem the logical conclusion of any strict interpretation of the social property relations approach that conceives the separation of coercive power and economic relations as the sine qua non of capitalist modernity, thereby making any war-assisted mode of capital accumulation seemingly irrational (see Balakrishnan 2004, 157–58; Allinson and Anievas 2010a). From such a perspective, however, how can one begin to understand, let alone respond politically to, events such as the 2003 Anglo-American invasion of Iraq or the US-Russian conflict over Georgia in 2008?

This all ties to a third difficulty with Teschke and Lacher's Political Marxism: the noncorrespondence (or misrecognition) of conceptual abstractions ("capital") and empirical realities (a conflictual states system). For the era of the two world wars, this is particularly problematic as this was an epoch firmly situated within capitalist modernity, despite Lacher's claims to the contrary (2006, 140–41), which view the interimperial rivalries of the time as bound to the protracted transition from absolutism to capitalism. One may then legitimately ask when reality might begin to impede upon our conceptions of it. The social realm is certainly a messy, complex affair; full of accidents, contingencies, and the untheorizable. A grand theory of everything is unlikely. Problems emerge, however, when the central objects of our theories (the modern states system, geopolitical rivalry, war) are considered pure contingencies in relation to the abstractions we seek to explain them with. Ellen Meiksins Wood, a fellow Political Marxist, once criticized the Althusserians as viewing the relationship between the state and mode of production within actually existing social formations as having "little to do" with capitalism's structural logic, thereby appearing "almost accidental" (Wood 1995, 55–56). Might not the same be said of Lacher and Teschke's conceptualization of the relationship between capitalism and the states system?

One final issue, relating to the preceding, is how Teschke and Lacher's Political Marxism is beset by theoretical indeterminacies, a certain form of Eurocentrism, and a near voluntaristic conception of political agency. Regarding the former, for Political Marxism, Marx's master concept the "mode of production"—conceived as the composite totality of relations encapsulating economic, legal, ideological, cultural, and political spheres—is reduced to the much thinner "social property relations" concept itself reduced to a form of exploitation (see Anievas and Nisancioglu 2013, from which the following three paragraphs draw). For Lacher and Teschke this has led to a substitution of Marx's "mode of production" with the much narrower "mode of exploitation" concept. The principal error here, one shared by Brenner, is to take a singular relation of exploitation (whether lord and peasant or capitalist and wage-laborer) as the most fundamental and axiomatic component of the mode of exploitation, which, in turn, constitutes the foundational ontology and analytical "building block" upon which ensuing theoretical and historical investigation is constructed. The result of this ontological singularity is a dual tunneling—both temporal and spatial—of our empirical field of vision and enquiry. *Temporally*, the history of capitalism's origins is reduced to the historical manifestation of one conceptual moment—the freeing of labor—and in turn explained by it. This is a "big bang" theory of the origins of capitalism, whereby capitalism's emergence is explained within a single conjuncture rather than a long, drawn-out process of increasing systemic complexification and consolidation continuing beyond the initial moment of its inception. For even after capitalist social relations have emerged and generalized within a single state, their systemic reproduction may rely for some time on the external sociohistorical environment as, for example, through such processes of colonialism and imperialism.

Spatially, for the Political Marxists, the genesis of capitalism is confined to a single geographical region—the English countryside—immune from wider intersocietal developments. Yet such tunneling cannot account for why the extensive presence of formally free wage labor prior to the sixteenth century (both inside and outside England) did not give rise to capitalism elsewhere (see Banaji 2011). Nor can it explain subsequent social developments. By obliterating the histories of colonialism, slavery, and imperialism, Brenner's account of the origins of capitalism, which Lacher and Teschke faithfully follow, "freezes" capitalism's history (Blaut 1991). This substantially narrows Marx's more robust conception of the process of so-called primitive accumulation that Brenner and his students give so much analytical weight in explaining capitalism's origins. As Marx wrote (1990, 915):

> The discovery of gold and silver in America, the expiration, enslavement and entombment in mines of the indigenous population of that continent, the beginnings of the conquest and plunder of India, and the conversion of Africa into a preserve for the commercial hunting of blackskins, are all things which characterize the dawn of the era of capitalist production. These idyllic proceedings are the chief moments of primitive accumulation. . . . The different moments of primitive accumulation can be assigned in particular to Spain, Portugal, Holland, France, and England, in more or less chronological order. These moments are systematically combined together at the end of the seventeenth century in England; the combination embraces the colonies, the national debt, the modern tax system, and the system of protection.

Here we see the much more temporally and spatially expansive conception of capitalism's emergence that Marx provides. The story of capitalism's genesis was not a national phenomenon, but, rather, an *intersocietal* one. It thus makes sense to follow Perry Anderson in viewing the origins of capitalism "as a value-added process gaining in complexity as it moved along a chain of interrelated sites" (Anderson 2005, 251).

By contrast, the Political Marxists *spatially* reduce capitalism's origins to processes that occurred solely in the English countryside. As such, towns and cities are omitted, Europe-wide dynamics are analytically active only as comparative cases, and the world outside of Europe does not figure at all. Similarly excluded are the numerous technological, cultural, institutional, and social relational discoveries and developments originating outside of Europe that were appropriated and adopted by Europe in the course of its capitalist development (see Hobson 2004). In short, Political Marxism neglects the determinations and conditions that arose from the social interactions *between* societies: "'political community' is subordinated to 'class' while classes are themselves largely conceptualised and studied within the empirical spatial limits of the political community in question" (Matin 2012, 45). As a consequence of this spatiotemporal tunneling there emerges a certain Eurocentrism within Political Marxists' accounts of the rise of capitalism and its spread. Temporal tunneling gives rise to the notion of historical priority (that is, developments within Europe are conceived as the primary "movers" of world history), while spatial tunneling gives rise to a methodologically internalist analysis. For Brenner's followers, these problems are only compounded as the possibility of the development of early capitalisms outside of the English countryside that Brenner allows for are rejected (compare Brenner 2001 to Wood 2002; Post 2002; Teschke 2003, 136). The notion of the origins of "capitalism in one country" is thus taken literally.

Finally, there is the issue of Teschke and Lacher's voluntaristic conception of political agency. In attempting to avoid any form of economic or technological reductionism associated with some variants of Marxism, Teschke and Lacher evacuate any causal role (direct or indirect) of Marx's forces of production from their theory of sociohistorical change. Before evaluating the consequences of this move, one first needs to dispel a common misperception of what the concept of the productive forces actually entails. For a frequent criticism of giving the productive forces any explanatory power (let alone primacy) is that it inevitably runs the risk of "technological determinism" vacating human agency in the process (see, for example, Lacher 2006, 30). Thus it is important to note that the productive forces not only took on different meanings relating to different historical contexts in Marx's writings (at one point being identified with early political communities) but, moreover, that they are not to be conflated with mere "technologies" (Marx 1973, 495; see Pijl 2007, 7–12). Rather, the forces of production refer to both the *means of production*—including "nature itself, the capacity to labour, the skills brought to the process, the tools used, and the techniques with which these tools are set to work"—and the *labor process*, "the way in which the different means of production are combined in the act of production itself" (Davidson 2012, 128). As this definition indicates, the forces of production (or "productive powers") cannot be subsumed under any "technodeterminist" interpretation: they are simultaneously *material* and *social* as, for example, the techniques by which tools are used necessarily imply both accumulated collective knowledge and a particular sociohistorical context in which they operate. To say then that there is a tendency for the forces of production to develop over time is to simply express that humans have been motivated to change them and have done so successfully in a way that the social productivity of labor has increased as a result (Davidson 2012, 512). Human agency is thus crucial in the process. By erasing the role of the productive forces, Lacher and Teschke thereby overlook the "limits" set by their development in explaining modal transitions, such as that between the feudal-absolutist epochs and capitalism. Moreover, the effects that the development of certain technologies (as an element of the productive forces) have on geopolitical strategizing and war-making are also ignored (Balakrishnan 2004; see also chaps. 3 and 5). Political Marxists' ability to offer a historical materialist account of geopolitics, the state, and war is thereby significantly hampered, for without *some* causal weight attributed to the development of the productive forces it becomes very difficult, if not impossible, to fully illuminate the sociomaterial contexts in which states function, foreign policymaking is made, and grand strategy executed, as well as their possibilities for success (see chap. 5). Moreover, in further loosening the perceived residual structuralism of Robert Brenner's (1986) concept of specific "rules of reproduction" for agents operating under capitalist conditions, Teschke and Lacher propose (2007, 571) "the more flexible and historically open term, 'ways of reproduction,'" circumventing Brenner's original concept's stipulation of an "analytically limited set of strategic options to class-specific reproduction." With this move, Teschke and Lacher have thus slipped into a voluntaristic understanding of political agency. For what purpose is there for a historical materialist theory of social structure and its system reproduction—not to mention the gauging of the possibilities for its transcendence—if not to understand and explain the range and limits of possible "strategic options to class-specific reproduction"? Of course, in no way should one deny the different means through which capitalists reproduce themselves, but they are nonetheless limited in their options by the determinations and pressures set by the competitive logic of capital accumulation, operating at multiple sociospatial scales (regional, national, international, global, and so on). Hence, as Callinicos rightly notes (2009b, 97)

> the whole thrust of Brenner's original work was to demonstrate the specific role played by what he calls social-property systems . . . in both setting limits to what specific categories of social actors can do and also, very importantly, endowing them with particular types of social capability and interests (captured by the concept of the rules of reproduction). In the absence of this theoretical construction, the entire argument for the specificity of capitalist economic development that has been one of the main themes of Political Marxism would collapse.

What we then find in Teschke and Lacher's rearticulation of Political Marxism is a structureless, inductive form of inquiry that does not quite add up to a theory of international relations at all. While offering a number of important insights into the evolving nature of social property relations and their relation to historically specific geopolitical systems, the end result is underwhelming in theoretical terms and questionable on some historical empirical claims as well— demonstrated, for example, in Teschke's contention (2003, 136) that the Low Countries did not undergo a capitalist transition before England. (In contrast, see Pepijn Brandon's [2011] judicial overview of the contemporary literature on the origins of Dutch capitalism.) Thus, whatever one makes of Teschke's criticisms of uneven and combined development, his alternative approach is an unhelpful starting point into understanding the geopolitics of the two world wars or, for that matter, the geopolitics of capitalist modernity more generally.

20. All the commonly identified "classical" Marxists recognized the manifold empirical links among imperialism, war, and revolution. Nonetheless, the theoretical exploration of a distinctive international sociality and its relationship to the causes of war and imperialism was never broached.

21. The problem of transhistorical overstretching is further addressed in Allinson and Anievas 2009, 2010a. For the purposes of explaining the geopolitics of the two world wars—an epoch firmly situated in capitalist modernity—much of the discussion is left aside here.

22. It is doubtful that Justin Rosenberg would disagree with much said here regarding the interweaving of the general and particular in social theoretic explanation, as an earlier discussion of Marx's method of abstraction illustrates (2000, 69–73). Nonetheless, the extent to which he has consistently followed this method is debatable (compare Justin Rosenberg 2007, 455, 456–57; 2006, 321, 323–24; 2008, 7–8, 20–21; 2010, 166–71; see also Allinson and Anievas 2009).

23. That said, the role that unevenness and combination played as causal conditions in the transition from feudalism to capitalism is a topic in need of further exploration. For an initial attempt at such an analysis, see Anievas and Nisancioglu 2013.

24. This can be seen as an example of Imre Lakatos's (1976, 82–99) "conceptstretching"—the expansion of a theoretical concept beyond its original range of explanatory hypotheses.

Chapter 3

1. There are, of course, limits to the explanatory scope of such a historically expansive account. This chapter does not seek to offer a "total history" of the origins of the 1914–18 war. Given the immensity of the historical literature, such a history would require a separate book. Moreover, I will not provide a detailed discussion of the day-to-day diplomatic activities of the July–August 1914 crisis. However, the chapter does crucially illustrate the framework's applicability in explaining the dominant causal forces shaping the chain of events leading to the war's outbreak. This is necessary given the decisive importance of the specificity of the war conjuncture in presenting a relatively short window of opportunity for the launching of a "preventive war," as emphasized in the historiographical literature. Thus, the road from Agadir to Sarajevo forms a central element of the later analysis.

2. For an interesting analysis of how uneven and combined development might be used to theorize contingencies, see Luke Cooper 2013.

3. Jack Levy (2011, 87) defines preventive war as "a state strategy to use military force to forestall an adverse shift in the distribution of power between two states . . . The logic of prevention is 'better now than later'—it is better to fight now and degrade the adversary's capabilities while the opportunity is still available, than to risk the consequences of continued decline." It is important to note that "preventive war" must not be confused with the normatively untenable concept of "defensive war." In IR, concepts such as "offense" and "defense" take different meanings from different timelines: an "offensive," forward invasion today could often be a response to decades of aggressive acts on the part of the target. While my use of *preventive war* is generally consistent with Levy's definition, two significant caveats must be noted. First, the concept must be rid of any realist assumptions of states as discretely formed entities whereby the logic of their competitive interaction autonomously (that is, theoretically isolated from their co-constitutive social structures) dictates their strategies. Second, and following from the first caveat, I expand the meaning of preventive war to incorporate the

destabilizing interaction of "external" and "internal" dynamics in producing different ramified social structures that came to feed back into causes of the war. As examined in this chapter, the German polity was in the midst of a severe domestic crisis that provided the ground on which the decision for war was made. I do *not* accept the stronger versions of a *Flucht nach vorn* (flight forward) thesis as a conscious strategy of "diversionary war" against revolution, but I do recognize the pressurized sociopolitical context affecting the decision (Eley 2014, 5).

4. Here I draw on the discussions of structural and conjunctural analysis in Callinicos 2005; Justin Rosenberg 2005.

5. Not only does a seemingly endless array of analytical dilemmas await any historical sociological investigation of precapitalist societies outside of Western Europe, but so too emerge a number of unresolved issues regarding the concept's appropriate spatial register of social relations. To put it in IR terms, what "level of analysis" does the mode of production seek to capture? Is a mode of production to be defined by the internal relations of territorially demarcated political spaces (the "nation-state" in its contemporary form) or from the world perspective, subsuming these international relations? Despite Marx's employment of the "pernicious postulate" of the nation-state framework, as Charles Tilly (1984, 11) terms it, historical materialism's guiding abstraction ("modes of production") in no way logically presupposes society in the ontological singular. As Eric Wolf (1997, 76) rightly claims, one of the advantages of the "mode of production" concept is that it "allows us to visualize intersystemic and intrasystemic relationships," with the former representing "interconnected systems in which societies are variously linked within wider "social fields."

6. For a discussion of this problem in relation to specific Marxist theories of IR, see Allinson and Anievas 2010a.

7. This follows the conceptual approach sketched by Justin Rosenberg (2008, 25–28) with significant alterations, among them its expanded geographical scope and inclusion of a third, "transatlantic" vector connecting the Anglo-Saxon empires.

8. On the rise of a distinct "Anglo world," see Belich 2009.

9. India and China are best described as cases of "*de*-development" resulting from European imperialism (see Mike Davis 2001).

10. In contrast to my analysis, Lebow conceptualizes the causal chains (three in his model) as independent in origin and effect.

11. This is a central argument of McDonald 1992 and is supported by Lieven 1983, Dietrich Geyer 1987, and Neilson 1995.

12. The global-colonial foundations of Britain's industrialization cannot be stressed enough. Likewise, capitalism did not emerge from developments *internal* to Europe. Unfortunately, these issues cannot be pursued further here (see Anievas and Nisancioglu 2013).

13. Trotsky (1918) set the precedent in this manner. Partial exceptions include Eley and Blackbourn 1984; Callinicos 2009a.

14. Here, it is only fair to note that Robert Gilpin (1981, 179) identifies Trotsky's

idea of uneven and combined development as a basis for his theorization. Yet nowhere does Gilpin employ "combined" social development in his analysis.

15. Astute British realist historian F. H. Hinsley, for example, criticized the classical Marxist explanation of war as the "inevitable" result of the monopoly capitalist epoch as fundamentally mistaken since war and imperialism were far more frequent among precapitalist societies than after capitalism had fully developed. He then went on to explain WWI as a consequence of "massive change in the criteria and distribution of power that was brought about from the 1870s, and especially after 1890s, by the uneven development, as between the different states, of industrialization based increasingly on technology and science" (Hinsley 1995, 6), Yet this leads to the question of what kind of *social structure* involves— indeed, demands—the systematic application of science and technology to spur this enormously dynamic but staggered process of industrialization. The ending of Europe's "insulation from the wider balance of power," as Hinsley (1995, 6) puts it, affected by the emergence of Japan and the United States as great powers, is thus only explicable as one aspect of a much wider process accompanying the rise of a distinctly *capitalist* world economy. For an appreciation of the differences among specific realist thinkers on technology, see Scheuerman 2009.

16. This was *despite* the fact that many contemporary technological developments actually favored "defensive" tactics. These were not, however, immediately apparent to many military strategists, who often interpreted them as favoring the "offensive." Further, although by 1914, most of the general staffs of the great powers anticipated a relatively long war, these expectations were not relayed to civilian policymakers lest the information deter them from going to war (Stevenson 1996; Förster 1999).

17. This is *not* to argue that Britain's empire had by this point turned into an absolute military or economic liability. The empire and dominion states made decisive contributions in material terms of soldiers, finances, industries, and raw materials to the British military efforts in both world wars. Moreover, during the Great Depression of the 1930s, imperial protectionism provided British capital with much-needed market outlets for its trade and investments (Saul 1960; Hobsbawm 1968, chap. 11; Cain and Hopkins 1993a, 109–12, 172–77; Mike Davis 2001, 296–301).

18. For Trotsky's analysis of German development in this international context, see 1971, 272–73.

19. On the emergence of the new radical nationalist Right and the drive for empire, see Eley 1980; Blackbourn 1986; Seligmann and McLean 2000, 81–91.

20. Making sense of the many "peculiarities" associated with Bismarck's revolution from above and its consequences for the trajectory of German development, Eley and Blackbourn write (1984, 85), requires "something like the classical Marxist concept of uneven and combined development." See also Mooers 1991, 143–46.

21. In addition to Perry Anderson 1974, the following account of German development draws on Wehler 1985; Blackbourn 2003.

22. For example, the Aniline violet dye and Gilchrist-Thomas processes from Britain and the fuchsine process from France (Trebilcock 1981, 64).

23. Hegemonic projects refer to specific political strategies formulated and pursued by social forces, including factions of capital in conjunction with public intellectuals, lobby groups, and other social organizations. For a hegemonic project to succeed, the dominant faction of capital or its "organic intellectuals" guiding the project must be able to unite other segments of capital and social forces under its "leadership." It must be able to reconcile its particular "economic-corporate" interests with the "universal" interests of the majority within the ruling social stratum (Gramsci 1971, 181, 370). Hegemonic projects are thus concerned with gaining a measure of consent and legitimacy, though always backed by force, among all social classes. A successful hegemonic project thus represents the strategic articulation of the interests of a historically concrete constellation of social forces under the leadership of specific factions of capital. At first sight, this might seem to contradict the emphasis on the potential for a divergence of interests between state managers and ruling classes. Yet the concept of a hegemonic *project* highlights the always *partial, incomplete,* and context-specific character of hegemony under world capitalist conditions. The triumph of a particular hegemonic project within a state (or multiple states) does *not* negate the continuing existence of intercapitalist, interbureaucratic, and/or geopolitical competitions that are often the source of "relatively autonomous" state interests. Rather, it *structures the contexts* in which these conflicts take place. The idea of different segments of capitals pursuing divergent hegemonic projects provides a less rigid analysis of the interconnections between state and capital by sensitizing the examination to the often open-ended and *partially* indeterminate interests of factions of capital vis-à-vis policymakers. The concept thus elucidates the fluid and unstable nature of intercapitalist competition in specific factions' attempts to secure and maintain a position of hegemony (Jessop 1990, 217).

24. To take one of many examples, after hearing a report about labor unrest at Augsburg and other places, the kaiser exclaimed, *"The Ministry of War has told me* that *at any time* I can declare a state of siege *throughout the Empire* (!!!). Until the Social Democratic leaders are fetched out of the Reichstag by soldiers and shot, no improvement can be hoped for." The following day, the kaiser reiterated his hope that a *"very* considerable blood-letting must be applied" in putting down the Socialists (Bülow 1931, 346).

25. For a good comparative analysis of different states' responses to the depression, see Gourevitch 1978.

26. See, for example, LaFeber 1998 on the United States; Lebovics 1988 on France; Berghahn 1993 on Germany; Hobsbawm 1968 on Great Britain.

27. On the effects of the depression and its relationship to economic groups and German foreign policy, see esp. Hans Rosenberg 1943; Gerschenkron 1966; Böhme 1967; Fischer 1975.

28. Some of the most important works include Mommsen 1973; Gordon 1974; Fischer 1975; Geiss 1976; Kehr 1977; Wehler 1985; Pogge von Strandmann 1988; Berghahn 1993.

29. This is covered in more detail later in chapter 3, under the heading "From Agadir to Sarajevo."

30. For the original Morgenthau quote, see http://www.gomidas.org/gida/in dex_and_%20documents/MorgRecords_index_and_documents/docs/Morgen thauDiaries1914.pdf. Further quotes by policymakers to this effect can be found in Geiss 1967, 65–68, docs. 3, 4; Fischer 1975, 172–74, 370–87; Berghahn 1993, 164–67, 203; Ferguson 1994, 144–45; Herrmann 1997, 136–37, 213–15; Copeland 2000, 64, 69–70, 83–84; Mombauer 2001, 122, 145, 173–79, 189.

31. Though as Marx noted at the time of the Franco-Prussian conflict, "If *Alsace* and *Lorraine* are taken, then *France* will later make war on *Germany in conjunction with Russia*" (quoted in Joll and Martel 2007, 56).

32. On the eve of the war, however, the French political milieu had witnessed a rightward nationalist shift demonstrated by the success of the Bloc Nationale in the 1912 elections. In office, Poincaré did little to relieve European tensions and, to this extent, his policies likely promoted war (Hayne 1993, 242–43; Strachan 2001, 28–29).

33. This is a key theme of Fischer 1975.

34. This conclusion is supported by the work of René Girault (1973) as discussed by Joll and Martel (2007). See also Collins 1973; Lieven 1983, 29–30; Dietrich Geyer 1987, 169–85; Spring 1988; Skålnes 2000, 71–107.

35. This section has greatly benefited from my many discussions with Jamie Allinson, whose dissertation (2012) applies uneven and combined development to the case of Jordan's state-formation process.

36. In the century before the First World War, the rate of growth of per capita gross domestic product for the Ottoman Empire remained between 1 and 2 percent, while differences in per capita income levels between the Middle East and high-income areas, such as Western Europe and the United States, widened (Pamuk 2006; see also table 1, on Austro-Hungarian growth).

37. The general contours of Trotsky's analysis of Russian development have been followed by subsequent scholars (see esp. Gerschenkron 1962; Trebilcock 1981).

38. The Schlieffen Plan was later altered by the younger Moltke. In this later incarnation, I therefore refer to it as the Schlieffen-Moltke Plan (Mombauer 2001).

39. Rather than viewing this process of policy alteration as derivative of an autonomously conceived changing balance of power (for example, Copeland 2000), it should instead be conceptualized in terms of the social-material dynamic standing behind these changes—that is, the uneven development between the European powers. In this sense, uneven development can be said to constitute an element determining the unconscious substratum of foreign policymaking (Paul M. Kennedy's "realities behind diplomacy") expressed by such metaphors as the "balance of power" employed by state and military managers.

40. In a 27 July 1911 telegram signed by leading steel magnates (including Thyssen, Rochling, and Kirdorf), the foreign minister was asked to defend the supply of raw materials from Morocco and the sale of German goods there "even if seri-

ous consequences ensue." Similarly, in a circular, a highly influential industrial lobby group, the CdI, wrote, "From the point of view of the German economy it is essential not only to preserve our German sphere of interest in Morocco but to safeguard for the future for reasons of economic and colonial policy the positions which our entrepreneurs have created there" (quoted in Fischer 1975, 80–81).

41. Diary entry, 4 October 1912, in Rathenau 1985, 167–68.

42. The positions of German and Habsburg policymakers during the July crisis were well summarized by Count Forgách in a private letter of 8 July 1914:

> The Minister [Berchtold] is determined . . . to use the horrible deed of Sarajevo for a military clearing-up of our impossible relationship with Serbia. The Austrian government, as well as of course the military and Bilinski . . . are in favour. Tisza, however, is opposed, wants to make only such demands of Serbia as will humiliate it but whose acceptance is not totally impossible, perhaps pose an ultimatum and only mobilize afterwards. With Berlin we are in complete agreement. Kaiser & Reich Chancellor etc. more decided than ever before; they take on board complete cover against Russia, *even at the risk of a world war which is not at all ruled out,* they consider the moment as favourable & advise to strike as soon [as possible] without asking or consulting the 2 other allies, Italy and the more than dubious Rumania, in any way. (quoted in Mombauer 2007, 84)

43. Muller's diary account of the meeting is reproduced in Röhl 1969, 662–63, from which the quotes are taken.

44. For contrasting interpretations of the War Council and its effects, compare the Fischer School's claims that the meeting set a precise "timetable for war" (Röhl 1969, 1994; Fischer 1975, 160–204; Geiss 1976) with the more cautious positions of Herwig (1991, 57–58), Mombauer (2001, 135–46), and skeptics such as Mommsen (1973, 12–14), Lambi (1984, 382–84), Berghahn (1993, 178–79), Stevenson (1996, 481), and Strachan (2001, 52–54). For the historiographical debates, see Mombauer 2002, 149–52.

Chapter 4

1. The peace treaties included Saint-Germain (with Austria), Neuilly (with Bulgaria), Trianon (with Hungary), Sèvres (with Turkey), and Versailles (with Germany). I generally use the "Paris Peace Conference" or "Versailles diplomacy" as shorthand for the combined outcome of all the treaties.

2. See the debate in Maier, Schuker, and Kindleberger 1981.

3. Within the historiographical literature, interpretations of U.S. diplomacy at Versailles have fallen into three broad schools of thought: realist, liberal, and revisionist. As their labels suggest, the first two overlap with IR approaches. Important realist works on Wilson and Versailles include Lippmann 1943; Kennan 1951; Morgenthau 1951; Osgood 1953; Ambrosius 1977, 2002; David M. Kennedy

1980; Trachtenberg 1980; Graebner 1984; Calhoun 1993; McDougall 1997; and Ross A. Kennedy 2009. The liberal interpretation is by far the most influential in the U.S. historiographical literature. Significant works here include those by Wilson's official biographer, Ray Stannard Baker (1924), Thomas Bailey (1944), John Milton Cooper (1969, 2001), Arthur Walworth (1977), Arthur Stanley Link (1979, 1982), Thomas Knock (1992), Frank Ninkovich (1999), Anne Pierce (2003), and many others. These approaches are discussed in this chapter. Revisionist approaches emphasize the importance of trade and economic concerns more generally in Wilson's diplomacy: see Mayer 1959, 1967; Levin 1968; Sidney Bell 1972; Williams 1972; Gardner 1984; Sklar 1988; Foglesong 1995; and Hoff 2008. Like any broad school, none of these approaches are monolithic. Within the revisionist school, for example, many works highlight the politically and economically progressive aspects of Wilson's diplomacy, sharing much with liberal approaches (Mayer 1959; Levin 1968; Gardner 1984; Bacino 1999), while others are more critical of Wilson's missionary exceptionalism, with more in common with realist interpretations (for example, Williams 1972; Emily S. Rosenberg 1982; LaFeber 1994; Foglesong 1995; Hoff 2008). My interpretation is closer to the latter but also draws on Lloyd Ambrosius's "realist" critique, which offers a useful supplement to those revisionists scholars neglecting the international sources of Wilsonian diplomacy. Given the tendency to automatically identify revisionist historians with (neo-)Marxism, it is worth noting that few actually identify themselves as such. The core theoretical assumptions of their works—specifically those associated with the "Wisconsin School" popularized by William Appleman Williams and his students—draw much less on Marxism than Progressive historians such as Frederick Jackson Turner and Charles Beard, offering an interpretation of U.S. history "quintessentially American in character" (Michael Cox and Kennedy-Pipe 2005, 98).

4. The following presents, in summary form, the "Kennan-Morgenthau" thesis. Kennan and Morgenthau diverged on many issues, however. Following a theory of "status quo" and "revisionist" powers, Morgenthau (1950, 849) saw the total victory against Germany as necessary to preventing its European hegemony. Kennan (1951, 55–56, 67) argued against total victory, looking favorably on the function of the prewar Kaiserreich in maintaining an equilibrium of power in Europe.

5. Numerous historical studies illustrate Wilson's "nonidealist" credentials, including the administration's penchants for unilateralism, power politics, military interventionism, and secret diplomacy (see esp. Safford 1978; David M. Kennedy 1980; Gardner 1984; Calhoun 1993; Foglesong 1995; Hannigan 2002; Ross A. Kennedy 2009).

6. For a fascinating exploration of the epistemological issues raised by realism's strategic rhetoricism, with specific reference to Carr, see Buzan, Little, and Jones (1993, pt. 3).

7. This form of realist explanation finds many resonances in the contemporary conjuncture, as illustrated in Mearsheimer and Walt's (2007) analysis of the

role of the Israeli lobby in the U.S. war on Iraq. The thematization of domestic/ societal factors in explaining U.S. foreign policy and its expansionist tendencies is taken much further by realists such as Fareed Zakaria (1998), Andrew Bacevich (2002), and Christopher Layne (2006). In attempting to escape the straitjacket of structural realism, these studies draw heavily on the Wisconsin School interpretation of U.S. foreign policy, emphasizing the importance of the Open Door strategy.

8. Perhaps this helps explain the tendency among self-proclaimed realist scholars cum policymakers to embrace Wilsonianism, as demonstrated in Kennan's (1991) about-face regarding his criticisms of Wilson (see also Kissinger 1994).

9. As Engels wrote in response to criticisms of Marx's theory as economically reductionist, "Force (that is, state power) is also an economic power!" (Marx and Engels 1983, 402).

10. Oren (1995), Michael Cox (2000), and Anthony (2008) are notable exceptions.

11. Quoted in "Farmers as Businessmen," *New York Times,* 27 July 1912.

12. The textual evidence of this "transcendental idealism of American exceptionalism" (Agnew 1987, 11) in Wilson's thinking is rife, but see esp. Wilson 1966–94, 18:87–95. Here and elsewhere, we see the heavy influence of Frederick Jackson Turner on Wilson's thinking. Both viewed American development as a microcosm of universal history, which represented Americanization writ large (see esp. Frederick Jackson Turner 1966, 10). "By mapping the space of the United States as stages of civilization," Christopher Hill notes (2008, 105), "Turner is able to explain the differences among the regions . . . as differences in degree of civilization. Turner explains away the unevenness of capitalist development by dividing national-historical space." A similar point applies to Wilson's conception of the "the international" as a condition of necessarily *temporary* difference.

13. This was one variation of a larger theme of the putative "harmony of interests" doctrine familiar among contemporary liberal internationalists (see Carr 1939). In the words of one Wilsonian, John Foster Dulles,

> those of us who are idealists must realize that it is the driving force of self-interest that most frequently achieves practical results . . . And fortunately we can very properly make appeal to our selfish interests without being false to our highest ideals. For in the realm of world economies there is no such thing as self-gain apart from gain to others. The world is an economic whole and any nation which intelligently advances its own interests cannot but thereby better the conditions of the world as a whole. ("America's Part in an Economic Conference," 19 January 1922, p. 12, Box 289, Dulles Papers, Mudd Library, Princeton University)

14. This conception of the national interest as universal and U.S. expansionism as missionary in purpose were common Wilsonian themes, as noted by Levin (1968, esp. 9–10, 16–18, 21, 26–27, 34, 126, 148, 249, 257) and others (Gardner 1984;

Offner 1986 [1975]; Sklar 1988; Ambrosius 1991; Tony Smith 1994). For further textual evidence see Wilson 1925, 3:61, 147–48, 4:44, 75, 123–24, 158, 171, 394.

15. A period of profound economic downturn, the formative moment of Wilson's political development was an "era of social upheaval" that saw unprecedented agrarian unrest and mass demonstrations. Between 1881 and 1900, the United States experienced 24,000 labor strikes and lockouts, while membership in the American Federation of Labor grew from 138,000 in 1886 to 1,500,000 in 1904. For the first time in U.S. history, mass radical and socialist parties emerged, threatening "proletarian revolution" (Schlesinger 1933, 161; U.S. Bureau of Labor Statistics 1970, 16–17; Slotkin 1998, 19).

16. On the racialist basis of the often-evoked "self-mastery" concept in contemporary discourses, see Hannigan 2002, 5–9.

17. In Wilson's words, "Business underlies every part of our lives; the foundation of our lives, of our spiritual lives included, is economic" (quoted in Sklar 1992, 108).

18. For Wilson's thought on this issue, see Wilson 1966–94, 15:143.

19. Here one must be careful not to think of the Open Door as the *only* purely capitalist model of expansionism, as do, for example, Wood (2003) and Gindin and Panitch (2004).

20. The British Empire's "imperialism of free trade" (Gallagher and Robinson 1953) during the 19th century was in many ways the real pioneer. However, the Open Door is *not* synonymous with Victorian free trade imperialism: the latter denoted low tariffs and the maintenance of special spheres of interests, whereas the former demanded equality of commercial opportunities.

21. It would be mistaken, however, to conceive of this racial dimension of U.S. foreign policy as somehow unique to U.S. imperialism. Modern racism was inextricably connected to the historical process through which capitalism emerged. The use of scientific and technological criteria in proving the superiority (and thus domination) of Europeans over non-European peoples became the norm from the late 18th century onward, reaching a high point in the era of classical imperialism. As material disparities between an industrial capitalist core and noncapitalist periphery developed, broader philosophical, religious, and cultural distinctions were superseded by those "based on things" (Adas 1989). This was one instance of a more general technological fetishism emerging with the rapid but uneven development of the productive forces under capitalism, whereby the level of technological development was perceived as determining the moral worth of a particular race and/or society. By the late 19th and early 20th centuries, these views were further buttressed and legitimized by the then fashionable "social Darwinist" theories applied to "civilized" countries' relations with the "backward" world. Racist in form and application, such bastardized Darwinistic theories formed one of the crucial assumptions of U.S. foreign policymaking (Hunt 1987; LaFeber 1993, Hannigan 2002). In these ways, modern racism can be viewed as developing with the *systematization of unevenness constitutive of the capitalist production mode.* In the context of U.S. imperialism, both the dispossession of the Native Americans and later interventionist policies abroad

were justified in similar terms. "Native Americans, like other less-powerful groups who possessed territory coveted by White Americans," Joseph Fry notes, "were declared racially inferior and *incapable of productive use of the land*" (2002, 44; emphasis added). As evocations of the "productive use of the land" make clear, communities that did not "adequately" develop the productive forces were judged unfit to live or in need of instructive rule from the morally and culturally superior "Western" society.

22. Wilson ordered more military interventions without declarations of war than any other U.S. president in the 20th century except Bill Clinton (Hoff 2008, 36). Even before Wilson's secret war against Bolshevik Russia, the administration organized military expeditions in Mexico (twice), Haiti, the Dominican Republic, and Nicaragua. As the president explained to a British official, the decision to intervene in Mexico was to "champion the open door"; to "secure Mexico a better government under which all contracts and business and concessions will be safer than they have been" (quoted in Hannigan 2002, 172). Whereas Theodore Roosevelt had "intervened cautiously, rarely, and in direct response" to potential extrahemispheric threats from European powers, Wilson "intervened repeatedly, violently, and excessively without ever facing a comparable threat of European military intervention" (Tilchin and Neu 2006, 149). If Roosevelt carried a stick, Wilson bore a two-by-four. The reasons for Wilson's interventionist impulse were not, however, narrowly economic. Rarely if ever did the administration intervene abroad on behalf of specific business interests or factions of capital. Wilson, for example, refused to support special financial interests in renewing the Six-Power Consortium in China (see Israel 1971). Rather, the use of force was intended "to protect American interests in the large sense" (Foglesong 1995, 16). This meant protecting U.S. property and the "rule of law" when threatened by revolutionary upheaval and securing the Open Door (Emily S. Rosenberg 1982, 64; cf. Levin 1968). Wilson personified, in action and ideology, what Engels refers to as the functions of the "ideal collective capitalist," acting on behalf of corporate capitalism *in general* rather than capitalists in particular.

23. Unfortunately, Bromley (2008) does not acknowledge the deeper historical origins of this uniquely American strategy, which stretch back to turn of the 20th century. Martin Sklar (1988, 82–83) convincingly demonstrates that the link between U.S. diplomacy and modernization theory dates to the McKinley administration.

24. Daniel Deudney conceptualizes these aspects of Wilsonianism in terms of a "Republican security agenda" seeking "*to populate the international system with republics and to abridge international anarchy in order to avoid the transformation of the American limited government constitutional order into a hierarchical state*" (2007, 186). His characterization of the Wilsonian strategy as aimed at ameliorating the negative effects of international anarchy (system-level) and securing American domestic order through the promotion of other nations' domestic (unit-level) transformation is indeed apt. However, I believe my alternative though complementary conceptualization is more appropriate given Deudney's dubious dating of this "Republic" security logic to the Greek polis, reflecting his U.S.-centric reading of the history of international relations.

25. As Randall Schweller (2001) has noted, there are surprisingly few substantive studies within IR specifically examining the making of peace settlements and particularly Versailles. But see Holsti 1991; Ikenberry 2001; Ripsman 2002; Dueck 2006.

26. See, for example, Holsti 1991; Ruggie 1998a; Kegley and Gregory 1999; Reus-Smit 1999; Ikenberry 2001.

27. On the transpartisan character of the debate on U.S. intervention in Bolshevik Russia, see Mayer 1967, 329-37.

28. Or, as Lenin repeatedly warned, "*Under all conceivable circumstances, if the German revolution does not come, we are doomed*" (Lenin 1960, 27:98).

29. From October 1918 onward, Germany experienced a blaze of revolutionary action that reached its apogee in late October and November 1918 and April-May 1919 and that witnessed the formation of the short-lived Bavarian Soviet Republic. Social revolutionary uprising also erupted at the two hearts of the dual monarchy, Vienna and Budapest. After a workers' and soldiers' uprising in the capital city overthrew the Habsburgs on 31 October, "Red Vienna" experienced a continual ebb and flow of revolutionary activities until early 1920 and remained a central outpost of socialist revolutionary agitation within Central Eastern Europe (Hautmann 1992). In Budapest, revolution in late October led to the formation of a liberal-democratic government. Under the impact of Romanian and Czech military incursions, this government gave way to a Bolshevik-style Hungarian Soviet Republic on 21 March 1919. The Soviet lasted until its military defeat by Romanian forces on 6 August 1919. During its short time, a similar regime was established in Slovakia under the auspices of the Hungarian Soviet (see Pastor 1988).

30. On Wilson's interventionist Russian policy forming the basis of post-World War II U.S. "modern methods of covert action," combining "idealistic publicity, secrecy, and circumscribed operations," see Foglesong 1995, 3, 12.

31. Before the war's start, President Wilson's de facto national security adviser, Colonel House, undertook a series of diplomatic missions to Europe on behalf of the administration in the early summer of 1914. During one of those missions, House met in England with Sir Edward Grey and other leading British elites to discuss plans for an informal entente among the advanced capitalist countries to collaborate in the development of the nonindustrialized world. Relaying the meeting's contents to Wilson, House had proposed that advanced capitalist powers such as Britain, the United States, and Germany "establish a plan by which investors" would be able to lend money "to develop, under favorable terms, the waste places of the earth" (House 1926-28, 2:264-65). Such a plan would not only reduce the sources of interstate conflict but also represent an advance toward bringing stability and better conditions to these societies. These designs held striking parallels with the "ultraimperialist" international order characterized by Marxist Karl Kautsky, whereby the imperialist powers would form a "holy alliance" in their mutual and peaceful exploitation of the Global South—House's "waste places of the earth" (Levin 1968, 24-29; Gardner 1993, 268-69).

32. Rosenberg is here referring to U.S. foreign policy in its post–Second World War manifestation, but the description aptly applies to the interwar period.

33. http://avalon.law.yale.edu/20th_century/leagcov.asp#art22.

34. As Erez Manela's (2007) fascinating study demonstrates, the disappointment with Wilson in the colonial world helped radicalize if not destabilize the region's politics.

35. By the end of 1918, there were approximately 118,000 Allied troops fighting in the Siberian theater.

36. During the war, the Wilson administration enacted a vast campaign of domestic repression and censorship against various leftist elements in response to the perceived fears of Bolshevik ideas spreading from Europe to the United States—specifically, through the conveyor belt of "foreign" elements within the body politic. Wilson showed particular concern about Bolshevism sparking "immigrant radicalism" and revolutionary tendencies among minority groups (Foglesong 1995, 36–40). On his way to Paris, Wilson told his doctor that "the American negro returning from abroad would be our greatest medium in conveying Bolshevism to America." The "poison" of Bolshevism was, as Wilson put it on another occasion, "running through the veins of the world" (Foglesong 1995, 42, 40).

37. On the role of U.S. policymaking in this process, see Costigliola 1984; Schmitz 1988; and Burke 1994.

Chapter 5

1. For example, "Hitler's unique pathologies were the single most important factor in causing both World War II in Europe . . . and Germany's eventual defeat" (Byman and Pollack 2001, 115).

2. According to Dale Copeland (2000, 122), "Most intentionalists would probably accept Alan Bullock's classical realist line that Hitler had a pathological lust for power." Significant contributions to the intentionalist school include Trevor-Roper 1972; Bracher 1973, 359–410; Hildebrand 1973; Hillgruber 1981; Weinberg 1995.

3. On the continuity debate, see Hildebrand 1973, esp. chap. 1; Jarausch 1979; Fischer 1986; Lee and Michalka 1987; Baranowski 2011.

4. For a fuller review and critique of these structural realist explanations of WWII, see chap. 1, at "World Wars as Balance-of-Power Crises"; chap. 6, at "IR Approaches to the Alliance Dynamics of the 1930s."

5. Inflation reduced the high debts incurred by the industrialists. Moreover, since prices for goods increased faster than nominal wages, inflation also acted to decrease relative labor costs. It has been shown that the inflation and hyperinflation of the period was a *calculated policy* jointly pursued by industrial and political leaders (particularly during the Cuno government) to demonstrate the country's inability to pay reparations and thereby scale down the overall amount (see Maier 1975; Marks 1976; Feldman 1977; Rupieper 1979; Schuker 1988).

6. According to Kurt Gossweiler (1971, 314–42), these industries were also linked to the Dresdner/DANAT financial group, which had strong ties to Anglo-American banking interests instrumental in the formulation of the Dawes Plan

in 1924 and its geopolitical corollaries, the Locarno Treaties (Pijl 1984, chap. 4; see also Gossweiler 1989; Simpson 2002).

7. That German heavy industry was relatively more labor-intensive than the dynamic, export-oriented sectors only *partially* explains their more combative stance toward labor. The tendency to blame labor costs for all of society's economic woes was more a result of long-held ideological dispositions than a realistic assessment of the structural problems besetting the industrial sector. The "profit squeeze" in heavy industry was above all an effect of a steep rise in *fixed costs* resulting from industrial overconcentration, rationalization, and cartel agreements perpetuating the conditions of chronic excess capacity aggravated by the war (Weisbrod 1990).

8. Until the Ruhr occupation of 1923, German foreign policy was largely protectionist and eastward-looking. To break out of the diplomatic and economic isolation in the West, policymakers and prominent business interests sought a rapprochement with their ideological and military enemy, the Soviet Union (see Carr 1979). Crucially, most German policymakers saw this Eastern-oriented strategy as a temporary *tactic* of frightening the Allies into treaty revisions. The policy assumed that the Bolshevik regime would soon collapse and thereby aimed to reconsolidate capitalist relations within Russia (Cameron 2005). This distinctly *social* logic of German diplomacy toward the Bolshevik regime sheds a somewhat different light on the traditional "balance of power" view of interwar Soviet-German relations as the "balance" German policymakers sought to achieve encompassed both domestic and international relations.

9. Whether the reconstruction of European capitalism through a revitalized German economy would be undergirded by a U.S.-led dollar or British-led sterling bloc linked to gold was, however, a major issue of contention between London and New York (Parrini 1969, chap. 4; Costigliola 1977, 1984, 127–31; Schuker 2003). An excellent summary from the period on the diverging U.S. and British interests over what form of the gold standard would be instituted after the war can be found in an exchange of letters between U.S. secretary of state Charles E. Hughes and Princeton economist Edwin W. Kemmerer. See Kemmerer to Hughes, 24 June 1924, RG 59, 462.00R296/386, U.S. National Archives; see also Arthur N. Young to Hughes, 9 June 1924, RG 59, 462.00R296/386. The persistence of Anglo-American rivalries throughout the interwar years is often not sufficiently emphasized. Anglo-American conflicts not only exacerbated world economic conditions during the 1920s but also led to a consistent inability to create a common front against German expansionism after the Nazis took power. But see Offner 1986 [1975].

10. On U.S. reparations and war debt policies, see Parrini 1969; Rhodes 1969; Van Meter 1971; Leffler 1979; Costigliola 1984; Schuker 1988; Hogan 1991. As Van Meter notes (1971, 254), U.S. policymakers offered war debt reductions only for a "shock therapy" list of items to the debtor countries aimed to facilitate the Open Door and reduce reparation claims.

11. Most emphatically stated by Costigliola (1976, 497): "Locarno was the po-

litical expression of the Dawes Plan." On the making of Locarno, see the indispensable Jacobson 1972 and the more recent Jacobson 2004; Cohrs 2006.

12. The "schizophrenic" character of U.S. hegemony of the interwar years was also essential to the cumulatively destabilizing economic-political effects on international order. Here, one must give leave to some of the revisionist U.S. diplomatic historiography; see Costigliola 1984; Kindleberger 1986; Offner 1986 [1975]; Ziebura 1990; Kent 1991; Artaud 1998.

13. At the same time, there is substantial evidence that the U.S. and European economies never fully recovered from WWI and before. The tendencies toward cartelization and scale economies as responses to problems of chronic overproduction and declining rates of profit were generalized if uneven developments characterizing all of the core capitalist economies but particularly the United States and Germany. Studies showing a general decline in the overall rate of profit in the United States from 1900 to 1929 include Mage 1963; Duménil, Glick, and Rangel 1987; Duménil and Lévy 1993.

14. Excellent discussions may be found in Weisbrod 1979; Geary 1983; and Mommsen 1996.

15. It is clear that the military was decisive in actually *installing* the Brüning dictatorship. The extent to which heavy industry was a passive or active force in the disintegration of Weimar democracy has been a topic of unusually heated debate (compare Stegmann 1973, 1976; Weisbrod 1979, 1981; Abraham and Feldman 1984; Henry Ashby Turner 1985, 100–111; Abraham 1986; Hayes 1987). On the particular issue of the grand coalition's collapse, I must take the boring middle position between Weisbrod's apparent exaggeration of heavy industry's political power and Turner's underestimation. But even if one accepts Turner's more conservative evaluation of heavy industry's role in undermining the Müller government, his account still shows that they were instrumental in sparking the crisis over welfare insurance that led to the cabinet's eventual collapse while quickly reconciling themselves to Brüning's dictatorship. More generally, Turner's main thesis that corporate capitalists played a fundamentally *passive* role in the events between 1930 and Hitler's appointment as chancellor in January 1933 is methodologically suspect (see esp. Henry Ashby Turner 1985, 340–59). Turner's argument rests primarily on an assessment of business leaders' financial contributions to the NSDAP and their relatively marginal role in the secret negotiations leading to Hitler's appointment rather than on an analysis of the overall effects of corporate capitalists' negative dispositions toward Weimar democracy in its final years. Examining the wealth of empirical evidence marshaled by Turner from this conception of capitalist agency one is inclined to draw a very different conclusion from Turner (see Childers 1988, 131–33; Geary 1990; Kolb 2005, 219–20).

16. Similarly, Zara Steiner writes (2005, 810), "If it had not been for the depression it is doubtful whether the Nazis . . . could have attracted over one-third of the German electorate in 1932. The depression, too, provided the opportunity for the traditional right-wing elite to gain power."

17. The identification of the Junker agrarians as *capitalists* is significant and

might raise some objections (Stegmann 1979). Yet it seems rather clear that Junker *production* methods were reconstituted on firmly capitalist foundations over the 19th century (cf. Perry Anderson 1974; Byres 1996; Blackbourn 2003). Irrespective of whether the Junkers retained some kind of precapitalist mentality (see chap. 1) they must be thus conceived as forming part of the capitalist class.

18. The analysis here draws on Kaiser 1990, 354–62.

19. Bernstein is summarizing the economic literature and does not view the issue of primary production as a central cause of the slump.

20. These included the "originating "belatedness" of Germany's dual transmutation into an industrialized and modern nation-state formation imparting its particularly hectic character; the commensurately increased role of state interventionism in achieving these goals in a time-compressed fashion through a "passive revolution" pressurized under the "external whip" of a geopolitically hostile environment; and the contradictory synthesis of the Junker-heavy industrial ruling bloc, ideologically amalgamating the "old and new" and contributing to the persistent weaknesses of German parliamentary traditions. All of these factors constitute the "national peculiarities" of German development that lent themselves to the rise of the fascist dictatorship.

21. The following use of Trotsky quotes is in no way intended to confer authority to my analysis or demonstrate Marxist orthodoxy. Rather, I aim to show how—*against* Trotsky's (1971) tendency toward a unit-homogenizing conception of fascism as the uniform consequence of capitalism in its "imperialist stage," in power representing the "most ruthless dictatorship of monopoly capital"—there is a more nuanced analysis to be immanently reconstructed from his writings.

22. See also Trotsky 1971, 339.

23. The 1933 census counted no fewer than 9.342 million people (or 29 percent of the population) employed in the agricultural sector (Tooze 2007, 167).

24. While incorporating a wide cross-section of German society, Nazism remained a movement primarily composed of the (old and new) *Mittelstand* and agrarian classes, which were overwhelmingly male and Protestant (Jones 1972; Stachura 1983; Childers 1984; Geary 1993, 24–26). Recent statements that it transcended class lines either before or (particularly) after taking power have been overstated (see Mühlberger 2003; Mann 2004, 139–55).

25. The "Bonapartist" label is used here simply to denote the unique circumstances in which both extreme divisions within the capitalist class *and* increased labor-capital struggles lead to the *temporary* intensification and relative autonomy of state power over and above these social forces. International factors often play a crucial in the balancing of opposing domestic forces. I do not, however, find the broader theory of Bonapartism particularly useful, since theorizing by historical analogy is always fraught with difficulties. See Dülffer 1976a; Linton 1989.

26. On Brüning's foreign and domestic policies, compare Kaiser 1980, chap. 2; Lee and Michalka 1987, 114–23; Weisbrod 1990; Kent 1991; Balderston 2002, 77–99; Patch 2006, 172–219.

27. For the contemporary debate, see Borchardt 1990; Holtfrerich 1990; and other contributions in Kruedener 1990.

28. This rendered the Brüning government partially dependent on the SPD. "Consequently," Abraham notes (1986, 256), "the SPD was able to participate indirectly in dismantling social programs even while exercising a considerable braking power that both limited the very dismantling and slowly undermining capital's confidence in Brüning's ability to get the job done." See also Patch 2006, 103–17.

29. Though the Nazi vote declined to 33.1 percent (196 seats) in the November 1932 elections, it remained the largest party in Parliament.

30. Reichstag election statistics in Stackelberg and Winkle 2002, 99–100, table 2.1.

31. According to Reinhard Neebe (1981), the general attack against the Brüning government launched by the "National Opposition" at Harzburg in October 1931 was at least indirectly supported by heavy industry. While the RDI refrained from participating at the Harzburg meeting, the North-West Employers' Association and the *Langnamverein* sent their representatives, Max Schlenker and Ludwig Grauert, who articulated heavy industry's interest in creating a "united front against the present 'system'" (quoted in Neebe 1981, 108). Schacht was nonetheless disappointed by the industrialists' "lack of courage to come out against" the government, which would "cost the industry its internal life" (Neebe 1981, 107; see also Stegmann 1976; Henry Ashby Turner 1985, 158–71).

32. Sohn-Rethel was a CPD member who got a job in 1932 as a staff writer for the MWT's paper, the *Deutschen Führerbriefe*. Henry Ashby Turner (1985, 466 n. 53) dismisses Sohn-Rethel as a "communist provocateur," pointing to inaccuracies in his account. Other historians have accorded more weight to Sohn-Rethel's work; see Frommelt 1977, 87–109; Stegmann 1978, 209–19; Neebe 1981, 123, 260–61 n. 3; Abraham 1986, xxxi–xliv; Seckendorf 1993; Thörner 2000; Gross 2005.

33. According to Abraham (1986), Silverberg was an important mediator between the more "progressive" dynamic-export and conservative heavy industrial factions; see also Neebe 1981; Geary 1990. On the controversial question of Silverberg's move to the Nazis, compare Neebe 1981, chaps. 7–8; Abraham 1986, 311–13; Mommsen 1996, 511–12; to Henry Ashby Turner (1985, 298–300).

34. Though quoting Sohn-Rethel (1978, 14) here, Neebe provides additional sources backing this claim, and his analysis generally complements Sohn-Rethel on this point (Neebe 1981, 123, 260–61 n. 3).

35. Only through an appreciation of national strength, Hitler declared (1994, 141), could "Germany take advantage of the political possibilities which, if we look far enough into the future, can place German life once more upon a natural and secure basis—and that means either new living space and the development of a great internal market or protection of German economic life against the world without and utilization of all the concentrated strength of Germany."

36. However, Henry Ashby Turner argues that corporate capitalist support peaked during the summer of 1932 and significantly waned thereafter (compare Turner 1985, 273–339; Stegmann 1973; Geary 1983; Abraham 1986, 271–318).

37. However, the key social force driving both Papen's and Schleicher's collapses was clearly the Junkers. Suffering from a massive contraction of world market, the agrarians demanded increased protectionism, debt relief, and a fundamental reorientation of German trade policy. While caving in to some of these demands, Brüning refused to compromise on tariff quotas, sparking a general revolt against the government from agrarian circles. His successors, von Papen and General von Schleicher, generally followed Brüning on the quota issue. Thus, von Papen's fall in 1932 was largely dictated by agrarian interests. When the 1932 elections failed to provide Papen with a reliable majority in the Reichstag, a number of industrialists, financiers, and particularly Junkers withdrew their support for the regime and began moving toward the idea of inclusion of the Nazis within a cabinet (Tooze 2007, 30; see also Geary 1990).

38. These terms are from Kershaw 1993, 108–9. The "intentionalist" explanations focusing on Hitler's idiosyncrasies have been most pronounced in foreign policy analysis, where liberal conceptions of the state and policymaking predominate.

39. A key inspiration of the structural-functionalist approach is Franz Neumann's (1944) classic study of the Third Reich, *Behemoth*. This work remains one of the most powerful interpretations ever written on the politics of the Nazi regime. Leading historians of the structural-functionalist school include Hans Mommsen (1976), Martin Broszat (1985), and Tim Mason (Mason and Caplan 1993).

40. This is in explicit contrast to those debates within IR, where *structure* refers to the distribution of power within the *international* system, which offensive and defensive realists conceive as decisive in explaining Nazi state action and the causes of the Second World War (Copeland 2000; Mearsheimer 2001).

41. On Americanism's cultural and material lure for interwar Europeans, see Costigliola 1984, chap. 6; De Grazia 2005.

42. For an analysis explicitly linking the causes of WWII to economies of scale, see Chase 2004; from a Marxist perspective, see Gowan 2010.

43. The dilemma of "inadequate *Lebensraum*" also created "difficult social problems" that Hitler identified with the socially explosive process of intensive industrialization-urbanization. Like everything else in Hitler's thinking, those social effects that could be associated with Germany's "uneven and combined development" took on viciously racist, anti-Semitic dimensions. For example, Hitler described the rapidly industrialized urban centers as "hotbeds of blood-mixing and bastardization, usually ensuring the degeneration of the race and resulting in that purulent herd in which the maggots of the international Jewish community flourish and cause the ultimate decay of the people. But it is precisely in this way that a decline is introduced . . . thus eliminating in the end the prerequisite [i.e., racial purity] needed in order for a *people to take on the final consequences in the struggle for the world market*" (Hitler 2003, 26–27).

44. Most prominent here was Professor Karl Haushofer, often identified as a central influence on Hitler's thinking. Haushofer's influence should not be exaggerated, however. In no way did he offer Hitler a set blueprint for action (Stoakes 1978; Murphy 1997, chap. 10; Herwig 1999).

45. Hitler refers to an "American union," as he anticipated that the United States would incorporate Canada into a single political bloc.

46. Hitler's perception of the potential *military* danger posed by U.S. power receded in the early years of the Third Reich as he began to refocus on the other peril, the rapidly industrializing Soviet menace. The U.S. threat would, however, reappear on the eve of war. Hitler's distorted ideological prism identified the Roosevelt administration with the vast anti-German world Jewish conspiracy connecting international bankers, liberals, socialists, and communists (see Tooze 2007, 282-84, 324-25, 407-8, 462, 502, 657-58, 664-65). The disparity of social forces subsumed under the unifying category of the "Jew" as external enemy attests to the malleability of the construct and thus its inherently ideological function.

47. On this matter, I therefore depart from Adam Tooze's otherwise excellent analysis of the Nazi drive to war, which understates the central significance of Soviet Russia in Hitler's grand strategy. For a useful corrective, see Riley forthcoming.

48. As is made clear by Stoakes (1986, 47-48, 154-55, 210, 216-17, 226), one of the two historical studies Copeland cites (2000, 281 n. 30).

49. See comments in Hitler 1973, 7, 75-76, 88-89, 322; Hitler 2001, 147, 326, 524, 655, 661-64; Stackelberg and Winkle 2002, docs. 4.15, 4.3.

50. Similarly, a month later, Hitler pronounced, "The Russian space is our India . . . our colonial expanse" (quoted in Kay 2006, 80).

51. Such a view was promoted by the *stamokap* (state monopoly capitalism) theories associated with the interwar communist parties. This took as an article of faith general secretary of the Comintern Georgi Dimitrov's definition of fascism in power "as the open terrorist dictatorship of the most reactionary, most chauvinistic and most imperialist elements of finance capital" (Dimitrov 1935). Against this crudely instrumentalist conception of Nazi state-capital relations, a "liberal consensus" emerging in the U.S. academy during the 1980s and 1990s stressed the more passive, acquiescent relationship of big business to an overbearing Nazi dictatorship (see, for example, Henry Ashby Turner 1985; Hayes 2001; James 2004; Feldman 2004). Such studies are "firmly rooted in a North American historiographical tradition and that of an anti-Marxist "corporate-culture" business history," Volker Berghahn (1991, 106) notes specifically regarding Peter Hayes's work. By emphasizing the role of big business as a passive object in the rise and consolidation of the Nazi dictatorship, this literature has clearly bent the stick too far. Few big capitalists were ever the helpless victims of the Third Reich; rather, they were willing collaborators (Leitz 2002, 56).

52. As is documented in a wealth of historical studies from different theoretical perspectives. See Volkmann 1990; Gregor 1998; Tooze 2001, 2007; Leitz 2004; Stokes 2004; Buchheim 2008.

53. The crucial figure here was Emil George von Strauss, Daimler-Benz's supervisory board chair and a prominent representative of Deutsche Bank, the leading financial interest dominating the board. He was a member of the infamous Kep-

pler circle, established by Schacht to influence Hitler's economic policies and facilitate connections between big business and Nazis. Strauss was a supporter of armaments and personally helped establish links between the Reichswehr, NS-DAP, and industrialists (Gregor 1998, 58; see also Henry Ashby Turner 1985, 142–44; James 2004, 39–41, 152–55).

54. In contrast to many of his latter-day liberal interpreters, Mason's thesis was *not* intended as license to erase the socioeconomic sphere from any measure of determinacy. Rather, Mason sought to conceptualize the exceptional socioeconomic conditions from which a radical autonomy of the political-ideological could emerge. Only through "far-reaching structural changes" in "the economy and in society" could the Nazi state "assume a fully independent role" (Mason 1995, 54–55).

55. This is what Bukharin (1973) referred to as the tendential fusion of state and capital; the supplanting or "nationalization" of private enterprises by the state, accompanied by the blurring of public and private power.

56. The following analysis draws on Callinicos 2001, 397–98; see also Gluckstein 1999.

57. On the latter, see Mason 1981; Salter 1981; Mason and Caplan 1993.

58. The best study of IG Farben's role in the Nazi economy remains Peter Hayes 2001, though I diverge from his overall interpretation of Nazi-business relations.

59. See, for example, Dahrendorf 1967; Schoenbaum 1980; Aly 2007.

60. The "capitalist peace" thesis has taken a variety of different forms. See Tony Smith 1994; Mandelbaum 2002; Weede 2005; Gartzke 2007, 2009.

61. Hitler's November 1937 "timetable" for war clearly stipulates this.

62. Hitler thought that by avoiding colonial expansionism—and thus not challenging the British Empire—British policymakers would allow Germany to expand to the east and attain hegemony on the European Continent.

63. On these economic dilemmas facing the regime in 1934, 1936–37, and 1939, see Kaiser 1980, 151–54, 167–69; Volkmann 1990, 240–44, 254–57, 262–63, 308–9, 354–55, 362–63, 365–72; Mason and Caplan 1993, 27, 170–72, 186–96, 232–40, 310–11, 316–17, 324–25, 328; Tooze 2007, 69–72, 114, 214–19, 230–34, 274–75, 300–303, 321–22, 328, 342–44, 663.

64. See also Kershaw 1992, 1999–2000, 2:529–91.

65. Only through an export drive could the Nazis accumulate the necessary foreign exchange reserves to pay for nondomestically produced raw materials and foodstuffs.

66. Given France and Britain's continuing unwillingness and inability to pursue anything nearing a comprehensive rearmament, the international arms race was predominantly between Germany and the USSR at this time. As Mark Harrison notes (1988, 178), "Only in the Soviet Union did defence production in the 1930s approach the same order of magnitude as that of Germany, and of all Germany's adversaries the Soviet economy devoted the highest peacetime proportion of national income to defence."

67. By September 1937, all armaments programs had fallen seriously behind

schedule. The consequence, General Bloomberg declared, would be "such a serious reduction in offensive readiness . . . that it could not but have implications for the freedom of action of the political leadership of the Reich" (quoted in Tooze 2007, 240).

68. For a discussion of the critical Hossbach memorandum recording the 5 November meeting and the historiographical debates surrounding it, see Wright and Stafford 1988. As they emphasize, the document must be read in the context of the disputes within the Nazi leadership over the pace of rearmaments in an overextended German economy.

69. On these economic-strategic motivations and benefits, see Kaiser 1980, 168-69; Kaiser 1989; Mason 1989; Messerschmid 1990, 650-51; Volkmann 1990, 323-36; Murray 1992.

70. However, British policymakers were in no sense ready to give up their appeasement efforts or pursue anything nearing a full-scale rearmament effort (see chap. 6).

71. Nazi policymakers' recognition of this *transnational space* of the British Empire—and its connection to the United States (the "transatlantic vector")—as a key factor in the military balance of power is particularly relevant for realist IR analyses. Hamstrung by a "nation-statist" ontology, many IR realists have discounted the massive financial-material resources afforded to Britain by the empire in leaders' quantitative calculations of the military balance of power on the eve of WWII. Their "deductive" theoretical hypotheses regarding the causes of war are thus suspect. Randall Schweller's "tripolarity" thesis, which completely erases Britain (and France) based on calculations of their levels of *national* power (that is, without reference to their empires) from the structure of the interwar international system, is one particularly extreme version of this more general tendency in structural realism (Schweller 1993, 1998).

72. This point is in agreement with Schweller (1993, 93) and Copeland (2000, 134-35) and has been well established by Tooze (2007, 318-21).

73. On the Roosevelt administration's increasing identification with the threat of "international Jewry" from late 1938 onward, see Tooze 2007, 282-83, 658-59.

74. On Hitler's perception of this quickly closing strategic window of opportunity, see Dülffer 1985, 167-68; Murray 1992, 89-91; Knox 2000, 105-6; Copeland 2000, 133-39; Tooze 2007, 322-24, 327-28, 334-35, 662-63.

75. Similarly, Hans-Erich Volkmann (1990) refers to the Nazi "war economy" as a "crisis economy."

76. But see Kaiser 1980, 180-82; Deist 1981, 111-12; Deist et al. 1985, 346-49; Dülffer 1985, 166-68; Kaiser 1989; Mason 1995, 299-322.

77. For an illuminating discussion of the nexus between economic interests and Nazi ideology, see Herbert 1993. Nonreductionist Marxist approaches can be found in Callinicos 2001; Milchman 2003; Traverso 2003.

78. On whether Hitler expected Britain to maintain neutrality, see Weinberg 1985a; Mason 1995, 37-38; Tooze 2007, 292-93; see also Hildebrand 1973, 86-89; Overy 1999a.

Chapter 6

1. See policymakers' quotes in Beck 1989; Record 2007.

2. Randall Schweller (1993, 257 n. 63) directs readers to E. H. Carr's *The Twenty Years' Crisis* as the "classic statement of the danger of interwar appeasement." Suffice to note that Carr actually endorsed Chamberlain's policy of appeasement. In the first edition of the *Twenty Years' Crisis,* Carr called the policy "a reaction of realism against utopianism" (1939, 14 n. 1). Seen within IR as one of the founding fathers of modern realism, the pro-appeasement themes throughout this work illustrate the problematic disassociation between realism's theoretic abstractions and its historically concrete explanations of foreign policies (see Pozo-Martin 2007).

3. That a few particular British policymakers (notably Winston Churchill and Robert Vansittart) viewed the Soviet Union as the lesser danger than the Nazis in the immediate context but were nevertheless vehemently anticommunist in no way invalidates this connection, which specifies a *general tendency.* As with any social theoretical inquiry applied to a particular historical case, it is entirely legitimate for specific exceptions to occur. Further, the Marxist framework elaborated here in no way denies the irreducible role of contingencies in theoretically informed historical analysis. The point of any good social theory is to identify the key structures, processes, and agents along with their main lines of interaction to generate adequate explanatory hypotheses (see Callinicos 1995).

4. The Court of Directors of the Bank of England was "chiefly composed" of those "members of the Accepting House Committee such as Barings, Rothschilds, Hambros, Morgan Grenfell, and Lazard Brothers" (Boyce 1987, 22). Staff exchanges between the Treasury and Bank of England were commonplace. During the interwar years, for example, two prominent Treasury officials, Sir Otto Niemeyer and Henry Arthur Siepmann, joined the Bank, helping to further "reinforce the relationship between the two institutions" (Forbes 2000, 13).

5. A note of caution is required here. Though I adopt the notion of a "City-Treasury-Bank" nexus playing a hegemonic role in British capitalism of the time, I subscribe neither to the definitional strictures of the original concept nor to the broader theses regarding the longer trajectory of British development put forth by proponents of this view. Two interconnected criticisms are particularly important for our purposes here. Most notable is the idea of an unbroken centuries-long persistence of an unreformed landowning aristocracy, eventually incorporating, both socially and culturally, City interests, which became hegemonic within the British ruling class. As Michael Barratt Brown (1988) has forcefully shown, this interpretation is dubious. Notions of a "gentlemanly" or "patrician" capitalism with a strict division between City and aristocratic landowning interests, on the one hand, and industrial capitalists, on the other, are untenable (Barratt Brown 1988; Daunton 1989). Second, and related, I reject the idea of the British state as some kind of anomalous, premodern archaism that had yet to modernize in the absence of a second bourgeois revolution. Without neglecting

the genuine peculiarities of British capitalism and the development of its state institutions, a more appropriate place to start would be an examination of the particularly early timing of its capitalist industrialization (the West-East vector) and its unusually internationalized nature (see Callinicos 1989b).

6. On these changes, see Emery 1988, 13–110.

7. The 1931 decision to abandon the gold standard was guided by strict financial orthodoxy: the maintenance of a fixed exchange rate was perceived as financially unsound since it would have to be defended by high interest rates, resulting in the loss of the benefits of cheap money (Cain and Hopkins 1993a, 76, 99; Cain 1996). Throughout the 1930s, the Bank of England thus ultimately sought "a reformed world gold standard: anything short of this could be only a temporary substitute" (Sayers 1986, 450).

8. The solidification of common interests was further accelerated by the changing structure of the British party system during the interwar period. See Middlemas 1979; Cain and Hopkins 1993a, 30.

9. On the foreign policy strategies and their supporting factions, see Gustav Schmidt 1986.

10. The literature on the state debate is massive. For overviews in their evolving states, see Holloway and Picciotto 1978; Peter B. Evans, Rueschemeyer, and Skocpol 1985; Clarke 1991; Barrow 1993; Wetherly, Barrow, and Burnham 2008.

11. This is a particularly important point in examining such cases as Nazi policymaking, where the broad impetus for nearly all major foreign policies lay with Hitler. Without a structural understanding of state agency as embedded within a "logic" of competitive capital accumulation—formed through the uneven and combined character of capitalist development—Nazi foreign policymaking is inexplicable without falling back on the historically suspect Marxist-Leninist theories of "state-monopoly capitalism" (see chap. 5).

12. For example, according to Alexander Gerschenkron's (1962) theory of late industrialization, the more "backward" a society is when it begins its industrialization, the more one can expect: (1) a rapid industrialization process, with relatively intensive growth spurts; (2) an emphasis on the production of capital goods (heavy industry) over consumer ones; (3) higher concentration and centralization of capital; (4) a smaller role played by agriculture in growth; (5) closely integrated banking and industrial sectors ("finance capital"); (6) a state-intensive developmental strategy; and (7) a "virulent" and nationalist ideology. Gerschenkron was familiar with Trotsky's work and likely influenced by it (Selwyn 2011). Whether one accepts every tenet of Gerschenkron's theory, it does capture the *effects* of the staggered and interactive process of capitalist industrialization in the differentiated forms of state-capital relations.

13. Murray's argument regarding the imperial sources of Britain's appeasement policy in diverting attention away from Britain's "continental commitment" is further illustrated in Bond 1980, 188, 257–58, 267–70, 338; Meyers 1983.

14. On U.S.-British relations, see esp. MacDonald 1981.

15. On these multiple aims, see Cain and Hopkins 1993a, 97; Forbes 2000, 97–132.

16. These assessments proved rather accurate, as examined in chapter 5.

17. British intelligence estimates of Soviet military power clearly emphasized the negative effects of Stalin's purges. Nonetheless, British strategists in 1938–39 continually stressed the necessity of Soviet cooperation for any effective defense of Eastern Europe. Drawing on interpretations of these reports offered by Keith Neilson (1993, 2006) and Michael Carley (1999b), it seems that Soviet military power was viewed as superior to Poland. Moreover, the effective use of Polish military capacities was largely (if not entirely) dependent on Soviet collaboration. Again, both factors point to the overwhelming importance of Soviet power as *the* decisive factor in calculating a potential balance of power against the Nazis in Eastern Europe.

18. This is contrary to constructivist approaches that treat ideological, cultural, and normative factors as (potentially) autonomous; see, for example, Ruggie 1998b; Alexander Wendt 1999; for a critique, see Bieler and Morton 2008. For a constructivist approach emphasizing the "autonomous" causal force of culture in determining British and French military strategies in the 1930s, see Kier 1997.

19. See Carley 1999a, 245.

20. See Yuen Foong Khong 1992.

21. Walt's assertion (1992, 452) that "the threat from Nazi Germany was anything but obvious" is unconvincing. British and French intelligence agencies provided ample evidence of the extent of the Nazi threat. See Robert J. Young 1978, 162–64; Paul M. Kennedy 1988, 316; Post 1993, 164–66; Peter Jackson 1998.

22. As emphasized in the revisionist historiographical literature against the "guilty men" thesis of the more "orthodox" interpretations. For a recent review of this literature, see Aster 2008.

23. As emphasized in a number of recent historical studies; see esp. Haslam 1984; Gorodetsky 1990; Roberts 1995; Uldricks 1996; Carley 1999a; Louise Grace Shaw 2003.

Conclusion

1. In their engagement with constructivism and related topics, Gramscian-inspired IR scholars have led the way. See, for example, Pijl 1998; Rupert 2000, 2010; Robert W. Cox and Schechter 2002; Bieler and Morton 2008; see also Laffey and Weldes 1997; Laffey 2000.

Bibliography

Abraham, David. 1986. *The Collapse of the Weimar Republic: Political Economy and Crisis*. 2nd ed. New York: Holmes and Meier.

Abraham, David, and Gerald D. Feldman. 1984. Debate: David Abraham's The Collapse of the Weimar Republic. *Central European History* 17 (2–3): 159–291.

Ádám, Magda. 2004. *The Versailles System and Central Europe*. Burlington, VT: Ashgate.

Adams, R. J. Q. 1993. *British Politics and Foreign Policy in the Age of Appeasement, 1935–39*. Stanford: Stanford University Press.

Adas, Michael. 1989. *Machines as the Measure of Men: Science, Technology, and Ideologies of Western Dominance*. Ithaca: Cornell University Press.

Agamben, Giorgio. 2005. *State of Exception*. Chicago: University of Chicago Press.

Agnew, John A. 1987. *The United States in the World-Economy: A Regional Geography*. Cambridge: Cambridge University Press.

Agnew, John A., and Stuart Corbridge. 1995. *Mastering Space: Hegemony, Territory and International Political Economy*. London: Routledge.

Aldcroft, Derek Howard. 1977. *From Versailles to Wall Street, 1919–1929*. London: Lane.

Alexander, Martin S. 1992. *The Republic in Danger: General Maurice Gamelin and the Politics of French Defence, 1933–1940*. Cambridge: Cambridge University Press.

Alexandroff, Alan, and Richard Rosecrance. 1977. Deterrence in 1939. *World Politics* 29 (3): 404–24.

Alker, Hayward R., Jr., and Thomas J. Biersteker. 1984. The Dialectics of World Order: Notes for a Future Archeologist of International Savoir Faire. *International Studies Quarterly* 28 (2): 121–42.

Allinson, Jamie C. 2012. The Social Origins of Alliances: Uneven and Combined Development and the Case of Jordan 1955–57. PhD diss., University of Edinburgh.

Allinson, Jamie C., and Alexander Anievas. 2009. The Uses and Misuses of Uneven and Combined Development: An Anatomy of A Concept. *Cambridge Review of International Affairs* 22 (1): 47–67.

Allinson, Jamie C., and Alexander Anievas. 2010a. Approaching "The International": Beyond Political Marxism. In *Marxism and World Politics: Contesting Global Capitalism*, edited by A. Anievas. London: Routledge.

Allinson, Jamie C., and Alexander Anievas. 2010b. The Uneven and Combined Development of the Meiji Restoration: A Passive Revolutionary Road to Capitalist Modernity. *Capital and Class* 34 (3): 469–90.

Aly, Götz. 2007. *Hitler's Beneficiaries: Plunder, Racial War, and the Nazi Welfare State*. New York: Metropolitan.

Ambrosius, Lloyd E. 1977. The Orthodoxy of Revisionism: Woodrow Wilson and the New Left. *Diplomatic History* 1 (3): 199–214.

Ambrosius, Lloyd E. 1987. *Woodrow Wilson and the American Diplomatic Tradition: The Treaty Fight in Perspective*. Cambridge: Cambridge University Press.

Ambrosius, Lloyd E. 1990. Imperialism and Revolution. In *Confrontation and Cooperation: Germany and the United States in the Era of World War I, 1900–1924*, edited by H.-J. Schröder. Providence, RI: Berg.

Ambrosius, Lloyd E. 1991. *Wilsonian Statecraft: Theory and Practice of Liberal Internationalism during World War I*. Wilmington, DE: SR Books.

Ambrosius, Lloyd E. 2002. *Wilsonianism: Woodrow Wilson and His Legacy in American Foreign Relations*. New York: Palgrave Macmillan.

Ambrosius, Lloyd E. 2007. Woodrow Wilson and "The Birth of a Nation": American Democracy and International Relations. *Diplomacy and Statecraft* 18 (4): 689–718.

Amin, Samir. 1977. *Imperialism and Unequal Development*. Hassocks: Harvester.

Anderson, Kevin. 2010. *Marx at the Margins: On Nationalism, Ethnicity, and Non-Western Societies*. Chicago: University of Chicago Press.

Anderson, M. S. 1966. *The Eastern Question, 1774–1923: A Study in International Relations*. London: Macmillan.

Anderson, Perry. 1974. *Lineages of the Absolutist State*. London: NLB.

Anderson, Perry. 1987. The Figures of Descent. *New Left Review* 16:20–77.

Anderson, Perry. 1992. *English Questions*. London: Verso.

Anderson, Perry. 2005. *Spectrum: From Right to Left in the World of Ideas*. London: Verso.

Anievas, Alexander. 2008. Theories of a Global State: A Critique. *Historical Materialism* 16 (2): 190–206.

Anievas, Alexander, and Kerem Nisancioglu. 2013. What's at Stake in the Transition Debate? Rethinking the Origins of Capitalism and the "Rise of the West." *Millennium: Journal of International Studies* 42 (1): 78–102.

Anthony, Constance G. 2008. American Democratic Interventionism: Romancing the Iconic Woodrow Wilson. *International Studies Perspectives* 9:239–53.

Arendt, Hannah. 1951. *The Origins of Totalitarianism*. New York: Harcourt.

Arrighi, Giovanni. 1978. *The Geometry of Imperialism: The Limits of Hobson's Paradigm*. London: NLB.

Arrighi, Giovanni. 1994. *The Long Twentieth Century: Money, Power, and the Origins of Our Times*. London: Verso.

Arrighi, Giovanni. 2005. Hegemony Unravelling—2. *New Left Review* 33:83–116.

Arrighi, Giovanni. 2007. *Adam Smith in Beijing: Lineages of the Twenty-First Century*. London: Verso.

Art, Robert J. 2003. *A Grand Strategy for America*. Ithaca: Cornell University Press.

Artaud, Denise. 1998. Reparations and War Debts: The Restoration of French Financial Power, 1919–1929. In *French Foreign and Defence Policy, 1918–1940: The Decline and Fall of a Great Power*, edited by R. W. D. Boyce. London: Routledge.

Ashman, Sam. 2006. From World Market to World Economy. In *100 Years of Permanent Revolution: Results and Prospects*, edited by B. Dunn and H. Radice. London: Pluto.

Ashman, Sam, and Alex Callinicos. 2006. Capital Accumulation and the State System: Assessing David Harvey's *The New Imperialism*. *Historical Materialism* 14:107–31.

Ashworth, Lucian M. 2002. Did the Realist-Idealist Great Debate Really Happen? A Revisionist History of International Relations. *International Relations* 16 (1): 33–51.

Aster, Sidney. 1973. *1939: The Making of the Second World War*. London: Deutsch.

Aster, Sidney. 2008. Appeasement: Before and after Revisionism. *Diplomacy and Statecraft* 19 (3): 443–80.

Bacevich, Andrew J. 2002. *American Empire: The Realities and Consequences of U.S. Diplomacy*. Cambridge: Harvard University Press.

Bacino, Leo J. 1999. *Reconstructing Russia: U.S. Policy in Revolutionary Russia, 1917–1922*. Kent, OH: Kent State University Press.

Bailey, Thomas Andrew. 1944. *Woodrow Wilson and the Lost Peace*. New York: Macmillan.

Bairoch, Paul. 1982. International Industrialization Levels from 1760 to 1980. *Journal of European Economic History* 11:269–333.

Bairoch, Paul. 1989. European Trade Policy, 1815–1914. In *Cambridge Economic History of Europe*, vol. 13, edited by P. Mathias and S. Pollard. Cambridge: Cambridge University Press.

Baker, Ray Stannard. 1922. *Woodrow Wilson and World Settlement*. 3 vols. Garden City, NY: Doubleday, Page.

Baker, Ray Stannard. 1924. *The Versailles Treaty and After*. New York: Doran.

Baker, Ray Stannard. 1927–39. *Woodrow Wilson: Life and Letters*. 8 vols. Garden City, NY: Doubleday, Page.

Balakrishnan, Gopal. 2004. The Age of Warring States. *New Left Review* 26:148–60.

Balderston, Theo. 2002. *Economics and Politics in the Weimar Republic*. Cambridge: Cambridge University Press.

Banaji, Jairus. 2011. *Theory as History*. Chicago: Haymarket Books.

Baranowski, Shelley. 2011. *Nazi Empire: German Colonialism and Imperialism from Bismarck to Hitler*. Cambridge: Cambridge University Press.

Barkawi, Tarak. 2006. *Globalization and War*. Lanham, MD: Rowman and Littlefield.

Barkawi, Tarak. 2010. Empire and Order in International Relations and Security

Studies. In *The International Studies Encyclopedia*, vol. 3, edited by R. A. Denemark. Chichester: Wiley-Blackwell.

Barkawi, Tarak, and Mark Laffey. 2006. The Postcolonial Moment in Security Studies. *Review of International Studies* 32 (2): 329–52.

Barker, Colin. 1978a. A Note on the Theory of Capitalist States. *Capital and Class* 2 (1): 118–26.

Barker, Colin. 1978b. State as Capital. *International Socialism* 2 (1): 16–42.

Barker, Colin. 1987. Comments on Base and Superstructure. *International Socialism* 2 (34): 125–27.

Barker, Colin. 2006. Beyond Trotsky: Extending Combined and Uneven Development. In *100 Years of Permanent Revolution: Results and Prospects*, edited by B. Dunn and H. Radice. London: Pluto.

Barratt Brown, Michael. 1970. *After Imperialism*. 2nd ed. New York: Humanities.

Barratt Brown, Michael. 1988. Away with All the Great Arches: Anderson's History of British Capitalism. *New Left Review* 167:22–51.

Barrow, Clyde W. 1993. *Critical Theories of the State: Marxist, Neo-Marxist, Post-Marxist*. Madison: University of Wisconsin Press.

Beck, Robert J. 1989. Munich's Lessons Reconsidered. *International Security* 14 (2): 161–91.

Beckett, I. F. W. 2007. *The Great War, 1914–1918*. New York: Longman.

Belich, James. 2009. *Replenishing the Earth: The Settler Revolution and the Rise of the Anglo-World, 1783–1939*. Oxford: Oxford University Press.

Bell, Duncan. 2008. Under an Empty Sky: Realism and Political Theory. In *Political Thought and International Relations: Variations on a Realist Theme*, edited by D. Bell. Oxford: Oxford University Press.

Bell, Duncan. 2009. Writing the World: Disciplinary History and Beyond. *International Affairs* 85 (1): 3–22.

Bell, P. M. H. 1986. *The Origins of the Second World War in Europe*. London: Longman.

Bell, Sidney. 1972. *Righteous Conquest: Woodrow Wilson and the Evolution of the New Diplomacy*. Port Washington, NY: Kennikat.

Berend, T. Iván, and György Ránki. 1979. *Underdevelopment and Economic Growth: Studies in Hungarian Social and Economic History*. Budapest: Akadémiai Kiadó.

Berghahn, Volker R. 1991. Big Business in the Third Reich. *European History Quarterly* 21:97–108.

Berghahn, Volker R. 1993. *Germany and the Approach of War in 1914*. 2nd ed. New York: St. Martin's.

Berghahn, Volker R. 1996. German Big Business and the Quest for a European Economic Empire in the Twentieth Century. In *Quest for Economic Empire: European Strategies of German Big Business in the Twentieth Century*, edited by V. R. Berghahn. Providence, RI: Berghahn.

Berki, R. N. 1971. On Marxian Thought and the Problem of International Relations. *World Politics* 24 (1): 80–105.

Bernstein, Michael A. 1987. *The Great Depression: Delayed Recovery and Economic Change in America, 1929–1939*. Cambridge: Cambridge University Press.

Bieler, Andreas, and Adam David Morton. 2008. The Deficits of Discourse in IPE: Turning Base Metal into Gold? *International Studies Quarterly* 52 (1): 103–28.

Blackbourn, David. 1986. The Politics of Demagogy in Imperial Germany. *Past and Present* 113:152–84.

Blackbourn, David. 2003. *History of Germany, 1780–1918: The Long Nineteenth Century*. 2nd ed. London: Blackwell.

Blackbourn, David, and Geoff Eley. 1984. *The Peculiarities of German History: Bourgeois Society and Politics in Nineteenth-Century Germany*. Oxford: Oxford University Press.

Blackbourn, David, and Richard J. Evans, eds. 1991. *The German Bourgeoisie: Essays on the Social History of the German Middle Class from the Late Eighteenth to the Early Twentieth Century*. London: Routledge.

Blaut, James M. 1991. Robert Brenner in the Tunnel of Time. *Antipode* 26 (4): 351–74.

Block, Fred L. 1987. *Revising State Theory: Essays in Politics and Postindustrialism*. Philadelphia: Temple University Press.

Böhme, Helmut. 1967. Big-Business Pressure Groups and Bismarck's Turn to Protectionism, 1873–79. *Historical Journal* 10 (2): 218–36.

Bond, Brian. 1980. *British Military Policy between the Two World Wars*. Oxford: Oxford University Press.

Booth, Ken. 1991. Security and Emancipation. *Review of International Studies* 17 (4): 313–26.

Borchardt, Knut. 1990. A Decade of Debate about Brüning's Economic Policy. In *Economic Crisis and Political Collapse: The Weimar Republic, 1924–1933*, edited by J. v. Kruedener. Oxford: Berg.

Boyce, Robert. 1987. *British Capitalism at the Crossroads, 1919–1932: A Study in Politics, Economics, and International Relations*. Cambridge: Cambridge University Press.

Boyce, Robert. 1989. World War, World Depression: Some Economic Origins of the Second World War. In *Paths to War: New Essays on the Origins of the Second World War*, edited by R. Boyce and E. M. Robertson. New York: St. Martin's.

Boyce, Robert. 2009. *The Great Interwar Crisis and the Collapse of Globalization*. Basingstoke: Palgrave Macmillan.

Bracher, Karl Dietrich. 1973. *The German Dictatorship: The Origins, Structure, and Effects of National Socialism*. New York: Penguin.

Brandon, Pepijn. 2011. Marxism and the "Dutch Miracle": The Dutch Republic and the Transition-Debate. *Historical Materialism* 19 (3): 106–46.

Brawley, Mark. 2009. Neoclassical Realism and Strategic Calculations: Explaining Divergent British, French, and Soviet Strategies towards Germany (1919–1939). In *Neoclassical Realism, the State and Foreign Policy*, edited by J. Taliaferro, S. Lobell, and N. Ripsman. Cambridge: Cambridge University Press.

Brechtefeld, Jörg. 1996. *Mitteleuropa and German Politics: 1848 to the Present*. New York: St. Martin's.

Brenner, Robert. 1985. The Agrarian Roots of European Capitalism. In *The Brenner Debate: Agrarian Class Structure and Economic Development in Preindustrial Eu-*

rope, edited by T. Ashton and C. Philpin. Cambridge: Cambridge University Press.

Brenner, Robert. 1986. The Social Basis of Economic Development. In *Analytical Marxism,* edited by J. Roemer. Cambridge: Cambridge University Press.

Brenner, Robert. 2001. The Low Countries in the Transition to Capitalism. *Journal of Agrarian Change* 1 (2): 169–241.

Brenner, Robert. 2006a. *The Economics of Global Turbulence: The Advanced Capitalist Economies from Long Boom to Long Downturn, 1945–2005.* London: Verso.

Brenner, Robert. 2006b. What Is, and What Is Not, Imperialism? *Historical Materialism* 14:79–105.

Brett, E. A. 1985. *The World Economy since the War: The Politics of Uneven Development.* Basingstoke: Macmillan.

Brewer, Anthony. 1990. *Marxist Theories of Imperialism: A Critical Survey.* 2nd ed. London: Routledge.

Bromley, Simon. 1994. *Rethinking Middle East Politics.* Austin: University of Texas Press.

Bromley, Simon. 2008. *American Power and the Prospects for International Order.* Cambridge: Polity.

Broszat, Martin. 1985. *The Hitler State: The Foundation and Development of the Internal Structure of the Third Reich.* London: Longman.

Broué, Pierre. 2005. *The German Revolution, 1917–1923.* Leiden: Brill.

Brown, Chris. 2001. *Understanding International Relations.* 2nd ed. New York: Palgrave.

Buchheim, Christoph. 2008. *German Industry in the Nazi Period.* Stuttgart: Franz Steiner Verlag Wiesbaden.

Bucholz, Arden. 1985. *Hans Delbrück and the German Military Establishment: War Images in Conflict.* Iowa City: University of Iowa Press.

Buckingham, Peter H. 1983. *International Normalcy: The Open Door Peace with the Former Central Powers, 1921–29.* Wilmington, DE: Scholarly Resources.

Bucklin, Steven J. 2001. *Realism and American Foreign Policy: Wilsonians and the Kennan-Morgenthau Thesis.* Westport, CT: Praeger.

Bukharin, Nikolai Ivanovich. 1973. *Imperialism and World Economy.* New York: Monthly Review Press.

Bukharin, Nikolai Ivanovich. 1982. *Selected Writings on the State and the Transition to Socialism.* Armonk, NY: M.E. Sharpe.

Bull, Hedley. 1977. *The Anarchical Society: A Study of Order in World Politics.* London: Macmillan.

Bülow, Prince von. 1931. *Memoirs: 1903–1909.* London: Putnam.

Bülow, Prince von. 1932. *Memoirs, 1909–1919.* London: Putnam.

Bunselmeyer, Robert E. 1975. *The Cost of the War, 1914–1919: British Economic War Aims and the Origins of Reparation.* Hamden, CT: Archon.

Burawoy, Michael. 1989. Two Methods in Search of Science: Skocpol versus Trotsky. *Theory and Society* 18 (6): 759–805.

Burk, Kathleen. 1992. The Lineaments of Foreign Policy: The United States and a "New World Order," 1913–1939. *Journal of American Studies* 26 (4): 377–91.

Burke, Bernard V. 1994. *Ambassador Frederic Sackett and the Collapse of the Weimar Republic, 1930–1933: The United States and Hitler's Rise to Power.* Cambridge: Cambridge University Press.

Buzan, Barry, Charles A. Jones, and Richard Little. 1993. *The Logic of Anarchy: Neorealism to Structural Realism.* New York: Columbia University Press.

Buzan, Barry, and Richard Little. 1999. Beyond Westphalia? Capitalism after the "Fall." *Review of International Studies* 25 (5): 89–104.

Byman, Daniel, and Kenneth M. Pollack. 2001. Let Us Now Praise Great Men: Bringing the Statesman Back In. *International Security* 25 (4): 107–46.

Byres, T. J. 1996. *Capitalism from Above and Capitalism from Below: An Essay in Comparative Political Economy.* Basingstoke: Macmillan.

Cain, P. J. 1996. Gentlemanly Imperialism at Work: The Bank of England, Canada, and the Sterling Area, 1932–1936. *Economic History Review* 49 (2): 336–57.

Cain, P. J., and A. G. Hopkins. 1993a. *British Imperialism: Crisis and Deconstruction, 1914–1990.* London: Longman.

Cain, P. J., and A. G. Hopkins. 1993b. *British Imperialism: Innovation and Expansion, 1688–1914.* London: Longman.

Calhoun, Frederick S. 1993. *Uses of Force and Wilsonian Foreign Policy.* Kent, OH: Kent State University Press.

Calleo, David P. 1978. *The German Problem Reconsidered: Germany and the World Order, 1870 to the Present.* Cambridge: Cambridge University Press.

Callinicos, Alex. 1987a. Imperialism, Capitalism, and the State Today. *International Socialism* 2 (35): 71–115.

Callinicos, Alex. 1987b. *Making History: Agency, Structure, and Change in Social Theory.* Ithaca: Cornell University Press.

Callinicos, Alex. 1989a. Bourgeois Revolutions and Historical Materialism. *International Socialism* 2 (43): 113–71.

Callinicos, Alex. 1989b. Exception or Symptom? The British Crisis and the World System. *New Left Review* 169:97–106.

Callinicos, Alex. 1995. *Theories and Narratives: Reflections on the Philosophy of History.* Durham: Duke University Press.

Callinicos, Alex. 2001. Plumbing the Depths: Marxism and the Holocaust. *Yale Journal of Criticism* 14 (2): 385–414.

Callinicos, Alex. 2004. *Making History: Agency, Structure, and Change in Social Theory.* 2nd rev. ed. Leiden: Brill.

Callinicos, Alex. 2005. Epoch and Conjuncture in Marxist Political Economy. *International Politics* 42 (3): 353–63.

Callinicos, Alex. 2007. Does Capitalism Need the State System? *Cambridge Review of International Affairs* 20 (4): 533–49.

Callinicos, Alex. 2009a. *Imperialism and Global Political Economy.* Cambridge: Polity.

Callinicos, Alex. 2009b. How to Solve the Many-State Problem: A Reply to the Debate. *Cambridge Review of International Affairs* 22 (1): 89–105.

Callinicos, Alex, and Justin Rosenberg. 2008. Uneven and Combined Development: The Social-Relational Substratum of "The International"? *Cambridge Review of International Affairs* 21 (1): 77–112.

Cambridge Review of International Affairs. 2009. Debating Uneven and Combined Development: Towards a Marxist Theory of "The International"? 22 (1): 7–110.

Cameron, J. David. 2005. To Transform the Revolution into an Evolution: Underlying Assumptions of German Foreign Policy toward Soviet Russia, 1919–27. *Journal of Contemporary History* 40 (1): 7–24.

Carley, Michael Jabara. 1993. End of the "Low, Dishonest Decade": Failure of the Anglo-Franco-Soviet Alliance in 1939. *Europe-Asia Studies* 45 (2): 303–41.

Carley, Michael Jabara. 1999a. *1939: The Alliance That Never Was and the Coming of World War II.* Chicago: Dee.

Carley, Michael Jabara. 1999b. "A Situation of Delicacy and Danger": Anglo-Soviet Relations, August 1939–March 1940. *Contemporary European History* 8 (2): 175–208.

Carling, Alan. 2002. Analytical Marxism and Social Evolution. In *Historical Materialism and Social Evolution,* edited by P. Blackledge and G. Kirkpatrick. Basingstoke: Palgrave Macmillan.

Carr, Edward Hallett. 1939. *The Twenty Years' Crisis, 1919–1939: An Introduction to the Study of International Relations.* London: Macmillan.

Carr, Edward Hallett. 1961. *What Is History?* London: Macmillan.

Carr, Edward Hallett. 1979. *German-Soviet Relations between the Two World Wars, 1919–1939.* New York: Arno.

Carsten, Francis. 1973. *The Reichswehr and Politics, 1918 to 1933.* Berkeley: University of California Press.

Chase, Kerry A. 2004. Imperial Protection and Strategic Trade Policy in the Interwar Period. *Review of International Political Economy* 11 (1): 177–203.

Chase-Dunn, Christopher. 1981. Interstate System and Capitalist World-Economy: One Logic or Two? *International Studies Quarterly* 25 (1): 19–42.

Chernow, Ron. 1990. *The House of Morgan: An American Banking Dynasty and the Rise of Modern Finance.* New York: Atlantic Monthly Press.

Chibber, Vivek. 2003. *Locked in Place: State-Building and Late Industrialization in India.* Princeton: Princeton University Press.

Chilcote, Ronald H. 1984. *Theories of Development and Underdevelopment.* Boulder: Westview.

Childers, Thomas. 1984. Who, Indeed, Did Vote for Hitler? *Central European History* 17 (1): 45–53.

Childers, Thomas. 1988. Review: Big Business, Weimar Democracy, and Nazism: Henry Turner's "German Big Business and the Rise of Hitler." *Business History Review* 62 (1): 128–33.

Childers, Thomas. 1990. The Social Language of Politics in Germany: The Sociology of Political Discourse in the Weimar Republic. *American Historical Review* 95 (2): 331–58.

Christensen, Thomas J. 1997. Perceptions and Alliances in Europe, 1865–1940. *International Organization* 51 (1): 65–97.

Christensen, Thomas J., and Jack Snyder. 1990. Chain Gangs and Passed Bucks:

Predicting Alliance Patterns in Multipolarity. *International Organization* 44 (2): 137–68.

Clark, Ian. 1997. *Globalization and Fragmentation: International Relations in the Twentieth Century*. Oxford: Oxford University Press.

Clark, Ian. 2007. *International Legitimacy and World Society*. Oxford: Oxford University Press.

Clarke, Simon. 1991. *The State Debate*. Basingstoke: Macmillan.

Clements, Kendrick A. 1992. *The Presidency of Woodrow Wilson*. Lawrence: University Press of Kansas.

Cohrs, Patrick O. 2006. *The Unfinished Peace after World War I: America, Britain, and the Stabilisation of Europe, 1919–1932*. Cambridge: Cambridge University Press.

Collins, D. N. 1973. The Franco-Russian Alliance and Russian Railways, 1891–1914. *Historical Journal* 16 (4): 777–88.

Colville, John Rupert. 1985. *The Fringes of Power: Downing Street Diaries, 1939–1955*. London: Hodder and Stoughton.

Coogan, John W. 1994. Wilsonian Diplomacy in War and Peace. In *American Foreign Relations Reconsidered, 1890–1993*, edited by G. Martel. New York: Routledge.

Cooper, John Milton. 1969. *The Vanity of Power: American Isolationism and the First World War, 1914–1917*. Westport, CT: Greenwood.

Cooper, John Milton. 2001. *Breaking the Heart of the World: Woodrow Wilson and the Fight for the League of Nations*. Cambridge: Cambridge University Press.

Cooper, Luke. 2013. Can Contingency Be "Internalised" into the Bounds of Theory? Critical Realism, the Philosophy of Internal Relations, and the Solution of "Uneven and Combined Development." *Cambridge Review of International Affairs* 26 (3): 573–97.

Copeland, Dale. 2000. *The Origins of Major Wars*. Ithaca: Cornell University Press.

Costigliola, Frank. 1976. The United States and the Reconstruction of Germany in the 1920s. *Business History Review* 50 (4): 477–502.

Costigliola, Frank. 1977. Anglo-American Financial Rivalry in the 1920s. *Journal of Economic History* 37 (4): 911–34.

Costigliola, Frank. 1984. *Awkward Dominion: American Political, Economic, and Cultural Relations with Europe, 1919–1933*. Ithaca: Cornell University Press.

Cox, Michael. 2000. Wilsonianism Resurgent? The Clinton Administration and American Democracy Promotion in the Late 20th Century. In *American Democracy Promotion: Impulses, Strategies, and Impacts,* edited by M. Cox, G. J. Ikenberry, and T. Inoguchi. Oxford: Oxford University Press.

Cox, Michael, G. John Ikenberry, and Takashi Inoguchi, eds. 2000. *American Democracy Promotion: Impulses, Strategies, and Impacts*. Oxford: Oxford University Press.

Cox, Michael, and Caroline Kennedy-Pipe. 2005. The Tragedy of American Diplomacy? Rethinking the Marshall Plan. *Journal of Cold War Studies* 7 (1): 97–134.

Cox, Robert W., and Michael G. Schechter. 2002. *The Political Economy of a Plural World: Critical Reflections on Power, Morals, and Civilization*. London: Routledge.

Craig, Gordon. 1955. *The Politics of the Prussian Army, 1640–1945*. Oxford: Clarendon.

Dahrendorf, Ralf. 1967. *Society and Democracy in Germany*. London: Weidenfeld and Nicolson.

Daunton, M. J. 1989. "Gentlemanly Capitalism" and British Industry, 1820–1914. *Past and Present* 122:119–58.

Daunton, M. J. 1996. How to Pay for the War: State, Society and Taxation in Britain, 1917–24. *English Historical Review* 111 (443): 882–919.

Daunton, M. J. 2002. *Just Taxes: The Politics of Taxation in Britain, 1914–1979*. Cambridge: Cambridge University Press.

Davenport, Andrew. 2013. Marxism in IR: Condemned to a Realist Fate? *European Journal of International Relations* 19 (1): 27–48.

Davidson, Neil. 2006. From Uneven to Combined Development. In *100 Years of Permanent Revolution: Results and Prospects*, edited by B. Dunn and H. Radice. London: Pluto.

Davidson, Neil. 2009. Putting the Nation Back into "The International." *Cambridge Review of International Affairs* 22 (1): 9–28.

Davidson, Neil. 2010. Many Capitals, Many States: Contingency, Logic, or Mediation? In *Marxism and World Politics: Contesting Global Capitalism*, edited by A. Anievas. London: Routledge.

Davidson, Neil. 2012. *How Revolutionary Were the Bourgeois Revolutions?* Chicago: Haymarket.

Davidson, Neil. 2014. The Far-Right and "the Needs of Capital." In *The Longue Durée of the Far-Right: An International Historical Sociology*, edited by A. Anievas, N. Davidson, A. Fabry, and R. Saull. London: Routledge (forthcoming).

Davis, Donald E., and Eugene P. Trani. 2002. *The First Cold War: The Legacy of Woodrow Wilson in U.S.-Soviet Relations*. Columbia: University of Missouri Press.

Davis, Mike. 2001. *Late Victorian Holocausts: El Niño Famines and the Making of the Third World*. London: Verso.

Day, Richard B., and Daniel Gaido, eds. 2009. *Witnesses to Permanent Revolution: The Documentary Record*. Leiden: Brill.

de Cecco, Marcello. 1984. *Money and Empire: The International Gold Standard*. New York: St. Martin's.

de Goede, Marieke. 2003. Beyond Economism in International Political Economy. *Review of International Studies* 29 (1): 79–97.

Deist, Wilhelm. 1981. *The Wehrmacht and German Rearmament*. Toronto: University of Toronto Press.

Deist, Wilhelm, Manfred Messerschmidt, Hans-Erich Volkmann, and Wolfram Wette. 1985. Causes and Preconditions of German Aggression. In *The German Military in the Age of Total War*, edited by W. Deist. Leamington Spa: Berg.

Deudney, Daniel. 2007. *Bounding Power: Republican Security Theory from the Polis to the Global Village*. Princeton: Princeton University Press.

Deudney, Daniel, and G. John Ikenberry. 1999. The Nature and Sources of Liberal International Order. *Review of International Studies* 25 (2): 179–96.

Deutscher, Isaac. 1984. *Marxism, Wars, and Revolutions: Essays from Four Decades*. Edited by T. Deutscher. London: Verso.

Diamond, William. 1943. *The Economic Thought of Woodrow Wilson*. Baltimore: Johns Hopkins Press.

Diaper, Stephanie. 1986. Banking in the Interwar Period: The Case of Kleinwort Sons & Co. *Business History* 28 (4): 55–76.

Dimitrov, Georgi. 1935. The Fascist Offensive and the Tasks of the Communist International in the Struggle of the Working Class against Fascism. In *Main Report delivered at the Seventh World Congress of the Communist International*. http://www.marxists.org/reference/archive/dimitrov/works/1935/08_02. htm.

Domhoff, G. William. 1983. *Who Rules America Now? A View for the '80s*. Englewood Cliffs, NJ: Prentice-Hall.

Doyle, Michael W. 1986. Liberalism and World Politics. *American Political Science Review* 80 (4): 1151–69.

Doyle, Michael W. 1997. *Ways of War and Peace: Realism, Liberalism, and Socialism*. New York: Norton.

Dueck, Colin. 2006. *Reluctant Crusaders: Power, Culture, and Change in American Grand Strategy*. Princeton: Princeton University Press.

Dülffer, Jost. 1976a. Bonapartism, Fascism, and National Socialism. *Journal of Contemporary History* 11 (4): 109–28.

Dülffer, Jost. 1976b. Der Beginn des Krieges 1939: Hitler, die innere Krise und das Mächtesystem. *Geschichte und Gesellschaft* 2 (4): 443–70.

Dülffer, Jost. 1985. Determinants of German Naval Policy, 1920–1939. In *The German Military in the Age of Total War*, edited by W. Deist. Leamington Spa: Berg.

Duménil, Gérard, M. Glick, and J. Rangel. 1987. The Rate of Profit in the United States. *Cambridge Journal of Economics* 11 (4): 331–59.

Duménil, Gérard, and Dominique Lévy. 1993. *The Economics of the Profit Rate: Competition, Crises, and Historical Tendencies in Capitalism*. Brookfield, VT: Elgar.

Eagleton, Terry. 2007. *Ideology: An Introduction*. London: Verso.

Eden, Anthony. 1962. *Facing the Dictators: The Eden Memoirs*. London: Cassell.

Einzig, Paul. 1941. *Appeasement Before, during and after the War*. London: Macmillan.

Eley, Geoff. 1980. *Reshaping the German Right: Radical Nationalism and Political Change after Bismarck*. New Haven: Yale University Press.

Eley, Geoff. 1983. What Produces Fascism: Preindustrial Traditions or a Crisis of a Capitalist State. *Politics and Society* 12 (3): 53–82.

Eley, Geoff. 1986. *From Unification to Nazism: Reinterpreting the German Past*. Boston: Allen and Unwin.

Eley, Geoff. 1996. *Society, Culture, and the State in Germany, 1870-1930*. Ann Arbor: University of Michigan Press.

Eley, Geoff. 2014. Germany, the Fischer Controversy, and the Context of War. In *Cataclysm 1914: World War I and the Making of Modern World Politics*, edited by A. Anievas. Leiden: Brill (forthcoming).

Elman, Colin. 1996. Horses for Courses: Why Not Neorealist Theories of Foreign Policy? *Security Studies* 6 (1): 7-53.

Emery, J. A. 1988. The Emergence of Treasury Influence in British Foreign Policy, 1914-1921. PhD diss., University of Cambridge.

Evans, Peter B., Dietrich Rueschemeyer, and Theda Skocpol. 1985. *Bringing the State Back In*. Cambridge: Cambridge University Press.

Evans, Richard J. 1983a. Review: From Hitler to Bismarck: "Third Reich" and Kaiserreich in Recent Historiography: Part I. *Historical Journal* 26 (2): 485-97.

Evans, Richard J. 1983b. Review: From Hitler to Bismarck: "Third Reich" and Kaiserreich in Recent Historiography: Part II. *Historical Journal* 26 (4): 999-1020.

Evans, Richard J. 1985. The Myth of Germany's Missing Revolution. *New Left Review* (149): 67-94.

Evans, Richard J. 2004. *The Coming of the Third Reich*. New York: Penguin.

Fabry, Adam. 2011. From Poster Boy of Neoliberal Transformation to Basket Case: Hungary and the Global Economic Crisis. In *First the Transition, Then the Crash: Eastern Europe in the 2000s*, edited by G. Dale. London: Pluto.

Feldman, Gerald D. 1970. German Business between War and Revolution: The Origins of the Stinnes-Legien Agreement. In *Entstehung und Wandel der modernen Gesellschaft*, edited by G. Ritter. Berlin: De Gruyter.

Feldman, Gerald D. 1977. *Iron and Steel in the German Inflation, 1916-1923*. Princeton: Princeton University Press.

Feldman, Gerald D. 2004. Financial Institutions in Nazi Germany: Reluctant or Willing Collaborators? In *Business and Industry in Nazi Germany*, edited by F. R. Nicosia and J. Huener. New York: Berghahn.

Ferguson, Niall. 1994. Public Finance and National Security: The Domestic Origins of the First World War Revisited. *Past and Present* 142:141-68.

Ferguson, Niall. 1999. *The Pity of War*. New York: Basic Books.

Ferguson, Niall. 2008. Earning from History? Financial Markets and the Approach of World Wars. *Brookings Papers on Economic Activities* 1:431-90.

Finney, Patrick. 1997. Introduction: History Writing and the Origins of the Second World War. In *The Origins of the Second World War*, edited by P. Finney. London: Arnold.

Fischer, Fritz. 1967. *Germany's Aims in the First World War*. London: Chatto and Windus.

Fischer, Fritz. 1974. *World Power or Decline: The Controversy over Germany's Aims in the First World War*. New York: Norton.

Fischer, Fritz. 1975. *War of Illusions: German Policies from 1911 to 1914*. New York: Norton.

Fischer, Fritz. 1984. World Policy, World Power, and German War Aims. In *The Origins of the First World War: Great Power Rivalry and German War Aims*, edited by H. W. Koch. Basingstoke: Macmillan.

Fischer, Fritz. 1986. *From Kaiserreich to Third Reich: Elements of Continuity in German History, 1871–1945*. London: Allen and Unwin.

Fischer, Fritz. 1990. The Foreign Policy of Imperial Germany and the Outbreak of the First World War. In *Escape into War?—The Foreign Policy of Imperial Germany*, edited by G. Schöllgen. Oxford: Berg.

Foglesong, David S. 1995. *America's Secret War against Bolshevism: U.S. Intervention in the Russian Civil War, 1917–1920*. Chapel Hill: University of North Carolina Press.

Forbes, Neil. 1987. London Banks, the German Standstill Agreements, and "Economic Appeasement" in the 1930s. *Economic History Review* 40 (4): 571–87.

Forbes, Neil. 2000. *Doing Business with the Nazis: Britain's Economic and Financial Relations with Germany, 1931–1939*. London: Cass.

Förster, Stig. 1999. Dreams and Nightmares: German Military Leadership and the Images of Future Warfare, 1871–1914. In *Anticipating Total War: The German and American Experiences, 1871–1914*, edited by M. F. Boemeke, R. Chickering, and S. Förster. Cambridge: Cambridge University Press.

Fracchia, Joseph. 2004. On Transhistorical Abstractions and the Intersection of Historical Theory and Social Critique. *Historical Materialism* 12:125–46.

French, David. 1982. *British Economic and Strategic Planning, 1905–1915*. London: Allen and Unwin.

Frommelt, Reinhard. 1977. *Paneuropa oder Mitteleuropa: Einigungsbestrebungen im Kalkül deutscher Wirtschaft und Politik, 1925–1933*. Stuttgart: Deutsche Verlags-Anstalt.

Fry, Joseph A. 1996. From Open Door to World Systems: Economic Interpretations of Late Nineteenth Century American Foreign Relations. *Pacific Historical Review* 65 (2): 277–303.

Fry, Joseph A. 2002. *Dixie Looks Abroad: The South and U.S. Foreign Relations, 1789–1973*. Baton Rouge: Louisiana State University Press.

Furner, James. 2008. Marx's Conception of Basis and Superstructure. PhD diss., University of Sussex.

Gallagher, John, and Ronald Robinson. 1953. The Imperialism of Free Trade. *Economic History Review* 6 (1): 1–15.

Gardner, Lloyd C. 1967. American Foreign Policy, 1900–1921: A Second Look at the Realist Critique of American Diplomacy. In *Towards a New Past: Dissenting Essays in American History*, edited by W. A. Williams. New York: Pantheon.

Gardner, Lloyd C. 1984. *Safe for Democracy: The Anglo-American Response to Revolution, 1913–1923*. Oxford: Oxford University Press.

Gardner, Lloyd C. 1993. The US, the German Peril and a Revolutionary World: The Inconsistencies of World Order and National Self-Determination. In *Confrontation and Cooperation: Germany and the United States in the Era of World War I, 1900–1924*, edited by H.-J. Schroder. Oxford: Berg.

Gartzke, Erik. 2007. The Capitalist Peace. *American Journal of Political Science* 51 (1): 166–91.

Gartzke, Erik. 2009. Production, Prosperity, Preferences, and Peace. In *Capitalism, Democracy, and the Prevention of War and Poverty,* edited by P. Graeff and G. Mehlkop. Milton Park, Abingdon: Routledge.

Geary, Dick. 1983. The Industrial Elites and the Nazis in the Weimar Republic. In *The Nazi Machtergreifung,* edited by P. Stachura. London: Allen and Unwin.

Geary, Dick. 1990. Employers, Workers, and the Collapse of the Weimar Republic. In *Weimar: Why Did German Democracy Fail?* edited by I. Kershaw. London: Weidenfeld and Nicolson.

Geary, Dick. 1993. *Hitler and Nazism.* London: Routledge.

Geiss, Imanuel, ed. 1967. *July 1914: Selected Documents.* London: Batsford.

Geiss, Imanuel. 1976. *German Foreign Policy, 1871–1914.* London: Routledge.

George, Margaret. 1965. *The Warped Vision: British Foreign Policy, 1933–1939.* Pittsburgh: University of Pittsburgh Press.

Germany, Auswärtiges Amt. 1949. *Documents on German Foreign Policy, 1918–1945.* Series D, vol. 7, August–September 1939. London: HMSO.

Gerschenkron, Alexander. 1962. *Economic Backwardness in Historical Perspective.* Cambridge: Harvard University Press.

Gerschenkron, Alexander. 1966. *Bread and Democracy in Germany.* New York: Fertig.

Gessner, Dieter. 1977. Agrarian Protectionism in the Weimar Republic. *Journal of Contemporary History* 12 (4): 759–78.

Gessner, Dieter. 1981. The Dilemma of German Agriculture during the Weimar Republic. In *Social Change and Political Development in Weimar Germany,* edited by R. Besel and E. J. Feuchtwanger. London: Croom Helm.

Geyer, Dietrich. 1987. *Russian Imperialism: The Interaction of Domestic and Foreign Policy, 1860–1914.* Leamington Spa, NY: Berg.

Geyer, Michael. 1983. Etudes in Political History: Reichswehr, NSDAP and the Seizure of Power. In *The Nazi Machtergreifung,* edited by P. Stachura. London: Allen and Unwin.

Geyer, Michael. 1985. The Dynamics of Military Revisionism in the Interwar Years. In *The German Military in the Age of Total War,* edited by W. Deist. Leamington Spa: Berg.

Giddens, Anthony. 1981. *A Contemporary Critique of Historical Materialism.* Berkeley: University of California Press.

Giddens, Anthony. 1987. *The Nation-State and Violence.* Berkeley: University of California Press.

Gilbert, Martin, and Richard Gott. 1963. *The Appeasers.* London: Weidenfeld and Nicholson.

Gilpin, Robert. 1981. *War and Change in World Politics.* Cambridge: Cambridge University Press.

Gilpin, Robert. 1987. *The Political Economy of International Relations.* Princeton: Princeton University Press.

Gilpin, Robert. 1988. The Theory of Hegemonic War. *Journal of Interdisciplinary History* 18 (4): 591–613.

Gindin, Sam, and Leo Panitch. 2004. *Global Capitalism and American Empire*. London: Merlin.

Girault, René. 1973. *Emprunts Russes et Investissements Français en Russie, 1887–1914: Recherches sur l'Investissement International*. Paris: A. Colin.

Glenn, John. 2012. Uneven and Combined Development: A Fusion of Marxism and Structural Realism. *Cambridge Review of International Affairs* 25 (1): 75–95.

Gluckstein, Donny. 1999. *The Nazis, Capitalism, and the Working Class*. London: Bookmarks.

Good, David F. 1984. *The Economic Rise of the Habsburg Empire, 1750–1914*. Berkeley: University of California Press.

Good, David F. 1986. Uneven Development in the Nineteenth Century: A Comparison of the Habsburg Empire and the United States. *Journal of Economic History* 46 (1): 137–51.

Gordon, Michael R. 1974. Domestic Conflict and the Origins of the First World War: The British and the German Cases. *Journal of Modern History* 46 (2): 191–226.

Gorodetsky, Gabriel. 1990. The Impact of the Ribbentrop-Molotov Pact on the Course of Soviet Foreign Policy. *Cahiers du Monde Russe et Soviétique* 31 (1): 27–41.

Gossweiler, Kurt. 1971. *Grossbanken, Industriemonopole, Staat: Ökonomie und Politik des Staatsmonoplistischen Kapitalismus in Deutschland, 1914–1932*. Berlin: Deutscher Verlag der Wissenschaften.

Gossweiler, Kurt. 1989. Economy and Politics in the Destruction of the Weimar Republic. In *Radical Perspectives on the Rise of Fascism in Germany, 1919–1945*, edited by M. N. Dobkowski and I. Wallimann. New York: Monthly Review Press.

Gourevitch, Peter. 1978. The Second Image Reversed: The International Sources of Domestic Politics. *International Organization* 32 (4): 881–912.

Gowan, Peter. 1987. The Origins of the Administrative Elite. *New Left Review* 162: 4–34.

Gowan, Peter. 2010. Industrial Development and International Political Conflict in Contemporary Capitalism. In *Marxism and World Politics: Contesting Global Capitalism*, edited by A. Anievas. London: Routledge.

Graebner, Norman A. 1984. *America as a World Power: A Realist Appraisal from Wilson to Reagan*. Wilmington, DE: Scholarly Resources.

Gramsci, Antonio. 1971. *Selections from the Prison Notebooks*. London: Lawrence and Wishart.

Grazia, V. D. 2005. *Irresistible Empire: America's Advance through Twentieth-Century Europe*. Cambridge: Harvard University Press.

Great Britain, Foreign Office, and E. L. Woodward. 1946. *Documents on British Foreign Policy, 1919–1939*. London: HMSO.

Green, Jeremy Bernard Rawson. 2012. Uneven and Combined Development and the Anglo-German Prelude to WWI. *European Journal of International Relations* 18 (2): 345–68.

Gregor, Neil. 1998. *Daimler-Benz in the Third Reich*. New Haven: Yale University Press.

Gross, Stephen. 2005. The Mitteleuropaeischer Wirtschaftstag and the Suedosteuropa-Gesellschaft: German Development Interests in the Balkans 1930 to 1945. Unpublished manuscript. University of California, Berkeley.

Haas, Mark L. 2005. *The Ideological Origins of Great Power Politics, 1789–1989*. Ithaca: Cornell University Press.

Hall, Martin. 1999. Review: International Relations and Historical Sociology: Taking Stock of Convergence. *Review of International Political Economy* 6 (1): 101–9.

Halliday, Fred. 1987. State and Society in International Relations: A Second Agenda. *Millennium—Journal of International Studies* 16:215–29.

Halliday, Fred. 1989. Theorizing the International. *Economy and Society* 18 (3): 346–59.

Halliday, Fred. 1999. *Revolution and World Politics: The Rise and Fall of the Sixth Great Power*. Durham: Duke University Press.

Halliday, Fred. 2002a. For an International Sociology. In *Historical Sociology of International Relations*, edited by S. Hobden and J. M. Hobson. Cambridge: Cambridge University Press.

Halliday, Fred. 2002b. The Persistence of Imperialism. In *Historical Materialism and Globalization*, edited by M. Rupert and H. Smith. London: Routledge.

Halperin, Sandra. 1996. The Politics of Appeasement: The Rise of the Left and European International Relations during the Interwar Period. In *Contested Social Orders and International Politics*, edited by D. Skidmore. Nashville: Vanderbilt University Press.

Halperin, Sandra. 2004. *War and Social Change in Modern Europe: The Great Transformation Revisited*. Cambridge: Cambridge University Press.

Hamilton, Richard F., and Holger H. Herwig, eds. 2003. *The Origins of World War I*. Cambridge: Cambridge University Press.

Hamilton, Richard F., and Holger H. Herwig. 2004. *Decisions for War, 1914–1917*. Cambridge: Cambridge University Press.

Hannah, Leslie. 1983. *The Rise of the Corporate Economy*. 2nd ed. London: Methuen.

Hannigan, Robert E. 2002. *The New World Power: American Foreign Policy, 1898–1917*. Philadelphia: University of Pennsylvania Press.

Hardach, Gerd. 1977. *The First World War, 1914–1918*. Berkeley: University of California Press.

Hardt, Michael, and Antonio Negri. 2000. *Empire*. Cambridge: Harvard University Press.

Hargrave, John. 1939. *Professor Skinner alias Montagu Norman*. London: W. Gardner.

Harman, Chris. 1982. *The Lost Revolution: Germany, 1918 to 1923*. London: Bookmarks.

Harman, Chris. 1986. Base and Superstructure. *International Socialism* 2 (32): 3–44.

Harman, Chris. 1991. The State and Capitalism Today. *International Socialism* 2 (51): 3–57.

Harrison, Mark. 1988. Resource Mobilization for World War II: The USA, UK, USSR, and Germany, 1938–1945. *Economic History Review* 41 (2): 171–92.

Hartz, Louis. 1955. *The Liberal Tradition in America: An Interpretation of American Political Thought since the Revolution.* New York: Harcourt.

Harvey, David. 2001. *Spaces of Capital: Towards a Critical Geography.* New York: Routledge.

Harvey, David. 2003. *The New Imperialism.* Oxford: Oxford University Press.

Harvey, Oliver. 1970. *The Diplomatic Diaries of Oliver Harvey, 1937–1940.* Edited by John Harvey. London: Collins.

Haslam, Jonathan. 1984. *The Soviet Union and the Struggle for Collective Security in Europe, 1933–39.* New York: St. Martin's.

Hautmann, H. 1992. Vienna: A City in the Years of Radical Change, 1917–1920. In *Challenges of Labour: Central and Western Europe, 1917–1920,* edited by C. Wrigley. London: Routledge.

Hayes, Peter. 1987. Review: History in an Off Key: David Abraham's Second "Collapse." *Business History Review* 61 (3): 452–72.

Hayes, Peter. 2001. *Industry and Ideology: IG Farben in the Nazi Era.* New ed. Cambridge: Cambridge University Press.

Hayne, M. B. 1993. *The French Foreign Office and the Origins of the First World War, 1898–1914.* Oxford: Clarendon.

Healy, David. 1970. *U.S. Expansionism: The Imperialist Urge in the 1890s.* Madison: University of Wisconsin Press.

Heckart, Beverly. 1974. *From Bassermann to Bebel: The Grand Bloc's Quest for Reform in the Kaiserreich, 1900–1914.* New Haven: Yale University Press.

Heckscher, August. 1991. *Woodrow Wilson.* New York: Scribner.

Hehn, Paul N. 2002. *A Low Dishonest Decade: The Great Powers, Eastern Europe, and the Economic Origins of World War II, 1930–1941.* New York: Continuum.

Heller, Henry. 2011. *The Birth of Capitalism.* London: Pluto.

Herbert, Ulrich. 1993. Labour and Extermination: Economic Interest and the Primacy of *Weltanschauung* in National Socialism. *Past and Present* 138:144–95.

Herrmann, David G. 1997. *The Arming of Europe and the Making of the First World War.* Princeton: Princeton University Press.

Herwig, Holger H. 1991. Industry, Empire, and the First World War. In *Modern Germany Reconsidered,* edited by G. Martel. London: HarperCollins.

Herwig, Holger H. 1994. Strategic Uncertainties of a Nation-State: Prussia-Germany, 1871–1918. In *The Making of Strategy: Rulers, States, and War,* edited by W. Murray, M. Knox and A. H. Bernstein. Cambridge: Cambridge University Press.

Herwig, Holger H. 1999. Geopolitik: Haushofer, Hitler, and Lebensraum. *Journal of Strategic Studies* 22 (2): 218–41.

Hewitson, Mark. 2004. *Germany and the Causes of the First World War*. Oxford: Berg.

Hildebrand, Klaus. 1973. *The Foreign Policy of the Third Reich*. London: Batsford.

Hildebrand, Klaus. 1989. *German Foreign Policy from Bismarck to Adenauer: The Limits of Statecraft*. London: Unwin Hyman.

Hill, Christopher L. 2008. *National History and the World of Nations: Capital, State, and the Rhetoric of History in Japan, France, and the United States*. Durham: Duke University Press.

Hillgruber, Andreas. 1981. *Germany and the Two World Wars*. Cambridge: Harvard University Press.

Hinsley, Fred. 1963. *Power and the Pursuit of Peace: Theory and Practice in the History of Relations between States*. Cambridge: Cambridge University Press.

Hinsley, Fred. 1995. The Origins of the First World War. In *Decisions for War,* edited by K. M. Wilson. New York: St. Martin's.

Hitler, Adolf. 1973. *Hitler's Table Talk, 1941–44: His Private Conversations*. 2nd ed. Translated by Norman Cameron and R. H. Stevens. Introduction and Preface by H. R. Trevor-Roper. London: Weidenfeld and Nicolson.

Hitler, Adolf. 1994. Adolf Hitler: Address to the Industry Club, 27 January 1932. In *The Weimar Republic Sourcebook,* edited by A. Kaes, M. Jay, and E. Dimendberg. Berkeley: University of California Press.

Hitler, Adolf. 2001. *Mein Kampf*. Boston: Houghton Mifflin.

Hitler, Adolf. 2003. *Hitler's Second Book: The Unpublished Sequel to Mein Kampf*. Edited by G. L. Weinberg. New York: Enigma.

Hixson, Walter L. 2008. *The Myth of American Diplomacy: National Identity and U.S. Foreign Policy*. New Haven: Yale University Press.

Hobsbawm, E. J. 1968. *Industry and Empire: An Economic History of Britain since 1750*. London: Weidenfeld and Nicolson.

Hobsbawm, E. J. 1987. *The Age of Empire, 1875–1914*. New York: Pantheon.

Hobsbawm, E. J. 1992. *Nations and Nationalism since 1780: Programme, Myth, Reality*. 2nd ed. Cambridge: Cambridge University Press.

Hobsbawm, E. J. 1994. *Age of Extremes: The Short Twentieth Century, 1914–1991*. London: Viking Penguin.

Hobson, John M. 1997. *The Wealth of States*. Cambridge: Cambridge University Press.

Hobson, John M. 1998a. The Historical Sociology of the State and the State of Historical Sociology in International Relations. *Review of International Political Economy* 5 (2): 284–320.

Hobson, John M. 1998b. For a "Second-Wave" Weberian Historical Sociology in International Relations: A Reply to Halperin and Shaw. *Review of International Political Economy* 5 (2): 354–61.

Hobson, John M. 2002. What's at Stake in Bringing Historical Sociology Back into International Relations? Transcending "Chronofetishism" and "Tempocentrism" in International Relations. In *Historical Sociology of International Relations,* edited by S. Hobden and J. M. Hobson. Cambridge: Cambridge University Press.

Hobson, John M. 2004. *The Eastern Origins of Western Civilization*. Cambridge: Cambridge University Press.

Hobson, John M. 2007. Back to the Future of "One Logic or Two"? Forward to the Past of "Anarchy versus Racist Hierarchy"? *Cambridge Review of International Affairs* 20 (4): 581–97.

Hobson, John M. 2011. What's at Stake in the Neo-Trotskyist Debate? Towards A Non-Eurocentric Historical Sociology of Uneven and Combined Development. *Millennium—Journal of International Studies* 40 (1): 147–66.

Hobson, John M., and George Lawson. 2008. What Is History in International Relations? *Millennium—Journal of International Studies* 37 (2): 415–35.

Hoff, Joan. 2008. *A Faustian Foreign Policy from Woodrow Wilson to George W. Bush: Dreams of Perfectibility*. Cambridge: Cambridge University Press.

Hoffmann, Stanley. 1977. An American Social Science: International Relations. *Daedalus* 106 (3): 41–60.

Hogan, Michael J. 1991. *Informal Entente: The Private Structure of Cooperation in Anglo-American Economic Diplomacy, 1918–1928*. Chicago: Imprint.

Holland, R. F. 1981. The Federation of British Industries and the International Economy, 1929–39. *Economic History Review* 34 (2): 287–300.

Holloway, John, and Sol Picciotto. 1978. *State and Capital: A Marxist Debate*. London: E. Arnold.

Holsti, K. J. 1991. *Peace and War: Armed Conflicts and International Order, 1648–1989*. Cambridge: Cambridge University Press.

Holsti, K. J. 1992. *International Politics: A Framework for Analysis*. 6th ed. Englewood Cliffs, NJ: Prentice Hall.

Holtfrerich, Carl-Ludwig. 1990. Was the Policy of Deflation in Germany Unavoidable? In *Economic Crisis and Political Collapse: The Weimar Republic, 1924–1933*, edited by J. v. Kruedener. Oxford: Berg.

Hoover, Herbert. 1958. *The Ordeal of Woodrow Wilson*. New York: McGraw-Hill.

Horn, Martin. 2005. J. P. Morgan & Co., the House of Morgan, and Europe, 1933–1939. *Contemporary European History* 14 (4): 519–38.

House, Edward Mandell. 1926–28. *The Intimate Papers of Colonel House*. Arranged by Charles Seymour. 4 vols. Boston: Houghton Mifflin.

Howard, Michael C., and J. E. King. 1989. *A History of Marxian Economics*. 2 vols. Princeton: Princeton University Press.

Hunt, Michael H. 1987. *Ideology and U.S. Foreign Policy*. New Haven: Yale University Press.

Hurrell, Andrew. 2007. *On Global Order: Power, Values, and the Constitution of International Society*. Oxford: Oxford University Press.

Ikenberry, G. John. 2001. *After Victory: Institutions, Strategic Restraint, and the Rebuilding of Order after Major Wars*. Princeton: Princeton University Press.

Ikenberry, G. John. 2004. Liberalism and Empire: Logics of Order in the American Unipolar Age. *Review of International Studies* 30 (4): 609–30.

Ikenberry, G. John, Thomas J. Knock, Anne-Marie Slaughter, and Tony Smith. 2009. *The Crisis of American Foreign Policy: Wilsonianism in the Twenty-First Century*. Princeton: Princeton University Press.

Ikenberry, G. John, and Charles A. Kupchan. 1990. Socialization and Hegemonic Power. *International Organization* 44 (3): 283–315.

Imlay, Talbot. 2007. Democracy and War: Political Regime, Industrial Relations, and Economic Preparations for War in France and Britain up to 1940. *Journal of Modern History* 79 (1): 1–47.

Ingham, Geoffrey K. 1984. *Capitalism Divided? The City and Industry in British Social Development*. New York: Schocken.

Irvine, William D. 1979. *French Conservatism in Crisis: The Republican Federation of France in the 1930s*. Baton Rouge: Louisiana State University Press.

Israel, Jerry. 1971. *Progressivism and the Open Door: America and China, 1905–1921*. Pittsburgh: University of Pittsburgh Press.

Jackson, Peter. 1998. French Intelligence and Hitler's Rise to Power. *Historical Journal* 41 (3): 795–824.

Jackson, Robert H. 2000. *The Global Covenant: Human Conduct in a World of States*. Oxford: Oxford University Press.

Jacobson, Jon. 1972. *Locarno Diplomacy: Germany and the West, 1925–1929*. Princeton: Princeton University Press.

Jacobson, Jon. 2004. Locarno, Britain, and the Security of Europe. In *Locarno Revisited: European Diplomacy, 1920–1929*, edited by G. Johnson. London: Routledge.

James, Harold. 2001. *The End of Globalization: Lessons from the Great Depression*. Cambridge: Harvard University Press.

James, Harold. 2004. *The Nazi Dictatorship and the Deutsche Bank*. Cambridge: Cambridge University Press.

Jameson, Fredric. 1981. *The Political Unconscious: Narrative as a Socially Symbolic Act*. Ithaca: Cornell University Press.

Jarausch, Konrad H. 1969. The Illusion of Limited War: Chancellor Bethmann Hollweg's Calculated Risk, July 1914. *Central European History* 2 (1): 48–76.

Jarausch, Konrad H. 1979. From Second to Third Reich: The Problem of Continuity in German Foreign Policy. *Central European History* 12 (1): 68–82.

Jászi, Oszkár. 1929. *The Dissolution of the Habsburg Monarchy*. Chicago: University of Chicago Press.

Jay, Martin. 1984. *Marxism and Totality: The Adventures of a Concept from Lukács to Habermas*. Berkeley: University of California Press.

Jervis, Robert. 1982. Deterrence and Perception. *International Security* 7 (3): 3–30.

Jessop, Bob. 1990. *State Theory: Putting the Capitalist State in Its Place*. Cambridge: Polity.

Joll, James, and Gordon Martel. 2007. *The Origins of the First World War*. 3rd ed. Harlow: Longman.

Jones, Larry Eugene. 1972. "The Dying Middle": Weimar Germany and the Fragmentation of Bourgeois Politics. *Central European History* 5 (1): 23–54.

Jordan, Nicole. 1992. *The Popular Front and Central Europe: The Dilemmas of French Impotence, 1918–1940*. Cambridge: Cambridge University Press.

Joseph, Jonathan. 2010. The Limits of Governmentality: Social Theory and the International. *European Journal of International Relations* 16 (2): 223–46.

Kaiser, David E. 1980. *Economic Diplomacy and the Origins of the Second World War: Germany, Britain, France, and Eastern Europe, 1930–1939*. Princeton: Princeton University Press.

Kaiser, David E. 1983. Germany and the Origins of the First World War. *Journal of Modern History* 55 (3): 442–74.

Kaiser, David E. 1989. Germany, "Domestic Crisis," and War in 1939. *Past and Present* 122 (1): 200–205.

Kaiser, David E. 1990. *Politics and War: European Conflict from Philip II to Hitler*. Cambridge: Harvard University Press.

Kandal, Terry R. 1989. Marx and Engels on International Relations, Revolution, and Counterrevolution. In *Studies of Development and Change in the Modern World*, edited by M. T. Martin and T. R. Kandal. Oxford: Oxford University Press.

Kasaba, Reşat. 1988. *The Ottoman Empire and the World Economy: The Nineteenth Century*. Albany: State University of New York Press.

Kay, Alex J. 2006. *Exploitation, Resettlement, Mass Murder: Political and Economic Planning for German Occupation Policy in the Soviet Union, 1940–1941*. New York: Berghahn.

Keeble, Curtis. 1990. *Britain and the Soviet Union, 1917–89*. New York: St. Martin's.

Kegley, Charles W., Jr. 1993. The Neoidealist Moment in International Studies? Realist Myths and the New International Realities. *International Studies Quarterly* 37 (2): 131–46.

Kegley, Charles W., Jr., and Gregory A. Raymond. 1999. *How Nations Make Peace*. New York: St. Martin's.

Kegley, Charles W., Jr., and Eugene R. Wittkopf. 2004. *World Politics: Trend and Transformation*. 9th ed. Belmont, CA: Thomson/Wadsworth.

Kehr, Eckart. 1977. *Economic Interest, Militarism, and Foreign Policy: Essays on German History*. Berkeley: University of California Press.

Keiger, John F. V. 1983. *France and the Origins of the First World War*. London: Macmillan.

Keiger, John F. V. 1997. *Raymond Poincaré*. Cambridge: Cambridge University Press.

Kemp, Tom. 1985. *Industrialization in Nineteenth-Century Europe*. 2nd ed. London: Longman.

Kennan, George F. 1951. *American Diplomacy, 1900–1950*. Chicago: University of Chicago Press.

Kennan, George F. 1991. Comments on the Paper Entitled "Kennan versus Wilson" by Professor Thomas J. Knock. In *The Wilsonian Era: Essays in Honor of Arthur S. Link*, edited by A. S. Link, J. M. Cooper, and C. E. Neu. Arlington Heights, IL: Harlan Davidson.

Kennedy, David M. 1980. *Over Here: The First World War and American Society*. New York: Oxford University Press.

Kennedy, Paul M. 1975. Idealists and Realists: British Views of Germany, 1864–1939. *Transactions of the Royal Historical Society* 25:137–56.

Kennedy, Paul M. 1980. *The Rise of the Anglo-German Antagonism, 1860–1914*. London: Allen and Unwin.

Kennedy, Paul M. 1981. *The Realities behind Diplomacy: Background Influences on British External Policy, 1865–1980*. London: Allen and Unwin.

Kennedy, Paul M. 1984. The First World War and the International Power System. *International Security* 9 (1): 7–40.

Kennedy, Paul M. 1988. *The Rise and Fall of Great Powers: Economic Change and Military Conflict from 1500 to 2000*. London: Fontana.

Kennedy, Ross A. 2009. *The Will to Believe: Woodrow Wilson, World War I, and America's Strategy for Peace and Security*. Kent, OH: Kent State University Press.

Kent, Bruce. 1991. *The Spoils of War: The Politics, Economics, and Diplomacy of Reparations, 1918–1932*. Oxford: Oxford University Press.

Keohane, Robert O. 1984. *After Hegemony: Cooperation and Discord in the World Political Economy*. Princeton: Princeton University Press.

Keohane, Robert O., ed. 1986. *Neorealism and Its Critics*. New York: Columbia University Press.

Keohane, Robert O., and Joseph S. Nye. 1977. *Power and Interdependence: World Politics in Transition*. Boston: Little, Brown.

Kershaw, Ian. 1992. Social Unrest and the Response of the Nazi Regime, 1934–36. In *Germans against Nazism: Nonconformity, Opposition, and Resistance in the Third Reich,* edited by F. R. Nicosia and L. D. Stokes. New York: Berg.

Kershaw, Ian. 1993. *The Nazi Dictatorship: Problems and Perspectives of Interpretation*. 3rd ed. London: E. Arnold.

Kershaw, Ian. 1999–2000. *Hitler*. 2 vols. New York: W.W. Norton.

Khong, Yuen Foong. 1992. *Analogies at War: Korea, Munich, Dien Bien Phu, and the Vietnam Decisions of 1965*. Princeton: Princeton University Press.

Kiely, Ray. 2006. United States Hegemony and Globalisation: What Role for Theories of Imperialism? *Cambridge Review of International Affairs* 19 (2): 205–21.

Kiely, Ray. 2012. Spatial Hierarchy and/or Contemporary Geopolitics: What Can and Can't Uneven and Combined Development Explain? *Cambridge Review of International Affairs* 25 (2): 231–48.

Kier, Elizabeth. 1997. *Imagining War: French and British Military Doctrine between the Wars*. Princeton: Princeton University Press.

Kindleberger, Charles P. 1981. Dominance and Leadership in the International Economy: Exploitation, Public Goods, and Free Rides. *International Studies Quarterly* 25 (2): 242–54.

Kindleberger, Charles P. 1986. *The World in Depression, 1929–1939*. Rev. and enl. ed. Berkeley: University of California Press.

Kirshner, Jonathan. 2007. *Appeasing Bankers: Financial Caution on the Road to War*. Princeton: Princeton University Press.

Kissinger, Henry. 1957. *A World Restored: Metternich, Castlereagh, and the Problems of Peace, 1812–22*. London: Weidenfeld and Nicolson.

Kissinger, Henry. 1994. *Diplomacy*. New York: Simon and Schuster.

Kitchen, Martin. 1968. *The German Officer Corps, 1890–1914*. Oxford: Clarendon.

Knei-Paz, Baruch. 1978. *The Social and Political Thought of Leon Trotsky*. Oxford: Oxford University Press.

Knock, Thomas J. 1992. *To End All Wars: Woodrow Wilson and the Quest for a New World Order*. New York: Oxford University Press.

Knox, MacGregor. 2000. *Common Destiny: Dictatorship, Foreign Policy, and War in Fascist Italy and Nazi Germany*. Cambridge: Cambridge University Press.

Koch, H. W., ed. 1984. *The Origins of the First World War: Great Power Rivalry and German War Aims*. 2nd ed. London: Macmillan.

Kocka, Jürgen. 1980. Ursachen des Nationalsozialismus. *Politik und Zeitgeschichte* 25 (80): 3–15.

Kocka, Jürgen. 1988. German History before Hitler: The Debate about the German Sonderweg. *Journal of Contemporary History* 23 (1): 3–16.

Kocka, Jürgen. 1999a. Asymmetrical Historical Comparison: The Case of the German Sonderweg. *History and Theory* 38 (1): 40–50.

Kocka, Jürgen. 1999b. *Industrial Culture and Bourgeois Society: Business, Labor, and Bureaucracy in Modern Germany*. New York: Berghahn.

Kolb, Eberhard. 2005. *The Weimar Republic*. 2nd ed. London: Routledge.

Kolko, Gabriel. 1963. *The Triumph of Conservatism: A Re-Interpretation of American History, 1900–1916*. New York: Free Press of Glencoe.

König, Wolfgang. 2004. Adolf Hitler vs. Henry Ford: The Volkswagen, the Role of America as a Model, and the Failure of a Nazi Consumer Society. *German Studies Review* 27 (2): 249–68.

Krasner, Stephen. 1978. *Defending the National Interest: Raw Materials Investments and U.S. Foreign Policy*. Princeton: Princeton University Press.

Kratochwil, Frederich. 1998. Politics, Norms and Peaceful Change. *Review of International Studies* 24:193–218.

Krause, Keith, and Michael C. Williams. 1997. *Critical Security Studies: Concepts and Cases*. Minneapolis: University of Minnesota Press.

Kruedener, Jürgen, ed. 1990. *Economic Crisis and Political Collapse: The Weimar Republic, 1924–1933*. Oxford: Berg.

Kubálková, V., and A. A. Cruickshank. 1989. *Marxism and International Relations*. Oxford: Oxford University Press.

Kuisel, Richard F. 1967. *Ernest Mercier: French Technocrat*. Berkeley: University of California Press.

Kupchan, Charles A., and Peter Trubowitz. 2007. Dead Center: The Demise of Liberal Internationalism in the United States. *International Security* 32 (2): 7–44.

Lacher, Hannes. 2002. Making Sense of the Modern International System: The Promises and Pitfalls of Contemporary Marxist Theories of International Relations. In *Historical Materialism and Globalization*, edited by M. Rupert and H. Smith. London: Routledge.

Lacher, Hannes. 2005. International Transformation and the Persistence of Territoriality: Toward a New Political Geography of Capitalism. *Review of International Political Economy* 12 (1): 26–52.

Lacher, Hannes. 2006. *Beyond Globalization: Capitalism, Territoriality, and the International Relations of Modernity*. London: Routledge.

LaFeber, Walter. 1993. *The American Search for Opportunity, 1865–1913.* 4 vols. Cambridge: Cambridge University Press.

LaFeber, Walter. 1994. *The American Age: United States Foreign Policy at Home and Abroad since 1750.* 2nd ed. 2 vols. New York: Norton.

LaFeber, Walter. 1998. *The New Empire: An Interpretation of American Expansion, 1860–1898.* Ithaca: Cornell University Press.

Laffey, Mark. 2000. Locating Identity: Performativity, Foreign Policy, and State Action. *Review of International Studies* 26 (3): 429–44.

Laffey, Mark. 2004. The Red Herring of Economism: A Reply to Marieke de Goede. *Review of International Studies* 30 (3): 459–68.

Laffey, Mark, and Jutta Weldes. 1997. Beyond Belief: Ideas and Symbolic Technologies in the Study of International Relations. *European Journal of International Relations* 3 (2): 193–237.

Lakatos, Imre. 1970. *Criticism and the Growth of Knowledge.* Edited by A. Musgrave. Cambridge: Cambridge University Press.

Lakatos, Imre. 1976. *Proofs and Refutations: The Logic of Mathematical Discovery.* Cambridge: Cambridge University Press.

Lambi, Ivo Nikolai. 1984. *The Navy and German Power Politics, 1862–1914.* Boston: Allen and Unwin.

Lammers, Donald N. 1966. *Explaining Munich: The Search for Motive in British Policy.* Stanford, CA: Hoover Institution on War, Revolution, and Peace, Stanford University.

Lammers, Donald N. 1973. Arno Mayer and the British Decision for War: 1914. *Journal of British Studies* 12 (2): 137–65.

Landes, David S. 2003. *The Unbound Prometheus: Technological Change and Industrial Development in Western Europe from 1750 to the Present.* 2nd ed. Cambridge: Cambridge University Press.

Lansing, Robert. 1971. *The Peace Negotiations: A Personal Narrative.* Westport, CT: Greenwood.

Lawson, George. 2005. Rosenberg's Ode to Bauer, Kinkel, and Willich. *International Politics* 42 (3): 381–89.

Layne, Christopher. 2006. *The Peace of Illusions: American Grand Strategy from 1940 to the Present.* Ithaca: Cornell University Press.

Lebovics, Herman. 1988. *The Alliance of Iron and Wheat in the Third French Republic, 1860–1914: Origins of the New Conservatism.* Baton Rouge: Louisiana State University Press.

Lebow, Richard Ned. 2000. Contingency, Catalysts, and International System Change. *Political Science Quarterly* 115 (4): 591–616.

Lee, Marshall M., and Wolfgang Michalka. 1987. *German Foreign Policy, 1917–1933: Continuity or Break?* New York: Berg.

Leffler, Melvyn P. 1972. The Origins of Republican War Debt Policy, 1921–1923: A Case Study in the Applicability of the Open Door Interpretation. *Journal of American History* 59 (3): 585–601.

Leffler, Melvyn P. 1979. *The Elusive Quest: America's Pursuit of European Stability and French Security, 1919–1933.* Chapel Hill: University of North Carolina Press.

Legro, Jeffrey. 2005. *Rethinking the World: Great Power Strategies and International Order*. Ithaca: Cornell University Press.

Leibovitz, Clement, and Alvin Finkel. 1998. *In Our Time: The Chamberlain-Hitler Collusion*. New York: Monthly Review Press.

Leitz, Christian. 2002. "Export or Die": Foreign Trade in the Third Reich. *Australian Journal of Politics and History* 48 (1): 52–64.

Leitz, Christian. 2004. *Nazi Foreign Policy, 1933–1941: The Road to Global War*. London: Routledge.

Lenin, Vladimir. 1960. *Collected Works*. 35 vols. Moscow: Foreign Languages Publishing House.

Lenin, Vladimir. 1969. *On the National Question and Proletarian Internationalism*. Moscow: Novosti Press Agency.

Levin, Norman Gordon. 1968. *Woodrow Wilson and World Politics: America's Response to War and Revolution*. New York: Oxford University Press.

Levy, Jack S. 1990. Preferences, Constraints, and Choices in July 1914. *International Security* 15 (3): 151–86.

Levy, Jack S. 2011. Preventive War: Concept and Propositions. *International Interactions* 37 (1): 87–96.

Lewis, W. Arthur. 1949. *Economic Survey, 1919–1939*. London: Allen and Unwin.

Lewis, W. Arthur. 1978. *Growth and Fluctuations, 1870–1913*. London: Allen and Unwin.

Lieven, D. C. B. 1983. *Russia and the Origins of the First World War*. London: Macmillan.

Linden, Marcel van der. 2007. The Law of Uneven and Combined Development: Some Underdeveloped Thoughts. *Historical Materialism* 15:145–65.

Lindqvist, Sven. 1996. *"Exterminate All the Brutes": One Man's Odyssey into the Heart of Darkness and the Origins of European Genocide*. New York: New Press.

Link, Arthur Stanley. 1979. *Woodrow Wilson: Revolution, War, and Peace*. Arlington Heights, IL: AHM.

Link, Arthur Stanley. 1982. *Woodrow Wilson and a Revolutionary World, 1913–1921*. Chapel Hill: University of North Carolina Press.

Link, Werner. 1986. *The East-West Conflict: The Organization of International Relations in the Twentieth Century*. New York: St. Martin's.

Linklater, Andrew. 1990. *Beyond Realism and Marxism: Critical Theory and International Relations*. Basingstoke: Macmillan.

Linklater, Andrew. 1998. *The Transformation of Political Community: Ethical Foundations of the Post-Westphalian Era*. Columbia: University of South Carolina Press.

Linton, Derek S. 1989. Bonapartism, Fascism, and the Collapse of the Weimar Republic. In *Radical Perspectives on the Rise of Fascism in Germany, 1919–1945*, edited by M. N. Dobkowski and I. Wallimann. New York: Monthly Review Press.

Lippmann, Walter. 1943. *U.S. Foreign Policy: Shield of the Republic*. Boston: Little, Brown.

Lippmann, Walter. 1944. *U.S. War Aims*. London: H. Hamilton.

Lisle-Williams, Michael. 1984. Merchant Banking Dynasties in the English Class

Structure: Ownership, Solidarity, and Kinship in the City of London, 1850–
1960. *British Journal of Sociology* 35 (3): 333–62.

Long, David. 1995. Conclusion: Inter-War Idealism, Liberal Internationalism,
and Contemporary International Relations. In *Thinkers of the Twenty Years'
Crisis: Inter-War Idealism Reassessed,* edited by D. Long and P. Wilson. Oxford:
Clarendon.

Long, David, and Brian C. Schmidt, eds. 2005. *Imperialism and Internationalism in
the Discipline of International Relations.* Albany: State University of New York
Press.

Lowe, John. 1994. *The Great Powers, Imperialism, and the German Problem, 1865–
1925.* London: Routledge.

Löwy, Michael. 1981. *The Politics of Combined and Uneven Development: The Theory
of Permanent Revolution.* London: NLB.

Luža, Radomír V., F. Gregory Campbell, and Anna M. Cienciala. 1985. Stages to
War: An Examination of Gerhard Weinberg's "The Foreign Policy of Hitler's
Germany." *Journal of Modern History* 57 (2): 297–315.

MacDonald, C. A. 1972. Economic Appeasement and the German "Moderates,"
1937–1939: An Introductory Essay. *Past and Present* 56:105–35.

MacDonald, C. A. 1981. *The United States, Britain, and Appeasement, 1936–1939.*
New York: St. Martin's.

Macfie, A. L. 1996. *The Eastern Question, 1774–1923.* Rev. ed. London: Longman.

Mage, Shane. 1963. "Law of the Falling Tendency of the Rate of Profit": Its Place in
the Marxist Theoretical System and Relevance to the U.S. Economy. PhD
diss., Columbia University.

Maier, Charles S. 1975. *Recasting Bourgeois Europe: Stabilization in France, Germany,
and Italy in the Decade after World War I.* Princeton: Princeton University Press.

Maier, Charles S., Stephen A. Schuker, and Charles P. Kindleberger. 1981. AHIR
Forum: The Two Postwar Eras and the Conditions for Stability in Twentieth-
Century Western Europe—Comments and Reply. *American Historical Review*
86 (2): 327–67.

Makki, Fouad. 2011. Empire and Modernity: Dynastic Centralization and Official
Nationalism in Late Imperial Ethiopia. *Cambridge Review of International Affairs* 24 (2): 265–86.

Mandel, Ernest. 1986. *The Meaning of the Second World War.* London: Verso.

Mandelbaum, Michael. 2002. *The Ideas That Conquered the World: Peace, Democracy, and Free Markets in the Twenty-First Century.* New York: Public Affairs.

Manela, Erez. 2006. Imagining Woodrow Wilson in Asia: Dreams of East-West
Harmony and the Revolt against Empire in 1919. *American Historical Review* 3
(5): 1327–51.

Manela, Erez. 2007. *The Wilsonian Moment: Self-Determination and the International Origins of Anticolonial Nationalism.* Oxford: Oxford University Press.

Mann, Michael. 1986. *The Sources of Social Power.* Vol. 1, *A History of Power from the
Beginning to AD 1760.* Cambridge: Cambridge University Press.

Mann, Michael. 1988. *States, War, and Capitalism: Studies in Political Sociology.* Oxford: Blackwell.

Mann, Michael. 1993. *The Sources of Social Power.* Vol. 2, *The Rise of Classes and Nation States, 1760–1914.* Cambridge: Cambridge University Press.

Mann, Michael. 2004. *Fascists.* Cambridge: Cambridge University Press.

Marks, Sally. 1976. *The Illusion of Peace: International Relations in Europe, 1918–1933.* London: Macmillan.

Marx, Karl. 1843. Marx to Ruge. *Letters from the Deutsch-Französische Jahrbücher.* http://www.marxists.org/archive/marx/works/1843/letters/43_09.htm#criticism.

Marx, Karl. 1970. *A Contribution to the Critique of Political Economy.* Moscow: Progress.

Marx, Karl. 1973. *Grundrisse: Foundations of the Critique of Political Economy.* Translated by Martin Nicolaus. London: Penguin.

Marx, Karl. 1976. *Capital: A Critique of Political Economy.* Vol. 1. Translated by Ben Fowkes. London: Penguin.

Marx, Karl. 1981. *Capital: A Critique of Political Economy.* Vol. 3. Translated by D. Fernbach. London: Penguin.

Marx, Karl, and Friedrich Engels. 1970. *The German Ideology.* London: Lawrence and Wishart.

Marx, Karl, and Friedrich Engels. 1983. *Letters on "Capital."* London: New Park.

Mason, Tim. 1981. The Workers' Opposition in Nazi Germany. *History Workshop* 11:120–37.

Mason, Tim. 1989. Germany, Domestic Crisis and War in 1939. *Past and Present* 122 (1): 205–21.

Mason, Tim. 1995. *Nazism, Fascism, and the Working Class.* Cambridge: Cambridge University Press.

Mason, Tim, and Jane Caplan. 1993. *Social Policy in the Third Reich: The Working Class and the National Community.* Providence, RI: Berg.

Matin, Kamran. 2007. Uneven and Combined Development in World History: The International Relations of State-Formation in Premodern Iran. *European Journal of International Relations* 13 (3): 419–47.

Matin, Kamran. 2012. Democracy Without Capitalism: Retheorizing Iran's Constitutional Revolution. *Middle East Critique* 21 (1): 37–56.

Matin, Kamran. 2013. Redeeming the Universal: Postcolonialism and the Inner Life of Eurocentrism. *European Journal of International Relations* 19 (2): 353–77.

Mayall, James. 1990. *Nationalism and International Society.* Cambridge: Cambridge University Press.

Mayer, Arno J. 1959. *Political Origins of the New Diplomacy, 1917–1918.* New Haven: Yale University Press.

Mayer, Arno J. 1967. *Politics and Diplomacy of Peacemaking: Containment and Counterrevolution at Versailles, 1918–1919.* New York: Knopf.

Mayer, Arno J. 1971. *Dynamics of Counterrevolution in Europe, 1870–1956: An Analytic Framework.* New York: Harper and Row.

Mayer, Arno J. 1977. Internal Crises and War since 1870. In *Revolutionary Situations in Europe, 1917–1922,* edited by C. Bertrand. Montreal: Interuniversity Centre for European Studies.

Mayer, Arno J. 1981. *The Persistence of the Old Regime: Europe to the Great War*. New York: Pantheon.

Mayer, Arno J. 1990. *Why Did the Heavens Not Darken?: The "Final Solution" in History*. New York: Pantheon.

Mayer, Arno J. 2000. *The Furies: Violence and Terror in the French and Russian Revolutions*. Princeton: Princeton University Press.

McCormick, Thomas J. 1967. *China Market: America's Quest for Informal Empire, 1893-1901*. Chicago: Quadrangle.

McDonald, David MacLaren. 1992. *United Government and Foreign Policy in Russia, 1900-1914*. Cambridge: Harvard University Press.

McDonough, Frank. 1997. *The Origins of the First and Second World Wars*. Cambridge: Cambridge University Press.

McDonough, Frank. 1998. *Neville Chamberlain, Appeasement, and the British Road to War*. Manchester: Manchester University Press.

McDougall, Walter A. 1978. *France's Rhineland Diplomacy, 1914-1924: The Last Bid for a Balance of Power in Europe*. Princeton: Princeton University Press.

McDougall, Walter A. 1979. Political Economy versus National Sovereignty: French Structures for German Economic Integration after Versailles. *Journal of Modern History* 51 (1): 4-23.

McDougall, Walter A. 1997. *Promised Land, Crusader State: The American Encounter with the World since 1776*. Boston: Houghton Mifflin.

McGraw, Roger 1983. *France, 1815-1914: The Bourgeois Century*. Oxford: Fontana.

McKercher, B. J. C. 1991. *Anglo-American Relations in the 1920s: The Struggle for Supremacy*. Basingstoke: Macmillan.

McNeil, William C. 1986. *American Money and the Weimar Republic: Economics and Politics on the Eve of the Great Depression*. New York: Columbia University Press.

McNeill, William H. 1982. *The Pursuit of Power: Technology, Armed Force, and Society since AD 1000*. Chicago: University of Chicago Press.

Mearsheimer, John J. 1990. Back to the Future: Instability in Europe after the Cold War. *International Security* 15 (1): 5-56.

Mearsheimer, John J. 2001. *The Tragedy of Great Power Politics*. New York: Norton.

Mearsheimer, John J., and Stephen M. Walt. 2007. *The Israel Lobby and U.S. Foreign Policy*. New York: Farrar, Straus, and Giroux.

Messerschmid, Manfred. 1990. Foreign Policy and Preparation for War. In *Germany and the Second World War: The Build-Up of German Aggression*, edited by W. Deist. Oxford: Clarendon.

Meyers, Richard. 1983. British Imperial Interests and the Policy of Appeasement. In *The Fascist Challenge and the Policy of Appeasement*, edited by H. Mommsen and L. Kettenacker. London: Allen and Unwin.

Middlemas, Keith. 1972. *Diplomacy of Illusion: The British Government and Germany, 1937-39*. London: Weidenfeld and Nicolson.

Middlemas, Keith. 1979. *Politics in Industrial Society: The Experience of the British System since 1911*. London: A. Deutsch.

Milchman, Alan. 2003. Marxism and the Holocaust. *Historical Materialism* 11 (3): 97-120.

Miliband, Ralph. 1969. *The State in Capitalist Society*. New York: Basic Books.

Miliband, Ralph. 1983. *Class Power and State Power*. London: Verso.

Mombauer, Annika. 2001. *Helmuth von Moltke and the Origins of the First World War*. Cambridge: Cambridge University Press.

Mombauer, Annika. 2002. *The Origins of the First World War: Controversies and Consensus*. London: Longman.

Mombauer, Annika. 2007. The First World War: Inevitable, Avoidable, Improbable, or Desirable? Recent Interpretations on War Guilt and the War's Origins. *German History* 25 (1): 78–95.

Mommsen, Hans. 1973. Domestic Factors in German Foreign Policy before 1914. *Central European History* 6 (1): 3–43.

Mommsen, Hans. 1976. National Socialism: Continuity and Change. In *Fascism: A Reader's Guide—Analyses, Interpretations, Bibliography*, edited by W. Laqueur. Berkeley: University of California Press.

Mommsen, Hans. 1981. The Topos of Inevitable War in Germany in the Decade before 1914. In *Germany in the Age of Total War*, edited by V. R. Berghahn and M. Kitchen. London: Croom Helm.

Mommsen, Hans. 1996. *The Rise and Fall of Weimar Democracy*. Chapel Hill: University of North Carolina Press.

Mooers, Colin. 1991. *The Making of Bourgeois Europe: Absolutism, Revolution, and the Rise of Capitalism in England, France, and Germany*. London: Verso.

Moore, Barrington. 1966. *Social Origins of Dictatorship and Democracy: Lord and Peasant in the Making of the Modern World*. Boston: Beacon.

Moravcsik, Andrew. 1991. Arms and Autarky in Modern European History. *Daedalus* 120 (4): 23–45.

Moravcsik, Andrew. 1997. Taking Preferences Seriously: A Liberal Theory of International Politics. *International Organization* 51 (4): 513–53.

Morgenthau, Hans J. 1948. *Politics among Nations: The Struggle for Power and Peace*. New York: Knopf.

Morgenthau, Hans J. 1950. The Mainsprings of American Foreign Policy: The National Interest vs. Moral Abstractions. *American Political Science Review* 44 (4): 833–54.

Morgenthau, Hans J. 1951. *In Defense of the National Interest: A Critical Examination of American Foreign Policy*. New York: Knopf.

Morgenthau, Hans J. 1977. The Pathology of American Power. *International Security* 1 (3): 3–20.

Morgenthau, Hans J. 1993. *Politics among Nations: The Struggle for Power and Peace*. Brief ed. Revised by Kenneth W. Thompson. New York: McGraw-Hill.

Morton, Adam David. 2007. Disputing the Geopolitics of the States System and Global Capitalism. *Cambridge Review of International Affairs* 20 (4): 599–617.

Mueller, John. 1988. The Essential Irrelevance of Nuclear Weapons: Stability in the Postwar World. *International Security* 13 (2): 55–79.

Mühlberger, Detlef. 2003. *The Social Bases of Nazism, 1919–1933*. Cambridge: Cambridge University Press.

Mulligan, William. 2010. *The Origins of the First World War*. Cambridge: Cambridge University Press.

Murphy, David Thomas. 1997. *The Heroic Earth: Geopolitical Thought in Weimar Germany, 1918–1933*. Kent, OH: Kent State University Press.

Murray, Williamson. 1984. *The Change in the European Balance of Power, 1938–1939: The Path to Ruin*. Princeton: Princeton University Press.

Murray, Williamson. 1992. Net Assessment in Nazi Germany in the 1930s. In *Calculations: Net Assessment and the Coming of World War II*, edited by W. Murray and A. R. Millett. New York: Free Press.

Murray, Williamson. 2005. The Industrialization of War, 1815–1871. In *The Cambridge History of Warfare*, edited by G. Parker. Cambridge: Cambridge University Press.

Nairn, Tom. 1977. *The Break-Up of Britain: Crisis and Neo-Nationalism*. London: NLB.

Narizny, Kevin. 2003. Both Guns and Butter, or Neither: Class Interests in the Political Economy of Rearmament. *American Political Science Review* 97 (2): 203–20.

Narizny, Kevin. 2007. *The Political Economy of Grand Strategy*. Ithaca: Cornell University Press.

Neebe, Reinhard. 1981. *Grossindustrie, Staat, und NSDAP, 1930–1933: Paul Silverberg und der Reichsverband der Deutschen Industrie in der Krise der Weimarer Republik*. Göttingen: Vandenhoeck and Ruprecht.

Neilson, Keith. 1993. Pursued by a Bear: British Estimates of Soviet Military Strength and Anglo-Soviet Relations, 1922–1939. *Canadian Journal of History* 28 (2): 189–222.

Neilson, Keith. 1995. *Britain and the Last Tsar: British Policy and Russia, 1894–1917*. Oxford: Oxford University Press.

Neilson, Keith. 2006. *Britain, Soviet Russia, and the Collapse of the Versailles Order, 1919–1939*. Cambridge: Cambridge University Press.

Néré, Jacques. 1975. *The Foreign Policy of France from 1914 to 1945*. London: Routledge and Kegan Paul.

Neumann, Franz L. 1944. *Behemoth: The Structure and Practice of National Socialism*. London: V. Gollancz.

Newton, Douglas J. 1997. *British Policy and the Weimar Republic, 1918–1919*. Oxford: Oxford University Press.

Newton, Scott. 1996. *Profits of Peace: The Political Economy of Anglo-German Appeasement*. Oxford: Clarendon.

Newton, Scott. 1997. The Anglo-German Connection and the Political Economy of Appeasement. In *The Origins of the Second World War*, edited by P. Finney. London: St. Martin's.

Nicolson, Harold. 1980. *Diaries and Letters, 1930–1964*. Edited and condensed by Stanley Olson. New York: Atheneum.

Ninkovich, Frank A. 1999. *The Wilsonian Century: U.S. Foreign Policy since 1900*. Chicago: University of Chicago Press.

Nisancioglu, Kerem. 2011. Rethinking Ottoman Decline: Uneven and Combined

Development in World History. Paper presented at the *Historical Materialism: Annual Conference*. SOAS, London.

Nisbet, Robert A. 1969. *Social Change and History: Aspects of the Western Theory of Development*. Oxford: Oxford University Press.

Noakes, Jeremy, and Geoffrey Pridham, eds. 1974. *Documents on Nazism, 1919–1945*. London: Cape.

Noakes, Jeremy, and Geoffrey Pridham, eds. 2001. *Nazism, 1919–1945: Foreign Policy, War, and Racial Extermination*. Exeter: University of Exeter Press.

Noble, Charles. 1985. Wilson's Choice: The Political Origins of the Modern American State. *Comparative Politics* 17 (3): 313–36.

Offer, Avner. 1989. *The First World War: An Agrarian Interpretation*. Oxford: Oxford University Press.

Offner, Arnold A. 1986 [1975]. *The Origins of the Second World War: American Foreign Policy and World Politics, 1917–1941*. Reprint ed. Malabar, FL: R.E. Krieger.

Ollman, Berttell. 1979. Marxism and Political Science: Prolegomenon to a Debate on Marx's Method. In *Social and Sexual Revolution: Essays on Marx and Reich*. London: Pluto.

Oneal, John R., and Bruce Russett. 1999. The Kantian Peace: The Pacific Benefits of Democracy, Interdependence, and International Organizations, 1885–1992. *World Politics* 52 (1): 1–37.

Oren, Ido. 1995. The Subjectivity of the "Democratic" Peace: Changing U.S. Perceptions of Imperial Germany. *International Security* 20 (2): 147–84.

Osgood, Robert Endicott. 1953. *Ideals and Self-Interest in America's Foreign Relations: The Great Transformation of the Twentieth Century*. Chicago: University of Chicago Press.

Otte, Thomas G. 2007. *The China Question: Great Power Rivalry and British Isolation, 1894–1905*. Oxford: Oxford University Press.

Ó Tuathail, Gearóid. 2006. Introduction to Part One: Imperialist Geopolitics. In *The Geopolitics Reader,* edited by G. Ó Tuathail, S. Dalby, and P. Routledge. New York: Routledge.

Overbeek, Henk. 1980. Finance Capital and the Crisis in Britain. *Capital and Class* 4 (2): 99–120.

Overy, Richard. 1995. *War and Economy in the Third Reich*. Oxford: Clarendon.

Overy, Richard. 1999a. Germany and the Munich Crisis: A Mutilated Victory? *Diplomacy and Statecraft* 10 (2–3): 191–215.

Overy, Richard. 1999b. Misjudging Hitler: A. J. P. Taylor and the Third Reich. In *The Origins of the Second World War Reconsidered: A. J. P. Taylor and the Historians,* edited by G. Martel. London: Routledge.

Owen, Roger. 1981. *The Middle East in the World Economy, 1800–1914*. London: Methuen.

Pamuk, Şevket. 2006. Estimating Economic Growth in the Middle East since 1820. *Journal of Economic History* 66 (3): 809–28.

Parker, R. A. 1993. *Chamberlain and Appeasement: British Policy and the Coming of the Second World War*. New York: St. Martin's.

Parrini, Carl P. 1969. *Heir to Empire: United States Economic Diplomacy, 1916–1923*. Pittsburgh: University of Pittsburgh Press.

Parrini, Carl P. 1976. Review: The United States and the Stabilization of Industrial Capitalism as a System after World War I. *Reviews in American History* 4 (3): 428–35.

Pastor, Peter, ed. 1988. *Revolutions and Interventions in Hungary and Its Neighbor States, 1918–1919*. New York: Columbia University Press.

Patch, William L. 2006. *Heinrich Brüning and the Dissolution of the Weimar Republic*. Cambridge: Cambridge University Press.

Peden, G. C. 1979. *British Rearmament and the Treasury, 1932–1939*. Edinburgh: Scottish Academic Press.

Peden, G. C. 2000. *The Treasury and British Public Policy, 1906–1959*. Oxford: Oxford University Press.

Peden, G. C. 2007. *Arms, Economics, and British Strategy: From Dreadnoughts to Hydrogen Bombs*. Cambridge: Cambridge University Press.

Peukert, Detlev. 1992. *The Weimar Republic: The Crisis of Classical Modernity*. New York: Hill and Wang.

Pierce, Anne R. 2003. *Woodrow Wilson and Harry Truman: Mission and Power in American Foreign Policy*. Westport, CT: Praeger.

Pijl, Kees van der. 1984. *The Making of an Atlantic Ruling Class*. London: Verso.

Pijl, Kees van der. 1998. *Transnational Classes and International Relations*. London: Routledge.

Pijl, Kees van der. 2007. *Nomads, Empires, States: Modes of Foreign Relations and Political Economy*. 3 vols. London: Pluto.

Plessis, Alain, and Olivier Feiertag. 1999. The Position and Role of French Finance in the Balkans from the Late Nineteenth Century until the Second World War. In *Modern Banking in the Balkans and West European Capital in the 19th and 20th Centuries*, edited by K. P. Kostis. London: Ashgate.

Pogge von Strandmann, Hartmut. 1988. Germany and the Coming of the First World War In *The Coming of the First World War*, edited by R. J. W. Evans and H. Pogge von Strandmann. Oxford: Oxford University Press.

Polanyi, Karl. 1957. *The Great Transformation*. Boston: Beacon.

Pollard, Sidney. 1981. *Peaceful Conquest: The Industrialization of Europe, 1760–1970*. Oxford: Oxford University Press.

Pomerance, Michla. 1976. The United States and Self-Determination: Perspectives on the Wilsonian Conception. *American Journal of International Law* 70 (1): 1–27.

Posen, Barry. 1984. *The Sources of Military Doctrine: France, Britain, and Germany between the World Wars*. Ithaca: Cornell University Press.

Post, Charles. 2002. Comments on the Brenner-Wood Exchange on the Low Countries. *Journal of Agrarian Change* 2 (1): 88–95.

Post, Gaines. 1993. *Dilemmas of Appeasement: British Deterrence and Defense, 1934–1937*. Ithaca: Cornell University Press.

Poulantzas, Nicos. 1973. *Political Power and Social Classes*. London: NLB.

Powell, Robert. 1996. Uncertainty, Shifting Power, and Appeasement. *American Political Science Review* 90 (4): 749–64.

Pozo-Martin, Gonzalo. 2007. Autonomous or Materialist Geopolitics? *Cambridge Review of International Affairs* 20 (4): 551–63.

Pradella, Lucia. 2013. Imperialism and Capitalist Development in Marx's *Capital*. *Historical Materialism* 21 (2): 117–47.

Prashad, Vijay 1995. Between Economism and Emancipation: Untouchables and Indian Nationalism, 1920–1950. *Left History* 3 (1): 5–30.

Price, Christopher. 2001. *Britain, America, and Rearmament in the 1930s: The Cost of Failure*. Basingstoke: Palgrave.

Price, Richard, and Christian Reus-Smit. 1998. Dangerous Liaisons? Critical International Theory and Constructivism. *European Journal of International Relations* 4 (3): 259–94.

Puhle, Hans-Jürgen. 1986. Comparative Approaches from Germany: The "New Nation" in Advanced Industrial Capitalism, 1860–1940—Integration, Stabilization and Reform. *Reviews in American History* 14 (4): 614–28.

Ránki, György. 1983. *Economy and Foreign Policy: The Struggle of the Great Powers for Hegemony in the Danube Valley, 1919–1939*. New York: Columbia University Press.

Rathenau, Walther. 1985. *Walther Rathenau: Notes and Diaries, 1907–1922*. Edited by Hartmut Pogge von Strandmann. New York: Clarendon.

Record, Jeffrey. 2007. *The Specter of Munich: Reconsidering the Lessons of Appeasing Hitler*. Washington, DC: Potomac.

Reus-Smit, Christian. 1999. *The Moral Purpose of the State: Culture, Social Identity, and Institutional Rationality in International Relations*. Princeton: Princeton University Press.

Reynolds, David. 2000. *Britannia Overruled: British Policy and World Power in the Twentieth Century*. London: Longman.

Rhodes, Benjamin D. 1969. Reassessing "Uncle Shylock": The United States and the French War Debt, 1917–1929. *Journal of American History* 55 (4): 787–803.

Richardson, Charles O. 1973. French Plans for Allied Attacks on the Caucasus Oil Fields, January–April, 1940. *French Historical Studies* 8 (1): 130–56.

Riley, Dylan. Forthcoming. The Third Reich as Rogue Regime: Adam Tooze's Wages of Destruction. *Historical Materialism*.

Ripsman, Norrin M. 2002. *Peacemaking by Democracies: The Effect of State Autonomy on the Post–World War Settlements*. University Park: Pennsylvania State University Press.

Ripsman, Norrin M., and Jack S. Levy. 2008. Wishful Thinking or Buying Time? The Logic of British Appeasement in the 1930s. *International Security* 33 (2): 148–81.

Risse-Kappen, Thomas. 1995. Democratic Peace—Warlike Democracies? *European Journal of International Relations* 1 (4): 491–517.

Ritschl, Albrecht. 1996. *Was Schacht Right? Reparations, the Young Plan, and the Great Depression in Germany*. London: London School of Economics.

Roberts, Geoffrey. 1995. *The Soviet Union and the Origins of the Second World War: Russo-German Relations and the Road to War, 1933–1941*. New York: St. Martin's.

Rogan, Eugene L. 1999. *Frontiers of the State in the Late Ottoman Empire: Transjordan, 1850–1921*. Cambridge: Cambridge University Press.

Röhl, John C. G. 1969. Admiral von Müller and the Approach of War, 1911–1914. *Historical Journal* 12 (4): 651–73.

Röhl, John C. G. 1994. *The Kaiser and His Court: Wilhelm II and the Government of Germany*. Cambridge: Cambridge University Press.

Rosecrance, Richard, and Arthur A. Stein. 1993. Beyond Realism: The Study of Grand Strategy. In *The Domestic Bases of Grand Strategy,* edited by R. Rosecrance and A. A. Stein. Ithaca: Cornell University Press.

Rosenberg, Emily S. 1982. *Spreading the American Dream: American Economic and Cultural Expansion, 1890–1945*. New York: Hill and Wang.

Rosenberg, Hans. 1943. Political and Social Consequences of the Great Depression of 1873–1896 in Central Europe. *Economic History Review* 13 (1–2): 58–73.

Rosenberg, Justin. 1994. *The Empire of Civil Society: A Critique of the Realist Theory of International Relations*. London: Verso.

Rosenberg, Justin. 1996. Isaac Deutscher and the Lost History of International Relations. *New Left Review* 215:3–15.

Rosenberg, Justin. 2000. *The Follies of Globalisation Theory: Polemical Essays*. London: Verso.

Rosenberg, Justin. 2005. Globalization Theory: A Post-Mortem. *International Politics* 42:2–74.

Rosenberg, Justin. 2006. Why Is There No International Historical Sociology? *European Journal of International Relations* 12 (3): 307–40.

Rosenberg, Justin. 2007. International Relations—The "Higher Bullshit": A Reply to the Globalization Theory Debate. *International Politics* 44 (4): 450–82.

Rosenberg, Justin. 2008. Anarchy in the Mirror of "Uneven and Combined Development": An Open Letter to Kenneth Waltz. Paper presented at the *British-German IR Conference BISA/DVPW*. Arnoldshain, Germany.

Rosenberg, Justin. 2010. Basic Problems in the Theory of Uneven and Combined Development, Part II: Unevenness and Political Multiplicity. *Cambridge Review of International Affairs* 23 (1): 165–89.

Rosenberg, Justin. 2012. Kenneth Waltz and Leon Trotsky: Anarchy in the Mirror of Uneven and Combined Development. Paper presented at the International Studies Association meeting, San Diego, CA.

Ruggie, John Gerard. 1983. Continuity and Transformation in the World Polity: Towards a Neorealist Synthesis. In *Neorealism and Its Critics,* edited by R. Keohane. New York: Columbia University Press.

Ruggie, John Gerard. 1993. *Multilateralism Matters: The Theory and Praxis of an Institutional Form*. New York: Columbia University Press.

Ruggie, John Gerard. 1998a. *Constructing the World Polity: Essays on International Institutionalization*. London: Routledge.

Ruggie, John Gerard. 1998b. What Makes the World Hang Together? Neo-Utilitarianism and the Social Constructivist Challenge. *International Organization* 52 (4): 855–85.

Ruggiero, John. 1999. *Neville Chamberlain and British Rearmament: Pride, Prejudice, and Politics*. Westport, CT: Greenwood.

Rupert, Mark. 1995. *Producing Hegemony: The Politics of Mass Production and American Global Power*. Cambridge: Cambridge University Press.

Rupert, Mark. 2000. *Ideologies of Globalization: Contending Visions of a New World Order*. London: Routledge.

Rupert, Mark. 2010. Post-Fordist Capitalism and Imperial Power: Toward a Neo-Gramscian View. In *Marxism and World Politics: Contesting Global Capitalism*, edited by A. Anievas. London: Routledge.

Rupieper, Hermann-Josef. 1979. *The Cuno Government and Reparations, 1922–1923: Politics and Economics*. Boston: M. Nijhoff.

Russett, Bruce M. 1993. *Grasping the Democratic Peace: Principles for a Post–Cold War World*. Princeton: Princeton University Press.

Ryan, David. 2000. *U.S. Foreign Policy in World History*. New York: Routledge.

Safford, Jeffrey J. 1978. *Wilsonian Maritime Diplomacy, 1913–1921*. New Brunswick, NJ: Rutgers University Press.

Salter, Stephen. 1981. Class Harmony or Class Conflict? The Industrial Working Class and the National Socialist Regime. In *Government, Party, and People in Nazi Germany*, edited by J. Noakes. Exeter: University of Exeter.

Saul, S. B. 1960. *Studies in British Overseas Trade, 1870–1914*. Liverpool: Liverpool University Press.

Sawer, Marian. 1977. The Genesis of State and Revolution. In *The Socialist Register 1977*, edited by R. Miliband and J. Saville. London: Merlin.

Sayer, Derek. 1979. *Marx's Method: Ideology, Science, and Critique in "Capital."* Atlantic Highlands, NJ: Humanities Press.

Sayer, Derek. 1991. *Capitalism and Modernity: An Excursus on Marx and Weber*. London: Routledge.

Sayers, R. S. 1986. *The Bank of England, 1891–1944*. Cambridge: Cambridge University Press.

Scally, Robert James. 1975. *The Origins of the Lloyd George Coalition: The Politics of Social-Imperialism, 1900–1918*. Princeton: Princeton University Press.

Scheuerman, William E. 2009. Realism and the Critique of Technology. *Cambridge Review of International Affairs* 22 (4): 563–84.

Schlesinger, Arthur M. 1933. *Political and Social Growth of the United States, 1852–1933*. Rev. ed. New York: Macmillan.

Schmidt, Brian C. 1998. Lessons from the Past: Reassessing the Interwar Disciplinary History of International Relations. *International Studies Quarterly* 42 (3): 433–59.

Schmidt, Gustav. 1983. The Domestic Background to British Appeasement Policy. In *The Fascist Challenge and the Policy of Appeasement*, edited by H. J. Mommsen and L. Kattenacker. London: Allen and Unwin.

Schmidt, Gustav. 1986. *The Politics and Economics of Appeasement: British Foreign Policy in the 1930s.* Leamington Spa: Berg.

Schmidt, Gustav. 1990. Contradictory Postures and Conflicting Objectives: The July Crisis, 1914. In *Escape into War? The Foreign Policy of Imperial Germany,* edited by G. Schollgen. Oxford: Berg.

Schmitz, David F. 1988. *The United States and Fascist Italy, 1922–1940.* Chapel Hill: University of North Carolina Press.

Schoenbaum, David. 1980. *Hitler's Social Revolution: Class and Status in Nazi Germany, 1933–1939.* New York: Norton.

Schuker, Stephen A. 1976. *The End of French Predominance in Europe: The Financial Crisis of 1924 and the Adoption of the Dawes Plan.* Chapel Hill: University of North Carolina Press.

Schuker, Stephen A. 1988. *American Reparations to Germany, 1919–33: Implications for the Third-World Debt Crisis.* Princeton: Princeton University.

Schuker, Stephen A. 1998. The Rhineland Question: West European Security at the Paris Peace Conference. In *The Treaty of Versailles: A Reassessment after 75 Years,* edited by M. F. Boemeke, G. D. Feldman and E. Gläser. Cambridge: Cambridge University Press.

Schuker, Stephen A. 2003. Money Doctors between the Wars: The Competition between Central Banks, Private Financial Advisers, and Multilateral Agencies, 1919–39. In *Money Doctors: The Experience of International Financial Advising, 1850–2000,* edited by M. Flandreau. London: Routledge.

Schuman, Frederick L. 1939. *Europe on the Eve: The Crises of Diplomacy, 1933–1939.* London: Knopf.

Schumann, Wolfgang, and Ludwig Nestler, eds. 1975. *Dokumente zu den Europa und Weltherrschaftsplänen des deutschen Imperialismus von der Jahrhundertwende bis Mai 1945.* Berlin: Deutscher Verlag der Wissenschaften.

Schwabe, Klaus. 1985. *Woodrow Wilson, Revolutionary Germany, and Peacemaking, 1918–1919: Missionary Diplomacy and the Realities of Power.* Chapel Hill: University of North Carolina Press.

Schweller, Randall L. 1993. Tripolarity and the Second World War. *International Studies Quarterly* 37 (1): 73–103.

Schweller, Randall L. 1998. *Deadly Imbalances: Tripolarity and Hitler's Strategy of World Conquest.* New York: Columbia University Press.

Schweller, Randall L. 2001. The Problem of International Order Revisited: A Review Essay. *International Security* 26 (1): 161–86.

Schweller, Randall L. 2004. Unanswered Threats: A Neoclassical Realist Theory of Underbalancing. *International Security* 29 (2): 159–201.

Seckendorf, Martin. 1993. Entwicklungshilfeorganisation oder Generalstab des deutschen Kapitals? Bedeutung und Grenzen des Mitteleuropäischen Wirtschaftstages. *Zeitschrift für Sozialgeschichte des 20. und 21Jahrhunderts* 8 (3): 10–33.

Segal, Paul H. 1987. *The French State and French Private Investment in Czechoslovakia, 1918–1938: A Study of Economic Diplomacy.* New York: Garland.

Seligmann, M. S., and R. R. McLean. 2000. *Germany from Reich to Republic, 1871–1918: Politics, Hierarchy, and Elites*. New York: St. Martin's.

Selwyn, Ben. 2011. Trotsky, Gerschenkron, and the Political Economy of Late Capitalist Development. *Economy and Society* 40 (3): 421–50.

Semmel, Bernard. 1960. *Imperialism and Social Reform: English Social-Imperial Thought, 1895–1914*. Cambridge: Harvard University Press.

Seton-Watson, R. W. 1914. *The War and Democracy*. London: Macmillan.

Shanin, Teodor. 1983. *Late Marx and the Russian Road: Marx and "The Peripheries of Capitalism."* New York: Monthly Review Press.

Shaw, Louise Grace. 2003. *The British Political Elite and the Soviet Union, 1937–1939*. London: Frank Cass.

Shaw, Martin. 1988. *Dialectics of War: An Essay in the Social Theory of Total War and Peace*. London: Pluto.

Shay, Robert Paul. 1977. *British Rearmament in the Thirties: Politics and Profits*. Princeton: Princeton University Press.

Shilliam, Robbie. 2009. The Atlantic as a Vector of Uneven and Combined Development. *Cambridge Review of International Affairs* 22 (1): 69–88.

Showalter, Dennis E. 1983. Army and Society in Imperial Germany: The Pains of Modernization. *Journal of Contemporary History* 18 (4): 583–618.

Simpson, Christopher, ed. 2002. *War Crimes of the Deutsche Bank and the Dresdner Bank: Office of Military Government (U.S.) Reports*. New York: Holmes and Meier.

Skålnes, Lars S. 2000. *Politics, Markets, and Grand Strategy: Foreign Economic Policies as Strategic Instruments*. Ann Arbor: University of Michigan Press.

Sklar, Martin J. 1988. *The Corporate Reconstruction of American Capitalism, 1890–1916: The Market, the Law, and Politics*. Cambridge: Cambridge University Press.

Sklar, Martin J. 1992. *The United States as a Developing Country: Studies in U.S. History in the Progressive Era and the 1920s*. Cambridge: Cambridge University Press.

Skocpol, Theda. 1973. A Critical Review of Barrington Moore's *Social Origins of Dictatorship and Democracy*. *Politics and Society* 4 (1): 1–34.

Skocpol, Theda. 1977. Review: Wallerstein's World Capitalist System: A Theoretical and Historical Critique. *American Journal of Sociology* 82 (5): 1075–90.

Skocpol, Theda. 1979. *States and Social Revolutions: A Comparative Analysis of France, Russia, and China*. Cambridge: Cambridge University Press.

Slotkin, Richard. 1998. *Gunfighter Nation: The Myth of the Frontier in Twentieth-Century America*. Norman: University of Oklahoma Press.

Smelser, Neil. 1992. External and Internal Factors in Theories of Social Change. In *Social Change and Modernity*, edited by H. Haferkamp and N. J. Smelser. Berkeley: University of California Press.

Smith, Neil. 2003. *American Empire: Roosevelt's Geographer and the Prelude to Globalization*. Berkeley: University of California Press.

Smith, Neil. 2006. The Geography of Uneven Development. In *100 Years of Permanent Revolution: Results and Prospects*, edited by B. D. H. Radice. London: Pluto.

Smith, Tony. 1994. *America's Mission: The United States and the Worldwide Struggle for Democracy in the Twentieth Century.* Princeton: Princeton University Press.

Smith, Tony. 1999. Making the World Safe for Democracy in the American Century. *Diplomatic History* 23 (2): 173–88.

Snow, Donald M., and Eugene Brown. 1996. *The Contours of Power: An Introduction to Contemporary International Relations.* New York: St. Martin's.

Snyder, Jack L. 1984. *The Ideology of the Offensive: Military Decision Making and the Disasters of 1914.* Ithaca: Cornell University Press.

Snyder, Jack L. 1991. *Myths of Empire: Domestic Politics and International Ambition.* Ithaca: Cornell University Press.

Sohn-Rethel, Alfred. 1978. *Economy and Class Structure of German Fascism.* London: CSE Books.

Speer, Albert. 2003. *Inside the Third Reich: Memoirs.* 2nd ed. London: Phoenix.

Spoerer, Mark 1998. Window-Dressing in German Inter-War Balance Sheets. *Accounting, Business, and Financial History* 8 (3): 351–70.

Spring, D. W. 1988. Russia and the Franco-Russian Alliance, 1905–14: Dependence or Interdependence? *Slavonic and East European Review* 66 (4): 564–92.

Stachura, Peter. 1983. The NSDAP and the German Working Class, 1925–1933. In *Towards the Holocaust: The Social and Economic Collapse of the Weimar Republic,* edited by M. N. Dobkowski and I. Walliman. Westport, CT: Greenwood.

Stackelberg, Roderick, and Sally Anne Winkle, eds. 2002. *The Nazi Germany Sourcebook: An Anthology of Texts.* London: Routledge.

Stedman Jones, Gareth. 1972. The History of American Imperialism. In *Ideology in Social Science,* edited by R. Blackburn. London: Fontana.

Stedman Jones, Gareth. 1977. Society and Politics at the Beginning of the World Economy. *Cambridge Journal of Economics* 1 (1): 77–92.

Stedman Jones, Gareth. 2008. Radicalism and the Extra-European World: The Case of Marx. In *Victorian Visions of Global Order: Empire and International Relations in Nineteenth Century Political Thought,* edited by D. S. Bell. Cambridge: Cambridge University Press.

Steel, David. 2010. A Combined and Uneven Development Approach to the European Neolithic. *Critique of Anthropology* 30 (2): 131–51.

Stegmann, Dirk. 1973. Zum Verhältnis von Großindustrie und Nationalsozialismus 1930–1933. *Archiv für Sozialgeschicht* 23:399–482.

Stegmann, Dirk. 1976. Kapitalismus und Faschismus in Deutschland, 1929–1934: Thesen und Materialien zur Restituierung des Primats der Großindustrie zwischen Weltwirtschaftskrise und beginnender Rüstungskonjunktur. *Gesellschaft: Beiträge zur Marxschen Theorie* 6:19–91.

Stegmann, Dirk. 1978. "Mitteleuropa," 1925–1934: Zum Problem der Kontinuität deutscher Außenhandelspolitik von Stresemann bis Hitler. In *Industrielle Gesellschaft und politisches System: Beiträge zur politischen Sozialgeschichte Festschrift für Fritz Fischer zum siebzigsten Geburtstag,* edited by D. Stegmann, B.-J. Wendt, and P.-C. Will. Bonn: Neue Gesellschaft.

Stegmann, Dirk. 1979. Comment on Abraham, "Constituting Hegemony." *Journal of Modern History* 51 (3): 434–37.

Steigerwald, David. 1999. The Reclamation of Woodrow Wilson. *Diplomatic History* 23 (1): 79–99.

Steiner, Zara S. 2005. *The Lights That Failed: European International History, 1919–1933*. Oxford: Oxford University Press.

Steiner, Zara S., and Keith Neilson. 2003. *Britain and the Origins of the First World War*. 2nd ed. New York: Palgrave Macmillan.

Stevenson, David. 1982. *French War Aims against Germany, 1914–1919*. Oxford: Clarendon.

Stevenson, David. 1988. *The First World War and International Politics*. Oxford: Oxford University Press.

Stevenson, David. 1996. *Armaments and the Coming of War: Europe, 1904–1914*. Oxford: Oxford University Press.

Stevenson, David. 1998. French War Aims and Peace Planning. In *The Treaty of Versailles: A Reassessment after 75 Years*, edited by M. F. Boemeke, G. D. Feldman, and E. Gläser. Cambridge: Cambridge University Press.

Stoakes, Geoffrey. 1978. The Evolution of Hitler's Ideas on Foreign Policy, 1919–1925. In *The Shaping of the Nazi State*, edited by P. D. Stachura. London: Croom Helm.

Stoakes, Geoffrey. 1986. *Hitler and the Quest for World Dominion*. Leamington Spa: Berg.

Stokes, Raymond. 2004. From the IG Farben Fusion the Establishment of BASF AG (1925–1952). In *BASF: Innovation and Adaptation in a German Corporation since 1865*, edited by W. Abelshauser. Cambridge: Cambridge University Press.

Stone, Norman. 2007. *World War One: A Short History*. London: Allen Lane.

Strachan, Hew. 2001. *The First World War*. Oxford: Oxford University Press.

Stürmer, Michael. 1990. A Nation State against History and Geography: The German Dilemma. In *Escape into War? The Foreign Policy of Imperial Germany*, edited by G. Schöllgen. Oxford: Berg.

Sugiyama, Shinya. 1988. *Japan's Industrialization in the World Economy, 1859–1899*. London: Athlone.

Sullivan, Brian R. 1999. More Than Meets the Eye: The Ethiopian War and the Origins of the Second World War. In *The Origins of the Second World War Reconsidered: A. J. P. Taylor and the Historians*, edited by G. Martel. London: Routledge.

Taylor, A. J. P. 1946. *The Course of German History: A Survey of the Development of Germany since 1815*. New York: Coward-McCann.

Taylor, A. J. P. 1983. *The Origins of the Second World War*. New York: Atheneum.

Teichova, Alice. 1979. Versailles and the Expansion of the Bank of England into Central Europe. In *Law and the Formation of the Big Enterprises in Nineteenth and Early Twentieth Centuries*, edited by N. Horn and J. Kocka. Göttingen: Vandenhoeck and Ruprecht.

Tenbruck, Friedrich. 1994. Internal History of Society or Universal History. *Theory, Culture, and Society* 11:75–93.

Teschke, Benno. 2003. *The Myth of 1648: Class, Geopolitics, and the Making of Modern International Relations*. London: Verso.

Teschke, Benno. 2008. Marxism. In *The Oxford Handbook of International Relations*, edited by D. Snidal and C. Reus-Smit. Oxford: Oxford University Press.

Teschke, Benno. 2011. Advances and Impasses in Fred Halliday's International Historical Sociology: A Critical Appraisal. *International Affairs* 87 (5): 1087–1106.

Teschke, Benno, and Hannes Lacher. 2007. The Changing "Logics" of Capitalist Competition. *Cambridge Review of International Affairs* 20 (4): 565–80.

Thomas, Martin. 1996. *Britain, France, and Appeasement: Anglo-French Relations in the Popular Front Era*. Washington, DC: Berg.

Thompson, John M. 1966. *Russia, Bolshevism, and the Versailles Peace*. Princeton: Princeton University Press.

Thompson, Neville. 1971. *The Anti-Appeasers: Conservative Opposition to Appeasement in the 1930s*. Oxford: Clarendon.

Thörner, Klaus. 2000. "Der ganze Südosten ist unser Hinterland": Deutsche Südosteuropapläne von 1840 bis 1945. PhD diss., Carl Von Ossietzky University, Oldenburg.

Thorsen, Niels. 1988. *The Political Thought of Woodrow Wilson, 1875–1910*. Princeton: Princeton University Press.

Tilchin, William N., and Charles E. Neu, eds. 2006. *Artists of Power: Theodore Roosevelt, Woodrow Wilson, and Their Enduring Impact on U.S. Foreign Policy*. Westport, CT: Praeger Security International.

Tilly, Charles. 1984. *Big Structures, Large Processes, Huge Comparisons*. New York: Russell Sage Foundation.

Tooze, Adam. 2001. Big Business and the Continuities of German History, 1900–1945. In *Weimar and Nazi Germany: Continuities and Discontinuities*, edited by P. Panayi. Edinburgh: Pearson.

Tooze, Adam. 2006a. Economics, Ideology, and Cohesion in the Third Reich: A Critique of Goetz Aly's *Hitlers Volksstaat*. http://adamtooze.commons.yale.edu/files/2012/10/Tooze-Article-on-Aly-for-Dapim-Lecheker-HaShoah-Sep-2006-Corrected.pdf.

Tooze, Adam. 2006b. Hitler's Gamble. *History Today* (11). http://www.historytoday.com/adam-tooze/hitler%E2%80%99s-gamble.

Tooze, Adam. 2007. *The Wages of Destruction: The Making and Breaking of the Nazi Economy*. New York: Viking.

Trachtenberg, Marc. 1980. *Reparation in World Politics: France and European Economic Diplomacy, 1916–1923*. New York: Columbia University Press.

Trachtenberg, Marc. 1990. The Meaning of Mobilization in 1914. *International Security* 15 (3): 120–50.

Trachtenberg, Marc. 1991. *History and Strategy*. Princeton: Princeton University Press.

Traverso, Enzo. 2003. *The Origins of Nazi Violence*. Translated by J. Lloyd. New York: New Press.

Trebilcock, Clive. 1981. *The Industrialization of the Continental Powers, 1780–1914*. London: Longman.

Treisman, Daniel. 2004. Rational Appeasement. *International Organization* 58 (2): 345–73.

Trevor-Roper, Hugh. 1972. A. J. P. Taylor, Hitler, and the War. In *The Origins of the Second World War: A. J. P. Taylor and His Critics,* edited by W. R. Louis. New York: Wiley.

Trotsky, Leon. 1918. *The Bolsheviki and World Peace.* New York: Boni and Liveright.

Trotsky, Leon. 1936. *The Third International after Lenin.* New York: Pioneer.

Trotsky, Leon. 1945. *The First Five Years of the Communist International.* New York: Pioneer.

Trotsky, Leon. 1957. *The History of the Russian Revolution.* 3 vols. Ann Arbor: University of Michigan Press.

Trotsky, Leon. 1959. *History of the Russian Revolution.* Garden City, NY: Doubleday.

Trotsky, Leon. 1962. *The Permanent Revolution and Results and Prospects.* London: Labor.

Trotsky, Leon. 1969. *1905.* Paris: Éditions de Minuit.

Trotsky, Leon. 1971. *The Struggle against Fascism.* New York: Pathfinder.

Trotsky, Leon. 1972a. *The First 5 Years of the Communist International.* 2 vols. New York: Monad Press.

Trotsky, Leon. 1972b. *Leon Trotsky Speaks.* New York: Pathfinder.

Trotsky, Leon. 1972c. *The Permanent Revolution and Results and Prospects.* 3rd ed. New York: Pathfinder.

Trotsky, Leon. 1972d. *Writings of Leon Trotsky [1932–1933].* New York: Pathfinder.

Trotsky, Leon. 1973. *Leon Trotsky on Britain, Volume 2.* New York: Monad Press.

Trotsky, Leon. 1976. *Leon Trotsky on China.* Introduction by Shu-tse Peng. Introduction by Leslie Evans, and Russell Block. New York: Monad.

Trotsky, Leon. 1998. *Trotsky's Notebooks, 1933–1935: Writings on Lenin, Dialectics, and Evolutionism.* New York: Columbia University Press.

Trotsky, Leon. 2007. *Terrorism and Communism.* Edited by S. Žižek. London: Verso.

Trotsky, Leon. 2008. *History of the Russian Revolution.* Chicago: Haymarket.

Turner, Frederick Jackson. 1966. *The Significance of the Frontier in American History.* Ann Arbor, MI: University Microfilms.

Turner, Henry Ashby. 1969. Big Business and the Rise of Hitler. *American Historical Review* 75 (1): 56–70.

Turner, Henry Ashby. 1985. *German Big Business and the Rise of Hitler.* New York: Oxford University Press.

Uldricks, Teddy J. 1996. Debating the Role of Russia in the Origins of the Second World War. In *The Origins of the Second World War Reconsidered,* edited by G. Martel. London: Routledge.

U.S. Bureau of Labor Statistics. 1970. Work Stoppages in Government. In *1958–68-1979: Report.* Washington, DC: U.S. Department of Labor.

Van Evera, Stephen. 1984. The Cult of the Offensive and the Origins of the First World War. *International Security* 9 (1): 58–107.

Van Evera, Stephen. 1998. Offense, Defense, and the Causes of War. *International Security* 22 (4): 5–43.

Van Evera, Stephen. 1999. *Causes of War: Power and the Roots of Conflict*. Ithaca: Cornell University Press.

Van Meter, Robert H., Jr. 1971. The United States and European Recovery, 1918–23: A Study of Public Policy and Private Finance, PhD Dissertation, University of Wisconsin.

Van Meter, Robert H., Jr. 1977. The Washington Conference of 1921–1922: A New Look. *Pacific Historical Review* 46 (4): 603–24.

Vasquez, John A. 1997. The Realist Paradigm and Degenerative versus Progressive Research Programs: An Appraisal of Neotraditional Research on Waltz's Balancing Proposition. *American Political Science Review* 91 (4): 899–912.

Veblen, Thorstein. 1915. *Imperial Germany and the Industrial Revolution*. New York: Macmillan.

Vitalis, Robert. 1995. *When Capitalists Collide: Business Conflict and the End of Empire in Egypt*. Berkeley: University of California Press.

Volkmann, Hans-Erich. 1990. The National Socialist Economy in Preparation for War. In *Germany and the Second World War: The Buildup of German Aggression*, edited by W. Deist. Oxford: Oxford University Press.

Vucetic, Srdjan. 2011. *The Anglosphere: A Genealogy of a Racialized Identity in International Relations*. Palo Alto, CA: Stanford University Press.

Walicki, Andrzej. 1969. *The Controversy over Capitalism: Studies in the Social Philosophy of the Russian Populists*. Oxford: Clarendon.

Walt, Stephen M. 1992. Alliances, Threats, and U.S. Grand Strategy: A Reply to Kaufman and Labs. *Security Studies* 1 (3): 448–82.

Waltz, Kenneth N. 1959. *Man, the State, and War: A Theoretical Analysis*. New York: Columbia University Press.

Waltz, Kenneth N. 1979. *Theory of International Politics*. Reading, MA: Addison-Wesley.

Waltz, Kenneth N. 1986. Reflections on Theory of International Politics: A Response to My Critics. In *Neorealism and Its Critics*, edited by R. Keohane. New York: Columbia University Press.

Waltz, Kenneth N. 1996. International Politics Is Not Foreign Policy. *Security Studies* 6 (1): 54–57.

Waltz, Kenneth N. 2008. *Realism and International Politics*. New York: Routledge.

Walworth, Arthur. 1977. *America's Moment, 1918: American Diplomacy at the End of World War I*. New York: Norton.

Walzer, Michael. 2006. *Just and Unjust Wars: A Moral Argument with Historical Illustrations*. 4th ed. New York: Basic Books.

Wark, Wesley K. 1985. *The Ultimate Enemy: British Intelligence and Nazi Germany, 1933–1939*. Ithaca: Cornell University Press.

Watt, Donald Cameron. 1989. *How War Came: The Immediate Origins of the Second World War, 1938–1939*. New York: Pantheon.

Weaver, Frederick. 1974. Relative Backwardness and Cumulative Change: A Comparative Approach to European Industrialization. *Studies in Comparative International Development* 9 (2): 70–97.

Webster, Richard A. 1975. *Industrial Imperialism in Italy, 1908–1915*. Berkeley: University of California Press.

Weede, Erich. 2005. *Balance of Power, Globalization, and the Capitalist Peace*. Potsdam: Liberal-Verl.

Wehler, Hans-Ulrich. 1970. Bismarck's Imperialism, 1862–1890. *Past and Present* 48:119–55.

Wehler, Hans-Ulrich. 1972. Industrial Growth and Early German Imperialism In *Studies in the Theory of Imperialism*, edited by R. B. Sutcliffe and R. Owen. London: Longman.

Wehler, Hans-Ulrich. 1985. *The German Empire, 1871–1918*. Leamington Spa, NY: Berg.

Wehler, Hans-Ulrich. 1996. A Guide to Future Research on the Kaiserreich? *Central European History* 29 (4): 541–72.

Weinberg, Gerhard L. 1985a. Hitler and England, 1933–1945: Pretense and Reality. *German Studies Review* 8 (2): 299–309.

Weinberg, Gerhard L. 1985b. Stages to War: Response. *Journal of Modern History* 57 (2): 316–20.

Weinberg, Gerhard L. 1995. *Germany, Hitler, and World War II: Essays in Modern German and World History*. Cambridge: Cambridge University Press.

Weisbrod, Bernd. 1979. Economic Power and Political Stability Reconsidered: Heavy Industry in Weimar Germany. *Social History* 4 (2): 241–63.

Weisbrod, Bernd. 1981. The Crisis of German Unemployment Insurance in 1928/29 and Its Political Repercussions. In *The Emergence of the Welfare State in Britain and Germany 1850–1950*, edited by W. Mommsen. Kent: Croom Helm.

Weisbrod, Bernd. 1990. Industrial Crisis Strategy in the Great Depression. In *Economic Crisis and Political Collapse: The Weimar Republic, 1924–1933*, edited by J. v. Kruedener. Oxford: Oxford University Press.

Weldes, Jutta. 1996. Constructing National Interests. *European Journal of International Relations* 2 (3): 275–318.

Wendt, Alexander. 1987. The Agent-Structure Problem in International Relations Theory. *International Organization* 41 (3): 335–70.

Wendt, Alexander. 1999. *Social Theory of International Politics*. Cambridge: Cambridge University Press.

Wendt, Bernd Jürgen. 1983. Economic Appeasement—A Crisis Strategy. In *The Fascist Challenge and the Policy of Appeasement*, edited by H. Mommsen and L. Kettenacker. London: Allen and Unwin.

Wetherly, Paul, Clyde W. Barrow, and Peter Burnham. 2008. *Class, Power, and the State in Capitalist Society: Essays on Ralph Miliband*. Basingstoke: Palgrave Macmillan.

Whealey, Robert H. 2005. *Hitler and Spain: The Nazi Role in the Spanish Civil War, 1936–1939*. Lexington: University Press of Kentucky.

Williams, William Appleman. 1972. *The Tragedy of American Diplomacy*. 2nd rev. and enl. ed. New York: Dell.

Williamson, Samuel R. 1991. *Austria-Hungary and the Origins of the First World War*. London: Macmillan Education.

Wilson, Woodrow. 1908. *Constitutional Government in the United States*. New York: Columbia University Press.

Wilson, Woodrow. 1925. *The Public Papers of Woodrow Wilson*. Edited by R. S. Baker, W. E. Dodd, and H. S. Leach. 6 vols. London: Harper.

Wilson, Woodrow. 1966–94. *The Papers of Woodrow Wilson*. Edited by A. S. Link. 69 vols. Princeton: Princeton University Press.

Winkler, Heinrich August. 1976. From Social Protectionism to National Socialism: The German Small-Business Movement in Comparative Perspective. *Journal of Modern History* 48 (1): 1–18.

Wolf, Eric R. 1997. *Europe and the People without History*. 2nd ed. Berkeley: University of California Press.

Wood, Ellen Meiksins. 1995. *Democracy against Capitalism: Renewing Historical Materialism*. Cambridge: Cambridge University Press.

Wood, Ellen Meiksins. 2002. The Question of Market Dependence. *Journal of Agrarian Change* 2 (1): 50–87.

Wood, Ellen Meiksins. 2003. *Empire of Capital*. London: Verso.

Wright, Jonathan. 2002. *Gustav Stresemann: Weimar's Greatest Statesman*. Oxford: Oxford University Press.

Wright, Jonathan, and Paul Stafford. 1988. A Blueprint for World War? Hitler and the Hossbach Memorandum. *History Today* 38 (3): 11–17.

Young, Robert J. 1978. *In Command of France: French Foreign Policy and Military Planning, 1933–1940*. Cambridge: Harvard University Press.

Young, Robert J. 1996. *France and the Origins of the Second World War*. New York: St. Martin's.

Young, William. 2006. *German Diplomatic Relations, 1871–1945: The Wilhelmstrasse and the Formulation of Foreign Policy*. Lincoln, NE: iUniverse.

Zakaria, Fareed. 1992. Realism and Domestic Politics: A Review Essay. *International Security* 17 (1): 177–98.

Zakaria, Fareed. 1998. *From Wealth to Power: The Unusual Origins of America's World Role*. Princeton: Princeton University Press.

Ziebura, Gilbert. 1990. *World Economy and World Politics, 1924–1931: From Reconstruction to Collapse*. Oxford: Berg.

Zolberg, Aristide R. 1981. Review: Origins of the Modern World System: A Missing Link. *World Politics* 33 (2): 253–81.

Index

Abraham, David, 250*n*28, 250*n*33
Absolutism, 31, 47, 68, 72, 73, 96, 135,
  224*n*35, 230-31*n*19, 233*n*19
Abyssinian War (1935-36), 176-77
"Advantages of priority," 41, 58, 68, 228*n*16
  and Britain, 62, 63-65, 69
Aehrenthal, Count Alois Lexa von, 101,
  102
Afghanistan, 97, 114
Agadir (*see also* Second Moroccan Crisis),
  100, 104, 235*n*1
Agamben, Giorgio, 183
Agency/agents, 218, 255*n*3
  and bourgeois revolutions, 222*n*10
  and capitalism, 230*n*19, 256*n*11
  and capitalists, 30, 169, 171, 191, 248*n*15
  of combined development, 47, 125
  and differentiation, 14, 52
  and German policymaking, 19, 135, 170
  homogenization of, 32-33
  and ideology, 221*n*2
  and military, 169
  and Nazi foreign policymaking, 162, 163,
    164, 169, 171, 256*n*11
  and policymakers, 100, 169
  and Political Marxism, 231*n*19, 233-
    34*n*19
  and "rules of reproduction," 233*n*19
  and the state, 30, 46, 127
  and system structure, 25, 67, 226*n*5
  and uneven and combined develop-
    ment, 45, 48-49, 228*n*17
Agnew, John, 63
Allinson, Jamie C., 239*n*35
Alsace-Lorraine, 85, 239*n*31
Allied war debts

and reparations, 146, 148-49, 247*n*10
Ambrosius, Lloyd, 240*n*3
American Civil War (1861-65), 124
"American exceptionalism," 115, 122
  and Wilson, 116-18, 124, 242*n*12
American Federation of Labor, 243*n*15
Anarchy, 4, 35, 62
  capitalist form, 3, 123
  culture of, 5
  and First World War, 26, 62
  and hierarchy, 123
  and Marxism, 36
  and realism, 14, 24-25, 28, 36, 50, 51, 52,
    67
  as self-help system, 25
  and social theory, 6
  and states, 2
  and uneven and combined develop-
    ment, 51, 117
  and Wilson(ianism), 117, 126, 132, 216,
    244*n*24
Ancien Régime thesis, 10, 16
  and Arno Mayer, 21
  critique of, 21-22
Anderson, Perry, 232*n*19
Anglo-American rivalry, 247*n*9
Anglo-Franco-Soviet Alliance, 188
  alliance negotiations, 211
  and anti-communist ideology, 209-11
  failure to form, 211, 218
Anglo-French Supreme War Council, 213
"Anglo-German Antagonism," 58, 66, 99
"Anglo-German Connection," 201-3, 206
Anglo-German Payments Agreement
  (1934), 203
Anglo-Japanese Alliance of 1902, 71

303